OXFORD STUDIES IN
EARLY MODERN PHILOSOPHY

OXFORD STUDIES IN EARLY MODERN PHILOSOPHY

VOLUME III

EDITED BY

DANIEL GARBER
(Princeton University)

AND

STEVEN NADLER
(University of Wisconsin, Madison)

CLARENDON PRESS · OXFORD

OXFORD
UNIVERSITY PRESS

Great Clarendon Street, Oxford OX2 6DP

Oxford University Press is a department of the University of Oxford.
It furthers the University's objective of excellence in research, scholarship,
and education by publishing worldwide in

Oxford New York

Auckland Cape Town Dar es Salaam Hong Kong Karachi
Kuala Lumpur Madrid Melbourne Mexico City Nairobi
New Delhi Shanghai Taipei Toronto

With offices in

Argentina Austria Brazil Chile Czech Republic France Greece
Guatemala Hungary Italy Japan Poland Portugal Singapore
South Korea Switzerland Thailand Turkey Ukraine Vietnam

Oxford is a registered trade mark of Oxford University Press
in the UK and in certain other countries

Published in the United States
by Oxford University Press Inc., New York

British Library Cataloguing in Publication Data

Data available

Library of Congress Cataloging in Publication Data

Data available

Typeset by Laserwords Private Limited, Chennai, India
Printed in Great Britain
on acid-free paper by
Biddles Ltd., King's Lynn, Norfolk

ISBN 0–19–920394–6   978–0–19–920394–9
ISBN 0–19–920393–8 (Pbk.)   978–0–19–920393–2 (Pbk.)

1 3 5 7 9 10 8 6 4 2

Contents

Contents

Note from the Editors

Oxford Studies in Early Modern Philosophy covers the period that begins, very roughly, with Descartes and his contemporaries and ends with Kant. It also publishes papers on thinkers or movements outside that framework (and including Kant), as long as they are important for illuminating early modern thought. The core of the subject matter is, of course, philosophy and its history. But the volume's papers reflect the fact that philosophy in this period was much broader in its scope than it is now taken to be, and included a great deal of what currently belongs to the natural sciences. Furthermore, philosophy in the period was closely connected with other disciplines, such as theology, and with larger questions of social, political, and religious history. While maintaining a focus on philosophy, the volume includes articles that examine the larger intellectual, social, and political context of early modern philosophy. While the articles in the volume are of importance to specialists in the various subfields of the discipline, our aim is to publish essays that appeal not only to scholars of one particular figure or another, but to the larger audience of philosophers, intellectual historians, and others who are interested in the period.

Oxford Studies in Early Modern Philosophy appears once a year in a single volume available in both hardback and paperback and containing roughly 250–350 pages. While everything will be published in English, essays may also be submitted in French, German, or Italian.

The editors of *Oxford Studies in Early Modern Philosophy* are Daniel Garber (Princeton University) and Steven Nadler (University of Wisconsin—Madison). The members of the editorial board are:

Theo Verbeek (Rijksuniversiteit te Utrecht, the Netherlands)
Catherine Wilson (CUNY Graduate Center, USA)

The editorial office is:

Oxford Studies in Early Modern Philosophy
Department of Philosophy
1879 Hall
Princeton University
Princeton, New Jersey 08544-1006
Email: dgarber@princeton.edu;smnadler@wisc.edu
Fax: 609-258-1502

Abbreviations

GASSENDI

Opera   *Opera Omnia*, 6 vols. (Lyon, 1658; repr. Stutt-
             gart: Frommann, 1964)

HOBBES

EW   Sir William Molesworth (ed.), *The English
             Works of Thomas Hobbes of Malmesbury*, 11 vols.
             (London, 1839–45)

LW   Sir William Molesworth (ed.), *Opera philosoph-
             ica quae Latine scripsit omnia*, 5 vols. (London,
             1839–45)

HUME

EHU   T. L. Beauchamp (ed.), *An Enquiry concern-
             ing Human Understanding* (Oxford: Clarendon
             Press, 2000)

EPM   T. L. Beauchamp (ed.), *Enquiry concerning the
             Principles of Morals* (Oxford: Clarendon Press,
             1998)

LDH   J. Y. T. Greig (ed.), *The Letters of David Hume*,
             2 vols. (Oxford: Clarendon Press, 1932)

Letter   *A Letter from a Gentleman to his Friend at Edin-
             burgh*

NLDH   R. Klibansky and E. C. Mossner (eds.), *New
             Letters of David Hume* (Oxford: Clarendon
             Press, 1954)

THN   D. F. Norton and M. J. Norton (eds.), *A
             Treatise of Human Nature* (Oxford: Oxford Uni-
             versity Press, 2000)

LEIBNIZ

A   Deutsche Akademie der Wissenschaften (ed.),
             *Gottfried Wilhelm Leibniz: Sämtliche Schriften und
             Briefe* (Berlin: Akademie Verlag, 1923–)

DM	*Discours de métaphysique*
GM	C. I. Gerhardt (ed.), *Mathematische Schriften*, 7 vols. (Berlin, 1849–63)
GP	C. I. Gerhardt (ed.), *Die philosophischen Schriften*, 7 vols. (Berlin, 1875–90)

LOCKE

E	John Locke, *Essay concerning Human Understanding*

MALEBRANCHE

LO	T. M. Lennon and P. J. Olscamp (tr.), *The Search after Truth and Elucidations of The Search after Truth* (Columbus: Ohio State University Press, 1980)
OC	André Robinet (ed.), *Malebranche: Œuvres complètes*, 20 vols. (Paris: J. Vrin, 1958–84)
Recherche	*Recherche de la vérité*

SPINOZA

C	Edwin Curley (tr.), *Collected Writings of Spinoza*, i (Princeton: Princeton University Press, 1984)
EIIP 13S	*Ethics* [part in roman numeral, followed by P (for proposition), D (for demonstration), S (for scholium), pref. (for preface), app. (for appendix), etc.]
G	Carl Gebhardt (ed.), *Spinoza Opera*, 4 vols. (Heidelberg: C. Winter, 1925)

I

Deflating Descartes's Causal Axiom

TAD M. SCHMALTZ

In a letter written in 1643, Princess Elisabeth told Descartes that 'I admit that it would be easier for me to concede matter and extension to the mind than it would be for me to concede to an immaterial thing the capacity to move the body and be moved by one' (AT iii. 661). This is of course the famous 'problem of Cartesian interaction'. More recently, this problem has been linked to the question of whether Descartes can allow in general for the interaction of objects with different natures.[1] The scholarly debate over this question has tended, particularly in the English-language literature, to focus on the connections of the more general problem for Cartesian interaction—dubbed by Robert Richardson 'the problem

---

[1] The most direct exchange is in a series of articles in the *Journal of the History of Philosophy*, 23 (1985): Daisie Radner, 'Is There a Problem of Cartesian Interaction?' ['Problem'] (35–49); Robert Richardson and Louis Loeb, 'Replies to Daisie Radner's "Is There a Problem of Cartesian Interaction?"' ['Replies'] (221–31); and Radner, 'Rejoinder to Professors Richardson and Loeb' ['Rejoinder'] (232–6). Radner's original article, which develops the position in her 'Descartes' Notion of the Union of Mind and Body', *Journal of the History of Philosophy*, 9 (1971), 159–70, is a response to views in Richardson's 'The "Scandal" of Cartesian Interaction' ['Scandal'], *Mind*, 91 (1982), 20–37, and Loeb's *From Descartes to Hume: Continental Metaphysics and the Development of Modern Philosophy* (Ithaca, NY: Cornell University Press, 1981). Relevant to this debate are Kenneth Clatterbaugh's 'Descartes' Causal Likeness Principle' ['Likeness'], *Philosophical Review*, 89 (1980), 379–402, Janet Broughton's 'Adequate Causes and Natural Change in Descartes' Philosophy' ['Adequate Causes'], in A. Donagan, A. N. Perovich, Jr., and M. V. Wedin (eds.), *Human Nature and Natural Knowledge: Essays Presented to Marjorie Grene* (Dordrecht: Reidel, 1986), 107–27, and Eileen O'Neill's 'Mind–Body Interaction and Metaphysical Consistency: A Defense of Descartes' ['Mind–Body Interaction'], *Journal of the History of Philosophy*, 25 (1987), 227–45. For more recent discussions that offer different reactions to this debate in the literature over the problem of Cartesian interaction, see my 'Sensation, Occasionalism, and Descartes' Causal Principles' ['Sensation'], in P. Cummins and G. Zoeller (eds.), *Minds, Ideas, and Objects: Essays on the Theory of Representation in Modern Philosophy* (Atascadero, Calif.: Ridgeview, 1992), 33–55, and Geoffrey Gorham's 'Causation and Similarity in Descartes' ['Causation'], in R. J. Gennaro and C. Huenemann (eds.), *New Essays on the Rationalists* (New York: Oxford University Press, 1999), 296–309.

of heterogeneity'[2]—to Descartes's own constraints on causation. The main culprit is Descartes's claim, which he introduced as an 'axiom or common notion', that 'whatever there is of reality or perfection in some thing, is formally or eminently in its first and adequate cause' (AT vii. 165; CSM ii. 116).[3] On one side of the debate, critics have argued not only that this axiom precludes heterogeneous interaction, but also that Descartes's recognition of this implication led him to admit the impossibility of at least certain forms of mind–body interaction.[4] On the other side, apologists have countered that Descartes never admitted the impossibility of mind–body interaction, and that he had no need to make such an admission since his causal axiom is perfectly consistent with heterogeneous interaction.[5]

This debate has been helpful in raising the question of the precise import of Descartes's causal axiom. Indeed, I hope to show that there are certain complications regarding this axiom that scholars involved in this debate have failed to appreciate. But I also want to step back a bit in order to consider whether this axiom is as central to Descartes's account of causation as the literature indicates.

In the first section of this chapter, I begin by considering in the context of Descartes's discussion of causation in the *Meditations* the meaning of the stipulation in his causal axiom that the cause contains the 'perfection or reality' of the effect 'formally or eminently'. I start by rejecting the strong deflationary thesis that the axiom in no case requires that an effect be similar in nature to its cause. I argue in particular that in certain of its applications, at least, Descartes's causal axiom requires that a cause that formally contains its effect have the same nature as that effect. Even so, I attempt to bolster the apologetic

---

[2] 'Scandal', 20.

[3] In contrast to the literature I consider, Descartes spoke of causal axioms or notions rather than of causal principles. But he did indicate in a 1646 letter to Clerselier that the term "principle" can be used for '*a common notion* that is so clear and so general that it can serve as a principle for proving the existence of all the beings, or entities, to be discovered later' as well as for '*a Being*, the existence of which is better known to us than any other, so that it can serve as a *principle* for knowing them' (AT iv. 444; CSMK 290). Although where possible I cite the standard English translation of passages from Descartes's texts, all translations are my own.

[4] The main versions of this position that I consider here are in Radner's 'Problem' and 'Rejoinder', and in Broughton's 'Adequate Causes'.

[5] The main version of this position that I consider is in Loeb's portion of Richardson and Loeb, 'Replies'.

argument that no such similarity is required in the case of eminent containment by offering an account of such containment in terms of containment in thought. If this account works, then with respect to Descartes's causal axiom, at least, the heterogeneity of cause and effect can be a problem in general only in cases where causes cannot eminently contain their effects.

The second section focuses on two such cases that commentators have taken to be particularly problematic for Descartes, namely, the causation of sensations by bodily motions and the causal interaction of bodies in collision. I argue that though his causal axiom does allow for some sort of causation in these cases, Descartes's remarks concerning these particular kinds of interaction reveal special problems for his treatment of causality. The cases illustrate that the apologetic claim that Descartes is entitled to his causal claims because no problems for such claims derive from his causal axiom accords too much importance to this axiom in his account of causal interaction. So in addition to deflating the causal axiom by claiming that it does not rule out all kinds of heterogeneous interaction, I argue that this axiom does not have the sort of importance that his critics and defenders alike have attributed to it. But I do not want to end simply with these negative and limiting points concerning the causal axiom. So I will offer in conclusion some more positive remarks that emphasize the contribution a consideration of this axiom can provide for an understanding of Descartes's theory of causation.

I. FORMAL AND EMINENT CONTAINMENT

In the Third Meditation, Descartes offered as a notion revealed as evident by the 'natural light' that 'there must be as much in the efficient and total cause, as in the effect of that cause' (AT vii. 40; CSM ii. 28). This 'reality principle', as it is called in the literature,[6] is said to follow from the fact that 'nothing can come from nothing, and that what is more perfect, that is, what contains more reality in itself, cannot come from what is less [perfect]' (AT vii. 41; CSM ii. 28). When challenged by Hobbes to explain what it could mean to say that reality admits of more or less, Descartes replied curtly

---

[6] See n. 13.

that 'substance is a greater thing than mode' and that 'if there is an infinite and independent substance, it is a greater thing than finite and dependent [substance]' (AT vii. 185; CSM ii. 130).[7] The following simple ontological hierarchy is suggested here.

God	infinite substance
minds	finite substance
bodies	
thoughts	modes of finite substance[8]
shapes, sizes, motions	

As Descartes's apologists have insisted, when perfection or reality is understood in terms of this simple ontological hierarchy, the reality principle does not preclude mind–body interaction.[9] Given this hierarchy, minds and bodies have the same amount of perfection or reality, and thus can interact given the reality principle. There is admittedly the claim in the literature that Descartes took particular bodies to be modes of the one corporeal substance, 'body taken in general'.[10] But even if this claim were correct, it would still be the case that bodily motions have the same modal status as the sensory or volitional thoughts. As far as the reality principle is concerned, then, motions can cause sensations and volitions can cause motions.

---

[7] Descartes also included in this hierarchy 'real accidents, or incomplete substances' that 'are greater things than modes, but less than complete substances' (AT vii. 185; CSM ii. 130). But he famously rejected the existence of scholastic bodily accidents that can subsist apart from corporeal substance. In Section 2.2 I return to this disagreement with the scholastic position.

[8] In a letter to Arnauld, Descartes emphasized that one must distinguish between thought or extension considered as an attribute that constitutes the nature of a substance and the variable modes of that attribute, such as particular acts of thinking or particular shapes, sizes, or motions (29 July 1648, AT v. 221; CSMK 357). On his official view, the attribute of thought or extension is only 'distinct by reason', and not distinct in reality from the substance to which it is attributed (see *Principles of Philosophy*, I. 62, AT viiia. 30; CSM i. 214–15). The attribute thus belongs on the same level of reality as its substance.

[9] See, for instance, Loeb, 'Replies', 228.

[10] Most famously, Martial Gueroult makes such a claim in *Descartes selon l'ordre des raisons* (Paris: Aubier, 1953), i. 107–18, and in *Spinoza* (Hildesheim: Georg Olms, 1968), vol. i, app. 10, pp. 540–55. The portion of this claim concerning 'body taken in general' (*corpus in genere sumptum*) is drawn from the Synopsis to the *Meditations* (AT vii. 14; CSM ii. 10). There is a more recent development of a monistic interpretation of Descartes's views on material substance in Thomas Lennon's 'The Eleatic Descartes', *Journal of the History of Philosophy*, 45 (2007).

In fact, however, Descartes indicated that matter is composed of parts that are themselves substances rather than modes. Thus, in the *Principles of Philosophy*, Descartes argued that since the particular parts of any corporeal substance can exist apart from each other, these parts are really distinct substances (*Principles of Philosophy*, I. 60, AT viiia. 28–9; CSM i. 213).[11] Just as minds are the subjects of various thoughts, so these parts of matter are the subjects of various shapes, sizes and motions.[12] Given this position, we have the following revised version of the simple ontological hierarchy.

God	infinite substance
minds	finite substances
parts of matter	
thoughts	modes of finite substances
shapes, sizes, motions	

In terms of this revised version, the reality principle would rule out only the causation of infinite substance by finite minds and substantial bodily parts and modes of these finite substances, and the causation of finite minds and substantial bodily parts by their modes. Once again, there is no general prohibition here of heterogeneous interaction.

In the same passage from the Third Meditation that introduces the reality principle, however, Descartes went on to say that a particular object such as a stone can in no way now begin to exist unless produced by a cause 'in which there is formally or eminently all that is found in the stone' (AT vii. 41; CSM ii. 28). More seems to be required here than the containment in the cause of the generic 'perfection or reality' of the effect. In particular, the cause needs to contain everything in its effect 'formally or eminently'. For this reason, Daisie Radner has argued that we need to distinguish in the *Meditations* the

---

[11] See also Descartes's claim in the *Sixth Replies* that the surface of a body cannot be a part of that body since it is a mode (AT vii. 433–4; CSM ii. 292–3). For an appeal to these considerations against Gueroult's interpretation of Descartes's account of material substance (cited in n. 10), see Paul Hoffman, 'The Unity of Descartes's Man', *Philosophical Review*, 95 (1986), 347–9.

[12] Descartes indicated that these substantial parts are the subjects of the modes rather than matter as a whole when he told More in a 1649 letter that properties such as tangibility and impenetrability 'have a relation to parts and presuppose the concept of division or termination', whereas 'we can conceive a continuous body of indeterminate magnitude, in which nothing is considered except extension' (AT v. 269; CSMK 361).

relatively weak reality principle, which requires the containment in the cause of only the reality of the effect, from a stronger 'containment principle', which requires further the containment in the cause formally or eminently of all features of the effect.[13]

In response, Louis Loeb has denied the distinction of the two principles Radner claims to find in Descartes on the grounds that what it is that is said to be contained formally or eminently in the cause is simply the perfection or reality that the reality principle concerns. In Loeb's view, then, to say that the cause must contain formally or eminently everything in the effect is just to say that the cause must be on either the same ontological level as (in the case of formal containment) or a higher ontological level than (in the case of eminent containment) its effect. Given this view, there is no problem for heterogeneous interaction since Descartes required not that the cause 'contain modes of the same kind' as it produces in the effect but merely that it contain the reality of the effect '*qua* degree of perfection'.[14]

Loeb's claim that the two causal principles are not ultimately distinct may seem to be supported by the fact that when attempting to formalize his system in the *Second Replies*, Descartes offered only one causal axiom, and explicated that axiom in terms of his simple ontological hierarchy. The causal axiom, which I cited at the outset, is that the 'first and adequate' cause contains formally or eminently 'whatever there is of reality or perfection in the effect'.[15] But this axiom is followed by a further axiom that explicates reality or perfection in terms of the fact that 'substance has more reality than accidents or modes, and infinite substance, than finite' (AT vii. 165; CSM ii. 117). So the suggestion here is that the reality that the cause formally or eminently contains is simply the reality of the effect as infinite substance, finite substance, or mode.

---

[13] 'Problem', 41. I take the labels from O'Neill's discussion of Radner's position in 'Mind–Body Interaction', 231–2. Radner calls the reality principle the 'at least as much principle', and the containment principle the 'pre-existence principle'. O'Neill is inclined to Radner's view that Descartes offered two distinct causal constraints; see 'Mind–Body Interaction', 232. Radner also takes Descartes to offer a distinct 'communication' principle on which the cause literally transfers to the effect what it contains in itself. In Section 2.2 I will consider Broughton's claim that Descartes was led by his causal axiom to accept such a principle in the case of body–body interaction.

[14] 'Replies', 228.

[15] I address presently the restriction of the axiom to the 'adequate' or, what is the same for Descartes, 'total' cause.

It must also be said that Loeb's deflationary version of the causal axiom suffices for the Third Meditation proof of the existence of God. The central premiss of this argument is that the cause must contain formally or eminently the reality that is present objectively in our idea of infinitely perfect substance. But to contain something at the same level of reality as infinitely perfect substance just is to contain formally the reality of infinite perfection itself.

Nonetheless, a more robust sort of formal containment seems to be required for the proof of the existence of the material world in the Sixth Meditation. Descartes concluded there that bodies are the causes that formally contain what is contained objectively in our sensory ideas of bodies. Contrary to Loeb's view, it does not seem to suffice that the causes contain something that contains the same reality '*qua* degree of perfection' as what is found objectively in those ideas. Otherwise, it would seem that non-bodily substances could count as formally containing the bodily modes that exist objectively in our sensory ideas simply in virtue of having something with the same level of reality on the simple ontological hierarchy, namely, its own modes. But the argument in the Sixth Meditation makes clear that it is only bodies that formally contain the reality that is present objectively in our sensory ideas. The implication here is that what formally contains the bodily features present objectively in our sensory ideas must have the same nature as body, and so must be actually extended.

There is a question—which I will just raise here and will explore in more detail later—whether Descartes held that a cause that formally contains an effect must actually possess something like the specific effect. It is often assumed that he did. However, there is the point, which Loeb has emphasized, that Descartes said that the cause contains not the effect itself, but only the 'reality or perfection' of the effect. I have already argued that given the remarks in the Sixth Meditation, this reality or perfection cannot be simply the level of reality or perfection on Descartes's simple ontological hierarchy. But there may be a more robust form of formal containment that falls short of the actual presence of features of the effect in the cause. Consider, for instance, the claim at the end of the proof of the existence of the material world that corporeal things possess 'all, considered generally, that is comprehended in the object of pure mathematics (*in purae Matheseos objecto comprehenduntur*)' (AT vii. 80; CSM ii. 55). On one reading, the suggestion here is that body possesses the reality or perfection of all features comprehended in the geometrical extension that constitutes its nature. This reading allows for cases in which body formally contains the reality of features it does not actually possess. There is admittedly a weaker reading of this passage, on which it claims only that all that a body in fact contains is comprehended in its nature as an extended thing. But we will discover presently that Descartes had reason to say that in certain cases, at least, not only bodies but also minds can formally contain the reality of features that they do not actually possess.

At this point, though, my main proposal is that Descartes offered a single causal axiom that requires that the cause contain the reality of the effect formally or eminently. Any apparent distinction of causal constraints derives from the fact that he sometimes needed to consider the reality or perfection of the effect only abstractly in terms of his simple ontological hierarchy, as in the case of the Third Meditation proof of the existence of God, whereas at other times he needed to consider the reality or perfection as reflected in the particular nature of the effect, as in the case of the Sixth Meditation proof of the existence of the material world. Given the latter consideration of reality or perfection, it cannot be said, *pace* Loeb, that Descartes did not require that a cause that formally contains the effect have the same nature as the effect. But this does not show, *pace* Radner, that Descartes required that in all cases the cause must have the same nature as the effect. For Descartes's axiom allows for cases where a cause contains its effect not formally but only eminently.

Radner has countered that Descartes's notion of eminent containment is so obscure that it does not reveal cases in which a cause and its effect differ in nature.[16] The challenge here is to offer an account of eminent containment that does not require that cause and effect have the same nature and that is both clear and fits the texts. Descartes's own official explication of formal and eminent containment is found in the *Second Replies*, where he stipulated that objects contain formally all that is 'such as (*talia ... qualia*) we perceive them', and contain eminently what 'indeed is not such [as we perceive], but greater, so that it is able to take the place of such a thing [that is as we perceive]' (AT vii. 161;

---

[16] 'Rejoinder', 232, 233–4.

CSM ii. 114). To say the least, this explication is less than transparent. We will see that in the case of sensation there are complications concerning the claim that objects formally contain what is 'such as we perceive them'. In order to address Radner's worry, however, we need to puzzle over what Descartes could have meant when he said that objects eminently contain what is not such as we perceive but is 'greater' than and 'able to take the place' of what we do perceive.

On one understanding, what is greater and able to take the place is simply the power to produce what we perceive. This understanding informs the analysis of eminent containment that Eileen O'Neill has offered recently. On this analysis, Descartes held that

a property ø is eminently contained in X if and only if: ø is not formally contained in X [i.e. X does not contain at least n degrees of ø]; X is an entity displaying a greater degree of relative independence than any possible Y which could contain ø formally (i.e., higher up the ontological hierarchy than any such Y); and X has the power to bring about the existence of ø.[17]

There is a weaker reading of the second clause, on which X is an entity displaying a greater degree of relative independence than ø, that is, is higher up in the ontological hierarchy than ø, as opposed to any possible Y that could contain ø formally. This weaker reading may seem to be supported by Descartes's comment in the Third Meditation that since 'extension, shape, position, and motion' are 'merely modes of a substance', they can be contained in him eminently given that he is thinking substance (AT vii. 45; CSM ii. 31).[18] In the Sixth Meditation, however, Descartes indicated that certain finite creatures can contain bodily effects eminently in virtue of the fact that they are 'more noble than' (*nobilior*) corporeal substance (AT vii. 79; CSM ii. 55). Here it is not just the fact that the effects are mere modes that allows for eminent containment in these other substances, but in addition the fact that these substances are more noble than the corporeal substances that contain the effects formally.[19]

---

[17] 'Mind–Body Interaction', 235. To my mind, O'Neill's analysis marks an advance over Clatterbaugh's view that ø is eminently contained in X if and only if X contains greater than n degrees of ø; see 'Likeness', 391.

[18] Thanks to David Ring, who pressed me to consider this point a number of years ago.

[19] Descartes could not have made this point that his mind is more noble than body in the Third Meditation because he had not yet provided an account of the nature of body and its distinction from the nature of mind.

An initial problem is that Descartes's simple ontological hierarchy suggests that mental and bodily substances have the same reality as finite substances. Given this hierarchy, it would seem that bodily effects cannot be contained eminently in a mental cause.[20] However, we could get around this problem by appealing to the suggestion in Descartes that mental substance is higher on the ontological scale of perfection than bodily substance. This suggestion is connected to his claim in the *Principles* that God is more perfect than body because he lacks the imperfection of divisibility that pertains to body in virtue of the fact that it is extended (*Principles of Philosophy*, I. 23, AT viiia. 13–14). Descartes had also insisted in the Sixth Meditation on the fact that 'there is a great difference between mind and body, inasmuch as body is by its very nature divisible, whereas mind is utterly indivisible' (AT vii. 85–6; CSM ii. 59). The implication is that though mind is below God since it is not infinite substance, it is above body since it is an indivisible substance. This gives us the following 'enhanced' ontological hierarchy.

God	infinite indivisible substance
minds	finite indivisible substances
parts of matter	finite divisible substances
thoughts	modes of finite substances
shapes, sizes, motions	

Given this enhanced hierarchy, O'Neill's analysis is consistent with the claim that substantial material parts and their modes can be contained eminently in finite minds.[21]

---

[20] On Gueroult's interpretation of Descartes (see n. 10), there would be no problem here for eminent containment in mind in so far as particular bodies, as modes, are lower in the ontological hierarchy than mental substances. But in the Sixth Meditation, the stress is on the fact that mental substances are more noble than the corporeal substances that formally contain what is present objectively in our sensory ideas.

[21] The eminent containment of the whole of matter in finite minds is more problematic given Descartes's view that this matter is an 'indefinite' rather than a finite substance. Indeed, he told Regius in correspondence that he could not think of indefinite extension 'unless the magnitude of the world also was or at least could be indefinite' (24 May 1640, AT iii. 64; CSMK 147). But the 'could be' suggests that there need not be anything indefinitely extended in order for our mind to think it. Moreover, there is the claim in the Fourth Meditation that our will is in some sense unrestricted, and is in fact the feature of our mind in virtue of which we understand ourselves to bear some image of God (AT vii. 56–7; CSM ii. 39–40). Given this feature of our mind, Descartes could perhaps allow that our

Even so, there remains a problem with the consequence of the last clause of O'Neill's definition that something can eminently contain ø only if it has the power to bring about the existence of ø. In defence of this clause, O'Neill appeals to the account of causation in the work of the early modern scholastic Francisco Suárez. In his 1597 *Disputationes metaphysicae*, Suárez offered a version of Descartes's causal axiom when he claimed that since 'to act is to communicate or to give *esse*', it must be the case that 'such *esse* be supposed actually to exist in the cause, either formally or eminently', given that 'nothing can give what it does not in any way have in itself'.[22] He noted that 'to contain eminently is to have a perfection of such a superior nature that it contains by means of power (*virtute*) whatever is in the inferior perfection', where this power is said to be the power 'to be able to create (*posse efficere*)' the effects of inferior perfection.[23] But though Descartes was obviously influenced by the scholastic claim that the effect is contained formally or eminently in its cause, there are reasons to think that he did not adopt Suárez's particular account of eminent containment. Whereas he held in the Third Meditation that his mind contains material things eminently, for instance, Descartes did not suggest there that he had the power to create the material world. Indeed, in a 1641 exchange with his critic 'Hyperaspistes', Descartes made clear that our mind has no such power. This critic claimed that in Descartes's view, 'since a corporeal thing is not more noble than the idea that the mind has of it, and mind contains bodies eminently, it follows that all bodies, and thus the whole of this visible world, can be produced by the human mind' (AT iii. 404). Such an implication is said to be objectionable in so far as it undermines our confidence that God alone created the visible world. In response,

---

mind contains even indefinite extension eminently. For discussion of the complications here, see Margaret Wilson, 'Can I Be the Cause of my Idea of the World? (Descartes on the Infinite and Indefinite)', in Wilson, *Ideas and Mechanisms: Essays on Early Modern Philosophy* (Princeton: University of Princeton Press), 108–25.

[22] *Disputationes metaphysicae* [*DM*], disp. 18, sect. 9, art. 8, in *Opera omnia* [*Opera*], xxv–xxvi, ed. C. Berton (Paris: Vivès, 1866), xxv. 670; tr. A. J. Freddoso in *On Efficient Causality: Metaphysical Disputations 17, 18, and 19* [*Efficient Causality*] (New Haven: Yale University Press, 1994), 226. Although I cite the English translation where applicable, the translations of passages from *DM* are my own. For Suárez's more extended argument that the effect cannot be 'more noble' than its total and principal efficient cause, see *DM* 26. 1. 1–2 and 5–8, *Opera* xxv. 916 and 917–19.

[23] *DM* 30. 1. 10, *Opera*, xxvi. 63. Cited in O'Neill, 'Mind–Body Interaction', 239.

Descartes protested that we can produce 'not, as objected, the whole of this visible world, but the idea of the whole of things that are in this visible world' (AT iii. 428; CSMK 193). The suggestion here is that even though the whole visible world is contained in our mind eminently, we do not have the power to produce its extra-mental existence.[24] Eminent containment would seem to be a necessary but not a sufficient condition for something to be able to produce features it does not formally contain.[25]

What then did Descartes take eminent containment to be? It seems best to start to answer this question by focusing on his own examples of such containment. In the Sixth Meditation, his primary examples are the containment of bodily effects in God and finite minds. Here I think it is significant that eminent containment involves containment in thought; indeed, I know of no case in which Descartes took a feature to be eminently contained in something other than a mind. It seems that we are to understand what is greater than and takes the place of the formally contained features in terms of the reality of those features as they are present objectively in thought. Then if we draw on the suggestion in Descartes that indivisible mental substance is higher on the ontological scale than divisible bodily substance, and if we retain the result of O'Neill's analysis that an object that contains a feature eminently is higher on the ontological scale than anything that contains that feature formally, we allow for the suggestion in Descartes that minds can contain eminently even features of body that they cannot create.

I say that we must 'understand' the eminently contained feature 'in terms of' the reality of that feature as present objectively in thought. I do not say that we can reduce the eminent containment of the reality of such a feature to the objective containment of this reality. I had better not say that, since Descartes himself explicitly distinguished objective and eminent containment. For instance, he emphasized in the *Principles* that the cause of the reality of a 'highly intricate machine' (*machina*

---

[24] But see the discussion in n. 21 of the problems deriving from Descartes's view that extension is indefinitely extended.

[25] Cf. the critique of O'Neill's account of eminent containment in Gorham, 'Descartes's Dilemma of Eminent Containment', *Dialogue*, 42 (2003), 3–25, at 11–13. Beyond objecting to the explication of eminent containment of an effect in terms of a causal power to produce that effect, however, Gorham rejects in general any account on which the eminently contained effect is to be reduced to other features that the cause formally contains. The alternative to O'Neill's account that I offer presently is reductionist in this sense.

valde artificiosa) must be present in its 'first and principal' cause 'not only objectively and representatively, but in reality formally or eminently' (*Principles of Philosophy*, I. 17, AT viiia. 11; CSM i. 198–9). My analysis in fact allows for cases in which something is contained objectively but not eminently in my mind, for example, God's infinite perfection. But I need to make a bit more explicit what the difference is between objective and eminent containment. Here I can draw on O'Neill's claim that X eminently contains ø only if it has the power to create ø. We have seen that this will not work, but what will work, I think, is the claim that X eminently contains ø only if it has the power that suffices to produce the reality objectively present in X's idea of ø. This further requirement is suggested by Descartes's analysis of the intricate machine. He noted in the passage from the *Principles* just cited that in order for the mind to be the cause of its idea of such a machine, there must be some mental feature, such as the experience of seeing 'such a machine made by someone else', a 'study of the science of mechanics', or the 'force of ingenuity (*ingenii*)', that explains how it could form this idea (AT viiia. 11; CSM i. 198). So what is greater than and takes the place of a formally contained feature is not simply that feature as represented by an idea, but in addition a mental power that has in itself what is required to produce the reality contained objectively in that idea.

In place of O'Neill's analysis of eminent containment quoted above, then, I offer the following:

> A property ø is eminently contained in X if and only if: ø is not formally contained in X; X is an entity displaying a greater degree of relative independence than any possible Y which could contain ø formally (i.e. higher up in the ontological hierarchy than any such Y); and X has a power that suffices to produce the objective reality that is present in X's idea of ø.

I do not commit myself here to O'Neill's explication of X's formal containment of ø in terms of X possessing 'at least n degrees of ø'.[26] I have indicated that there may be some cases in which Descartes must allow that X can formally contain the reality of ø without actually possessing ø. But more importantly, I think it is X's power to produce

---

[26] O'Neill speaks of an object's formally 'containing' at least *n* degrees of ø, but uses as an example of such containment a body's actually possessing at least *n* degrees of motion ('Mind–Body Interaction', 236).

the objective reality present in its idea of ø, rather than the power to produce ø itself, that is essential to eminent containment. Thus, for our mind to contain the visible world eminently, it is not necessary that it be able to create the visible world; all that is required is that it have in itself a power that suffices to create the objective reality of our idea of the visible world.

Even so, on both O'Neill's analysis and mine, Descartes's causal axiom allows for the eminent containment of effects that differ in nature from their cause. For O'Neill, this is because there is nothing in the axiom that rules out the fact that a cause has the power to produce something lower in the ontological hierarchy that differs in nature from it. For me, it is because there is nothing in the axiom that rules out the fact that the mind has the power to produce the objective reality present in its idea of something lower in the ontological hierarchy that differs in nature from it.

It might be thought that even if this account of eminent containment works for finite minds, it does not work for God's eminent containment of his effects. For surely Descartes held that God has the power to produce not only the objective reality of his idea of the world, but also the actual existence of that world, that is, its formal reality. I would of course agree that Descartes took God to have this greater power. But here we must take into account his claim in a 1644 letter that in the case of the 'universal and indeterminate cause', that is, a cause not limited to particular effects, it is a common notion that 'whatever can do the greater can do the lesser' (AT iv. 111; CSMK 231). God's greater power to create the formal reality of the world includes the lesser power to create the objective reality of this world as it exists in his idea.[27] But Descartes's exchange with Hyperaspistes makes clear that we cannot infer from the fact that the mind that eminently contains the visible world has the lesser power of creating the objective reality of the idea of this world that it has the greater power of creating that world's formal reality. So although God has the

---

[27] The fact that the power to create the formal reality of an object is greater than the power to create its objective reality is indicated by Descartes's indication in the Third Meditation that the mode of being of that which exists objectively in the intellect is more imperfect than the mode of that object in so far as it has formal reality (AT vii. 41; CSM ii. 29).

greater power, only the lesser power can be essential to eminent containment.

Even though our mind can have this lesser power in certain cases, however, there is no case in which bodies can. In Descartes's view, bodies are extended non-thinking things, and so cannot possess the power to create the objective reality of their ideas. Eminent containment therefore cannot be involved when bodies act on minds or on each other. Descartes's causal axiom would seem to require that in such cases a bodily cause formally contain what it brings about in its effect. But formal containment would appear to be ruled out in the case of the action of body on mind in sensation. For bodies simply cannot formally contain (even in the weak sense of comprehending in their nature) anything resembling the various sensations they produce in the mind. Formal containment does not seem to be ruled out in the same way in the case of body–body interaction; bodies surely can formally contain the aspects of motion that they produce in other bodies through collision. Nevertheless, Descartes seems to have allowed for particular instances of collision where the bodily cause does not actually possess something similar to what it produces as its effect. Moreover, Descartes critics from his time to our own have held that Descartes's causal axiom requires an implausible model of body–body causation.

Janet Broughton has taken the fact that Descartes adhered to his containment constraints on causation even in the face of these difficulties to indicate that he had 'an underlying and thoroughgoing commitment to the conception of causality articulated in the adequacy principle [i.e. Descartes's causal axiom]'.[28] I argue on the contrary that the difficulties can be mitigated to a considerable extent, and that a closer consideration of Descartes's own remarks concerning the particular cases of body-to-mind action and body–body interaction reveals that the central problems for his claims concerning causal interaction lie elsewhere. Even so, it is telling that Descartes has the most difficulty in cases where his causal axiom requires formal containment. Though critics such as Radner have tended to focus on the obscurity of his notion of eminent containment, it is cases involving formal containment that seem to be most problematic for him.

---

[28] 'Adequate Causes', 107.

2. TWO CASES OF CAUSAL INTERACTION

2.1. *First case: body-to-mind action*

We have already encountered Descartes's conclusion in the Sixth Meditation that bodies must exist as causes that formally contain what is present objectively in our sensory ideas. This conclusion is not unproblematic. For starters, there is scholarly disagreement over whether Descartes even allowed that bodily features are contained objectively in sensory ideas. I myself take the Sixth Meditation proof of the material world to indicate clearly enough that he did intend to allow for such containment. After all, the emphasis there is on the fact that sensory ideas must be produced by bodies that formally contain what is in these ideas objectively. Even so, it must be admitted that Descartes indicated none too clearly how the aspect objectively contained in the sensory ideas is related to the aspect formally contained in bodies. Recall his claim in the *Second Replies* that features that exist formally in objects are 'such as we perceive them' (AT vii. 161; CSM ii. 114). The problem is that he cannot take bodily features to be such as we sense them. Indeed, Descartes himself noted after presenting the Sixth Meditation proof that bodies may not exist 'in a way that is entirely such as (*talia omnino ... qualia*) the senses comprehend them, in so far as the comprehension of the senses is in many cases very obscure and confused' (AT vii. 80; CSM ii. 55). It would seem, then, that bodies cannot formally contain the qualities that we sense in a confused and obscure manner, and thus that there is no need for an external cause in the case of such sensations.[29]

I think we can go some way towards reconciling the Sixth Meditation proof with the subsequent comment concerning the confused and obscure comprehension of the senses by emphasizing the following claim elsewhere in the Sixth Meditation:

from the fact that I sense diverse colours, sounds, odours, tastes, heat, hardness and the like, I correctly conclude that there are other things in bodies from which these various sensory perceptions come (*adveniunt*), variations corresponding to them [i.e. to the variations among the sensations], though perhaps not similar to them. (AT vii. 81; CSM ii. 56)

---

[29] Here I draw on my discussion of this problem in 'Sensation'.

This passage indicates that sensory ideas that do not resemble bodily qualities nonetheless are systematically correlated with them. Because of these correlations, particular ideas can direct the mind to certain bodily qualities rather than others. Of course, we cannot know, simply by introspection, which qualities these ideas represent; that is why Descartes called the ideas confused and obscure. Even so, the ideas can represent the qualities in the broad sense just indicated. In virtue of the fact that the ideas so represent, they possess some sort of objective reality. Bodies formally contain what is in the sensory ideas objectively, then, in the sense that they possess the qualities to which these ideas direct the mind.

Admittedly, this reading stretches thin the claim in the *Second Replies* that features contained objectively in the mind are contained formally in bodies only when they exist outside of the mind in a way that is 'such as we perceive them'. But I take Descartes's own remarks concerning confused and obscure sensory ideas to suggest a thin notion of being 'such as' these ideas reveal. Moreover, this thin notion allows for the passage from the *Second Replies* to be reconciled with the suggestion in the Sixth Meditation that even though the objective reality of sensory ideas corresponds to the formal reality of bodily qualities, these qualities are often 'not entirely such as' they are comprehended by sense.

Even if this move works, however, there still seems to be a difficulty deriving from the fact that what is formally contained in the body does not resemble what is objectively contained in the idea. The causal axiom specifies that *everything* in the effect must be contained in its cause formally or eminently.[30] But it seems that given this requirement, the non-resembling features of sensory ideas, what is not 'entirely such as' are found in bodies, cannot 'come from' bodies. This axiom therefore seems to reveal the need to qualify the conclusion in the Sixth Meditation that sensory ideas 'have been emitted (*emitti*) from corporeal things' (AT vii. 79; CSM ii. 55).

Broughton argues that Descartes's commitment to the causal axiom drove him to claim in his later writings 'that the mind alone causes sensations'. Her principal text is the 1647 *Comments on a Certain Broadsheet*,

---

[30] In particular, the claim is that the stone, for example, must be produced 'by another thing in which there is formally or eminently *all* that is found in the stone' (AT vii. 165; CSM ii. 116; my emphasis).

in which Descartes addressed the thesis of his wayward Dutch disciple Henricus Regius that all ideas are 'engraved in the mind' by means of experience. In response, Descartes made the startling claim that everything in sensory ideas except 'circumstances pertaining to experience' is innate to mind in so far as it derives from an innate mental faculty, the operation of which is 'occasioned' by the presence of motions in the brain. There is an appeal here to the result in the *Dioptrics* that ideas of shapes and motions, and 'all the more' ideas of pain, colours, and sounds, are not exactly similar to the motions that occasion the activity of the innate mental faculty (AT viiib. 358–9; CSM i. 304).[31]

Here is Broughton's take on this passage:

> the formal containment principle [i.e. the causal axiom as it concerns cases where eminent containment in the cause is ruled out] applied to brain movements as the cause of sensation yields this requirement: Brain movements must contain exactly what is in the objects of sensation. Thus Descartes has shown in the [*Comments*] passage that a necessary condition for causation, as well as origination, has not been met. By showing that sensations do not originate from brain movements, Descartes has also shown that they are not *caused* by brain movements.
>
> ... The formal containment principle plus the [*Comments*] argument entail a denial that brain movements cause sensations.[32]

We need to distinguish two questions that Broughton's commentary raises: (1) Does Descartes's causal axiom plus his argument in the *Comments* entail the denial that brain movements cause sensations? and (2) Is there even an implicit appeal in the *Comments* to the causal axiom?

First question first. An initial point against Broughton is that Descartes restricted his causal axiom in a relevant way. In response to the objection that the sun and rain do not satisfy the axiom since they do not formally or eminently contain the animals they help to produce, he noted: 'It is certain that there is nothing in the effect *that is not contained formally or eminently in its* EFFICIENT *and* TOTAL *cause*, which two words I have added expressly. But the sun and the rain are not the

---

[31] For a more complete discussion of this passage and its context, see my 'Descartes on Innate Ideas, Sensation, and Scholasticism: The Response to Regius', in M. A. Stewart (ed.), *Studies in Seventeenth-Century European Philosophy* (Oxford: Clarendon Press, 1997), 33–73.

[32] 'Adequate Causes', 118–19. Cf. the similar reading of the *Comments* passage in Gorham, 'Causation', 304–6.

total causes of the animals they generate' (AT iii. 274; CSMK 166). So the causal axiom is restricted here to total or, as Descartes called them in the *Second Replies*, adequate causes (AT vii. 165; CSM ii. 116). The suggestion in the passage above is that it does not apply fully to merely partial causes of an effect.[33] Thus, even if brain movements do not formally contain everything that comes about in the mind, the causal axiom does not rule out the claim that such movements are *partial* efficient causes of sensory ideas. Perhaps the total and efficient cause in this case is the combination of the motions and the mental faculty.[34]

One might wonder whether the innate mental faculty responsible for forming sensory ideas can contain formally or eminently those features of the ideas not contained formally in motions in the brain. Descartes indicated in the *Comments* that prior to their formation intellectual ideas exist merely potentially in the faculty that forms them (AT viiib. 361; CSM i. 305), and he presumably thought that prior to their formation sensory ideas exist in the same way in the innate mental faculty. So if formal containment requires the actual presence of what is formally contained, prior to their formation sensory ideas cannot be formally contained in the faculty that forms them. But on the account of eminent containment that I attribute to Descartes, they cannot be eminently contained in that faculty either, since they are not features of objects lower on the ontological scale than minds.

At this point, we can draw on the suggestion above that there may be a weaker sense of formal containment than actual possession. Even if those features of sensory ideas that derive from the innate mental

---

[33] For more on the distinction between total/adequate and partial causes in Descartes and its connection to this distinction in Suárez, see Vincent Carraud, *Causa sive ratio: La Raison de la cause de Suarez à Leibniz* (Paris: PUF, 2002), 177–84.

[34] Steven Nadler has taken Descartes's claim in the *Comments* that brain motions provide the 'occasion' for the production of sensory ideas to indicate that these motions are not efficient causes at all, but rather a special kind of 'occasional cause' that serves merely as a remote condition for the action of the efficient cause; see 'Descartes and Occasional Causation', *British Journal of the History of Philosophy*, 2 (1994), 35–54. As Nadler notes, I had suggested that the bodily motions are remote causes in my 'Sensation'. However, I now think (but cannot argue in detail here) that Descartes's account in the *Comments* of the production of sensory ideas is consistent with the claim that brain motions are proximate, albeit only partial, efficient causes that act simultaneously with the innate mental faculty to produce sensory ideas. Such a claim is in line with the suggestion in several of Descartes's texts, early and late, that motions give rise immediately to sensory experience. Thanks to Andrew Chignell for discussion of this issue.

faculty are not present prior to their formation by the mind, the reality of those features could be present in so far as it is 'comprehended in' the reality of the innate mental faculty that forms them. It might seem that Descartes himself precluded this option when he insisted in the Third Meditation that 'the objective being of [an] idea can be produced not by potential being (*esse potentiali*), which strictly speaking is nothing, but only by actual or formal (*actuali sive formali*)' (AT vii. 47; CSM ii. 32). Given the claim here, it may seem as if the reality of sensory ideas as present potentially in the innate mental faculty could not play a role in the causation of the ideas themselves.[35] In this particular passage, however, the items that are 'strictly speaking nothing' are divine perfections that cannot be contained in a finite mind. What worried Descartes was that there would be certain features of the reality contained in the idea of God that would have no foundation in the reality of its cause. But it seems that the reality of the sensory ideas that the mind has a faculty to produce does have a foundation in an actual being, namely, in the mental faculty that forms them. If so, then the mind could be said to contain formally the reality of those features of its sensory ideas that do not derive from motions in the brain.[36] The total and efficient cause of these ideas, consisting of motions in the brain and the innate mental faculty, could be said to contain formally all of the effect produced, and thus the causal axiom would be satisfied.

Someone might well protest at this point that the innate mental faculty all by itself could be the total or adequate cause of sensory ideas. Why is there a need to appeal at all to the causality of the brain motions? There is the claim in the *Comments* that the innate faculty forms the ideas 'at this time rather than another' owing to the motions. So the causal activity of the motions could explain the fact that the ideas are formed at a particular moment. But more than this, such activity could explain why the ideas direct the mind to certain features of the external world rather than to others. Descartes did indicate in the *Comments* that the motions in our brain that derive from its

---

[35] Thanks to Dan Kaufman for this objection.

[36] In contrast, Suárez held that in all cases of immanent action, the action of the faculty that produces the effect is equivocal, and thus the faculty itself only eminently contains the effect; see *DM* 18. 9. 10, *Opera*, xxv. 671; *Efficient Causality*, 228. We saw in Section 1 that there are reasons to think that Descartes could not accept Suárez's account of eminent containment. I provide further reasons in Section 2.2 below.

interaction with the external world are (to use the language of the *Second Replies*) not 'entirely such as' we perceive them to be. But if I am correct that there is a much weaker sense in which the bodily features are 'such as' we perceive them to be, then this text does not rule out the claim that bodies are partial efficient causes that formally contain some, though not all, of what is produced in the mind in sensation.

The passage from the *Comments* does say that with the exception of judgements pertaining to experience, 'there is *nothing* in our ideas that was not innate to the mind or the faculty of thinking' (AT viiib. 358; CSM i. 304; my emphasis), and this may seem to preclude motions in the brain from contributing anything to sensation.[37] As I indicate presently, however, Descartes seems to have been most concerned here to deny that the mind literally sees anything in the brain. It is also significant that he continued to claim in this text that brain motions 'transmit something' (*aliquid immiserunt*) that triggers the formation of sensory ideas by the innate mental faculty (AT viiib. 359; CSM i. 304). So there seems to be an indication here that brain motions do contribute something to sensory experience and, as we have seen, Descartes's causal axiom does not rule out the position that this contribution is a causal one.[38]

But is there even an implicit appeal to this axiom in the *Comments*? This was our second question. Here it is important to follow up on the reference in this text to the account of sensation Descartes had 'explicated at length in *Dioptrics*'. In this earlier text, appended to the 1637 *Discourse on the Method*, he had argued that we do not

---

[37] Thanks to Gonzalo Rodriguez-Pereyra for this objection.

[38] For the point that Descartes allowed in the *Comments* for some sort of causal transmission from bodily motions to mind in sensory experience, see David Scott, 'Occasionalism and Occasional Causation in Descartes' ['Occasionalism'], *Journal of the History of Philosophy*, 38 (2000), 503–28. Scott is particularly concerned in the second section of his paper to counter the account of Descartes's 'occasional causation' in the work of Steven Nadler cited in n. 34. In contrast to the view I offer against Nadler in this note, however, Scott claims that transmission is to be contrasted with 'efficacious or productive agency' and that it occurs at a 'pre-efficiency' stage 'immediately prior to the actual production of ideas by the mind' (ibid. 520). Also, Scott does not suggest the position, to which I am inclined, that what the brain motions transmit is the special sort of objective reality present in sensory ideas. For yet another interpretation of the *Comments* passage, on which Descartes held that the motions serve as causal triggers but do not produce the content of sensory ideas, see Marleen Rozemond, 'Descartes on Mind–Body Interaction: What's the Problem?', *Journal of the History of Philosophy*, 37 (1999), 435–67.

perceive an object by viewing pictures of it in the brain, 'as if there are other eyes in our brain with which we could perceive it' (AT vi. 130; CSM i. 167). In this passage Descartes was not concerned to argue that a picture (or set of motions) in the brain cannot cause the perception; on the contrary, he explicitly claimed there that motions 'act immediately on our soul' (AT vi. 130; CSM i. 167). His point was merely that the mind does not come to have the perception by viewing pictures composed of motions in the brain. The reference in the *Comments* to this earlier account of sensory perception indicates that the appeal to the formation of sensory ideas by an innate mental faculty is a development of the claim in the *Dioptrics* that the soul is instituted by nature to have certain sensations when bodily motions act on it. We are far here from considerations involving the causal axiom, or indeed from the conclusion that bodily motions play no causal role in the production of sensory ideas.

There still is the question of how precisely motions in the brain cause the operation of the innate mental faculty. It seems to me that this question is not directly addressed in the *Comments*, or in the *Dioptrics* for that matter. In the *Comments*, for instance, we are simply told dogmatically that motions serve as the occasion for the production of the ideas by triggering the operation of the innate mental faculty at a particular time, and that is that. But some commentators have claimed that there is in fact no problem here for Descartes. For example, Robert Richardson has argued that he was perfectly entitled to posit a distinctive form of causation in the case of body-to-mind action in sensation. Richardson emphasizes in particular Descartes's response to the objection from Princess Elisabeth concerning mind–body interaction that I quoted at the outset. In this response, Descartes claimed that the notion of mind–body interaction must be understood in terms of a 'primitive' notion of mind–body union that is distinct from primitive notions that apply to mind alone and to body alone, noting that

of the soul and the body together, we have only that of their union, on which depends that of the force (*force*) which the soul has to move the body, and the body to act on the soul, in causing its sensations and passions (*et le corps d'agir sur l'ame, en causant ses sentiments et ses passions*). (AT iii. 665; CSMK 218)

According to Richardson, the suggestion here is that we posit special kinds of forces to explain body-to-mind and mind-to-body action.

He takes the burden to be on the critic to show that Descartes was not entitled to posit such forces. In Richardson's terms:

There is no logical incoherence in such a position. A multiplicity of forces is no less coherent than a single force in nature. To posit such a multiplicity may be less parsimonious, but to admit that is hardly to admit that there is a serious principled or logical objection to Cartesianism.[39]

I agree that Descartes's causal axiom presents no insuperable barrier to the positing of a special sort of bodily force to act on mind. As long as body contains at least some of the reality of what is produced in the mind, and as long as some other efficient cause formally or eminently contains the rest of what is produced, the basic requirements of the axiom have been met. But it is too much to suggest, as I take Richardson to do, that Descartes has no burden of justification in positing these forces. For surely Descartes needs to show that his metaphysical principles allow for the purported dictate of experience that our body has a force to act on our soul in causing its sensations. In particular, he must show that this experience is consistent with his official doctrine that the nature of body consists in extension alone.[40] As we will see presently, though, the case of body–body interaction serves to indicate even more clearly the manner in which Descartes's doctrine creates problems for the attribution of causal powers to bodies. It is significant that this case is problematic even though, in contrast to the case of body-to-mind action, there is no general difficulty concerning the formal containment of the effect in the cause.

2.2. Second case: body–body interaction

Descartes's claim in the Sixth Meditation that bodies 'emit' sensory ideas suggests, problematically, that bodily causes produce sensations by literally sending them to the mind. Similarly, some of his remarks concerning body–body interaction suggest, again problematically, that motion is literally transferred from one body to another in collision. This is what Broughton calls the 'migration theory of motion',

---

[39] From 'Replies', 222.

[40] There is a similar problem with the appeal in the Sixth Meditation proof of the existence of the material world to the fact that bodies possess an 'active faculty' for producing sensory ideas (AT vii. 79–80; CSM ii. 55).

according to which motion is transferred in collision by means of the migration of a particular mode of motion from one body to another.[41] Broughton takes this theory to be suggested by Descartes's claim in the *Principles* that '[God] conserves motion, not as always fixed in the same parts of matter, but as it mutually is passing from some to others (*sed ex unis in alias ... mutuo ... transeuntem*) as they encounter each other' (*Principles of Philosophy*, II. 42, AT viiia. 66; CSM i. 243).[42] Her proposal is that Descartes was led to this theory by the fact that his causal axiom requires that in cases of formal containment, the cause not only contains something similar to what is found in the effect, but also imparts *the very same thing it formally contains* to its effect.[43]

As we have seen, Descartes offered in the *Comments* a more nuanced version of the view that bodies transmit ideas to the mind. It might be thought that he could also accept a more nuanced version of motion transfer than we find in the passage from the *Principles* that Broughton cites. With respect to this point, it is worth considering the case of Suárez. As I have noted, Suárez accepted a version of Descartes's causal axiom. Yet he also emphasized in his *Disputationes metaphysicae* that an efficient cause is 'extrinsic' since it does 'not communicat[e] its own proper and (as I will put it) individual *esse* to the effect, but instead some other really flowing forth (*profluens*) and proceeding (*manans*) from such a cause by means of an action'.[44] The basic point is that the efficient cause that formally contains its effect does not pass on the very same feature that it contains; rather, it only produces a feature of the same type.

For Suárez, the type here is the particular form or quality that the cause induces in its effect. A paradigmatic case would be one in which fire generates the same kind of 'real quality' of heat in something else that it itself possesses.[45] But Suárez allowed that in the case of

---

[41] 'Adequate Causes', 120–1.

[42] She also cites a passage from Descartes's *Le Monde* (AT xi. 11; CSM i. 85), and from a 1639 letter (AT ii. 543; CSMK 135).

[43] 'Adequate Causes', 120–1. This is similar to Radner's view that Descartes was committed to a 'communication principle'; see n. 13.

[44] *DM* 17. 1. 6, *Opera*, xxv. 582; *Efficient Causality*, 10. The contrast here is with formal and material causes, which are 'intrinsic' in the sense that they produce an effect not by an action that brings about something extrinsic to them, but by a 'formal and intrinsic union' to which they contribute their own being.

[45] Suárez held that with respect to the Aristotelian predicables, only qualities, and not quantities and relations, can be principles of action. Among the qualities, principles of

bodily interactions there can be cases where the 'principal'[46] efficient cause does not possess the same kind of quality, but is an 'equivocal' cause that contains the quality it induces only eminently. He held, for instance, that heated water contains the quality of coldness 'virtually' in so far as it has by its nature the active power to cool.[47] Descartes of course rejected the whole category of real qualities and active powers that informs Suárez's account of efficient causality on the grounds that all accidents are mere modes of substance.[48] But he thereby also rejected the view that there can be qualities or powers in bodies 'more noble than' bodily effects that also eminently contain these effects. For Descartes held that all alterable features of body have the same kind of reality as modes of extension, and that only infinite or finite indivisible minds can be more noble than bodily substances and their modifications.[49] Thus, he could not have accepted Suárez's position that there can be adequate bodily causes that eminently contain their effects.

---

action include active (vs. passive) *potentiae*, habits and dispositions that yield specific actions (as opposed to general states), and sensible qualities. Among the sensible qualities, some such as colours can effect 'intentional species' of themselves but not qualities similar to themselves, whereas others such as heat and light can effect both intentional species of themselves and qualities similar to themselves. Significantly enough with respect to later developments in Descartes, Suárez explicitly denied that either shapes (in the category of quality) or local motions (as well as alteration in quality, augmentation in quantity, and substantial generation) can serve as *per se* principles of action. See *DM* 18. 4, *Opera*, xxv. 624–7; *Efficient Causality*, 111–20.

[46] As opposed to instrumental; Suárez allowed that the instrumental cause can contain its effect neither formally nor eminently, but nonetheless insisted that in cases of instrumental causality there must be some cause or causes that so contains whatever the instrumental cause does not; see *DM* 18. 2. 22–6, *Opera*, xxv. 606–8; *Efficient Causality*, 69–74.

[47] *DM* 18. 3. 4 and 18. 7. 19, *Opera*, xxv. 616 and 635–6; *Efficient Causality*, 32 and 143. For Suárez's account of equivocal causality, see *DM* 17. 2. 21, *Opera*, xxv. 591–2; *Efficient Causality*, 32.

[48] See, for instance, Descartes's claim in a 1643 letter to Mersenne that 'I do not suppose any *real qualities* in nature, which are joined to substance, as little souls to their bodies, and which can be separated from it by divine power, and thus I attribute to motion or to all the other varieties of substance that one calls qualities no more reality than the philosophers commonly attribute to shape, which they call not *real quality* but only *mode*' (AT iii. 648–9; CSMK 216). For discussion of Descartes's deep differences from the scholastics on this point, see Stephen Menn, 'The Greatest Stumbling Block: Descartes' Denial of Real Qualities', in R. Ariew and M. Grene (eds.), *Descartes and his Contemporaries: Meditations, Objections, and Replies* (Chicago: University of Chicago Press, 1995), 182–207.

[49] It is telling that in the passage quoted in n. 48, Descartes assumed that his scholastic opponents must conceive of bodily qualities that are 'more noble than' mere modes as 'little souls' joined to bodies.

Even so, Suárez's analysis of efficient causation serves to counter Broughton's suggestion that Descartes's causal axiom, when applied to the case of body–body interaction, requires a migration theory of motion. It seems that Descartes could have held that a body that is an efficient cause of motion itself contains a motion that has the same features as, but nonetheless is numerically distinct from, the motion it induces in another body. Indeed, in a passage from his 1649 correspondence with Henry More that Broughton herself cites, Descartes explicitly rejected the migration theory of motion. No doubt prompted by the passage from the *Principles* that is suggestive of the migration theory, More protested that a mode of motion cannot 'pass over' (*transet*) or 'migrate' (*migret*) from one corporeal subject to another (AT v. 382). Descartes responded:

this is not what I have written; indeed I think that motion as a mode continually changes. ... But when I said that the same motion always remains in matter, I understood this to concern the force impelling its parts (*de vi eius partes impellente*), which force applies itself now to one part of matter, now to another, in accord with the laws proposed in articles 45 and following in the Second Part [of the *Principles*]. (AT v. 405; CSMK 382)

Given the passage from the *Principles* previously cited, it was somewhat disingenuous of Descartes to claim that he had never written that motion can be passed from one body to another. But his main point is perhaps that when he wrote that, he meant only that the force that causes motion is redistributed in a particular manner. And in the Second Part of the *Principles*, Descartes did indeed emphasize that changes in the speed or direction of motion derive from 'the quantum of force (*quantum ... virium*) in [bodies], either to move, or to resist motion' (*Principles of Philosophy*, ii. 45, AT viiia. 67; CSM i. 244).

Nevertheless, there remains the requirement of Descartes's causal axiom that the adequate or total bodily cause of changes in motion contain formally or eminently all of its effects in other bodies. If my analysis above is correct, eminent containment cannot be at issue here. So the question is whether the formal containment requirement is satisfied in cases of body–body interaction. In most of the basic cases of such interaction that he considered, Descartes could allow that the efficient cause actually contains something similar to what it produces in its effect. In his discussion in the *Principles* of the seven rules of collision, he indicated that in all cases where a moving body collides either with a moving body smaller than or equal to itself or with a smaller body at rest, the bodily cause contains modes of the same type as those it produces. In particular, in these cases the cause contains at least the *n* degrees of speed (to use O'Neill's language[50]) and the directional determination of the motion that it produces in the body with which it collides.[51] Matters are less straightforward, however, in cases where a moving body collides with a body at rest that is either larger than or equal in size to it. Descartes's fourth and sixth rules of collision require that the body at rest produce an instantaneous change in the direction of the motion of the moving body in such cases, even though the resting body does not actually possess any motion, and thus does not possess the particular directional determination it produces in the moving body.[52] So in these cases, the resting body that serves as the efficient and apparently total or adequate cause of the reversal of the moving body[53] seems not to contain formally or eminently everything that it produces in the effect.

It can still be said that the resting body contains the reality of extension, and this reality in some sense 'comprehends' the reality of the determination in a certain direction that this body imposes on the moving body. But more than this, Descartes held in the *Principles* that the resting body that causes a change possesses an amount of 'force

[50] See the passage quoted in the text to n. 17.

[51] The original version of the seven rules is set out in the Latin edition of the *Principles of Philosophy* (II. 46–52, AT viiia. 68–70). My comment applies to the following rules: the first rule, which covers the collision of bodies moving in opposite directions with equal sizes and speeds; the second rule, which covers the collision of a larger body with a smaller body moving in the opposite direction with the same speed; the third rule, which covers the collision of bodies moving in opposite directions with equal sizes but different speeds; the fifth rule, which covers the collision of a larger moving body with a smaller body at rest; and the seventh rule, which covers the collision of bodies with varying sizes or speeds that are moving in the same direction.

[52] These cases are covered by the fourth and sixth rules. There is a much expanded version of the rules that cover collisions involving bodies at rest in the 1647 French edition of the *Principles* (AT ixb. 90–2), which was preceded by a reconsideration of such collisions that Descartes offered in a 1645 letter to Clerselier (AT iv. 183–7; CSMK 246–8). For a helpful discussion of the evolution of Descartes's views concerning such collisions, see Daniel Garber, *Descartes' Metaphysical Physics* [*Metaphysical Physics*] (Chicago: University of Chicago Press, 1992), ch. 8. Cf. the complications indicated in n. 56.

[53] With respect to bodies, at least; here I bracket God's contribution as 'universal and primary cause' to changes in motion.

for resisting' (*vis ad resistendum*) equal to or greater than the amount of 'force for acting' (*vis ad agendum*) that is found in the moving body. So the resting body could be said to contain formally the reality of motion determined to a certain direction in the sense that it has a force at least as great as the force of the moving body to proceed with the same speed and direction.[54]

The suggestion here that prior to its production the reality of the directional determination of motion is formally contained in the force for resisting in the resting body that produces this determination is similar to my previous suggestion that prior to their formation the reality of sensory ideas is formally contained in the innate mental faculty that produces them. In both cases, formal containment of the reality need not involve the actual possession of the feature contained. To this extent I can side with Loeb's deflationary view of the causal axiom. Nonetheless, both of these cases respect the requirement that the cause and the effect it formally contains have the same nature. For both the innate mental faculty and the sensory ideas the mind formally contains must be conceived in terms of the thought that constitutes nature of mind, whereas both the force for resisting and the directionally determined motion the body formally contains must be conceived in terms of the extension that constitutes the nature of body.

There is admittedly some question whether the various bodily forces that Descartes posited both in the *Principles* and in his correspondence with More can be conceived in terms of extension alone. For extension seems to comprehend only passive modes and to exclude all active qualities and principles. Given this consideration, some have argued that it is plausible to think that Descartes in fact denied that bodies actually have any sort of force, and so have claimed that he could not allow that bodies can serve as true efficient causes of changes that follow on their collisions with other bodies. Here the appeal is to his claim in the Second Part of the *Principles* that God is 'the general cause of all the motions in the world' (*Principles of Philosophy*, ii. 36, AT viiia. 61; CSM i. 240). Drawing on such a claim, Daniel Garber has recently argued that

---

[54] In the *Principles*, the resting body is said to have the force 'for persevering in its state of rest', whereas the moving body is said to have the force 'for persisting in its motion, that is, in motion with the same speed and toward the same part' (*Principles of Philosophy*, ii. 43, AT viiia. 66–7; CSM i. 243–4).

Descartes regarded the bodily forces that he used to explain changes in motion 'simply as ways of talking about how God acts, resulting in the lawlike behavior of bodies'. In Garber's view, Descartes held that the forces themselves are '*nowhere*, strictly speaking, not in God, who is the real cause of motion in the inanimate world, and not in bodies, which are the recipients of the motion that God causes'.[55]

Even if Descartes denied that bodies are real efficient causes in collision, it seems that he could have held that the formal containment requirement is still satisfied. For the main point of this requirement is to rule out cases where the effect is disproportionate to the cause. Even given that there are no forces in the moving and resting bodies, there still is some sort of measurable modal quantity (size x speed in the case of the moving body, size x speed of colliding body in the case of the resting body[56]) that is at least as great in the agent as it is in the patient. In this sense the quantity produced in the effect can be said to be present in its bodily 'cause'.

But I suspect that Descartes would not have thought that the scare quotes are needed here. We have seen that even when he proposed an alternative to a transmission theory of sensation in the *Dioptrics*, he spoke of bodily motions as 'acting immediately on our soul'.[57] So also,

---

[55] *Metaphysical Physics*, 298. Cf. the 'occasionalist' interpretation of Descartes's views on body–body interaction in Gary Hatfield, 'Force (God) in Descartes' Physics', *Studies in History and Philosophy of Science*, 10 (1979), 113–40.

[56] This account of the quantities is suggested in the discussion of the collision rules in the 1644 Latin edition of the *Principles*. In the 1647 French edition of this text, however, there seems to be the more complicated position that in the case of collisions involving bodies at rest, the force for resisting is measured by the product of the size of the resting body and the quantity of motion that this body would receive were the moving body able to impose it, whereas the force for acting is measured by the product of the size of the moving body and the quantity of motion that body would have were it able to impose enough motion on the resting body for both to move subsequently at the same speed. For the claim that there is an evolution in Descartes's thought on this point, see Garber, *Metaphysical Physics*, 240–2, 250–1, 358 n. 16. But for an interpretation on which Descartes's account of the forces is more stable, see Alan Gabbey, 'Force and Inertia in the Seventeenth Century' ['Force'], in Stephen Gaukroger (ed.), *Descartes: Philosophy, Mathematics and Physics* [*Descartes*] (Brighton: Harvester; Totowa, NJ: Barnes & Noble, 1980), 230–320, at 269–70.

[57] Garber has argued that though Descartes started as a mind–body interactionist, he shifted over time to an occasionalist account of body-to-mind action; see 'Descartes and Occasionalism', in S. Nadler (ed.), *Causation and Early Modern Philosophy* (University Park: Pennsylvania State University Press, 1993), 9–26. There is an extended and, I think, convincing critique of Garber's position in Scott, 'Occasionalism', 504–15.

the suggestion in the *Principles* and the correspondence with More that forces are real quantities in bodies is reinforced by his comment in a 1640 letter to Mersenne that

it is certain that from the fact alone that a body begins to move, it has in itself the force to continue to move (*il a en soy la force de continuer à se mouvoir*); just as, from the fact alone that it is stopped in a certain place, it has the force to continue to remain there. (AT iii. 213; CSMK 155)

And Descartes might have thought that he was entitled to causal realism, at least in the case of body–body interaction, given the premiss in the *Principles* that motive forces derive from the tendency all bodies have to persist in the state they are in so far as they can (*quantum in se est*) (*Principles of Philosophy*, ii. 43, AT viiia. 66; CSM i. 243).[58]

Whether or not this tendency in bodies provides an adequate foundation for real bodily forces is a topic for another place.[59] The main point here is that a consideration of this question takes us beyond issues involving the containment constraints deriving from Descartes's causal axiom. It seems open to Descartes to overcome problems pertaining to these constraints by holding that bodies are partial causes that formally contain only certain features of sensory ideas, and that resting bodies are causes of aspects of motion that they themselves do not actually possess but only comprehend in the quantities that express their (actual or fictional) force for resisting. Even if he made these moves, though, the question about the legitimacy of the appeal to bodily forces would remain. In order to get to the source of the troubles with Descartes's treatment of causal interaction, we need to go beyond the sort of issues concerning his causal axiom that have exercised his critics and defenders.

These are the deflationary conclusions that I promised at the outset. But I promised as well some non-deflationary claims regarding Descartes's causal axiom. Here they are: First, *pace* Loeb, I have

---

[58] The classic defences of a realist interpretation of Descartes's account of body–body interaction are found in Martial Gueroult, 'The Metaphysics and Physics of Force in Descartes', in Gaukroger (ed.), *Descartes*, 196–229, and Gabbey, 'Force'. See also my defence of such an interpretation in 'Cartesian Causation: Body–Body Interaction, Motion, and Eternal Truths', *Studies in History and Philosophy of Science*, 34 (2003), 737–62.

[59] An important question here is whether Descartes is entitled to take the existence of body to involve more than the instantiation of a geometrical nature. His suggestion in the *Principles* is that existence carries with it a tendency to continue to exist in the same state, but it is perhaps not obvious that existence must include this additional tendency.

suggested that formal containment requires more than the presence of something at the same level of reality as the effect, but also, *pace* many other interpreters of Descartes, less than the actual presence of the effect in the cause. What is crucial in all cases of such containment is merely that the reality of the effect be present in some feature of the cause. As we have seen, this feature might be an innate mental faculty or some bodily quantity that is not the very same kind of thing as the effect. Second, I have argued on the basis of Descartes's own examples that eminent containment is to be understood in terms of the containment of effects in thought, and more particularly in a mental power that by itself suffices to produce the objective reality of ideas of those effects. The consequence here, in line with the view of Descartes's apologists, is that the causal axiom does not rule out heterogeneous interaction in cases involving eminent containment. Finally, there is the non-apologetic point that formal containment is in important respects more problematic for Descartes than eminent containment. The most serious problems concern the cases of body-to-mind action and body–body interaction, which ultimately require an appeal to bodily powers. We have seen that these problems do not derive directly from Descartes's causal axiom. But though a consideration of this axiom cannot uncover the roots of Descartes's theory of causation, it can at least show us where to start digging.[60]

Duke University

[60] I presented earlier versions of this chapter at Harvard University, the University of Oxford, and the University of Washington. My thanks to the audiences there for helpful discussion. I have mentioned in the notes the contributions of several individuals, for which I am grateful. Thanks also to Dan Garber, Andrew Janiak, and Steve Nadler for their comments on the chapter.

The Dustbin Theory of Mind:
A Cartesian Legacy?

LAWRENCE NOLAN AND JOHN WHIPPLE

I. INTRODUCTION

It is part of the lore of Descartes's philosophy that he subscribed to
what might be termed the 'Dustbin Theory of Mind'. According
to this traditional picture, Descartes's conception of the mental was
determined by his prior conception of matter as pure extension, shorn
of the various sensible qualities familiar from our ordinary experience
of the physical world. Having banished these qualities from nature,
and finding no other place to locate them, Descartes swept them
into the dustbin of the mind. The mind thus became a repository of
heterogeneous items—colours, sounds, odours, heat and cold, pains,
beliefs, intellections, etc.[1]

This interpretation of Descartes's theory of the mental has given
birth to several criticisms. One in particular has a long history,
dating back to Descartes's unorthodox disciple Nicolas Malebranche.
Descartes and his more orthodox followers purport to have a clear
and distinct idea of the mind, but Malebranche argues that this

---

[1] Without using the term 'Dustbin Theory' as such, Ryle's *Concept of Mind* (Chicago:
University of Chicago Press, 1949), esp. 20 and 199, contains the seminal statement of this
interpretation within analytic philosophy, though as we indicate below the general view
can be traced to Malebranche, Descartes's successor. Nicholas Jolley was perhaps the first
to discern this interpretation of Descartes in Malebranche, *The Light of the Soul* (Oxford:
Clarendon Press, 1990), and concurs in this interpretation himself: 'Descartes subscribed to
what might be called a dustbin or grab bag conception of the mind. The items that fall
under the umbrella of the mental, for Descartes, are whatever is left over from the picture of
the world once matter is defined in purely geometrical terms' ('Malebranche on the Soul',
in Steven Nadler (ed.), *The Cambridge Companion to Malebranche* (New York: Cambridge
University Press, 2000), 57). Also see Monte Cook, 'Descartes and the Dustbin of the Mind'
['Descartes and the Dustbin'], *History of Philosophy Quarterly*, 13 (1996), 17–33, and Richard
Rorty, *Philosophy and the Mirror of Nature* (Princeton: Princeton University Press, 1979).

claim is belied by their practice. To determine whether colours and other sensible qualities[2] are modifications of the mind, they do not consult their idea of mind; rather they consult the idea of body as pure extension and reason as follows: 'Heat, pain, and color cannot be modifications of extension, for extension can have only various figures and motion. Now there are only two kinds of beings, minds and bodies. Therefore, pain, heat, color, and all other sensible qualities belong to the mind' (Elucidation XI, OC iii. 165; LO 634).[3] Malebranche concludes that the Cartesians themselves lack a distinct idea of the mind, for if they had such an idea, they would not need such a circuitous route to establish that sensible qualities are mental items. We shall refer to this circuitous way of arguing, which Malebranche attributes to the Cartesians, as the 'Indirect Argument'.[4]

Despite Malebranche's claims, Descartes never explicitly articulates a version of the Indirect Argument.[5] The important question to consider, however, is whether there are any features of Descartes's philosophical system that commit him to it. Tad Schmaltz has argued that Descartes's account of material falsity, which stresses the obscurity and confusion that attends our sensations, should have led him to embrace the Indirect Argument, on the ground that our confused perception of the qualities of sense conceals their ontological status from us. We can know that sensible qualities are modes of the mind only indirectly, by first examining our distinct idea of body.[6] One

---

[2] Malebranche uses the term 'sensible qualities' (qualitez sensibles) to refer exclusively to colours, sounds, heat and cold, odours, etc. We follow his usage in this chapter.

[3] This chapter uses the following abbreviations: LO: T. M. Lennon and P. J. Olscamp (tr.), The Search after Truth and Elucidations of The Search after Truth (Columbus: Ohio State University Press, 1980). TFI: On True and False Ideas: New Objections to Descartes's Replies, tr. E. J. Kremer (Lewiston, NY: Edwin Mellen Press, 1990). We sometimes diverge from the translations in CSM(K) and LO.

[4] Malebranche's objection here is part of a larger critique of Descartes's account of knowledge of the mind. We defend Descartes against this critique in 'Self-Knowledge in Descartes and Malebranche', Journal of the History of Philosophy, 43 (2005), 55–81. Here we are concerned with Malebranche's Indirect Argument more narrowly, as it bears on the question of whether Descartes holds a Dustbin Theory of Mind. For recent discussions of the Indirect Argument, see Cook, 'Descartes and the Dustbin'; Jolley, 'Malebranche on the Soul'; Andrew Pyle, Malebranche (New York: Routledge, 2003), 186–208; and Tad Schmaltz, Malebranche's Theory of the Soul: A Cartesian Interpretation (New York: Oxford University Press, 1996).

[5] Ferdinand Alquié and Geneviève Rodis-Lewis claim to detect an indirect argument in the Passions of the Soul. We consider and reject this claim in n. 29.

[6] Schmaltz, Malebranche's Theory of the Soul, 81–2.

might also argue that if Descartes were a dustbin theorist, then he ought to have been committed to the Indirect Argument. For again, according to this traditional interpretation, Descartes the scientist started with a positive conception of matter and then conceived of the mind in negative terms as whatever body is *not*. If this interpretation were correct, then the argument for the mental status of sensible qualities would simply be an instance of this general strategy. Malebranche's claim that the Cartesians themselves lack a clear idea of mind would thus be vindicated.

But contrary to Malebranche and to more recent critics,[7] Descartes has principled reasons for rejecting both the Indirect Argument and the Dustbin Theory of Mind, as we shall argue. There are two general considerations, stemming from his philosophical system, which will help us to uncover these reasons: first, his diagnosis of why our ideas of mind and body, and our sensations,[8] are confused prior to philosophizing, and, second, his primary strategy for clarifying these ideas. Sections 2 and 3 take up each of these points respectively. These considerations will reveal three distinct (albeit related) reasons why Descartes would reject the Indirect Argument and the Dustbin Theory.

2. DESCARTES'S DIAGNOSIS OF CONFUSED THOUGHT

2.1. *Embodiment and false judgements as the source of confusion*

Descartes's account of how our sensations become confused presupposes an account of how confusion infects the ideas of mind and body. So we begin our discussion with the latter. Descartes maintains that our ideas of mind and body are given to us as confused, largely as a result of our 'embodiment'. This is one of the watchwords of recent Cartesian studies. Commentators are beginning to concur that the doctrine of mind–body union constitutes one of the keys to Descartes's philosophy. Although the mind is a substance really

---

[7] See n. 1.

[8] Descartes often uses the terms 'sensation' and 'sensory idea' interchangeably. In this chapter, we shall use the term 'sensation' exclusively. Descartes distinguishes these mental effects from (1) the motions in our sense organs that occasion them and from (2) the judgements about things outside us that often accompany our sensations (see AT vii. 436–7; CSM ii. 294–5). As we shall see below, the latter play a crucial role in his account of how our sensations become confused.

distinct from the body, and thus can exist apart from it, the body strongly influences the mind and the two are so intimately related in this life that it is difficult to understand one without the other. As is to be expected then, mind–body union figures prominently in Descartes's account of confused thought. One of the most immediate consequences of mind–body union, familiar to readers of the *Meditations*, is that from its infancy the mind is immersed in the senses and the ways in which the body is being affected by things outside it: 'In its first state (*primā aetate*) the mind was so closely tied to the body that it had no leisure for any thoughts except those by means of which it had sensory awareness of what was happening to the body' (AT viiia. 35; CSM i. 218).[9] At this point, we had no purely intellectual thoughts—no thoughts of the mind as a purely thinking thing and no understanding of body as pure extension. All we had was a confused perception of ourselves as a union of mind and body.

This sensory, pre-philosophical perception of union is not something we can improve upon through meditation or intellectual endeavour. In an oft-cited passage from a letter to Elisabeth, Descartes asserts that the union of mind and body is 'known very clearly' through the senses but 'known only obscurely by the intellect'. Whereas the mind is known best by the intellect, and body by the intellect aided by the imagination, one is best able to perceive how the soul acts on the body, and vice versa, through 'the ordinary course of life and conversation' (AT iii. 691–2; CSM iii. 227). According to Descartes's technical definitions of clarity and distinctness (and their correlatives), if something is obscure to the intellect, then it is also confused or indistinct.[10] This implies that, in addition to being obscure, the union of mind and body is conceived of only confusedly by the intellect. As Descartes asserts in the Sixth Replies: 'I had from my earliest years conceived of my mind and body as a unity of some sort (for I had a confused awareness that I was composed of mind and body)' (AT vii. 445; CSM ii. 300). This confused conception makes it extremely difficult to conceive of the real distinction between mind and body, and 'many more people make the mistake of thinking that the soul is

---

[9] CSM translates *primā aetate* here as 'early childhood', but we think the more literal translation is appropriate, for we take it that on Descartes's view the ideas of mind and body are given to us as confused at birth (or even in the womb) as a result of the union.

[10] See *Principles of Philosophy*, I. 45, AT viii. 22; CSM i. 207–8.

not really distinct from the body than make the opposite mistake of admitting their distinction and denying their union' (letter to Regius, January 1642, AT iii. 508; CSMK 209).[11] Descartes's view then is that our ideas of mind and body are confused as a result of our ordinary, pre-philosophical awareness of ourselves as a union. This point is highly significant for it suggests that the confusion attending these ideas consists in their being confounded *together*. We draw out several consequences of Descartes's analysis below, after discussing the source of confused *sensory* thought.

It is standardly held that the obscurity and confusion attending Cartesian sensations is intrinsic and thus incapable of being remedied. This standard reading is based on Descartes's remarks about materially false ideas in the Third Meditation. There Descartes proffers as examples of material falsity the sensations of heat and cold, and says that such ideas 'contain so little clarity and distinctness' that one cannot tell whether 'cold is merely the absence of heat or vice versa, or whether both of them are real qualities, or neither is' (AT vii. 43–4; CSM ii. 30). Some influential commentators have taken such remarks to imply that sensations have a deceptive presentational character that inclines us to make false judgements about the properties of external objects. Although we can guard against making such judgements, we cannot ameliorate the obscurity and confusion that naturally attends our sensations.[12]

The received view of material falsity has recently come under fire. At least two commentators have argued convincingly that our sensations are not inherently deceptive and that the obscurity and confusion attending our sensations, prior to philosophizing, is the result of habits of judgement formed in childhood and reinforced by scholastic science.[13] On this view, the sensory perception of a red apple is confused not because the idea itself has a misleading

---

[11] Also see *Fourth Replies*, AT vii. 228–9; CSM ii. 160.

[12] The classic formulation of this interpretation can be found in Margaret Wilson, *Descartes* (London: Routledge & Kegan Paul, 1978), 101–19. Schmaltz presupposes an interpretation of material falsity along these lines when he suggests that this feature of Descartes's system should have led him to endorse the Indirect Argument. See n. 6.

[13] See Lilli Alanen, 'Sensory Ideas, Objective Reality, and Material Falsity', in John Cottingham (ed.), *Reason, Will, and Sensation* (New York: Clarendon Press, 1994), 229–50, and especially Alan Nelson, 'The Falsity in Sensory Ideas: Descartes and Arnauld', in Elmar Kremer (ed.), *Interpreting Arnauld* (Toronto: Toronto University Press, 1996), 13–32.

presentational character, but because the perception is compounded with the false judgement that redness is a quality in the apple. Such judgements are so habituated that we fail to realize that we are making them. Nevertheless, these judgements are voluntary and therefore fully correctable.

This revisionist interpretation of material falsity has several attractive features *as* an account of material falsity and it is one that we accept.[14] It is also attractive for at least one external reason, more directly relevant to the concerns of this chapter. The revisionist interpretation explains Descartes's remarks in the *Principles of Philosophy*, I. 68, that our sensations of pain and colour are clear and distinct when they are regarded merely as thoughts, and not judged to resemble anything in bodies:

> In order to distinguish what is clear in this connection from what is obscure, we must be very careful to note that pain and color and so on are clearly and distinctly perceived when they are regarded merely as sensations or thoughts. But when they are judged to be certain things existing outside our mind, there is no way of understanding what sort of things they are … (AT viiia. 33; CSM i. 217)

Proponents of the standard view of material falsity are forced to maintain that Descartes is not entitled to say that sensations can be clearly and distinctly perceived, or that what he says here is inconsistent with his remarks in the *Meditations*, for on their view sensations are intrinsically confused and this confusion cannot be remedied.

But to suppose that Descartes is inconsistent here would also require one to suppose that he is inconsistent in the *Meditations* itself. For in the Sixth Meditation he says that although certain things appear to have been taught to us by nature or by the senses themselves—such as that heat or colour is in body—such beliefs are in fact the result of 'a habit of making ill-considered judgments' (AT vii. 82; CSM ii. 56). Descartes appeals here to the very same account of sensory confusion that one finds in the *Principles*, in terms of habits of judgements formed in early childhood. Indeed, while considering another example in the same context, he notes that

> although a star has no greater effect on my eye than the flame of a small light, that does not mean that there is any real or positive inclination in me

---

[14] See Nelson, 'The Falsity in Sensory Ideas', for an enumeration of these attractions.

to believe that the star is no bigger than the light; I have simply made this judgment from childhood onwards without any rational basis. (AT vii. 83; CSM ii. 57)

Descartes is quite explicit that the source of the confusion is not something 'real or positive' in the sensation itself, which inclines me to judge falsely. Rather I make this judgement because of a habit of doing so that was developed in childhood and that has become ingrained. In the articles surrounding *Principles* I. 68 (especially article 71), we get a more detailed account of how these habits of judgement are formed and thus of how our sensations become confused. We turn now to that discussion.

As with his diagnosis of how our ideas of mind and body become confused, Descartes's account of the genesis of confused sensory thought relies on the doctrine of mind–body union. Descartes explains that, in our infancy, when immersed in the senses and the ways our body was being affected, we did not 'refer' our sensations of pain, colour, smell, etc. to anything outside ourselves. However, this is not to say that we attributed them exclusively to the mind. Because our ideas of mind and body were confounded together we regarded 'ourselves' not as minds, but as mind–body unions. We thereby falsely attributed our sensations to the union, rather than to the mind alone.[15]

At this very early stage, the mind also perceived shapes, sizes, and motions, etc. that were presented to it 'not as sensations but as things, or modes of things, existing (or capable of existing) outside thought' (AT viiia. 35; CSM i. 219). However, at this point, we did

---

[15] Some commentators have argued that Cartesian sensations are, in fact, modes of the union rather than of the mind. For a range of positions like this, see John Cottingham, 'Cartesian Trialism', *Mind*, 94 (1985), 218–30; Paul Hoffman, 'Cartesian Passions and Cartesian Dualism', *Pacific Philosophical Quarterly*, 71 (1990), 310–33; R. C. Richardson, 'The "Scandal" of Cartesian Interactionism', *Mind*, 91 (1982), 20–37; and Tad Schmaltz, 'Descartes and Malebranche on Mind and Mind–Body Union', *Philosophical Review*, 101 (1992), 281–325. The purported texts in favour of such 'trialist' interpretations, however, all admit of alternative readings consistent with Descartes's official dualism; for example, in places where some of these commentators read Descartes as saying that sensations are modes of the union, he can be taken to mean that they are modes of mind *caused by* the mind's union with the body or, more precisely, *caused by* the body and produced in the mind as a result of the union (see e.g. AT viiia. 23; CSM i. 209). As Marleen Rozemond has shown, trialist interpretations also suffer from philosophical problems and saddle Descartes with serious inconsistencies. See *Descartes's Dualism* (Cambridge, Mass.: Harvard University Press, 1998), 191–2.

not fully understand the difference between sensations and external things. As the body began to develop such that it could pursue what was beneficial and avoid what was harmful to the union, the mind 'began to notice that the objects of this pursuit or avoidance had an existence outside itself' (ibid.). It then attributed to these objects 'not only sizes, shapes, motions, and the like, which it perceived as things, or modes of things, but also tastes, smells and so on, the sensations of which were, it realized, produced by the objects in question' (AT viiia. 36; CSM i. 219). We thus came to form many false judgements concerning the things causing our sensations. In particular, we judged that there were things in bodies—which we *called* 'colours', 'sounds', 'odours', etc.—that resemble our sensations.[16] Our sensations became further confused as a result of such false judgements, and our ideas of mind and body became further confused together.

Descartes calls these false judgements—by which we attribute colours, sounds, and odours to external things—'prejudices', where the Latin *praejudicia* literally means to 'prejudge'. In general, the prejudices of childhood are the 'chief cause of error'. They are formed when we are not in full command of our reason, but are difficult to relinquish later when we reach intellectual maturity because they become habituated.[17] 'Forgetting that they were adopted without sufficient examination', we regard them 'as known by the senses or implanted by nature', accepting them 'as utterly true and evident' (AT viiia. 36; CSM i. 218–19). As a result of these prejudices, and our preoccupation with the senses and the imagination, 'most people have nothing but confused perceptions [of all their ideas] throughout their entire lives' (AT viiia. 36; CSM i. 220).

This discussion has important consequences for the issue of whether Descartes holds a Dustbin Theory of Mind and for whether he is committed to Malebranche's Indirect Argument. First, it shows that Descartes and Malebranche have very different diagnoses of the source

---

[16] AT viiia. 216; CSM i. 216. Also see AT viiia. 318, 322; CSM i. 282, 285, for Descartes's account of how we come to apply the terms 'colour', 'smell', 'taste', 'sound', etc. to properties of bodies.

[17] '... we are therefore in the habit of judging of these things not on the basis of present perception but from preconceived opinion' (AT viiia. 37; CSM i. 220). For a more complete treatment of the role of habits in confused thought, see Lawrence Nolan, 'The Ontological Argument as an Exercise in Cartesian Therapy', *Canadian Journal of Philosophy* (forthcoming).

of our confusion. Malebranche attributes our sensory confusion to the fact that we lack a clear and distinct idea of the mind.[18] But Descartes will not accept that verdict. On the contrary, he has his own highly sophisticated account of our confusion that attempts to explain how it infects all of our ideas, prior to philosophizing, and that depends on theses about mind–body union that he shares with Malebranche. If anything, one wonders why Malebranche rejected his account in favour of a verdict that appears, from a strictly Cartesian perspective, rather hasty.

Second, Descartes thinks that the confusion attending our pre-philosophical idea of mind and our sensations is a contingent matter, resulting in the first case from our embodiment and in the second from habitual false judgements, and not from something intrinsic to these ideas. Although it requires great effort and training, and most people never succeed, the dedicated meditator is capable of dispelling the confusion infecting all of these ideas. Malebranche, by contrast, assumes that our confusion about the nature of the mind is inevitable and incurable.

Third, although Descartes and Malebranche agree that the ordinary person and the scholastic falsely attribute colours, sounds, odours, etc. to external things, they have different accounts of the content of such judgements. According to Malebranche, the common person supposes that the very qualities she senses are in external objects: it is a 'prejudice common to all men, *that their sensations are in the objects they sense*' (*Recherche*, i. 16, OC i. 169; LO 75). Descartes, by contrast, holds that the common person makes two other mistakes: first, rather than (properly) attributing sensations to the mind, she attributes them to the union. Second, she supposes there are things (that she calls 'colours', 'sounds', 'tastes', etc.) in external objects that resemble her sensations.

It is highly significant that Descartes thinks the common person makes this second mistake, for it shows that he does *not* identify colour or sound sensations with the 'colours', 'sounds', etc. that the common person attributes to external things. The latter are *not* sensations, but things the confused person takes to *resemble* her sensations. This

---

[18] 'Now the reason why all men do not immediately see that colors, odors, tastes, and all other sensations are modifications of their soul is that we have no clear idea of our soul' (*Recherche*, i. 12, OC i. 139; LO 58).

reveals the first of three main reasons why Descartes would reject both the Indirect Argument and the Dustbin Theory. The Dustbin Theory presupposes, and the Indirect Argument seeks to prove, that the sensible qualities that we pre-philosophically attribute to external bodies are really just modes of mind. But if Descartes does not identify those qualities with sensations, as we have suggested, then he would regard the Indirect Argument as unsound. Quite simply, these so-called 'qualities' are not modes of body *or* mind; they are merely the products of confused judgement.[19]

From Descartes's perspective, another problem with Malebranche's Indirect Argument is that it presupposes a distinct idea of body that is ready to hand and to which even the philosophically benighted person can appeal to establish the mental status of sensible qualities. But, according to Descartes's diagnosis, prior to philosophizing the ordinary person's ideas of mind and body are both highly confused, and this confusion consists in their being literally confounded together. Thus, there is no prior idea of body that is given to us as distinct. In Section 3, we attempt to explain Descartes's positive strategy for clarifying our ideas. As we shall see, to achieve distinct ideas of both mind and body, one must carefully and methodically tease them apart. This means that clarifying these ideas is a single process, and one does not achieve a *fully* clear and distinct idea of the one without also achieving such an idea of the other. But once one has a fully clear and distinct idea of the mind, then one can determine the ontological status of any mode of mind *directly*. Before turning to that discussion, however, in the next subsection we address the question of why Malebranche assumes that the ordinary person has a distinct idea of extension, prior to philosophizing. This will further expose the philosophical divide that separates him from Descartes.

2.2. Malebranche's distinction between the idea of body and the idea of extension

It is puzzling that Malebranche singles out the lack of a distinct idea of the mind as the primary reason we mistakenly attribute sensible

---

[19] For an account of the ontological status of Cartesian sensible qualities that complements the claims of this chapter, see our 'The Bogey of Cartesian Qualia' (unpub.).

qualities to bodies. On Descartes's view, this mistake results in part from having confused ideas of both mind and body. Short of taking that position, it seems more plausible to locate the source of our error in the idea of body. In his defence of Descartes, Arnauld rightly observes that people who think that sensible qualities are in corporeal objects do not have a clear and distinct idea of body.[20] In Elucidation XI Malebranche attempts to address this objection by drawing a distinction between the idea of body and the idea of extension: some people 'might have doubts as to whether or not body is capable of sensations, or of receiving some sensible quality; but this is because they understand body as something other than extension' (OC iii. 167; LO 635). However, even if they conceive of body in this confused manner, the idea of extension 'is so clear that everyone agrees on what it contains and what it excludes' (ibid.). Arnauld dismisses Malebranche's response here as a pure equivocation. Those who distinguish body from extension do not 'have a clear idea of extension, since they do not know that body and extension are the same thing' (TFI 130). In other words, if one does not recognize that extension just is the essence of body, then one does not have a clear idea of extension.

Arnauld plainly gets the better of Malebranche on this point. But what is motivating Malebranche's tenuous distinction between the idea of body and the idea of extension? Consider the following passage from Elucidation XI:

If the nature of the soul is better known than the nature of any other thing, if the idea we have of it is as clear as the idea we have of the body, then I ask only this: how is it that there are so many people who confuse the two? Is it possible to confuse two entirely different clear ideas? Those who are not of our opinion are as reasonable as we, they have the same ideas of things, they participate in the same reason. Why, then, do they confuse what we distinguish? Have they ever confused two different numbers? Have they ever taken a square for a circle? Yet the soul is more different from the body than a square is from a circle, for they are substances that agree in nothing, and yet these people confuse them. There is, then, some difficulty in recognizing

---

[20] '... those who think that the sensible qualities do not belong to the soul believe that they belong to the body. Therefore they do not have a clear idea of the body, since according to him [i.e. Malebranche], in order for an idea to be clear, we must be able to perceive, by a simple vision, *what it contains and what it excludes*' (TFI 134–5).

their difference. ... The idea of extension must be carefully consulted, and it must be seen that extension is not a mode of bodies but body itself ... and thus, since the modes of which a body is capable are in no way related to sense qualities, the subject of these qualities ... must be very different from body. Such arguments must be produced in order to avoid confusing the soul with the body. But if we had a clear idea of the soul, as we do of the body, we certainly would not have to take such a roundabout way to distinguish it from the body. We could do so at a single glance, as easily as we see that a square is not a circle. (*OC* iii. 170–1; LO 637–8)

This passage is quite striking given our earlier discussion of Descartes's account of how the ideas of mind and body are confused. Malebranche begins by acknowledging Descartes's point that people often confound these ideas together, but rather than attributing this confusion to our pre-philosophical conception of union, he insists that this too is due to our lack of a clear (and distinct) idea of mind. He also claims that the idea of extension remains perfectly clear. This strains credulity, for we are told here that extension just is body ('extension is not a mode of bodies but body itself'). To press Arnauld's point, how could one have a distinct idea of extension if she did not know that body just is extension? Once more, the idea of extension *is* the idea of body, and if this idea were distinct, one would not confuse the idea of the mind with it.

Malebranche thinks he is entitled to say that we have a clear and distinct idea of extension—even while confusing the ideas of body and mind—because the primary notions in geometry and arithmetic are immediately distinct and readily agreed upon by everyone. He is treating mathematical knowledge as the paradigm of knowledge through clear and distinct ideas and emphasizing what he takes to be a revealing asymmetry with knowledge of mind. People do not (generally) confuse geometrical figures or numbers, but (almost) everyone confuses the mind with the body. If we had a clear and distinct idea of the mind then we would be able to see immediately that sensible qualities are modes of the mind and that the mind is really distinct from the body—just as we see that a square is not a circle.

The appeal to mathematical knowledge fails to validate Malebranche's distinction between the idea of body and the idea of extension, for the reasons already given. In particular, it does not address Arnauld's point that people who attribute sensible qualities to body do not have a clear idea of extension. Malebranche insists on making the idea of mind (or the lack thereof) the culprit, but this is implausible. Following Descartes, it is more reasonable to say that such people lack clear and distinct ideas of both mind and body (extension). Malebranche thus fails to locate an asymmetry between our knowledge of body and our knowledge of mind. At most, he identifies an interesting asymmetry between knowledge of mind and body on the one hand and mathematical knowledge on the other. Generally speaking, only knowledge of the latter sort is immediately clear and distinct (or so it seems). One might well wonder why this is.

In the *Sixth Replies*, Descartes offers an interesting explanation of this epistemic disparity that again relies (implicitly) on our status as embodied creatures.

It is true that, before freeing myself from prejudices acquired from the senses, I did perceive correctly that two and three make five ... and many things of this kind; and yet I did not think that the soul of man is distinct from his body. But I do not find this surprising. For I can easily see why it happened that, when still an infant, I never made any false judgments about propositions of this sort, which everyone accepts; the reason was that I had no occasion to employ these propositions, since children do not learn to count two and three until they are capable of judging whether they make five. (AT vii. 445; CSM ii. 299–300)

If we juxtapose this passage with the ones considered earlier from the *Principles* and elsewhere, we begin to get a very full and nuanced account of the genesis of confused thought and of the sense in which mathematical knowledge is privileged for Descartes, if it is privileged at all. In our earliest years, when immersed in the senses and the ways in which our body was being affected by external things, we formed many false judgements about the nature of the mind and the nature of corporeal objects. However, at that stage we were so concerned with preserving our union and pursuing what was beneficial to it that we never had occasion to make judgements about mathematical propositions; a fortiori we had no occasion to make *false* judgements that would later become habituated. As a result, we never formed prejudices about the primary notions in mathematics. We only began making judgements in mathematics after we were already in full command of our reason. Once we have an idea of a simple mathematical truth, it is immediately clear and distinct. It turns out that on Descartes's view, the disparity between our mathematical knowledge and other types of knowledge is completely innocuous, and even complements his treatment of why the ideas of mind and body are confused. By failing to consider this account or to provide adequate responses to Arnauld's objections, Malebranche's own conclusions appear rash and forced.

3. HOW OUR CONFUSED IDEAS BECOME CLEAR AND DISTINCT

We now turn to Descartes's primary strategy for clarifying our pre-philosophically confused sensations and ideas of mind and body. This strategy follows naturally from his account of how these ideas are confused, as explained in Section 2.1. Since the ideas of mind and body are given to us as confused, *and* this confusion consists in their literally being confounded together, the primary strategy for dispelling this confusion is to tease these ideas apart very carefully and methodically: 'it happens in almost every case of imperfect knowledge that many things are apprehended together as a unity, though they will later have to be distinguished by a more careful examination' (AT vii. 445; CSM ii. 300). Simply put, the ideas of mind and body become distinct (in Descartes's technical sense of 'distinctness') by being distinguished from each other.[21] It is precisely because these ideas are confused together that the only way to make them distinct is by teasing them apart. This is a single process and a gradual one: these ideas become distinguished by degrees, and one does not achieve fully clear and distinct ideas of mind and body until one has completely distinguished them from each other.[22]

---

[21] In the *Principles* Descartes explains that 'a perception is "distinct" if, as well as being clear, it is so sharply separated from all other perceptions that it contains within itself only what is clear' (AT viiia. 22; CSM i. 207–8).

[22] One might object that this assertion contravenes Descartes's boast in the Second Meditation that mind is better known than body. If our ideas in this case become clear and distinct by means of a single process, then at most Descartes should claim that mind and body are known equally well. To blunt this objection, it helps to recall that by the end of the *Meditations* Descartes does think that our knowledge of mind and our knowledge of body are on a par, in the sense that we have metaphysical certainty about the existence and nature of both substances. In keeping with this point, Descartes's stronger thesis is

In fact, one could read the *Meditations* as a whole as aiming towards this goal. The meditator begins this process in the Second Meditation, but does not complete it until the Sixth Meditation, where she excludes the ideas of mind and body from each other in thought. This final step of the process plays a central role in Descartes's proof of the real distinction between mind and body.

If this reading is correct, it highlights the second main reason that Descartes would reject both the Indirect Argument and the Dustbin Theory. As we have seen, the latter presuppose that the idea of body (or extension) is given to us as distinct and is prior to any idea of mind. But Descartes maintains that both ideas are highly confused prior to philosophizing and, moreover, that one cannot achieve a *fully* clear and distinct idea of the one without also achieving such an idea of the other.

In this section we shall develop and defend our interpretative hypothesis concerning the way in which clear and distinct ideas of mind and body are achieved. This discussion will also reveal the third main reason that Descartes would reject the Indirect Argument. He maintains that the ontological status of any mode can only be known *directly*, and prescribes a method for accomplishing this that consists in perceiving a given mode through a substance's 'principal' attribute.

We have suggested that a central aim of the *Meditations* is to help the sympathetic reader tease her ideas of mind and body apart from each other. Many of the moves Descartes deploys to help the meditator attain this end are quite familiar. Using the method of universal doubt, he teaches the meditator to withdraw from the senses and to meditate carefully on the ideas of mind and body individually. In the Second Meditation, the meditator discovers that she can conceive of her mind as a thinking thing and the wax as an extended thing. The nuances of the *cogito*, the *res cogitans*, and the wax passage have been discussed at great length in the secondary literature. Such details need not be discussed here, for our perspective is much broader. We shall focus on the *function* of the various cognitive exercises prescribed for the meditator in the Second Meditation.

often interpreted to mean either (1) that body is known through the mind or (2) that in the context of the Second Meditation, the existence and nature of mind is certain while that of body remains dubitable. But both of these interpretations are compatible with the claim that the ideas of mind and body are not fully clear and distinct until they have been completely teased apart.

Descartes makes some revealing remarks about this function in the following passages from the Second Replies and the Synopsis of the *Meditations*:

All our ideas of what belongs to the mind have up till now been very confused and mixed up with the ideas of things that can be perceived by the senses. This is the first and most important reason for our inability to understand with sufficient clarity the customary assertions about the soul and God. *So I thought I would be doing something worthwhile if I explained how the properties or qualities of the mind are to be distinguished from the qualities of the body.* Admittedly, many people had previously said that in order to understand metaphysical matters the mind must be drawn away from the senses; but no one, so far as I know, had shown how this could be done. The correct, and in my view unique, method of achieving this is contained in my Second Meditation. But the nature of the method is such that scrutinizing it just once is not enough. *Protracted and repeated study is required to eradicate the lifelong habit of confusing things related to the intellect with corporeal things, and to replace it with the opposite habit of distinguishing the two.* (AT vii. 131; CSM ii. 94; our emphasis)

In the Second Meditation, the mind uses its own freedom and supposes the non-existence of all the things about whose existence it can have even the slightest doubt; and in so doing the mind notices that it is impossible that it should not itself exist during this time. *This exercise is also of the greatest benefit, since it enables the mind to distinguish without difficulty what belongs to itself, i.e. to an intellectual nature, from what belongs to the body.* (AT vii. 12; CSM ii. 9; our emphasis)

These texts cohere nicely with the thesis argued for in Section 2.1, namely that prior to meditation the ideas of mind and body are confused by their having been naturally confounded together. This is most explicit in the first passage where Descartes speaks of the 'lifelong habit of confusing things related to the intellect with corporeal things'. Descartes wants to help the meditator replace this habit 'with the opposite habit of distinguishing the two'. Similarly, in the second passage Descartes describes the application of the method of doubt as being 'of the greatest benefit' because it allows the meditator to distinguish what belongs 'to an intellectual nature, from what belongs to the body'.

We want to underscore the fact that in each of these texts Descartes presents his Second Meditation strategies as directly combating the confusion that infects the ideas of mind and body. One virtue of applying the method of doubt as directed in the Second Meditation is that it allows the meditator to tease her ideas of mind and body apart. Indeed, the texts cited above, taken in conjunction with Descartes's previously discussed remarks on how the ideas of mind and body are given to us as confused, strongly suggest that the Second Meditation is carefully crafted with precisely this end in mind.

We now turn our attention to the real distinction argument of the Sixth Meditation. As mentioned above, this is where the final step in the process of distinguishing the ideas of mind and body takes place. Needless to say, a complete discussion of Descartes's real distinction proof exceeds the scope of this chapter. For our present purposes, we need focus only on how to understand Descartes's claim that mind can be clearly and distinctly understood apart from body. This assertion constitutes an important part of the real distinction proof. It is a particular instance of a general principle that Descartes sets forth at the beginning of his proof: 'the fact that I can clearly and distinctly understand one thing apart from another is enough to make me certain that the two things are distinct' (AT vii. 78; CSM ii. 54). At first glance, the phrase 'clearly and distinctly understanding one thing apart from another' seems ambiguous. To use the case of mind and body, it is not clear whether considering mind apart from body requires attending to the idea of the mind alone, or attending to the ideas of both mind and body.

Arnauld, in his well-known objection to the real distinction argument in the *Fourth Set of Objections*, assumed that Descartes was claiming the former. He thought that to perceive mind apart from body was just to think of the mind without thinking of body. Arnauld suggested that one could clearly and distinctly perceive a right-angled triangle without knowing that the Pythagorean theorem is one of its properties. This would seem to be a case of clearly and distinctly understanding one thing—a right-angled triangle—apart from another, namely the Pythagorean property. But of course the Pythagorean theorem *is* a property of a right-angled triangle. Thus, in this case perceiving one thing apart from another does not seem to be sufficient for demonstrating distinctness. But if this is so, why should our perception of the mind apart from body have to entail that mind and body are really distinct substances?

Although I clearly and distinctly know my nature to be something that thinks, may I, too, not perhaps be wrong in thinking that nothing else belongs to my nature apart from the fact that I am a thinking thing? Perhaps the fact that I am an extended thing may also belong to my nature. (AT vii. 203; CSM ii. 142–3)

Descartes provides a two-part rejoinder to Arnauld's objection. In each part he attempts to establish a disanalogy between the right-angled triangle and the Pythagorean theorem, on the one hand, and the distinction between mind and body, on the other. Here we shall focus only on Descartes's second response.[23] However, in order to understand it we must briefly sketch a distinction Descartes draws between two kinds of mental operation—abstraction and exclusion. Although this important distinction is at work in Descartes's real distinction argument, he does not formally expound it in the *Meditations*. The only place the distinction is explicitly set forth is in a letter to Gibieuf. He tells Gibieuf that abstraction is an intellectual operation which consists in concentrating one's attention on one aspect of some rich idea while ignoring or turning one's thought away from its other aspects. For example, if one were to 'consider a shape without thinking of the substance or the extension whose shape it is', one would be performing an abstraction (19 January 1642, AT iii. 475; CSMK 202). By contrast to abstraction, exclusion is a matter not simply of ignoring certain aspects of an idea, but of actively denying them. For example, one could exclude from a circle the properties of a square. Exclusion thus requires that one attend to what is being excluded. When one performs such an exclusion clearly and distinctly, one establishes that what has been excluded is not contained in the idea in question. If it were so contained, then it would not be possible to perform the exclusion (clearly and distinctly). For example, although one can attend to the particular shape of a corporeal substance without attending to the substance itself (as mentioned above), it is impossible to understand the shape if one excludes the substance. Abstraction

---

[23] Descartes's first point is that mind and body can be conceived as complete things, while neither a right-angled triangle nor the Pythagorean theorem can be conceived as complete things (AT vii. 224; CSM ii. 158). To conceive the mind as a complete thing is just to conceive mind as a substance, that is, as something capable of existing independently (of any other *finite* substance). In contrast, Descartes does not think that a right-angled triangle or the Pythagorean theorem can be conceived as capable of independent existence.

is thus a weaker intellectual operation than exclusion—it does not follow from the fact that A can be clearly and distinctly abstracted from B that A can be clearly and distinctly excluded from B.[24]

We are now well placed to understand the second part of Descartes's response to Arnauld. Descartes concedes to Arnauld that one can clearly and distinctly understand a right-angled triangle without recognizing that the Pythagorean theorem is one of its properties. In the technical terminology set forth above, one is merely considering the idea of a right-angled triangle in abstraction from the Pythagorean theorem. Performing such an abstraction does not prove that the Pythagorean theorem is not a property of a right-angled triangle. In order to establish that conclusion one would have to clearly and distinctly *exclude* the Pythagorean theorem from the idea of a right-angled triangle. But this, of course, cannot be done: 'it is not intelligible that this ratio should be denied of the triangle' (AT vii. 227; CSM ii. 159).

In contrast, Descartes explains that clearly and distinctly understanding mind apart from the body involves more than just thinking of the mind in abstraction from the body: 'not only do we understand it [the mind] to exist without the body, but, what is more, all the attributes which belong to a body can be denied of it. For it is of the nature of substances that they should mutually exclude one another' (AT vii. 227; CSM ii. 159). Contrary to Arnauld's assumption, clearly and distinctly understanding mind apart from body involves attending to the ideas of both mind and body. More precisely, it involves excluding the ideas of mind and body from each other in thought.[25] It is by performing this exclusion operation that

---

[24] For more on this distinction, see Dugald Murdoch, 'Exclusion and Abstraction in Descartes's Metaphysics', *Philosophical Quarterly*, 43 (1993), 38–57.

[25] That exclusion is an essential feature of this proof is further confirmed by Descartes's brief discussion of real distinction in the *Principles*. There he states that 'from the mere fact that each of us understands himself to be a thinking thing and is capable, in thought, of excluding (*excludere*) from himself every other substance, whether thinking or extended, it is certain that each of us, regarded in this way, is really distinct from every other thinking substance and from every corporeal substance' (AT viiia. 29; CSM i. 213). Furthermore, although the real distinction passage in the Sixth Meditation makes no explicit mention of exclusion, a careful reading shows it to be implicit in this text as well: 'On the one hand I have a clear and distinct idea of myself, in so far as I am simply a thinking, non-extended thing; and on the other hand I have a distinct idea of body, in so far as this is simply an extended, non-thinking thing. And accordingly, it is certain that I am really distinct from my body, and can exist without it' (AT vii. 78; CSM ii. 54). We must be careful not to

one completes the process of distinguishing the ideas of mind and body from each other—thereby achieving fully clear and distinct ideas of these substances simultaneously.[26]

To perform this exclusion operation, it suffices to exclude the essences of mind and body from each other, for in excluding the essences one also excludes the modes of each substance. This result follows from Descartes's conception of the metaphysical relation between the modes of a substance and its essence. Cartesian created substances are simple in an important way: minds are purely thinking things and bodies are purely extended things. But they are simple in another sense too: the 'modes' or affections of a substance are merely determinations of its essence. For example, modes of body such as size, shape, position, etc. are determinations of extension. Clearly, Descartes chose the term 'mode' (*modus*), which literally means 'way', to indicate this relation. Modes are *ways* of being an extended or thinking thing. As Daniel Garber has observed, Descartes's view that there must be a very intimate relation between the modes of a

misread this passage. When Descartes claims to have an idea of the mind as 'a thinking, non-extended thing', and of body as 'an extended, non-thinking thing', he is not attributing negative properties to the ideas of mind and body. He is not saying that it is part of the idea of mind that it is non-extended, or that it is part of the idea of body that it is non-thinking. Rather, he is claiming that these two ideas can be mutually excluded from each other in thought.

[26] It is natural to ask whether this exclusion can be performed earlier in the *Meditations*—perhaps by the end of the Second Meditation. To be sure, the meditator achieves clear and distinct ideas of mind and body in the Second Meditation, but it is not clear whether *fully* clear and distinct ideas of mind and body can be achieved at this point. On the one hand, Descartes does not speak of mutual exclusion in the Second Meditation or in any of his replies to objections concerning it. Nevertheless, he does occasionally use language that is suggestive of mutual exclusion prior to the Sixth Meditation (see e.g. AT vii. 44; CSM ii. 30). If a meditator were to perform the relevant exclusion operation prior to the Sixth Meditation, she would achieve fully clear and distinct ideas of mind and body. We see no reason for Descartes to deny that *some* meditators might do this. But the important issue here is not whether mutual exclusion is first performed in the Second or Sixth Meditations. Descartes emphasizes mutual exclusion in the Sixth Meditation because it is only at this point that the attainment of fully clear and distinct ideas of mind and body will have ontological implications. Descartes is seeking *scientia* of the respective natures of mind and body, and this is not possible until one has secured a divine guarantee and the rule for truth, for without these things we cannot be sure 'whether things do in reality correspond to our perception of them' (AT vii. 226; CSM ii. 159). Fully clear and distinct ideas of mind and body must be attained in order to prove that mind and body are really distinct substances, but this conclusion cannot be established until the sceptical doubts raised in the First Meditation have been defeated.

substance and its essence contrasts sharply with the scholastic account of substance, which it is likely targeting. The scholastics countenanced a very loose connection between the essence of a substance and its non-essential or accidental properties, such that the latter are merely 'tacked on' to an underlying substratum, but this is something that Descartes could not abide. The only properties of a Cartesian substance are its essence and the modes, or ways, of being that essence.[27]

The metaphysical priority of essences to modes grounds a corresponding conceptual or epistemic priority. In fact, as a consequence of his understanding of the relation between a substance and its properties, Descartes is committed to an important epistemic principle, namely that the modes of a substance can be clearly and distinctly understood *only* through the essence or what he calls the 'principal attribute' of that substance.

A substance may ... be known through any attribute at all; but each substance has one principal property which constitutes its nature and essence, and to which all its other properties are referred. Thus extension ... constitutes the nature of corporeal substance; and thought constitutes the nature of thinking substance. Everything else which can be attributed to body presupposes extension, and is merely a mode of an extended thing; and similarly, whatever we find in the mind is simply one of the various modes of thinking. (AT viiia. 25; CSM i. 210)

In his subsequent discussion, Descartes makes clear that what it means to say that the modes of a substance are 'referred' to its principal attribute is that they are *understood or conceived of through* that attribute. For example, 'shape is unintelligible except in an extended thing ... [and] imagination, sensation, and will are intelligible only in a thinking thing' (AT viiia. 25; CSM i. 210–11). Despite the centrality of this epistemic principle to Descartes's philosophy, and his explicit statement of it in pivotal texts, it is widely under-appreciated.[28] Indeed, Malebranche failed to grasp its centrality, for it provides Descartes with a direct method for determining the ontological status of any mode

---

[27] This paragraph has greatly benefited from Garber's discussion of this issue. See *Descartes's Metaphysical Physics* (Chicago: Chicago University Press, 1992), 68–9.

[28] Descartes's most careful presentation of this epistemological principle is in the *Principles* (AT viiia. 25; CSM ii. 210). Less formal statements of the principle can be found in the *Sixth Replies* (AT vii. 444; CSM ii. 299), and in *Comments on a Certain Broadsheet* (AT viiib. 350; CSM i. 298).

whatsoever: if a mode can be conceived of through the attribute of thought, then it is a mode of mind; if it can be conceived of through the attribute of extension, then it is a mode of body. However, this method cannot be applied unless one has a clear and distinct idea of the substance in question. An indirect argument purporting to establish that sensations (or any other modes) are modes of mind *in the absence of a clear and distinct idea of the mind* is thus impossible in principle.[29] This is the third and final reason that Descartes would reject both the Indirect Argument and the Dustbin Theory.

4. CONCLUSION

We have argued, contrary to a long-standing myth, that Descartes is not committed to the Dustbin Theory of Mind and, correlatively, that he would reject Malebranche's Indirect Argument. If this were a

[29] Geneviève Rodis-Lewis and Ferdinand Alquié claim to detect an indirect argument in the following passage from the *Passions of the Soul*: 'Thus, because we have no conception of the body as thinking in any way at all, we have reason to believe that every thought present in us belongs to the soul' (AT xi. 329; CSM i. 329). We find this suggestion implausible, especially given the larger context in which this passage appears. Descartes is attempting to distinguish the functions of the soul from the functions of the human body (AT xi. 328; CSM i. 328). In article 3, just before the passage at issue, he presents a 'rule' that will enable us to accomplish this task: 'anything we experience as being in us, and which we see can also exist in wholly inanimate bodies, must be attributed only to our body. On the other hand, anything in us which we cannot conceive in any way as capable of belonging to a body must be attributed to our soul' (AT xi. 329; CSM i. 329). Descartes maintains that an application of this rule will disabuse the scholastically trained reader of the 'serious error' of thinking that 'the soul gives movement and heat to the body', which he takes to be the primary reason previous philosophers failed to give a satisfactory explanation of the passions: 'we must believe that all the heat and all the movements present in us, insofar as they do not depend on thought, belong solely to the body' (here the 'us' refers to the union of mind and body, and 'heat' to the cause of the sensation) (AT xi. 329–30; CSM i. 329). One cannot help noticing that this application of the rule runs in the other direction than the Indirect Argument—from mind to body! If Descartes were articulating an indirect argument in these passages it would have to operate in both directions, given his statement of the rule. But what would this mean by Malebranche's reasoning, *that we lack distinct ideas of both mind and body*? Fortunately, there is a better explanation of this text. Descartes does not say here what grounds the rule for distinguishing the functions of mind and body, but it is natural to suppose that he sees himself as relying on the results of his mature philosophy, especially the proof of real distinction. Indeed, in applying the rule one is, in effect, rehearsing one of the main steps of that proof, namely the mutual exclusion of mind and body in thought. See Ferdinand Alquié, *Le Cartesianisme de Malebranche* (Paris: J. Vrin, 1974), 99, and Rodis-Lewis's editorial remarks on the *Recherche*, OC iii. 367 n. 91. Also see Schmaltz, *Malebranche's Theory of the Soul*, 256 n. 125, who agrees with us that Descartes does not intend to articulate an indirect argument in this passage.

Cartesian legacy, then Descartes would have to concede Malebranche's contention that he lacks a clear and distinct idea of mind. Our interpretation spares him from having to concede anything here.

The strategy of our argument has been to develop two general considerations stemming from Descartes's philosophical system: first, his diagnosis of the confusion infecting our ideas of mind and body, and our sensations, and, second, his method for dispelling this confusion. These considerations reveal three independent reasons that Descartes would reject the Dustbin Theory and the Indirect Argument.

First, the Dustbin Theory and the Indirect Argument presuppose that the qualities we pre-philosophically attribute to external things just are modes of mind. Descartes rejects this presupposition. According to his diagnosis, these purported qualities are not modes of body *or* mind, but the products of confused judgement that result from the ordinary person's tendency to posit things in bodies that resemble his sensations. Thus, rather than reducing these so-called 'things' or 'qualities' to modes of mind, Descartes eliminates them from his ontology entirely.

Second, it is a presupposition of the Dustbin Theory and the Indirect Argument that the idea of body is epistemically prior to the idea of mind. But for Descartes the ideas of mind and body are confused together, prior to meditating, and one cannot achieve a fully clear and distinct idea of body until one also has a clear and distinct idea of mind and vice versa.

Third, Descartes holds that the *only* way to establish the ontological status of any mode is by conceiving of it through the principal attribute of the substance that it modifies. In the case of mind, this requires that one conceive of the mode in question through the attribute of thought. This procedure is *direct*, and can only be performed if one has a clear and distinct idea of the mind as a purely thinking substance. This means that an indirect argument for the claim that sensible qualities are modes of mind is impossible in principle.[30]

California State University, Long Beach
University of California, Irvine

[30] We would like to thank Paul Hoffman, Nicholas Jolley, Thomas Lennon, Steven Nadler, Alan Nelson, Tad Schmaltz, Russell Wahl, June Yang, and referees for this volume for comments on earlier drafts of this chapter. We are also indebted to audiences at the University of North Carolina, Chapel Hill (Nov. 2002) and at the American Philosophical Association meeting in San Francisco (Mar. 2003).

3

Is Descartes a Libertarian?

C. P. RAGLAND

In his *Theodicy*, Leibniz complains: 'M. Descartes demands a freedom which is not needed, by his insistence that the actions of the will of man are altogether undetermined, a thing which never happens.'[1] According to Spinoza, Descartes believes that 'man ... has absolute power over his actions, and is determined by no other source than himself.'[2] The view of freedom that Leibniz and Spinoza attribute to Descartes strongly resembles what philosophers now call *libertarianism*: the view that people have free will, that free will is incompatible with determinism, and hence that determinism is false.[3] Leibniz and Spinoza were not alone in attributing this view to Descartes,[4] and today, too,

---

[1] GP vi. 89. Citation from M. Huggard (ed. and tr.), *Theodicy* (La Salle, Ill.: Open Court, 1985), 112 (Preliminary Dissertation 69).

[2] Preface to *Ethics*, Part III, C i. 229.

[3] Throughout this chapter, I employ common terms from contemporary discussions about free will. I define *determinism* below, at the beginning of Section 1. *Compatibilists* believe that free will can coexist with determinism, while *incompatibilists* think that freedom requires the absence of determinism. There are two kinds of incompatibilists: *libertarians* (who think that we are free and therefore also think that determinism is false) and *hard determinists* (who believe in determinism and hence deny the reality of free will).

[4] Theo Verbeek reports that in Holland in the late 1640s, 'many people felt that [Descartes's] interpretation of human freedom was a dangerous case of Pelagianism', a Christian heresy that strongly emphasizes the role of human freedom—conceived along libertarian lines—in the process of salvation (*Descartes and the Dutch: Early Reactions to Cartesian Philosophy, 1630–1650* (Carbondale: Southern Illinois University Press, 1992), 5). Revius, regent of the theological college in Leiden, went so far as to declare that Descartes's doctrine 'exceeds all forms of Pelagianism: it eliminates God and places free will upon His throne' (Verbeek, *Descartes and the Dutch*, 42). For a similar criticism by Revius' colleague Triglandius, see Adrien Baillet, *La Vie de Monsieur Des-Cartes* (New York: Garland, 1987), ii. 315. Even Arnauld, who was generally very sympathetic to Descartes's philosophical programme, wrote that Descartes was unenlightened in matters of religion because his letters 'are full of Pelagianism' (Arnauld, *Œuvres de Messire Antoine Arnauld*, 43 vols. (Lausanne,

many take Descartes to be a libertarian.[5] Nevertheless, a libertarian reading of Descartes is far from obviously correct. Commentators have drawn widely divergent conclusions from Descartes's scattered and puzzling remarks about freedom. Some suggest that he considered freedom to be compatible with certain kinds of determinism.[6] Others claim that his view of freedom changed over time,[7] or that his position

1775), i. 671; see also Stephen Menn, *Descartes and Augustine* (Cambridge: Cambridge University Press, 1998), 70).

[5] See Robert Sleigh, Jr., Vere Chappell, and Michael Della Rocca, 'Determinism and Human Freedom', in Daniel Garber and Michael Ayers (eds.), *The Cambridge History of Seventeenth-Century Philosophy* (Cambridge: Cambridge University Press, 1998), 1195–1278, at 1206. John Cottingham says that several important passages 'strongly suggest that [Descartes] belongs with the partisans of full-blooded libertarian free will' (John Cottingham (ed. and tr.), *Descartes' Conversation with Burman* (Oxford: Clarendon Press, 1976), p. xl). In *Descartes and the Enlightenment* (Kingston: McGill–Queen's University Press, 1989) Peter Schouls argues that Descartes already embraced the notions of libertarian freedom, mastery, and progress characteristic of the Enlightenment *philosophes*. Other commentators who read Descartes as a libertarian include: Jean Laporte, 'La Liberté selon Descartes' ['La Liberté'], in Laporte, *Études d'histoire de la philosophie française au XVIIe siècle* (Paris: J. Vrin, 1951), 37–87; Jean-Marc Gabaude, *Liberté et raison (La Liberté cartésienne et sa réfraction chez Spinoza et chez Leibniz)*, i: *Philosophie réflexive de la volonté* (Toulouse: Association des publications de la Faculté des lettres et sciences humaines de Toulouse, 1970), 161–97; Robert Imlay, 'Descartes and Indifference' ['Indifference'], *Studia Leibnitiana*, 14 (1982), 87–97; Georges J. D. Moyal, 'The Unity of Descartes' Conception of Freedom' ['Unity'], *International Studies in Philosophy*, 19 (1987), 33–51, and 'Magicians, Doubters and Perverts' ['Magicians'], *Revue Internationale de Philosophie*, 50 (1996), 73–107; Lilli Alanen, 'Intuition, Assent, and Necessity: The Question of Descartes' Psychologism' ['Intuition'], *Acta Philosophica Fennica*, 64 (1999), 99–121, and 'Descartes on the Will and the Power to Do Otherwise' ['Otherwise'], in Henrik Lagerlund and Mikko Yrjönsuuri (eds.), *Emotions and Choice from Boethius to Descartes* (Dordrecht: Kluwer, 2002), 279–98.

[6] James Petrik, *Descartes' Theory of the Will* (Durango, Colo.: Hollowbrook, 1992); Joseph Keim Campbell, 'Descartes on Spontaneity, Indifference, and Alternatives' ['Spontaneity'], in Rocco J. Gennaro and Charles Huenemann (eds.), *New Essays on the Rationalists* (Oxford: Oxford University Press, 1999), 179–99; Charles Larmore, 'Descartes' Psychologistic Theory of Assent' ['Psychologistic'], *History of Philosophy Quarterly*, 1/1 (1984), 61–74; Anthony Kenny, 'Descartes on the Will' ['Will'], in R. J. Butler (ed.), *Cartesian Studies* (Oxford: Blackwell, 1972), 1–31; Jean-Marie Beyssade, *La Philosophie première de Descartes: Le Temps et la cohérence de la métaphysique* (Paris: Flammarion, 1979), 177–214; Vere Chappell, 'Descartes's Compatibilism' ['Compatibilism'], in John Cottingham (ed.), *Reason, Will, and Sensation: Studies in Descartes's Metaphysics* (Oxford: Clarendon Press, 1994), 177–90.

[7] Alexander Boyce Gibson, *The Philosophy of Descartes* [*Descartes*] (London: Methuen, 1932), 332–9; Michelle Beyssade, 'Descartes's Doctrine of Freedom: Differences between the French and Latin Texts of the Fourth Meditation' ['Doctrine'], in Cottingham (ed.), *Reason, Will, and Sensation*, 191–206.

was logically incoherent.[8] One even suggests that Descartes had no real view about the nature of freedom.[9]

In this chapter, I argue that Descartes embraced a libertarian account of freedom throughout his career. I begin by showing that Descartes denied three important forms of determinism (Section 1). Then I examine whether he took the falsehood of determinism—particularly intellectual determinism—to *follow from* the truth of free will. I show that Descartes considered the will's freedom to consist in its 'two-way' power to either do something or not (Section 2). Because he also thought that the will would lose this two-way power if its actions were *always* determined by the intellect, Descartes is an incompatibilist (Section 3). However, for Descartes, freedom does not require that the will's actions *never* be determined by the intellect (Section 4). Descartes believes that the will controls how we direct our attention, and this leads him to think that we remain free and self-determining even when clear perceptions in the intellect determine the will (Section 5).

1. DESCARTES AND DETERMINISM

An event E is *determined* just in case the causes of E make the non-occurrence of E impossible—i.e. just in case the conditions causally necessary for E are also *sufficient* for E. *Determinism* is the view that *every* event is determined. Descartes's ontological framework raises the possibility of three specific sorts of determinism. The first is physical determinism, according to which the past states of extended things (together with the laws of nature) causally determine all their present

---

[8] Lucien Laberthonnière (*Études sur Descartes*, in *Œuvres de Laberthonnière*, ed. Louis Canet (Paris: J. Vrin, 1935), i. 418–31) and Joel T. Tierno (*Descartes on God and Human Error* (Atlantic Highlands, NJ: Humanities Press, 1997), 48–55) both accuse Descartes of holding a self-contradictory view. So do Imlay ('Indifference') and Kenny ('Will'). Randal Marlin defends Descartes against Kenny's criticisms, but raises some worries of his own about the coherence of Descartes's view ('Cartesian Freedom and the Problem of the Mesland Letters', in Georges J. D. Moyal and Stanley Tweyman (eds.), *Early Modern Philosophy: Metaphysics, Epistemology, and Politics* (Delmar, NY: Caravan Books, 1985), 195–216).

[9] Étienne Gilson, *La Liberté chez Descartes et la théologie* [*La Liberté*] (Paris: Alcan, 1913).

states. The second is intellectual determinism, according to which the intellectual states of thinking things always determine their acts of will. The third is theological determinism, according to which God causally determines *every* event, whether mental or physical. A brief survey of the evidence suggests that Descartes rejected all three forms of determinism.

Descartes believed that 'everything that happens comes *entirely* from [God]' (letter to Elisabeth, 6 October 1645, AT iv. 314; CSMK 272; my emphasis). Therefore, as he says in the *Passions of the Soul*, 'nothing can possibly happen other than as it has been *determined* from all eternity by [God's] Providence; so that providence is like a fate or immutable *necessity*' (AT xi. 438; CSM i. 380; my emphasis).[10] Such remarks suggest that God determines everything. But in fact Descartes exempts free choices from such determinism. The *Passions* continues: '*except for those things that [Providence] has willed to depend on our free will*, we must consider everything ... to occur of necessity and as it were by fate' (AT xi. 439; CSM i. 380; my emphasis). More importantly, in the *Principles of Philosophy*, Descartes says:

We can easily get ourselves into great difficulties if we attempt to reconcile ... divine preordination with the freedom of our will, or attempt to grasp both these things at once ... But we shall get out of these difficulties if we remember that our mind is finite, while the power of God is infinite ... We may attain sufficient knowledge of this power to perceive clearly and distinctly that God possesses it; but we cannot get a sufficient grasp of it to see how it *leaves the free actions of men undetermined*. (AT viiia. 20; CSM i. 206; my emphasis)

Descartes's considered position seems to be that God can providentially arrange our free choices without causally determining them.[11]

Next, with respect to physical determinism, Descartes says in the *Principles* that laws of nature derived from God's immutability govern the motions of bodies (AT viiia. 61–6; CSM i. 240–3). Concerning these laws, Descartes says: 'there is nothing in the whole of nature (nothing, that is, which should be referred to purely corporeal causes, *i.e. those devoid of thought and mind*) which cannot be deductively

---

[10] See also AT iv. 314; CSMK 272.

[11] For a detailed discussion of this issue, see my 'Descartes on Divine Providence and Human Freedom', *Archiv für Geschichte der Philosophie*, 87/2 (2005), 159–88.

explained on the basis of these selfsame principles' (AT viiia. 315; CSM i. 279; my emphasis). Descartes's parenthetical remark suggests that the laws of nature do not govern physical events directly caused by minds, such as intentional movements of the human body. Descartes confirms this later in *Passions of the Soul*. He suggests that while physical laws of nature govern 'every movement we make without any contribution from our will', they do not cover bodily events directly caused by the will, such as 'when our merely willing to walk has the consequence that our legs move and we walk' (AT xi. 341–3; CSM i. 335). So Descartes rejects the view that *every* physical event is causally determined by past physical events; the laws of nature govern only events resulting solely from bodily causes.

Finally, consider intellectual determinism. Like the scholastics, Descartes took the mind's own free actions to involve the inter-action of two faculties: intellect and will.[12] Scholastics distinguished between 'elicited' acts (acts performed by the will itself, e.g. choosing to raise one's hand) and 'commanded' acts (acts of the body or the intellect caused by the will's choice, e.g. actually raising one's hand, or imagining doing so).[13] Descartes's standard examples of elicited acts are pursuit and avoidance (choices regarding practical courses of action) and affirmation and denial (judgements about propositions).[14]

Descartes thinks that in human beings, the intellect is prior to the will, in the sense that the will cannot elicit an act unless the intellect first presents it with a potential course of action or a proposition. Descartes says that '[intellectual] perception ... is a prerequisite of judgment' (*Comments on a Certain Broadsheet*, AT viiib. 363; CSM i. 307), and more generally that 'when we direct our will towards

---

[12] See *Principles of Philosophy*, I. 32 (AT viiia. 17–18; CSM i. 204) and the parallel part of the Fourth Meditation (AT vii. 56–62; CSM ii. 39–43).

[13] Aquinas makes the distinction between elicited and commanded acts in *Summa theologiae*, part II–I, question 6, article 4. For a good discussion of the distinction, see the Introduction to Luis de Molina, *On Divine Foreknowledge (Part IV of the Concordia)*, ed. and tr. Alfred J. Freddoso (Ithaca, NY: Cornell University Press, 1988), 25.

[14] See the Fourth Meditation (AT vii. 57; CSM ii. 40) and the 9 February 1645 letter to Mesland (AT iv. 173; CSMK 245). In considering acts of judgement to be acts of will, Descartes departs from scholastic tradition, which considered them to be acts of the intellect commanded by the will. For more on Descartes's differences from the scholastics regarding the commanded/elicited distinction, see Chappell, 'Compatibilism', 179–80. See also Francisco Suárez, *On Efficient Causality: Metaphysical Disputations 17, 18, and 19*, tr. Alfred J. Freddoso (New Haven: Yale University Press, 1994), 328.

something, we always have some sort of understanding of some aspect of it' (*Fifth Replies*, AT vii. 377; CSM ii. 259).[15] If Descartes believes that the intellectual conditions necessary for our eliciting any particular volition are also *sufficient* for it, then he is an intellectual determinist.

Though Descartes may think that the contents of the intellect *sometimes* determine the will to act in a particular way, he clearly does not think they *always* do so. In the Fourth Meditation, he insists that God 'has given me the freedom to assent or not assent in those cases where he did not endow my intellect with a clear and distinct perception' (AT vii. 61; CSM ii. 42).[16] In such cases, the will has 'the freedom to direct itself, without the determination of the intellect, towards one side or the other' (*Fifth Replies*, AT vii. 378; CSM ii. 260). Descartes denies intellectual determinism.

In taking Descartes to be an indeterminist, then, Leibniz and Spinoza were correct. But this does not yet prove that Descartes was a libertarian, for libertarians think not only that determinism is false, but also that its falsehood is entailed by the truth of freedom: they think that freedom cannot possibly exist in a deterministic world. So to determine whether Descartes is a libertarian, we need to understand how he conceives of freedom. Did he think it could coexist with determinism?

2. DESCARTES AND THE PRINCIPLE OF ALTERNATIVE POSSIBILITIES

Descartes's only explicit definition of free will comes from the Fourth Meditation:

[1] the will, or freedom of choice ... simply consists in this: that we are able to do or not do (that is, to affirm or deny, to pursue or avoid); [2] or rather (*vel potius*), simply in this: that we are carried in such a way toward what the intellect proposes for affirmation or denial or for pursuit or avoidance, that we feel ourselves determined to it by no external force. (AT vii. 57; CSM ii. 40; my translation)

One important point about this definition is very clear: Descartes uses the terms 'will' (*voluntas*) and 'freedom of choice' (*arbitrii libertas*)

---

[15] See also AT viiia. 18; CSM i. 204.
[16] See also AT vii. 377–8; CSM ii. 259–60 and AT viiia. 6, 19–20; CSM i. 194, 205–6.

interchangeably because he thinks that freedom is essential to the will: necessarily, *every* voluntary act is free.[17]

It is less clear, however, whether this definition endorses what we now call the *principle of alternative possibilities* (PAP): the idea that doing something freely requires being able to do otherwise. The first clause of the definition seems to assert PAP by identifying freedom with a 'two-way' power to do or not do, but the 'or rather' introduces ambiguity: does it *retract* the two-way power requirement and replace it with a more accurate one (contained in the second clause), or does it *explain* more clearly the sense in which two-way power is required?

A retraction reading of the 'or rather' can appear quite plausible. Since Descartes thought that the will is free with respect to all its acts, if he believed PAP, then he should conclude that the will enjoys two-way power with respect to all its acts. But Descartes seems to deny this conclusion. In the Fifth Meditation, he says: 'My nature is such that so long as I perceive something very clearly and distinctly I cannot but believe it to be true' (AT vii. 69; CSM ii. 48); and according to the *Second Replies*, 'The will of a thinking thing is drawn voluntarily and freely (for that is the essence of will) but nevertheless infallibly (*infallibiliter*), towards a clearly known good' (AT vii. 166; CSM ii. 117; my translation). These and many similar passages[18] seem to teach a *doctrine of clear and distinct determinism* (CDD): whenever the intellect clearly and distinctly perceives a truth or good, the will cannot but assent or pursue.[19] CDD implies that the will does *not* enjoy two-way power with respect to all its acts. Since PAP implies the very opposite, it is natural to conclude that Descartes rejected PAP: the 'or rather' and second clause must mean that two-way power is not necessary for freedom.[20]

---

[17] Descartes reiterates the essential freedom of the will in several other places: AT vii. 166, CSM ii. 117; AT vii. 191, CSM ii. 134; AT xi. 359, CSM i. 343.

[18] See also AT iii. 64, CSMK 147; AT vii. 58–9, 145, CSM ii. 41, 104; AT viiia. 21, CSM i. 207; AT iv. 116, CSMK 233.

[19] In Section 5 below I argue that though Descartes accepts a version of CDD, he does not accept the simple version stated here. However, since this version is naturally gleaned from an initial reading of many passages, and is attributed to Descartes by many commentators, it proves useful in the initial stages of my argument.

[20] Tartaglia, a censor who examined the *Meditations* as part of the process leading up to the Roman Catholic Church's condemnation of Descartes's works in 1663, read the 'or rather' in just this way, declaring that 'any freedom from necessity is removed from our will, and is replaced simply by a freedom from constraint' (Jean-Robert Armogathe and Vincent

This conclusion leads to what I call the 'asymmetrical' interpretation of Cartesian freedom, best expressed by Anthony Kenny.[21] On this view, freedom is essentially the ability to get things right. In cases where unclear perception makes it possible for us to go wrong, freedom requires that we *also* be able to *avoid* going wrong, and so consists in the ability to 'do or not do'. But in cases where clear perceptions determine the will to get things right, freedom does *not* require such two-way power.

This reading fits very well with Descartes's insistence that 'the blessed' in heaven, who have 'nothing in the intellect except light' are nevertheless free (letter to Mesland, 2 May 1644, AT iv. 116−17; CSMK 234). In the Fourth Meditation, Descartes considers *hypothetical* 'enlightened' agents, and insists that they would be free.

God could easily have brought it about that without losing my freedom, and despite the limitations in my knowledge, I should nonetheless never make a mistake. He could, for example, have endowed my intellect with a clear and distinct perception of everything about which I was ever likely to deliberate. (AT vii. 61; CSM ii. 42)

Read with CDD in mind, this passage suggests freedom is *in principle* compatible with intellectual determinism. If God had given us a constant stream of clear perceptions, these perceptions would have determined our every volition, but we would still have been free.

If the asymmetrical reading is correct, then Descartes cannot be a standard libertarian. For a standard libertarian would argue against intellectual determinism in the following way:

(1) The human will is free.
(2) No free will can be subject to intellectual determinism.
(3) Therefore the human will is not subject to intellectual determinism.

Carraud, 'The First Condemnation of Descartes's *Œuvres*: Some Unpublished Documents from the Vatican Archives', in Daniel Garber and Steven Nadler (eds.), *Oxford Studies in Early Modern Philosophy*, i (Oxford: Oxford University Press, 2003), 67−109, at 83).

[21] Kenny, 'Will', 18−20. For similar readings, see Gilson, *La Liberté*, 310; M. Beyssade, 'Doctrine', 194, 206; and Larmore, 'Psychologistic', 67. For conceptions of freedom similar to the one Kenny attributes to Descartes, see Anselm, *De libertate arbitrii*, in *Opera omnia*, ed. F. S. Schmitt (Edinburgh: Nelson, 1946), i. 225; and Susan Wolf, 'Asymmetrical Freedom', *Journal of Philosophy*, 77 (1980), 151−66.

But, on the asymmetrical reading, Descartes rejects (2)—the core incompatibilist premiss—and reasons in this way:

(4) The human will is free but labours under unclear perceptions.

(5) No free will *that labours under unclear perceptions* can be subject to intellectual determinism.

(6) Therefore the human will is not subject to intellectual determinism.

Descartes reaches the same conclusion as the standard libertarian, but does not share the libertarian's conviction that freedom is *in principle* incompatible with intellectual determinism.

Two important passages work against the asymmetrical interpretation by suggesting that the will enjoys two-way power even in cases of clear and distinct perception. First, in the *Principles of Philosophy*, Descartes says:

It is a supreme perfection in man that he acts voluntarily, that is, freely; this makes him in a special way the author of his actions and deserving of praise for what he does. We do not praise automatons for accurately producing all the movements they were designed to perform, because the production of these movements occurs necessarily. It is the designer who is praised ... for in constructing [automatons] he acted not out of necessity but freely. By the same principle, when we embrace the truth, our doing so voluntarily is much more to our credit than would be the case if we could not do otherwise (*quam si non possemus non amplecti*). (AT viiia. 19; CSM i. 205)

The earlier lines of this passage say that an action is free only if it does not occur necessarily. The last line suggests that if our action does not occur necessarily, then we could have done otherwise. Therefore, the passage as a whole suggests that freedom implies the ability to do otherwise. Could Descartes be describing the two-way power that (according to the asymmetrical interpretation) we exercise only in cases of obscure perception? No, because Descartes is describing a case in which we *deserve credit* for embracing the truth, and he thinks that we deserve credit for embracing a truth only if we *clearly perceive* that truth. As he says a bit later in the *Principles*: 'when we give our assent to something which is not clearly perceived, this is always a misuse of our judgment, even if by chance we stumble on the truth' (AT viiia. 21; CSM i. 207). So, in the passage above, Descartes envisions a case in which we clearly perceive some truth. In this case, our freedom entails being able *not* to embrace (*non amplecti*) the truth, i.e. being able to *withhold* our assent.

Second, in what I call the 'two-senses' passage from a 1645 letter to Mesland, Descartes discusses 'a positive faculty of determining oneself to one or other of two contraries, that is to say, to pursue or avoid, to affirm or deny'. Of this faculty, he says:

I do not deny that the will has this positive faculty. Indeed, I think it has it not only with respect to those actions to which it is not pushed by any evident reasons on one side rather than on the other, but also with respect to all other actions; so that when a very evident reason moves us in one direction, although *morally speaking* we can hardly move in the contrary direction, *absolutely speaking* we can. For it is always open to us to hold back from pursuing a clearly known good, or from admitting a clearly perceived truth, provided we consider it a good thing to demonstrate the freedom of our will by so doing. (AT iv. 173; CSMK 245; my emphasis)

Here Descartes *explicitly* says that the will enjoys two-way power with respect to *all* its acts, including the ones undertaken 'when a very evident reason'—i.e. a clear perception—moves us. Descartes here affirms PAP, and seeks to avoid contradicting CDD by invoking two different senses of the word 'can': CDD is true 'morally speaking', while PAP is true 'absolutely speaking'. Whatever this distinction turns out to mean, it is clear that when Descartes wrote the *Principles* and this letter to Mesland, he accepted PAP and hence did *not* hold the asymmetrical view of freedom.

However, he may have held the asymmetrical view in an earlier stage of his thought. Some scholars claim that in the *Meditations* (1640) Descartes rejected PAP in favour of the asymmetrical view of freedom, but came to affirm PAP in the *Principles* (1644) and later texts.[22] Although Descartes's 1645 letter to Mesland purports to clarify his earlier remarks in the *Meditations*, there is reason to be suspicious: Descartes was addressing a Jesuit, and Jesuits were fierce partisans of the will's two-way power. For political reasons, Descartes may have misrepresented his earlier views in order to feign agreement with the

---

[22] See Gilson, *La Liberté*, 310–19; Gibson, *Descartes*, 332–9; Beyssade, 'Doctrine', 191–206.

Jesuits.[23] However, a careful reading of the *Meditations* reveals that Descartes accepted PAP even there.

Just before defining freedom, Descartes says:

It is above all in virtue of the will that I understand myself to bear in some way the image and likeness of God. For although God's will is incomparably greater than mine, both in virtue of the knowledge and power that accompany it and make it more firm and efficacious, and also in virtue of its object, in that it ranges over a greater number of items, nevertheless it does not seem any greater than mine when viewed as will formally and precisely in itself (*in se formaliter & praecise spectata*). (AT vii. 57; CSM ii. 40; my translation)

Descartes claims that the essence of divine freedom and the essence of human freedom have something in common (just as in the *Principles*, the definitions of created and uncreated substance share the idea of ontological independence; AT viiia. 24–5; CSM i. 210).[24] He then introduces the definition of the will in order to explain the point of similarity: '*This is because* the will simply consists in this: that we are able to do or not do, or rather ...' (AT vii. 57; CSM ii. 40).

In this context, the reader expects the first clause to identify the *essence* of will: what the will is when viewed 'formally and precisely in itself'. But on the asymmetrical interpretation, the first clause does *not* identify the will's essence. On that interpretation, Descartes holds that two-way power is *not* essential to the will. Therefore, because the first clause identifies freedom with two-way power, it fails to give a formal and precise definition of human will, and consequently fails to explain why God's will, *qua* will, is no greater than ours. If the 'or rather' retracts PAP, then in context the overall force of the definition is something like this: 'the point of similarity between divine and human freedom is two-way power; well, no—actually it is something else'. If this were Descartes's position, why didn't he simply erase the first clause?[25] The asymmetrical interpretation requires us to believe

---

[23] Gilson advances this sort of argument. For an excellent summary of Gilson's position, see Imlay, 'Indifference', 90.

[24] Descartes does not mean that the divine and human will share the same essence (AT vii. 433; CSM ii. 292), but he thinks their distinct essences share a common feature so that there is an *analogy* between divine and human wills, just as there is an analogy between divine and created substance.

[25] For a similar criticism, see Jean Laporte, *Le Rationalisme de Descartes*, 3rd edn. [*Le Rationalisme*] (Paris: PUF, 1988), 271. For a different criticism of the retraction reading, see Imlay, 'Indifference', 91.

that Descartes let stand a clause that is not only stylistically awkward, but also downright misleading![26]

It is much more plausible to suppose that the 'or rather' means something like 'or in other words', so that the definition's two parts explicate the very same concept in two different ways: the first states that the freedom common to God and humans is a two-way power, and the second explains more precisely what kind of two-way power human freedom consists in.

Furthermore, in the Fourth Meditation, Descartes already implicitly uses modal terms like 'can' in two different senses, as he does explicitly in the letter to Mesland. Descartes associates the first sense of 'can' with indifference, a kind of multidirectional inclination in the will (AT vii. 58; CSM ii. 40).[27] Wondering whether or not he is identical to a body, Descartes says:

I am making the further supposition that my intellect has not yet come upon any persuasive reason in favor of one alternative rather than the other. This obviously implies that I am indifferent as to whether I should assert or deny either alternative, or indeed refrain from making any judgment on the matter. What is more, this indifference does not merely apply to cases where the intellect is wholly ignorant, but extends in general to every case where the intellect does not have sufficiently clear knowledge at the time when the will deliberates. For although probable conjectures may pull me in one direction, the mere knowledge that they are simply conjectures, and not certain or indubitable reasons, is itself quite enough to push my assent the other way. (AT vii. 59; CSM ii. 41)

Unclear perception implies multidirectional inclination, which in turn implies the ability to choose in more than one way. In this first sense, to say 'I could have chosen otherwise' implies 'I had some *inclination* to choose otherwise'. If freedom requires being 'able to do or not do' in *this* sense, then freedom requires indifference.

But in the Sixth Replies, Descartes says explicitly that freedom does *not* require indifference:

---

[26] For a more detailed discussion of how Descartes's analogy between divine and human freedom works against the retraction reading, see my 'Alternative Possibilities in Descartes' Fourth Meditation', *British Journal for the History of Philosophy* (forthcoming).

[27] Descartes comments on his use of the term indifference in letters to Mesland from 1644 (AT iv. 115; CSMK 233) and 1645 (AT iv. 173–4; CSMK 245–6).

Indifference does not belong to the essence of human freedom, since not only are we free when ignorance of what is right makes us indifferent, but we are also free—indeed at our freest—when a clear perception impels us to pursue some object. (AT vii. 433; CSM ii. 292)[28]

We can now see why Descartes's definition of freedom contains the seemingly awkward 'or rather'. Just after defining freedom as the ability to 'do or not do', Descartes realized that his readers might—mistakenly—conclude that freedom requires indifference. So he quickly added the 'or rather' and the second clause to convey the true sense in which freedom requires alternative possibilities. We are 'able to do or not do' in the sense required for freedom just in case 'we are carried in such a way toward what the intellect proposes ... that we feel ourselves determined to it by no external force' (AT vii. 57; CSM ii. 40).

Descartes invokes these same two senses of two-way power in what I call the 'great light' passage:

I could not but judge something which I understood so clearly to be true; not because I was compelled so to judge by any external force, but because a great light in the intellect was followed by a great inclination in the will, and thus I have believed this more spontaneously and freely as I have been less indifferent to it. (AT vii. 58–9; CSM ii. 41; my translation)

Descartes suggests that the great light in his intellect gave his will just one inclination: to assent. So in the sense of 'can' that means 'is motivated', Descartes could not do otherwise than assent. However, in the sense of 'can' connected to self-determination, he could have done otherwise because he was not determined by an external force. Descartes assumes that if one is not externally determined to perform an action, then (in a sense) one could *not* perform it. As he says in a 1644 letter to Mesland: 'God cannot have been determined to make it true that contradictories cannot be true together, and therefore ... he could have done the opposite' (AT iv. 118; CSMK 235).

As Robert Imlay says, the 1645 letter to Mesland 'does no more than spell out in somewhat more detail a current of thought already to be found in [the Fourth] Meditation'.[29] For Descartes, the will

---

[28] See also AT iv. 116, CSMK 234; and AT vii. 58, CSM ii. 40.
[29] 'Indifference', 92.

enjoys an 'absolute' two-way power with respect to all its acts. This absolute power depends not on being indifferent, but on satisfying the conditions laid down in the second part of the definition of freedom: we must be carried towards what the intellect puts forward in such a way that we feel we are not determined by any external force. What exactly does Descartes mean by this requirement?

Descartes could be taken to mean that we are free just in case we *feel* undetermined (even if *in fact* external forces determine our action), but three things work against this interpretation. First, when the great light passage refers back to the second clause, it mentions *actual* non-determination, not the *feeling* of non-determination. Second, Descartes frequently says that we know our own freedom from an inner feeling or experience.[30] Descartes thinks that this experience of freedom is clear and distinct, and therefore veridical. So in the definition of freedom, when he says 'we feel (*sentiamus*) that we are determined by no external force', this implies that we *really are* undetermined.[31] Third, in the Fourth Meditation, Descartes aims to show that because we err freely, God cannot be held responsible for our errors.[32] But if freedom were a mere feeling, consistent with behind-the-scenes divine control, then Descartes could not sensibly appeal to our freedom as a way of getting God off the hook. So I think the second clause of Descartes's definition of freedom requires the *actual* absence of external determination.

What is the metaphor of *carrying* supposed to convey? Translated most literally, the sentence just following the definition of freedom reads: 'For in order to be free it is not necessary that I can be carried (*ferri posse*) in both directions, but on the contrary, the more I incline (*propendeo*) in one direction ... the more freely do I choose it' (AT

---

[30] AT vii. 56, 191, 377, CSM ii. 39, 134, 259; AT viiia. 6, CSM i. 194; AT iv. 332, CSMK 277; AT v. 159, CSMK 342. See also Campbell, 'Spontaneity', 181.

[31] See especially *Principles of Philosophy*, I. 39 (AT viiia. 19–20; CSM i. 205–6). See also AT iii. 161, CSMK 161; AT vii. 191, CSM ii. 134; and Campbell, 'Spontaneity', 181.

[32] As *Principles* I. 29 says: 'God is not the Cause of our Errors' (AT viiia. 16; CSM i. 203). See also *Principles of Philosophy*, I. 31 and I. 38, and the Fourth Meditation (AT vii. 54, 60; CSM ii. 38, 41). For a good discussion of Descartes's appeal to free will in response to his epistemological version of the problem of evil, see Michael Latzer, 'Descartes's Theodicy of Error', in Elmar Kremer and Michael Latzer (eds.), *The Problem of Evil in Early Modern Philosophy* (Toronto: University of Toronto Press, 2001), 35–48. See also my 'Descartes' Theodicy' (unpub.).

vii. 57–8; CSM ii. 40; my translation). We can be carried in both directions only if we are inclined in both directions. Therefore, what carries us must be an inclination or desire. When the intellect proposes an object for judgement or choice, this object produces at least one inclination in the will. The inclination upon which the will acts is the one that 'carries' us.

The phrase 'determined by no external force' is ambiguous in two important respects. First, the 'external' could mean either 'external to the will' (in which case the intellect would count as an external force) or 'external to the mind' (in which case the intellect would not count as 'external'). Second, 'determined' can be given a compatibilist or incompatibilist reading. To understand these two readings, we must first distinguish between direct and indirect external causal determination.

In *direct* determination, an external force sufficiently causes an act of will to occur, thereby preventing internal forces (i.e. the will's own inclinations) from determining the act (as would be the case if, for example, Descartes was inclined not to read the Bible, but God caused him to do it anyway). In *indirect* determination, the external force acts not *in spite of* the will's inclinations, but *through* them: the act of will is determined by inclinations, which are in turn determined by *prior* external forces (as would be the case if God caused Descartes to have an overpowering desire to read the Bible).

On an incompatibilist reading of 'determined', Descartes means to rule out both direct and indirect external determination. On such a reading, Descartes thinks that free agents must be the *ultimate* causal sources of their free actions. However, on a compatibilist reading of 'determined', Descartes means to rule out only *direct* determination. On this reading, the will's inclinations must be a source of free actions, but they need not be the *ultimate* source. Let us explore the compatibilist reading further.

3. ABSOLUTE POWER AS HYPOTHETICAL

On the compatibilist reading, to say that an act of will is 'determined' is to say that it would have occurred *no matter what* the will's internal inclinations were. Therefore, agents performing some act of will A at time T are 'undetermined' or 'free' just in case they satisfy the following condition: *if* their inclinations had been sufficiently different at T, they could have failed to perform A. Agents satisfying this condition enjoy what I call *hypothetical* two-way power with respect to A.

The two-senses passage suggests that this (or a similar) condition is crucial to Descartes's understanding of 'absolute' two-way power. Descartes first claims that we can *always* withhold our assent, even from clear perceptions. Then he explains this claim by noting that a 'very evident reason' cannot compel our assent *if* we consider it good to demonstrate our freedom (by withholding assent from clear perceptions). Since we do not always desire to prove our freedom, Descartes must mean that our absolute two-way power depends on what we could have done *if* we had so desired.[33]

On a compatibilist reading of the two-senses passage, when we clearly and distinctly perceive that P, and no other motives, are present, our only inclination will be to assent to P. Given this one-way inclination, our assent is determined: we are 'morally speaking' unable to do otherwise. But 'absolutely speaking' we can withhold our assent because *if* we had wanted to withhold it, we could have (morally speaking): if we had desired to prove our freedom, not even a clear perception could have determined us to assent.[34]

A number of Descartes's theological claims appear to support this interpretation. In the Fourth Meditation, he says that God's grace produces a great light in the intellect without threatening freedom (AT vii. 58; CSM ii. 40), and also that God—without removing our freedom—could have ensured that we never err, by always giving us clear and distinct perceptions (AT vii. 58, CSM ii. 40; AT vii. 61, CSM ii. 42). These passages make it appear that in some cases God—an external force—indirectly determines the act of will: God causes clear perceptions, which then cause certain internal motivational states, which in turn determine the act of will. Descartes insists that we remain free in such cases, so he must think

---

[33] For a similar suggestion about the nature of Cartesian two-way power, and a similar (though slightly different) reading of the 'two senses' passage, see Campbell, 'Spontaneity', 193–4.

[34] Interestingly, in his 'Summary of the Controversy', appendix to *Theodicy*, Leibniz seems to use the terms 'morally necessary' and 'absolutely necessary' in just this sense, and even mentions the desire to prove freedom (GP vi. 379–81).

that freedom is compatible with indirect external determination and requires only hypothetical two-way power. On the other hand, some of Descartes's *other* theological remarks call into question this case for the compatibilist interpretation.[35]

More importantly, Descartes's reply to Gassendi's *Fifth Objections* undermines such an interpretation. In his objections, Gassendi does not reject Descartes's picture of intellectual states influencing choices *by means of* the will's own inclinations. Instead, he criticizes Descartes from within his own framework, arguing that the intellect always determines the will's choice. If the intellect sees 'reasons of equal weight on either side, or no reasons at all', Gassendi claims, then 'no judgment follows' (AT vii. 315; CSM ii. 219). Furthermore, if the intellect takes proposition P to be the most probable of the alternatives, it cannot but judge that P 'irrespective of whether it accords with the truth of the matter or not'. Thus Gassendi concludes:

This means that we do not have the power so much to guard against error as to guard against persisting in error; and if we want to use our judgment correctly, we should not so much restrain our will as apply our intellect to develop clearer awareness, *which the judgement will always then follow.* (AT vii. 317; CSM ii. 220; my emphasis)

Gassendi suggests that intellectual states always determine the will's motivational state, which in turn always determines judgement (or the absence thereof). This intellectual determinism is indirect, coming via the will's own inclinations. Therefore, if Descartes had a compatibilist understanding of external determination, he should not find Gassendi's picture threatening to freedom.

But in fact, Descartes rejects Gassendi's picture of the will: 'You may be unfree if you wish, but I am very pleased with my freedom since I experience it within myself.' Descartes insists that when presented with obscure perceptions, a truly free will can 'be directed towards an object which the intellect does not impel it towards'. In

---

[35] For instance, in the *Second Replies*, Descartes suggests that the impulses of divine grace can be resisted (AT vii. 147–9; CSM ii. 105–6), and in a letter to Mesland he points out that he never said that grace entirely prevents indifference (AT iv. 117–18; CSMK 234). So divine grace may not create genuine cases of indirect determinism. Similarly, as I show below in Section 5, Descartes probably does *not* think that by giving us a constant stream of clear perceptions, God necessarily determines our acts of will.

other words, the will has 'the freedom to direct itself, without the determination of the intellect, towards one side or the other' during obscure perception (AT vii. 377–8; CSM ii. 259–60). At least in cases of obscure perception, the determinism Gassendi proposes—though indirect—would destroy freedom.

By rejecting Gassendi's picture, Descartes implicitly answers our two questions about the terms in his definition of freedom. First, he must consider the intellect (as Gassendi pictures it) an external force; for if it were internal, it would be no threat to freedom.[36] For Descartes, an 'external force' is external to the *will*, not to the mind. Second, and more importantly, Descartes rejects indirect external determination as incompatible with freedom. He must think that freedom requires the absence of both direct *and indirect* external determination. In other words, he must have intended the 'no external determination' clause to be given an *incompatibilist* reading.

Of course, Descartes does *not* say that Gassendi's intellectual determinism would destroy freedom in cases of *clear* perception. So the reply to Gassendi leaves open the following possibility: Descartes may think that the will cannot be free if determined by *obscure* intellectual perceptions, but remains free if determined by *clear* perceptions. Descartes may have intended the 'no external determination' clause to have incompatibilist implications *only* for cases of obscure perception. However, this suggestion begins to look rather implausible when we read the reply to Gassendi together with the two-senses passage.

Descartes tells Gassendi that the will has 'the freedom to *direct itself*, without the determination of the intellect, towards one side or the other (*se ipsam sine determinatione intellectus in unam aut alteram partem movendi*)' (AT vii. 378; CSM ii. 260; my emphasis). In cases of unclear perception, Descartes thinks that the will is *self-determining*: it is the causal *origin* of its own acts, in the sense that its acts cannot be traced back to the prior sufficient causal influence of the intellect. In the two-senses passage, Descartes once again invokes the notion of self-determination: 'perhaps others mean by "indifference" a positive faculty of *determining oneself* to one or other of two contraries, that

---

[36] On the basis of the reply to Gassendi, I disagree with Vere Chappell's suggestion that the intellect is *always* an 'internal' force (see Chappell, 'Compatibilism', 186). However, there is reason to think that for Descartes the intellect is *sometimes* as internal force. I discuss this further below, early in Section 5.

is to say, to pursue or avoid, to affirm or deny (*positiva facultas se determinandi ad utrumlibet e duobus contrariis*)' (AT iv. 173; CSMK 245; my emphasis). He goes on to say that the will has this positive power of self-determination in all cases, even ones involving clear and distinct perception. For Descartes, the will somehow remains the causal origin of its own acts even in cases of clear perception. For freedom, Descartes demands something more metaphysically robust than hypothetical two-way power.

4. ABSOLUTE POWER AS IMMEDIATE

On the 'radical libertarian' interpretation, advanced by Alquié, Moyal, and Alanen, Descartes identifies freedom with what I call *immediate two-way power*. An agent A has this power with respect to act of will W elicited at time T if and only if given everything in the actual world through time T (except W itself), A can fail to elicit W. Since, for Descartes, the will is always free, this interpretation implies that the will's actions are *never* determined, not even by clear and distinct perceptions.[37]

On this interpretation, when the two-senses passage says, 'morally speaking we can hardly move' against a 'very evident reason', it means simply that morality or reason requires us to follow the evident reason. Similarly, all the passages that seem to assert CDD actually make an exclusively *normative* claim (that the will *ought* to follow 'a great light in the intellect') rather than a descriptive claim about human psychology (that the great light determines the will).[38] These texts describe how we behave *if* we are rational.[39] We are 'absolutely speaking' able to resist evident reasons because it is up to us whether we will be rational: we can hold back from obeying evident rules of reason, or perhaps can even disobey them.[40]

---

[37] Moyal, 'Unity', 38.

[38] For this reading of the necessity involved in the CDD texts, see ibid. 38–40, 46–7, and Moyal, 'Magicians', 89–93; Alanen, 'Intuition', 109–12; see for contrast Larmore, 'Psychologistic', 61.

[39] Moyal, 'Magicians', 101–2.

[40] Ferdinand Alquié (*La Découverte Métaphysique de l'homme chez Descartes*, 2nd edn. (Paris: PUF, 1966), 286) and Moyal ('Unity', 35 and 45, and 'Magicians', 78) both suggest that we have the power to deny clear and distinct perceptions. Alanen ('Otherwise', 294) insists that we cannot deny them but still retain the power to withhold assent from them.

Descartes's distinction between 'moral' and 'absolute' certainty in the French version of the *Principles* may support this interpretation:

Moral certainty is certainty which is sufficient to regulate our behavior, or which measures up to the certainty we have on matters relating to the conduct of life which we never normally doubt, though we know that it is possible, absolutely speaking, that they may be false. (AT ixb: 323; CSM i. 289 n. 2)[41]

It is very unusual (and perhaps practically irrational), but nevertheless possible, to doubt a morally certain claim. The radical libertarian reading proposes a very similar meaning for the term 'morally' in the two-senses passage: we are morally necessitated to assent to a proposition just in case it would be very unusual (and indeed irrational)—but still possible—not to believe it. But despite this apparent support from the *Principles*,[42] the radical libertarian reading will not work.

Before explaining my own reasons for rejecting the radical libertarian reading, I want to consider Anthony Kenny's argument against it:

To abandon the theory that clear and distinct perception necessitates the will is to call in question the whole validation of reason in which the *Meditations* culminates. ... the only way to find out which ideas are clear and distinct is to do our damnedest to doubt them and fail to do so. But if clear and distinct ideas can be doubted at the moment they are intuited, we should never have genuine and certain knowledge of anything ... [43]

Descartes's goal, Kenny assumes, is to build a validation of reason on *psychologically certain* propositions: claims that 'however much we may exercise our free will' we find ourselves compelled by our nature to believe.[44] If the will always enjoys immediate two-way power, then it will never be compelled to believe anything. There will be no psychologically certain bedrock on which to erect the edifice of knowledge.

Kenny's argument here depends on a rather uncharitable reading of Descartes's project. Descartes cannot be satisfied to build his system

---

[41] Descartes also distinguishes between moral and absolute certainty in the *Discourse* (AT vi. 37–8; CSM i. 130).

[42] Moyal ('Magicians', 91–3) seems to take the parallelism with the *Principles* as conclusive proof.

[43] Kenny, 'Will', 29.

[44] Ibid.

on mere psychological certainties, because they could be false. As Descartes himself noted, our inability to doubt a proposition (such as 'a manifest contraction cannot be true'; Third Meditation, AT vii. 36; CSM ii. 25) does not prove its truth. Our creator may have built us to go wrong: we might be forced by our very nature to assent to the false.[45] Kenny can suggest (as many interpreters do) that Descartes tries to move from an initial position of psychological certainty to a position of *normative* certainty, in which there is no longer any reason to doubt his nature's reliability. By constructing a proof that he was created by a veracious God, Descartes removes his reasons for doubt. However, this attempt to reach normative certainty seems doomed to failure (this is the problem of the Cartesian circle). For if the *premisses* of Descartes's argument for God's existence are somewhat doubtful, then the *conclusion* will be just as doubtful. As Michael Della Rocca says: 'If Descartes is, prior to the conclusions of his theological argument ... at most psychologically (and thus not normatively) certain of propositions in general, then Descartes cannot by means of argument go on to acquire normative certainty.'[46]

Della Rocca proposes that Descartes did not in fact engage in such a quixotic venture, for Descartes considered himself to be—from the beginning—normatively certain of all currently perceived clear and distinct perceptions. Descartes uses the argument for God's existence and veracity not to *gain* normative certainty, but to *extend* it from currently perceived to merely remembered clear and distinct perceptions. Like Della Rocca, I think that Descartes takes himself to *start off* with normative certainty of some (clear and distinct) propositions, because he is aware of a *normative* property in them—the fact that he *ought* to assent to them. Descartes can be aware of this fact even if clear perceptions do not determine his assent, and so Kenny's criticism of the radical libertarian reading fails.

Though I am not convinced by Kenny's argument, I think his conclusion is correct: the radical libertarian interpretation will not work. For, as I read him, when Descartes says that we sometimes 'cannot but' assent to clear and distinct perceptions, the 'cannot'

---

[45] AT vii. 21, CSM ii. 14; AT vii. 36, CSM ii. 25. On this point, see Alan Gewirth, 'The Cartesian Circle', *Philosophical Review*, 50 (1941), 371.

[46] Michael Della Rocca, 'Descartes, the Cartesian Circle, and Epistemology without God', *Philosophy and Phenomenological Research*, 70 (2005), 1–33.

functions *both* normatively and descriptively. Descartes thinks that in some circumstances, we not only *ought* to assent to a clear and distinct perception, but also are determined (by the very nature of the will) to do so.

My interpretation follows straightforwardly from Descartes's picture of how volition relates to intellection and inclination. Like Aquinas,[47] Descartes considers the will a rational appetite for goodness and truth.[48] As Descartes says in the *Sixth Replies*, the will 'cannot tend toward anything else' other than truth or goodness (AT vii. 432; CSM ii. 292). The will cannot tend—i.e. incline—towards affirming a proposition unless the intellect first represents the proposition as at least possibly true. Similarly, we cannot be inclined towards a course of action unless it seems to us somehow good.

Because the will's natural orientation affects inclination, it also limits choice. In the *Passions of the Soul*, Descartes says: 'if we were wholly certain that what we are doing is bad, we would refrain from doing it, since the will tends only towards objects that have some semblance of goodness' (AT xi. 464; CSM i. 392). And in a May 1637 letter to Mersenne, he says: 'If the intellect never represented anything to the will as good without its actually being so, the will could never go wrong in its choice' (AT i. 366; CSMK 56). These passages, from both early and late in Descartes's career, make clear that we cannot choose to do something unless we are inclined to do it, and we cannot be inclined to do it unless it appears somehow good.[49]

Now suppose that the intellect considers course of action A—and thinks of nothing else. If perception of A is obscure, then according to Descartes the intellect will find some goodness in all three of its options: pursuing A, avoiding A, or doing nothing (postponing a decision). Consequently, the will has motivation and immediate

---

[47] 'In order that the will tend to anything, it is requisite ... that it be apprehended as good' (*ST* II–I q. 8 a. 1; citation is from the first complete American edition, tr. Fathers of the English Dominican Province (New York: Benziger Brothers, 1947–8)).

[48] 'The will does not tend toward evil except in so far as it is presented to it by the intellect under some aspect of goodness' (AT i. 366; CSMK 56).

[49] Descartes also presents the will as oriented towards truth (AT vii. 431–3; CSM ii. 291–2), yielding the parallel claim that we cannot assent to a proposition unless the intellect presents it as at least possibly true. But for the sake of simplicity in the argument that follows, I describe assent as an action aimed at the good—specifically, the good of believing or knowing the truth.

power to go in any of these directions. However, if the intellect clearly and distinctly perceives that A is good, then it represents only pursuing A as good. In this case, the will would be inclined only towards pursuing A, and would clearly lack what Aquinas called the *liberty of specification*—the ability to pursue A or some different course B. But would the will retain liberty with regard to the *exercise* of its act—the ability to pursue A or not (by 'holding back' or doing nothing at all)?[50]

As Lilli Alanen has recently noted, Duns Scotus and other later medieval voluntarists insisted that the will always has a 'positive power' to elicit or not elicit its own acts. Therefore, Scotus would claim that even when presented with a clear good, the will enjoys the power to hold back from pursuit by doing nothing at all. Alanen notes that Descartes's characterization of the will as *positiva facultas se determinandi* resembles some of Scotus' remarks,[51] and concludes that Descartes takes the Scotistic position: he thinks that even when the will is inclined only in one direction, it still has an immediate two-way power to either go in that direction, or hold back.[52] However, two things work against Alanen's interpretation.

First, the Scotistic position requires a sharp distinction between liberty of specification (e.g. pursuing vs. fleeing) and liberty of exercise (pursuing vs. doing nothing). But in his definition of freedom, Descartes runs together the ability to 'do or not do' with the ability to 'pursue or flee' or to 'affirm or deny'. For Descartes, holding back is just as much a positive course of action as pursuing or fleeing. Therefore, if the will is to have the immediate power to hold back, the intellect must first represent holding back as somehow good.[53] As Descartes says in the two-senses passage, 'it is always open to us to hold back from pursuing a clearly known good, or from admitting a clearly perceived truth, *provided we consider it a good thing to demonstrate the*

---

[50] For more on the specification–exercise distinction, see Aquinas, *ST* II–I q. and 9 a. 1, Garber and Ayers (eds.), *The Cambridge History of Seventeenth-Century Philosophy*, ii. 1198–9.

[51] Descartes refers to the will's 'positive power' in AT iv. 116, 173–4; CSMK 234, 245. For a more detailed summary of Scotus' position and use of similar terminology, see Alanen, 'Otherwise', 287–91.

[52] Alanen, 'Otherwise', 294.

[53] In his discussion of indifference just following the great light passage, Descartes presents 'refraining from making a judgment' as an option on a par with affirming or denying (AT vii. 59; CSM ii. 41).

freedom of our will by so doing' (AT iv. 173; CSMK 245; my emphasis).[54] If Descartes thought that the will enjoys liberty of exercise no matter what is in the intellect, he would not have needed to add the italicized proviso.

Second, in the great light passage, where Descartes does seem to imply the specification–exercise distinction, he suggests that clear and distinct perception (at least sometimes) rules out *both* kinds of immediate power. He says that he was 'not able not to judge true' (*non potui ... non judicare*) what he clearly and distinctly perceived. Not only could he not deny it, he could not even refrain from assenting to it.

So Descartes thinks that in at least some cases, clear and distinct perceptions in the intellect provoke only a single inclination in the will, and thereby determine the will's choice. How then can Descartes claim that the will maintains an incompatibilist two-way power in such cases?

5. ABSOLUTE POWER AS DERIVATIVE

For many libertarians, free choices may be determined by some factor other than the will (e.g. the agent's moral character), *provided* that the free agent herself brought about that factor through earlier undetermined free choices (e.g. through shaping her own character).[55] On this view, some free choices can be determined, but only if some earlier free choices were *not* determined. These earlier choices ensure that (in an indirect way) the will is still the ultimate causal origin of its acts.

I think Descartes held this kind of libertarian view. For Descartes, to be free with respect to a volition, we must have *self-determining* two-way power with respect to that volition. There are two ways to be self-determining: either by having immediate two-way power with respect to the volition (direct self-determination), or by having *derivative* two-way power with respect to it (indirect self-determination). An

---

[54] This passage explains why the will always enjoys 'a positive faculty' of *determining itself* 'to one or other of two contraries' and so is clearly relevant to Alanen's interpretation.

[55] See Robert Kane, *The Significance of Free Will* (Oxford: Oxford University Press, 1996), 32–40. Descartes's contemporary John Bramhall held a similar position. See Vere Chappell (ed.) *Hobbes and Bramhall on Liberty and Necessity* (Cambridge: Cambridge University Press, 1999), 52.

agent A has derivative two-way power with respect to a volition V_1 at time T_1 if and only if: (i) A does not have immediate power with respect to V_1 at T_1; (ii) at an earlier time T_0, A elicited another volition V_0 that contributes causally to A's eliciting of V; and (iii) A had *immediate* power with respect to V_0.

In the two-senses passage, when Descartes says that 'morally speaking' we cannot withhold assent from a clearly perceived truth, he describes a case in which we are determined to assent by a one-way inclination in the will. However, even when thus determined, we are 'absolutely speaking' able to hold back because we satisfy two conditions. First, in a relevantly similar alternative scenario, we would enjoy the immediate power to hold back (for example, if our clear perception were accompanied by the thought that it would be good to prove our freedom, we could hold back). Second, at some time in the past we had it in our immediate power either to bring about that alternative scenario, or not. The first of these conditions resembles hypothetical two-way power, but the second condition adds an incompatibilist element: the alternative scenario must have been (at some point) *genuinely accessible* to the agent.

The notion of indirect self-determination resolves a lingering puzzle about the meaning of 'external force' in the second part of the definition of freedom. In the great light passage, the intellect indirectly determines the will's act without removing freedom. Since, for Descartes, indirect determination by external forces removes freedom, this suggests that the intellect must not be an external force. But as I argued above, Descartes's reply to Gassendi suggests that the intellect's indirect determination *would* remove freedom, and so *is* an external force. The best way to harmonize these passages is to suppose that, for Descartes, the intellect can be either internal or external, depending on the situation. A force counts as 'internal' just in case it is either in the will, or *under the will's influence*. In the great light passage, Descartes's clear perceptions are 'internal' forces because they were brought about by an earlier act of will that was *not* determined by the intellect's contents. Thus if we trace the chain of sufficient causes back far enough, we find that it originates in the will. By contrast, in Gassendi's picture, the will is never self-determining with respect to the intellect, so that the chain of sufficient causes must ultimately originate *outside* the will, in the intellect.

At the end of his 1645 letter to Mesland, Descartes says: 'freedom considered in the acts of the will at the moment when they are elicited' does not involve two-way power of any kind, because 'what is done cannot remain undone as long as it is being done' (AT iv. 174; CSMK 246). However, Descartes insists that *prior* to the moment of choice the will always has a positive power of self-determination 'to one or other of two contraries' (AT iv. 173; CSMK 245). So, for Descartes, freedom after the moment of choice is always *derivative* on an earlier two-way power.

Similarly, our 'absolute' two-way power at the time of choice sometimes derives from our earlier immediate power to direct our *attention* in various ways. Descartes's definition of clear perception in the *Principles* seems to make such perception always contingent on attention: 'I call a perception "clear" when it is present and accessible to the attentive mind (*menti attendenti*)' (AT viiia. 22; CSM i. 207; see also AT x. 368; CSM i. 14).[56] And the following passage from a letter to Mesland suggests that our control over attention is, as Jean Laporte says, 'the foundation of our merit'.[57]

And one does not cease to merit, although seeing very clearly what must be done, one does it infallibly, and without any indifference, as Jesus Christ did in this life. Since Man cannot always attend perfectly to what we ought to do, it is a good action to pay attention and thus to ensure that our will follows so promptly the light of our understanding that there is no longer any indifference at all. (AT iv. 117; CSMK 234)

It seems that, for Descartes, Christ earns merit because the infallible determination of his will towards right action is not absolute, but depends on a prior exercise of immediate two-way power: his decision to pay attention exclusively to the best course of action.

As I understand it, the 'absolute' two-way power essential to Cartesian freedom cannot be hypothetical two-way power. Hypothetical power is consistent with universal determinism by intellect, a kind of determinism that Descartes considered inconsistent with freedom (as the reply to Gassendi demonstrates). Therefore Descartes is not a compatibilist, but some kind of incompatibilist about freedom and

---

[56] See Laporte, 'La Liberté', 62–4.
[57] Laporte, *Le Rationalisme*, 273.

determinism. But neither can Cartesian freedom consist in immediate two-way power: Descartes thinks that the intellect can sometimes determine the will without removing freedom, but such determination *would* remove immediate two-way power. So Descartes is not a radical libertarian who believes that the will can never be determined in its choices. Rather, he is a more moderate libertarian, who believes that the will is always either directly or indirectly self-determining. In cases where a clear perception in the intellect determines the will, the will is somehow responsible for bringing about that clear perception in the first place through selective direction of attention.

Descartes's claims about hypothetical enlightened agents might seem to undermine my interpretation.[58] Recall that enlightened agents would enjoy clear and distinct perceptions all the time, with regard to anything they might ever deliberate about. But if clear perceptions always determine the will, as so many passages suggest, then enlightened agents would always have their will determined by their intellect. The fact that the will controls the direction of attention would make no difference, because Descartes must think that, like other acts of will, decisions about how to direct attention are responses to prior perceptions in the intellect.[59] So the will of an enlightened agent could never be either directly or indirectly self-determining (it is in the same predicament as the will on Gassendi's model). So if my reading were correct, we would expect Descartes to deny that enlightened agents are free. But in fact he *affirms* this.

If Descartes's doctrine of clear and distinct determinism (CDD) is that clear perceptions *always* determine the will, then he could not (on pain of contradiction) accept the view of freedom I attribute to him. However, the two-senses passage shows that Descartes did not accept such a strong version of CDD. In that passage, Descartes suggests that we can have two things in mind at once: (1) a 'very evident

---

[58] Though the blessed in heaven are enlightened agents (see letter to Mesland, 2 May 1644, AT iv. 116; CSMK 234), they do not present a problem for my interpretation because they were not *always* enlightened. Their post-mortem enlightened freedom could be derivative from their ante-mortem, immediate two-way power of choice.

[59] Laporte himself acknowledges this, but he also attributes CDD to Descartes (*Le Rationalisme*, 273). So for the reasons sketched in this paragraph, I think that Laporte's interpretation of Descartes founders on the texts about the freedom of enlightened agents. For other criticisms of Laporte, see Campbell, 'Spontaneity', 192; Imlay, 'Indifference', 93; Moyal, 'Unity', 42–3.

reason' (a clear and distinct perception); and (2) the thought that it would be good to prove our freedom by not acting on that reason. In my view, the thought of proving freedom is just an example of a *counter-motive*: an apparent good which the intellect presents alongside the clear perception, and which motivates us to hold back from the course of action towards which the clear perception pushes us.[60] Counter-motives are evidentially neutral: they do not bear at all on the truth or falsehood of the 'evident reason'. Since they do nothing to call the 'evident reason' into doubt, they do nothing to diminish its clarity and distinctness,[61] and yet they give us the immediate power to hold back. In cases of counter-motivation, clear perceptions do *not* determine the will.

My reading of the two-senses passage is controversial. According to Kenny, Descartes does not mean that we can hold back from a clear perception at the moment we perceive it clearly. He means rather that thinking of a counter-motive distracts our attention from the original perception, so that we no longer perceive it clearly. Only then can we hold back. For support, Kenny cites the following passage from the 1644 letter to Mesland:[62]

I agree with you when you say that we can suspend our judgement; but I tried to explain in what manner this can be done. For it seems to me certain that 'a great light in the intellect is followed by a great inclination in the will'; so that upon seeing very clearly that a thing is good for us, it is very difficult, and even, as I believe, impossible, while one remains in this thought, to stop the course of our desire. But the nature of the soul is such that it hardly attends for more than a moment to a single thing; hence, as soon as our attention turns (*se detoume*) from the reasons which show us that the thing is good for us, and we merely keep in our memory the thought that it appeared desirable to us, we can call up before our mind some other reason to make us doubt it, and so suspend our judgement, and perhaps even form a contrary judgement. (AT iv. 116; CSMK 233–4)

Kenny assumes that this passage describes the same power (to resist an evident reason) as the two-senses passage, and he gives this passage

---

[60] Campbell ('Spontaneity', 194) agrees that it is just an example. Imlay ('Indifference', 94) suggests that the desire to prove freedom is the only possible motive that could work in the way Descartes describes.

[61] My interpretation here is in contrast to Kenny, 'Will', 29.

[62] Kenny, 'Will', 28–9.

interpretative priority because it seems to reveal the psychological mechanism behind the power.

However, the 1644 passage and the two-senses passage do not describe the very same power. In the *Second Replies*, Descartes distinguishes between *per se* and *per aliud* clear and distinct perceptions. *Per se* clear and distinct perceptions 'are so transparently clear and at the same time so simple that we cannot ever think of them without believing them to be true', whereas *per aliud* truths 'are perceived very clearly by our intellect so long as we attend to the arguments on which our knowledge of them depends' (AT vii. 145–6; CSM ii. 104). The 1644 passage explains how to suspend judgement with respect to pursuing an object that is good *per aliud* (by turning our attention 'from the reasons which show us that the thing is good for us'), but it does not show how we could suspend judgement with respect to *per se* clear and distinct truths. The two-senses passage, by contrast, concerns a power the will *always* has, even with respect to *per se* clear perceptions.

So my reading of the two-senses passage is not undermined by the 1644 letter. Furthermore, my reading has textual support from elsewhere in Descartes's correspondence. Furthermore, my reading has textual support from elsewhere in Descartes's correspondence. In the two-senses passage, Descartes speaks of 'the positive power we have of following the worse although we see the better (*sequendi deteriora, quamvis meliora videamus*)' (AT iv. 174; CSMK 245). Descartes alludes here to a famous line from Ovid: 'I see and approve the better, I follow the worse.'[63] In a much earlier letter to Mersenne (May 1637), Descartes explains how he understands the Ovid passage: 'the intellect often represents different things to the will at the same time (*diverses choses en même temps*); and that is why they say, "I see and praise the better, but I follow the worse"' (AT i. 366; CSMK 56). This text merely reinforces the most natural reading of the two-senses passage: when we perceive a clear good, but at the same time also consider a counter-motive, we can, at that moment, go either way (we have immediate two-way power to pursue or to hold back).

Descartes's true doctrine of clear and distinct determinism (CDD) is not that clear perceptions always determine the will, but that they

---

[63] *Metamorphoses* 7. 20: 'video meliora proboque, deteriora sequor'.

always do so *if* the contents of the intellect are limited to exclude counter-motives. In the passages that assert CDD, Descartes does not mention this condition because he simply *assumes* that it has been fulfilled: he assumes that no counter-motives are present. For example, as Alanen points out, the will Descartes considers in the *Meditations* 'is essentially a will of a meditator in search of certain knowledge'.[64] The meditator is concerned only with believing the truth, to the exclusion of counter-motives.

The 1644 letter to Mesland also suggests that Descartes usually assumes the absence of counter-motives. Descartes says there that 'upon seeing very clearly that a thing is good for us', the will is determined to pursue that thing. But surely it is possible for both of two incompatible courses of action to be good for us, in different ways. If we clearly perceived both of them, Descartes's remark would imply that our will would be determined to both at once, which is absurd. Perhaps we could avoid this result by supposing that 'good' really means 'best',[65] but Descartes does not think the will must always choose the best option (as the references to Ovid show). The only charitable way around this difficulty is to suppose that Descartes here *assumes* that the clearly perceived good is the *only* one we perceive. His point is that when our attention is limited to a single good, if that good is clearly perceived, it inspires one-way inclination in the will, thereby determining it (whereas if a single good is obscurely perceived, it inspires ambivalent inclinations and so does not determine the will).

Because Descartes does not think clear perceptions *always* determine the will, his views about enlightened agents do not necessarily conflict with his incompatibilist account of freedom. For Descartes may have held that the human intellect has a natural tendency towards pragmatic multiplicity: unless the will intervenes to prevent it, the intellect displays many incompatible, apparently good, potential courses of action for the immediate future. In other words, the intellect is naturally geared to explore alternative answers to the question 'What shall I do next?' Given this assumption about the intellect, hypothetical enlightened human agents would *start out* perceiving at least two

---

[64] Alanen, 'Intuition', 111.

[65] Though I suspect the problem might arise again from the possibility of decision situations where two options tie for best.

incompatible courses of action as somehow good. Since, for Descartes, the will is not forced to choose the greatest good, even if enlightened agents saw clearly which course was best overall, they would still enjoy immediate two-way power in this initial situation. Among the courses of action open to such agents, some might involve suspending the intellect's consideration of future action and instead concentrating completely on a present activity. With their attention narrowed in this way, enlightened agents would sometimes lack immediate two-way power (e.g. when they are considering whether or not to believe a clear and distinct proposition). But even so they would retain *derivative* two-way power, because they brought about this narrowed attention state through an earlier exercise of immediate two-way power.

Though Descartes never explicitly says that the intellect naturally starts out considering multiple goods, this idea fits well with his visual metaphors for cognition. For example, in the Ninth of his *Rules for the Direction of the Mind*, he says:

Craftsmen who engage in delicate operations, and are used to fixing their eyes on a single point, acquire through practice the ability to make perfect distinctions between things, however minute and delicate. The same is true of those who never let their thinking be distracted by many different objects at the same time, but always devote their whole attention to the simplest and easiest of matters: they become perspicacious. (AT x. 401; CSM i. 33)[66]

If the intellect starts out presenting multiple practical options analogous to an entire visual field, then to become perspicacious—that is, to have our will determined by a great light in the intellect—we must first fix our eyes on a single point by devoting *all* of our attention to a particular project.

My interpretation is similar to the radical libertarian reading in emphasizing the normative force of clear and distinct perceptions. On both interpretations, we can withhold assent from clear and distinct propositions (though I do not think that in Descartes's view we can *deny* such propositions). On my reading, we can withhold assent during clear and distinct perception by firmly keeping a counter-motive in mind. But notice that we can do so only by keeping our distance

---

[66] Descartes employs the same metaphor again later, in *Principles* I. 45 (AT viiia. 22; CSM i. 207).

from a certain norm-guided project—the Cartesian project of trying to believe only what is true. What distinguishes clear and distinct ideas from obscure ones is not their psychological force *simpliciter*, but their psychological force *in the normative context* of the Cartesian project. My interpretation incorporates this key strength of the radical libertarian reading, while avoiding its weaknesses. I will close by considering three more objections to my interpretation.

First, in the 1645 letter to Mesland, Descartes defines 'indifference' as 'that state of the will when it is not impelled one way rather than another by any perception of truth or goodness' (AT iv. 173; CSMK 245). This suggests that 'indifference' means 'multidirectional motivation in the will'. Since, on my interpretation, freedom could not exist without such multidirectional motivation (at least at the initial level of pragmatic options), my reading makes freedom depend on indifference. But as we have seen, Descartes says explicitly that freedom does not require indifference. Furthermore, enlightened agents could never enjoy the multidirectional motivation I attribute to them, because, for Descartes, man 'is never indifferent except when he does not know which of the two alternatives is better or truer, or at least when he does not see this clearly enough to rule out any possibility of doubt' (*Sixth Replies*, AT vii. 433; CSM ii. 292).

When Descartes defines indifference, he mentions not only ambivalent motivation, but also the absence of perception, and most of his references to indifference also mention ignorance or a lack of clarity in our perceptions. This suggests that, for Descartes, 'indifference' means not just 'multidirectional motivation', but 'multidirectional motivation produced by ignorance'. On this reading, Descartes's claim that we are never indifferent except when we are ignorant does *not* imply that two-way motivation is impossible without ignorance. Rather, it implies that the sort of two-way motivation we sometimes experience during clear perception (as in the case of proving our freedom) does not count as 'indifference'. Indifference is the ambivalence we feel when we search for the truth, but cannot be sure we have found it. It is *not* the ambivalence we feel when trying to decide whether to search for truth in the first place. On my interpretation, Cartesian freedom depends on two-way motivation, but not on indifference.

My preferred interpretation of 'indifference' might seem to conflict with this claim from the Fourth Meditation: 'if I always saw clearly what was true and good, I would never deliberate about what is to be judged or chosen (*nunquam de eo quod esset judicandum vel eligendum deliberarem*); and in that case, although completely free, still I could never be indifferent' (AT vii. 58; CSM ii. 40; my translation). This might be taken to suggest that an enlightened agent would never deliberate, and so would never experience simultaneous motivations towards incompatible options. But in fact, the passage says that enlightened agents do not need to deliberate about 'what is to be judged or chosen'. Descartes's point is that enlightened agents always know clearly what ought to be done, or what option is best. This does not imply that they cannot be inclined, at the same time, in other directions. Indifference is the ambivalence we feel when we are committed to doing whatever is best but cannot figure out what it is, not the ambivalence we feel when choosing between the best option and another that is merely good.

Second, some libertarians might object that the view of freedom I attribute to Descartes is not sufficiently robust. For Cartesian freedom, on my reading, is not the power to *deny* the clear and distinct, or to *pursue* the evil, but merely to *hold back* from a clearly known truth or good. Because they would never be indifferent, enlightened agents would be unable to sin, as the following passage from the 1644 letter to Mesland shows:

Wherever there is an occasion for sinning, there is indifference; and I do not think that in order to do wrong it is necessary to see clearly that what we are doing is evil. It is sufficient to see it confusedly, or merely remember that we once judged it to be so, without in any way seeing it—that is, without paying attention to the reasons which prove it to be so. For if we saw it clearly, it would be impossible for us to sin, as long as we saw it in that fashion; that is why they say that whoever sins does so in ignorance. (AT iv. 117; CSMK 234)

Although enlightened agents might be self-determining in the sense of choosing one of many possible good paths of life, they would still 'never make a mistake' (Fourth Meditation, AT vii. 61; CSM ii. 42). The freedom enjoyed by enlightened agents would not be 'morally significant' in Alvin Plantinga's sense: it would not be a power to choose between good and evil.[67]

---

[67] Alvin Plantinga, 'God, Evil, and the Metaphysics of Freedom', in Robert and Marilyn Adams (eds.), *The Problem of Evil* (Oxford: Oxford University Press, 1990), 85.

It is important to see that, for Descartes, the freedom we wield here and now, in the actual world, *is* accompanied by indifference, and so is morally significant. Descartes suggests that God may have given us this morally significant freedom in order to make the world as a whole better, though he clearly thinks that *we* would have been better off with the morally insignificant freedom of enlightened agents (Fourth Meditation, AT vii. 61; CSM ii. 42). To some, this last thought may seem odd, but if it is a problem, it is a problem for Descartes, not for my interpretation.

Finally, some might object that my interpretation is too speculative. To make all the texts hang together, I have assumed that, for Descartes, the intellect naturally presents multiple pragmatic options unless the will steps in to limit the scope of attention. And though this assumption fits both Descartes's emphasis on the role of attention and his visual metaphors for cognition, there is no *explicit* textual evidence for it.

As someone who thinks that interpreters should stick as closely as possible to the evidence, I am deeply sympathetic to this objection. However, I think that the only feasible alternative to my reading is a rather grim one for Descartes: his collected remarks about freedom really are basically unsystematic, and indeed self-contradictory. Descartes placed a high value on freedom, remarking to Queen Christina in 1647 that 'Free will is in itself the noblest thing we can have, since it makes us in a way equal to God and seems to exempt us from being his subjects; and so its correct use is the greatest of all the goods we possess' (AT v. 85; CSMK 326). Therefore, it would be a shame if Descartes had no sincerely held or coherent view about the nature of freedom. So though the textual evidence remains somewhat ambiguous, that other great guide of interpretation—the principle of charity—works in favour of my reading.[68]

Saint Louis University

[68] I am grateful to Saint Louis University for the Mellon summer stipend that supported my writing of this chapter. I am indebted to the editors of this volume and to many others for helpful feedback on earlier drafts, including the organizers of and participants in the Mid-Atlantic Seminar in Modern Philosophy at Rutgers University in November 2004, Shelly Kagan, Sukjae Lee, Dan Kaufman, Marilyn Adams, Nicholas Zavediuk, and an anonymous referee for *Oxford Studies in Early Modern Philosophy*. I owe very special thanks to Michael Della Rocca and Robert Adams, both of whom gave me extensive comments on numerous early versions of the chapter.

4

The Scholastic Resources for Descartes's Concept of God as *Causa Sui*

RICHARD A. LEE, JR.

I. INTRODUCTION

The debate between Caterus and Arnauld on one side and Descartes on the other about whether God is *causa sui* has been seen as marking the distinction between scholastic and modern thought.[1] This debate, which arises initially out of an issue that is not even central to Descartes's proof for the existence of God, has Descartes insisting that we must understand God as *causa sui* in the positive sense that God's essence is something like an efficient cause of God's existence, and Arnauld and Caterus, scholastic as they are, insisting that no philosopher holds such an incomprehensible position.

Caterus and Arnauld stand in a long tradition, stemming all the way back to Aristotle, that denies the possibility that something can be the cause of itself. This tradition, as will be shown, has two main features. First, it denies the possibility that something can move itself, in the sense of either local motion, alteration, or augmentation. Second, it denies the specific notion that something can move itself as an efficient cause of itself because that would require a thing to be in potency and in actuality at the same time with regard to the same thing. However, beginning at least with Duns Scotus, scholastic philosophers did argue that God's being must be *a se* or *ex se*, i.e. from itself. While many would maintain, as does Caterus, that this is to be understood negatively in that God's existence needs no other cause

[1] Étienne Gilson, *Études sur le rôle de la pensée médiévale dans la formation du système Cartésien*, 3rd edn. (Paris: J. Vrin, 1967), 226, but see also Jean-Luc Marion, 'The Essential Incoherence of Descartes' Definition of Divinity', in Amélie Oksenberg Rorty (ed.), *Essays on Descartes' 'Meditations'* (Berkeley: University of California Press, 1986).

besides the divine essence, the question that Descartes raises is, How do we give an account of that very fact? Descartes's insistence is that a thorough proof for the existence of God demands that one supply a reason or cause for God's existence, or a reason or cause why God needs no such cause. God is from Godself because God has an infinite power that entails that nothing could be repugnant to that existence.[2]

In what follows, I would like to look at the classic scholastic rejection of *causa sui*. I will use Scotus and Aquinas as emblematic of these arguments, and I will trace their influence on Suárez's understanding of how God is *a se*. I am not merely interested in the rejection of the notion. Rather, I want to show how medieval thinkers, primarily Aquinas and Scotus, seem to require a concept very much like *causa sui* in order to bring together God's existence with God's infinity especially when treating the power of God that grounds God's independence. While I am primarily interested in showing the Scotistic origins for Descartes's ability to posit that God is *causa sui*,[3] I will first set the stage by addressing Aquinas' arguments against the notion of *causa sui* within his proof for the existence of God in *Summa contra gentiles*. I want to pay attention to two features of these discussions: first, while medieval thinkers (and here Aquinas and Scotus are particularly instructive examples) roundly denied the cogency of the notion *causa sui*, they developed the means that Descartes will use in his positing of God as *causa sui*. Second, I want to show how those concepts that Descartes mobilizes in making sense of *causa sui* were developed not in proofs for the existence of God based on causation, but with reference to God's infinity, power, and perfection. What I hope to show is that Descartes is able to argue

[2] In this way, I disagree both with Gilson's contention that Descartes has no predecessors in claiming that God is *causa sui* and with Marion's claim that there is a fundamental incoherence in Descartes's concept and definition of God.

[3] Roger Ariew (*Descartes and the Last Scholastics* (Ithaca, NY: Cornell University Press, 1999)) has brought more attention to the scholastic influences on Descartes. In particular, he has shown that much of the scholastic thought with which Descartes was familiar carried much of Scotus' thought in a Thomistic wrapper. 'Contra Gilson, an analysis of Eustachius's works quickly shows that every doctrine one would call Scotist was held by him. ... It is clear that Eustachius was propounding common Parisian doctrines ...' (p. 2). Ariew lists several 'Scotist' positions that 17th-century scholastic philosophers held and that Descartes himself adopts. Here I am interested in the link between perfection, infinity, and the existence of God that is found in Scotus. It is this connection that brings him close to Descartes's notion of God as *causa sui*.

that God is *causa sui*, precisely because his argument turns on the notions of infinity and infinite perfection, and that these are thought by him to be related to power. This same kind of argument is found in Scotus (and, to a certain extent in Suárez), where we also have a proof for the existence of God that is both ontological (proving the existence of something from its mere concept) and cosmological (proving the existence of a first cause). It is this kind of argument that allows Descartes to make sense of the concept of *causa sui* in a way that medieval thinkers could not.

2. AQUINAS ON GOD AS FIRST CAUSE

If one compares the structures of Aquinas' *Summa theologiae* with his *Summa contra gentiles*, one notices remarkable differences.[4] One reason, perhaps even the major reason, for these differences is the different intentions that Aquinas announces for each work.[5] The *Summa theologiae* was a textbook in theology, his attempt to write a replacement for Peter Lombard's *Sentences*.[6] Because it is a beginning textbook in theology, the structure of this text is designed to exhibit what one might call the internal coherence of the Catholic faith. That is, Aquinas is not concerned there to demonstrate the external validity of the faith, but merely to bring its exposition to sufficient clarity.[7] The *Summa contra gentiles* (*SCG*), however, as its title indicates, is a book written to arm the faithful with arguments against non-believers.[8]

---

[4] For the text of the *Summa theologiae*, I rely on the text of Thomas Aquinas edited by Commissio Leoninis, *Sancti Thomae Aquinatis opera omnia iussu impenasque Leonis XIII P.M.*, xiii–xv (Rome: Commissio Leoninis, 1882). For the *Summa contra gentiles*, I use Thomas Aquinas, *Liber de veritate catholicae fidei contra errores infidelium, seu 'Summa contra gentiles'*, ed. Ceslai Pera, Petro Marc, and Petro Caramello (Rome: Marietti, 1961). References to this text will use book number followed by chapter number.

[5] On the task and procedure of the *SCG*, see Norman Kretzmann, *Metaphysics of Theism: Aquinas's Natural Theology in Summa contra Gentiles I* [*Aquinas*] (Oxford: Clarendon Press, 1997); and Mark Jordan, 'The Protreptic Structure of the *Summa contra Gentiles*', *Thomist*, 50 (1986), 173–209.

[6] The intention, announced in the prologue of the *ST*, is 'to treat those things that pertain to the Christian religion in that way that is congruent with the learning of a beginner'.

[7] Again in the Prologue, Aquinas complains that other textbooks in theology (perhaps primarily Lombard's *Sentences*) do not treat the subject according to the 'order of the discipline'.

[8] 'Our intention is to show, according to our measure, the truth, which the Catholic faith declares by eliminating contrary errors' (*SCG* I. 2).

Aquinas states that his intention is to provide rational demonstrations of those truths of the faith that are able to be demonstratively proven and to provide reasons, though not demonstrative, for those truths that cannot be demonstratively proven (SCG I. 9). Precisely because it is written against those who do not accept the faith, it cannot assume any elements deriving simply from the faith, but must speak to its external validity.

I point to this structure because I think it helps to account for a striking dissimilarity between these two texts on the issue of proving the existence of God. One can notice immediately that when Aquinas addresses the question 'whether God exists' in ST he offers five proofs for the existence of God. These five proofs are offered there as five ways to show one and the same thing, namely that God exists. The five ways, then, stand side by side with one another, each achieving its result independently of the other. That is to say, at the moment they are offered, there is no internal relation between them, and Aquinas makes no attempt, *philosophically*, to show an internal relationship among the five arguments.[9] While the relationship between the first efficient cause of all things and the governor of all things is clear from within the faith, Aquinas does not prove this immediately when he gives his five proofs. From the point of view of the Catholic faith, a point of view that is presupposed in ST, the identity is already obvious. Now this procedure is valid in a text designed to explicate the contents of the faith, but it is invalid in a text that attempts to show the external validity of those contents. In SCG, Aquinas offers four proofs, two of them from motion (I. 13). Not only are the two other proofs remarkably short, but they are both taken as arguments produced by others and their material is covered again in more detail later in the text.[10] For example, the proof that there is a governor of

---

[9] Kretzmann (*Aquinas*, 54) argues that the proofs for the existence of God are not even necessary to the task of ST.

[10] This is a fact that Kretzmann does not point out in his discussion of these arguments. Indeed, he argues that, from a more contemporary point of view, it is not the case that a demonstration of the existence of God must be carried out before any other task of natural theology. I would argue that it is not the conclusion 'God exists' that Aquinas needs, but rather the proof itself and its notions of causation, motion, first cause, etc. that Aquinas relies on in the remainder of book I of SCG. On the relation between these arguments and those of SCG, see Scott MacDonald, 'Aquinas's Parasitic Cosmological Argument', *Medieval Philosophy and Theology*, I (1991), 119–55.

the universe is treated in much more detail in chapter 63 of book I of *SCG*. This is because in showing the external validity of the faith, Aquinas attempts to demonstrate all these facts about God from out of the very notion that God is the first mover of all things. In other words, the *SCG* has a structure that is attempting to follow the flow of logical consequences of the notion that there must be a first mover, something that would be awkward, and maybe even misleading, in a text that merely attempts to give an intelligible explication to the contents of the faith.

Before moving to the proof of the existence of God, Aquinas first addresses the question of whether the proposition 'God exists' is demonstrable at all. He takes up two sets of arguments that the existence of God is indemonstrable. The second group argues that the proposition 'God exists' is held only by faith and therefore cannot be demonstrated. The first group, on the other hand, argues that the existence of God is a self-evident proposition and as such cannot be demonstrated. A self-evident proposition would be indemonstrable because there is no middle term between the subject and the predicate that would make a demonstration possible. 'It follows, then, that in all our inquiries we inquire either (a) whether there is a *middle* or (b) what the *middle* is; for the cause is a *middle*, and in all cases this is what is sought.'[11] Aquinas, like many medieval philosophers, considers Anselm's ontological argument to show that the proposition 'God exists' is self-evident, and therefore indemonstrable. Aquinas does not disagree that in itself the proposition is self-evident. 'Certainly *simpliciter* that God is self-evident, because this itself that God is God's being. But because we cannot conceive by the mind this itself that God is, it remains unknown for us' (*SCG* I. II). This lack of knowledge allows an a posteriori demonstration of the existence of God, a demonstration that would use the effects of God in place of a definition and would have, as a result, a proper middle term for the demonstration. Aquinas rejects Anselm's argument and puts in its

---

[11] Aristotle, *Posterior Analytics* 89^{b}5 ff.; tr. Hippocrates Apostle (Grinell, La.: Peripatetic Press, 1981), 48. On the role of the middle in Aristotle's theory of demonstration, see Patrick Byrne, *Analysis and Science in Aristotle* (Albany: SUNY Press, 1997), 103–22. On the question of self-evident propositions in Aquinas, see my *Science, the Singular, and the Question of Theology*, New Middle Ages, ed. Bonnie Wheeler (New York: Palgrave, 2002), 33–57, but esp. 34 ff.

place a cosmological argument that does not turn on the mere concept of God.

The basic structure of the argument in *SCG* is quite simple:

(1) Everything that is moved is moved by another.
(2) It is obvious, at least from sensation, that something is moved (like the sun).
(3) Either that other that moves the first is moved, or not.
(4) If it is not moved, then there is a first mover that is immobile, namely God.
(5) If it is moved, therefore it is moved by another.
(6) Either this process goes on to infinity, or it stops at some immobile mover.
(7) It cannot go on to infinity; therefore it is necessary to posit some first immobile mover.

This argument, as Aquinas indicates, makes two presuppositions that are themselves in need of proof, namely that everything that is moved is moved by another and that the relation of moved to mover cannot proceed to infinity. He therefore embarks on demonstrations of each of these in turn. At least one of these arguments concerns not just local motion but causation itself—it shows that nothing can be *causa sui*.[12]

Aquinas gives three arguments that nothing can move itself. The first one has to do with the impossibility of any whole that is made of parts moving itself as a whole rather than parts moving the whole. Aquinas concludes that in such things, a part will always move the whole, and so the whole will not be *causa sui*. The second argument looks at all the kinds of motion that Aristotle posits: accidental, *per se*, by violence, and by nature, and he shows that according to none of these is it possible for something to move itself.

It is the third argument that is most significant in the history of the concept of *causa sui*. It has its origins in Aristotle's notion of actuality

---

[12] I assume that a self-mover would be *causa sui* inasmuch as Aquinas, like Aristotle, takes motion in the broad sense that encompasses local motion, alteration, increase and decrease, and perhaps even all forms of efficient causation. Furthermore, because this proof for the existence of God turns ultimately on production, and Aquinas links the concept of self-production to *causa sui*, this identification of *causa sui* with self-mover is entirely warranted. In short, while every self-mover might not be cause of itself, except in terms of its motion, every cause that causes itself would be a self-mover.

and potentiality. This argument shows that built into the notion of *causa sui* would be the fundamental contradiction that something would be in actuality and potency at the same time with regard to the same. In outline, the argument runs:

(1) Nothing is at the same time in act and in potency with respect to the same.

(2) Everything that is moved, in so far as it is moved, is in potency, because motion is the act of something existing in potency in so far as it is moving.

(3) Everything that would be a mover is in act, because nothing acts unless to the extent that it is in actuality.

(4) Therefore, nothing is, with respect to the same, actually moving and moved, and thus nothing moves itself.

Clearly this argument would apply not only to motion but also to causation in general. Since all causation, according to both Aristotle and Aquinas, can be understood as the 'reduction' of potency to actuality, any cause that is in potency and in actuality in the same way, that is, any *causa sui*, will be a violation of the principle of non-contradiction. This makes sense only given this specific sense of the term *potentia*. The argument, then, states that to be reduced from potentiality into actuality requires some cause that is itself in actuality in the same way. That is, actuality is prior to potentiality and therefore to assume that a being is *causa sui* would be tantamount to assuming that it is prior to itself—an obvious, at least to Aquinas, contradiction.

It is only when causation as a whole is thought on the model of actuality and potentiality, that is, as the leading out of potentiality into actuality, that the notion of *causa sui* presents itself as a violation of the principle of non-contradiction.[13] If potentiality is not thought in this way, we are not forced into saying that something is both A (potential) and not A (actual) at the same time and in the same way. It is central to Aquinas' argument that the potency relevant to causation is always considered in relation to actuality, or, as he most

---

[13] While I cannot pursue the question in detail here, one might be able to argue that Descartes's main disagreement with Caterus and Arnauld is that Descartes thinks of cause in terms of power, while Caterus, at least, still thinks of it in terms of Suárez's 'real influx of being', which is the bringing of something from potency into act. This is perhaps why God's power functions so importantly in Descartes's response to both Arnauld and Caterus.

often puts it, 'Actuality is prior to potentiality.'[14] Because he considers causation to be this movement from potency to actuality, and because he considers potency to be always 'not yet this actuality', he finds the notion of *causa sui* to be an obvious contradiction. We would have to say that the wood is potentially fire and not potentially fire at the same time in the same way.

It should be clear that if some concept of *causa sui* is to be developed that does not lead to this contradiction, causation will have to be recast outside the model of potency–actuality. Such an alternative is not unknown in the Middle Ages, for creation itself as a whole resists this model. There is no way to think that prior to creation there was something that was potentially a cosmos, or any member of the cosmos. For if that were the case, then that potency would have to be ascribed to God, and to ascribe potency in this sense to God is tantamount to saying that God is mutable. Conversely, one could argue that some potency is co-eternal with God and that creation is nothing other than God bringing actuality to that potency. Such a position obviously violates the notion of creation *ex nihilo*. However, medieval thinkers, including Aquinas, use this same term *potentia* to describe the characteristic that belongs to God that allows God to do or make things in a way other than by leading them from potentiality to actuality. That is, *power* is ascribed to God as that which allows God to create *ex nihilo*. This sense of *potentia* is not opposed to actuality, but rather belongs to a being that is already in act. Aquinas often calls this 'active potency' as opposed to the 'passive potency' that belongs to matter and is the potency that is led out into actuality in causation.

Related to God's *potentia* is what Aquinas calls a *virtus essendi*, a power of being. These two related notions of power become relevant when Aquinas comes to consider God's perfection. Since God is the first cause, Aquinas argues, God did not begin to be. However, the fact that God is the first cause does not immediately entail that God is also unable to cease to be. Aquinas argues that God is unable to cease to be because God has the power of always being. How are we to understand this power to be? Aquinas contrasts this *virtus essendi* directly with the potency that is relevant in causation: 'if it is conceded

---

[14] The notion that potency can be led into actuality only by something actual *in the same way* is central to many of the arguments of the first book of *SCG*.

that in the celestial body there is no potency in the sense of being passive to being, which is the potency of matter, still in it there is a potency in the sense of being active, which is the power of being' (*SCG* I. 20). This active potency that the celestial body has is the 'power always to be'. The heavenly body has an infinite power of being and therefore it is of infinite duration. As Aquinas argues in his commentary on *The Book of Causes*, something with an infinite power of being will be able to last an infinite time because the more power of being something has, the longer it is able to last.[15]

This ability to last that results from a thing's *virtus essendi* has both a positive and a negative sense. Positively, the *virtus essendi* is the active potency that arises not from matter, but from the form of the thing. 'Therefore, to the extent and while any given thing has being, to that extent is the power of its form.'[16] The power of being of any given thing is the power of being always, or for some determinate time.[17] Negatively, or seen from the other side, this *virtus essendi* also is the power to resist corruption, either externally or internally (*SCG* III. 5). That is, while the power of being is an active potency that derives from the form of the thing, it is what accounts for the determinate or infinite duration of the thing precisely because it is able to resist corruption.[18] The power of being of a thing resists corruption because

[15] Thomas Aquinas, *Super librum de causis expositio*, ed. H. D. Saffrey (Fribourg: Société philosophique-Nauwelaerts, 1954), *lectio* 4. On the concept of *virtus essendi* in Aquinas, see Étienne Gilson, 'Virtus essendi', *Medieval Studies*, 26 (1964), 1–11; as well as Fran O'Rourke, *Pseudo-Dionysius and the Metaphysics of Aquinas* (Leiden: E. J. Brill, 1992). Here I am stressing the origin of this concept in the context of discussions (perhaps begun by Averroes) on why a heavenly body, though not eternal, is not subject to corruption. The reason for this will become clear below.

[16] Thomas Aquinas, *Commentarium in De caelo*, ed. Commissio Leonis, *Sancti Thomae Aquinatis opera omnia iussu impenasque Leonis XIII P.M.*, iii (1886), 1–257, *lectio* 6 n. 5: 'Unde tantum et tamdiu habet unaquaeque res de esse, quanta est virtus formae eius.'

[17] Thomas Aquinas, *Super III Sententiis*, ed. M. F. Moos, *S. Thomae Aquinatis scriptum super Sententiis Magistri Petri Lombardi*, iii (Paris: P. Lethielleux, 1956), d. 23 q. 1. Aquinas traces the notion of power of being back to Aristotle's *De caelo*. See his commentary on that text (cited above) for the origin of this concept in relation to the heavenly body. *Virtus essendi* also has roots in the Pseudo-Dionysius, and many commentators (e.g. O'Rourke) treat that link as more crucial. As is indicated here, however, in this context, Averroes is certainly the source. The importance of the function of *virtus essendi* in discussions of the incorruptibility of the heavens is indicated by Suárez, who raises that question no less than four times in his discussion of proofs for the existence of God.

[18] It should be clear that I do not fully agree with Kretzmann's translation of *virtus essendi* as 'capacity of being', and his subsequent interpretation of this notion. Aquinas himself

it gives to the thing actuality over potentiality. It resists corruption externally by being stronger than the *virtutes* of other things.

It is this *virtus essendi* that allows Aquinas to prove that God is universally perfect. Aquinas begins by arguing that the excellence (*nobilitas*) of any given thing belongs to it according to its being. 'For a thing, to the extent that its being is contracted to some special mode of nobility, greater or lesser, it is said to be according to this greater or lesser' (*SCG* I. 28). Since nobility belongs to a thing according to its being, 'if something is to which belongs the whole *virtus essendi*, no power of nobility would be lacking for it' (ibid.). Aquinas immediately replaces *virtus* with *potestas*:

> But to the thing that is its being belongs being according to its whole power (*potestas*); just as if there would be some separated whiteness, no power of whiteness could be lacking for it. For something of the power of whiteness could be lacking for something white from the defect of the thing receiving whiteness … (ibid.)

The power of whiteness is delimited not in itself, but by the thing that receives whiteness. If there were (*per impossibile*) separated whiteness, it would contain the entire power of whiteness. God's perfection, therefore, lies in the fact that God has complete *virtus essendi*. That is, when viewed from the side of efficient causality, nothing is *causa sui*, yet when viewed from the side of perfection, or what Scotus will come to call eminence, God has the whole power of being. Aquinas does not combine perfection and causation in his proofs for the existence of God, but it is not difficult to see that when one does, the infinite *virtus essendi* of God will be tied more closely to God's causation, including the causation of Godself.

Let me sum up the conclusion of Aquinas' rejection of *causa sui*. First, he rejects the consistency of the notion because it is in and of itself a manifest contradiction. This contradiction arises, however, only when causation is thought on the model of the movement from

---

clearly links the notion of *virtus essendi* with *potentia* in this active sense, and furthermore with the ability to resist corruption. Finally, when Aquinas derives from the *virtus essendi* a thing's determinate or indeterminate existence, it seems clear that he cannot mean here simply 'capacities' (though it certainly can include capacities). In this way, I would say that wisdom (an example Kretzmann uses) might be a *virtus essendi* of being human but only to the extent that it allows for humans to resist corruption.

passive potency to actuality. Aquinas recognizes that God is peculiar in that God has an active power of being that is infinite, and hence God is eternal and cannot not exist. God has the power to resist all corruption. This last point, however, is already a step on the road towards the very way in which Descartes and Spinoza will come to think *causa sui*. Duns Scotus, while following Aquinas in many ways, will develop this road a bit further towards the notions we find operating in Descartes by bringing together the orders of efficient causation and the orders of eminence in his proof.

3. DUNS SCOTUS AND ORDERS OF CAUSALITY

Scotus has offered what must be counted as the most thorough examination of the relation between a causal order and its first cause.[19] His argument brings together elements of Aquinas' five ways so as to show that in three significant kinds of order—efficient causation, final causation, and eminence—there must be a first, and the first in any one of these orders must be identical to the first in any of the other three orders. The overall structure of the argument shows that there is a first efficient cause, a first final cause, and a first eminent being, that each of these is identical with the other, and that there can be only one such triply first being. What is crucial is that Scotus is proving the existence of a unique *infinite* being. Beginning with the notion of an infinite being is precisely what necessitates the combination of these orders, resulting in an argument that is both ontological and cosmological. Scotus is one of the few medieval thinkers who does not reject Anselm's argument and who also does not think that it shows that the proposition 'God exists' is self-evident. This allows him to use the results of a cosmological argument as a premiss in an ontological argument.

On his way to proving his conclusion, Scotus will show that in each order there is a something that is simply first, it is uncaused,

---

[19] Versions of this argument are found in several places in Scotus' works. The two most extended treatments of this topic are found in John Duns Scotus, *Ordinatio liber primus distinctio prima et secunda* [*Ordinatio*], ed. Commissio Scotistica, *Ioannis Duns Scoti opera omnia*, ii (Vatican City: Typis Polyglottis Vaticanis, 1950), d. I d. 2 qq. 1–2, and in John Duns Scotus, *A Treatise on God as First Principle* [*De primo principio*], tr. Allan B. Wolter (Chicago: Franciscan Herald Press, 1966). I rely in what follows primarily on the *Ordinatio* version, with supplements from some of the others.

and it actually exists. If we pay attention to this structure, it becomes apparent that since the final conclusion in each case will be that such a first actually exists, the other conclusions will have to be proven merely on the basis of the concept. That is, Scotus will show that the very concept of efficient cause, final cause, or eminence does not contradict the possibility of there being some first in each of these orders, and that the concept itself includes the conclusion that this possible first will also be uncaused. Only then does Scotus go on to prove that such a possible first in each order actually exists. Just as in a traditional ontological argument, Scotus' argument proceeds merely from the concept of causation and then goes on to show that there actually is some being that is shown to be possible on the basis of the concept of efficient cause, final cause, or eminence.

The argument about a first efficient cause shows this clearly. Scotus' proof that there must be a first efficient cause begins with the claim that 'some being is effectible', i.e. some being can be an effect (*Ordinatio*, 151). Scotus does not posit that there is actually some effect in existence. Rather, he simply says that there is no contradiction in positing that some being is effectible. The meaning of 'effectible' demands that such a being would be 'from itself, from nothing, or from something else' (ibid.). From here, the argument proceeds much like that of Aquinas: it cannot be from nothing, because that which is nothing is the cause of nothing; it cannot be from itself, because there is no thing that makes or generates itself. Therefore, it must be from another. From the concept of effect alone, Scotus has shown that what is an effect must be from another. If we turn our attention to that other, we run the same argument again. If it is not an effect, then it is first and we have our conclusion. If it is also an effect, then we run our argument again. Since this cannot proceed to infinity, there must be some first efficient cause.

Scotus, unlike Aquinas, recognizes that there is nothing objectionable in general about a series of causes and effects running to infinity. Rather, he argues that only in what he calls an 'essential order' of causes is an infinite regress impossible. In a series of causes and effects that is accidentally ordered, there certainly can be an infinite series of causes and effects. The terms 'accidental' and 'essential' modify the *kind of order* that obtains among the causes in that order. Scotus' general definition of 'order' is that it is a 'relation of priority and posteriority' (*De primo principio*, 1. 5). So the difference between these two kinds of order will be a difference in how priority and posteriority are understood. In an accidental order, there is an order established between the being of one cause and the being of another. The priority and posteriority is either temporal, or ontological. For example, a child is the effect of its parents (thus the parents are ontologically prior to the offspring), its parents are effects of their parents, and so on back to the first humans. Each cause in this temporal chain is required to produce the ultimate effect, but their connection to one another is merely that one is required in order for the next to exist. In this way the first cause causes something to exist and that causes something else to exist and so on until the effect under consideration is reached. In an essential order, however, the causes are related *in their causation*, and not just in their being. Such an order is an interrelation among various causes, *all of which produce one and the same effect*. So in an accidental order, only the last cause causes the effect, whereas in an essential order of causes, all causes produce the effect. Aristotle's famous four causes are an example of a kind of essential order, for each is related to the others in terms of priority and posteriority understood not ontologically, but in terms of superiority and inferiority. Matter alone cannot cause anything, but requires something prior, and therefore superior, in order to bring about any effect. From this, Scotus draws out three characteristics that distinguish an essential order from an accidental: (1) in an essential order a second cause, *in so far as it causes*, depends on the first, whereas in an accidental order, a second cause depends on the first only in being; (2) in an essential order each cause causes in a different way, because if two causes caused in the same way, one of them would be superfluous; (3) every cause in the essential order is required at the same time for bringing about the effect (*Ordinatio*, 154–5).

If this distinction is to prove helpful to Scotus' argument, he must show that in an essential order an infinite chain of causes and effects is impossible and also that an accidental order of causes is impossible without an essential order. Scotus offers three conclusions to prove the necessity of a first cause in an essential order. He shows (1) that in an essential order there must be a first; (2) in an accidental order there must be recourse to some essential order, and thus the first argument

applies; (3) that the rejection of essential order is self-defeating.[20] It is
the argument for the first conclusion that concerns us most. Scotus'
argument turns on an undefended rejection of the notion of *causa sui*.
He argues that in any essential order of causes, the first must itself stand
outside that order. If it did not, then the order, viewed as a whole,
would be *causa sui*. For example, if the object seen and the organ of
vision are essentially ordered causes of vision, then, according to the
characteristics of an essential order of causes, they each would cause
vision in a different way, each would be required at the same time,
and each must be something that is not caused by another cause in the
essential order.[21] If we imagine, for example, that the organ of sense
is caused by the thing seen, then seeing would be, in a way, *causa sui*,
because the order would cause an element of that very order, and that
element would in turn be essential to causing the effect. In this way,
whenever a visible object would exist, vision would be self-caused by
that object. Here we see first that Scotus simply denies that the notion
of *causa sui* is tenable, but also that an essential order of causes requires
always some cause that is eminent to the order. If six causes are in an
essential order that, as an order, produces some effect, there must be

[20] This argument often goes unexamined in commentaries on Scotus. The structure of
his argument is indeed quite complex. The overall structure has three steps: (1) in the orders
of efficient causation, final causation, and eminence there is some first actually existing;
(2) what is first according to one concept of primacy is first according to the others;
(3) that that triple primacy belongs to only one nature. It is on the way to proving the first
conclusion that Scotus demonstrates nine theses, three in each order: (1) something is simply
first; (2) the simply first is incausable; (3) the simply first actually exists. Scotus' reliance on
an essential order would prove the existence of this triply first being only if such an essential
order of causes actually exists. That is why, it seems to me, he shows that you cannot
posit an infinite accidental order of causes without recourse to an essential order. In this
way, it makes no difference whether one can actually find such an essential order, because
an infinite accidental order will require one to posit an essential order. John Reading is
quite clear about this argument: 'An infinity of others succeeding an individual cannot be
produced or be unless by another thing of another order existing at the same time with
the whole succession' (Girard J. Etzkorn, 'John Reading on the Existence and Unicity of
God, Efficient and Final Causality', *Franciscan Studies*, 41 (1981), 137). In this way I disagree
with the statement made by Rega Wood ('Scotus's Argument for the Existence of God',
Franciscan Studies, 47 (1987), 261) that 'Unless we accept Scotus's picture of the physical
world, his arguments against an infinite regress and in support of the first conclusion do not
show that a simply-first effective being actually exists.'

[21] 'Uncontroversial examples of essentially ordered causes are notoriously difficult to find'
(Wood, 'Scotus's Argument for the Existence of God', 259). Wood, in fact, gives examples
that are acknowledged not to fit the exact definition of an essential order of causes. I think
my example does fit the bill, though even if it does not, it, like Wood's examples, is still
illustrative.

something, according to Scotus, that is not among those six that, as it were, underlies and orders the causes in an essential order. In fact, for Scotus an essential order of causes is always an order of eminence, because in an essential order there is still a priority that makes the order what it is. According to Scotus, the prior cause in the order is always superior to the posterior.[22] Since, then, an essential order of causes turns out to be a relation of superiority and inferiority among causes, all of which together produce an effect, an essential order turns out always to point to some one cause that is eminent to, i.e. beyond and yet containing, the essential order of causes.

After showing that there must be some first efficient cause in an essential order, Scotus now turns to showing that that first cause is itself uncausable. Scotus' main argument here is that what cannot be an effect of any cause is independently effective. That is, the first in the order of efficient causes is not only uncaused, but its causation cannot be in virtue of another, but only in virtue of itself.[23] If it were uncaused, but acted as a cause only in virtue of another, then it would not be first, because it would require that other for its causing. So the first in the essential order of efficient causes must cause only in virtue of itself. Here again, the fact that the first cause in the order of efficient causation is uncaused and causes only in virtue of itself rules out even the possibility that it is *causa sui*.

Since Scotus has started merely from the possible existence of some effect, his conclusions up to this point show only that the concept of efficient cause requires that there be some simply first being. That is, he has not yet shown that this first actually exists, but only that it is possible. In order to show that the first in the order of efficient causation actually exists—and that there is some nature that is truly effective—Scotus now has to consider the way in which this first exists. Again, beginning with the concept of cause and effect, Scotus argues that if it is repugnant to the very concept of something to be from another, that thing must be 'able to be from itself', if it is able to be at all (*Ordinatio*, 164).[24] The first two conclusions have shown

---

[22] This is shown clearly by John of Reading in his interpretation of the argument.

[23] With this appeal to independence, a concept that will now be crucial to the proof, Scotus begins to show the coherence of those elements Marion labels as incoherent and show himself, to a certain extent, to be a predecessor of Descartes.

[24] '... illud si potest esse, potest esse a se'.

us that it is possible for there to be a first in the order of efficient causation and that it is repugnant to that being to be from another. So, we have a being that is able to be, and yet cannot be from another, therefore it must be 'from itself'. This means that this first effective being is able to be '*ex se*'.

But is not this notion of being 'from itself' the very notion of *causa sui*?[25] Scotus goes on to claim that what is not actually 'from itself' is not able to be 'from itself', for that would mean that non-being would produce something in being.[26] That is, if something does not actually exist that is 'from itself', then it cannot come into being from itself, for then what is nothing would produce something. Furthermore, it would also mean that it would cause itself. But if it is cause of itself, then it would not be entirely uncausable. On the one hand, something that is able to be from itself and yet does not exist, is not able to exist, and therefore is not even possible. On the other hand, what is able to be from itself must exist, if it is possible.

How are we to understand this notion of a being 'from itself', if we do not understand that it is cause of itself? If Scotus wants to rule out that *potest esse ex se* means *causa sui*, then it could only mean that it belongs to its nature or quiddity to exist. That is, if we ask why it is at all, we only have recourse to its very nature so as to say that it exists from or by its very nature.

Recall that what Scotus is trying to prove is that the first in the order of efficient causation that has been shown to be possible and to be uncausable also actually exists. That is, the first two steps in the argument show merely that it is possible that there be an uncausable first efficient cause. Without this last step, namely the proof that it actually exists, Scotus has not sufficiently made his case. Or, more precisely, this extended excursion into the order of efficient causality turns out to be nothing other than a complicated version of Anselm's

---

[25] On this question in relation to Plotinus and Descartes, see Jean-Marc Narbonne, 'Plotin, Descartes, et la notion de *causa sui*', *Archives de Philosophie*, 56 (1993), 177–95, and its companion essay Jean-Marc Narbonne, 'La Notion de puissance dans son rapport à la *causa sui* chez les Stoïciens et dans la philosophie de Spinoza', *Archives de Philosophie*, 58 (1995), 35–53, which links the notion of *causa sui* with the notion of power in Spinoza and the Stoics.

[26] 'Quod non est a se non potest esse a se, quia tunc non-ens produceret aliquid ad esse, quod est impossibile.'

ontological argument—complicated in that it runs through the notion of causation. Its basic form would be:

(1) An effect is possible; therefore a first efficient cause is possible.
(2) The first efficient cause must be uncausable.
(3) It belongs to the very nature of an uncausable first efficient cause to exist.

The ontological portion of the argument comes in the demonstration of (3). If Scotus means that the first efficient cause is from itself as from its very nature, then his argument is that the order of efficient causation leads to the possibility of a first efficient cause, and if it is possible, then it must be actual because of the very concept of a possible but uncaused efficient cause. The argument shows that an uncausable first efficient cause cannot be caused nor cause in virtue of another, so it must be from itself.

This notion of being 'from itself', in turn, becomes crucial to his demonstration that the three firsts (efficient cause, final cause, most eminent being) are one and the same being. It is in this argument that Scotus turns to something very much like Aquinas' *virtus essendi*. There he argues that 'nothing is able not to be unless something incompossible, either privatively or positively, to it is able to be, but nothing can be incompossible, either privatively or positively, to that which is from itself and incausable' (*Ordinatio*, 170). The being of this first is thought both in relation to its cause (or lack of cause) and in relation to the possibility of its destruction. The first cause that is from itself and incausable cannot have another with which it is incompossible because that other would either be able to be from itself or it would be from another. If it is from itself, then neither would exist at all because each one would destroy the other. On the other hand, if it were from another, then we have one being that is from itself and another that is purported to be able to destroy it that is not from itself but from another. 'But no cause is able to destroy some being on account of a repugnance of its effects to that other being, unless it would give more intense and perfect being to its effect than would be the being of that other destructible thing' (*Ordinatio*, 171).[27] However, no being that is from another is able to be more noble

---

[27] '... nulla causa potest destruere aliquod ens propter repugnantiam sui effectus ad illud nisi suo effectui perfectius et intensius esse det quam sit esse illius alterius destructibilis'.

than that whose being is necessary from itself, because the former has dependent being while the latter has independent being (*Ordinatio*, 171). Notice that at this point Scotus has brought together perfection, independence (aseity), and power. Since the proof is that a unique, infinite being exists, Scotus has already demonstrated the fundamental coherence of all those elements that Marion claims are incoherent in Descartes.[28] If the question is which of these is prior or anterior or ground of the others, Scotus' argument shows (albeit implicitly) that it is power. Thus, the first efficient cause exists because it gives itself, or has from itself, a more intense and perfect form of being than that which is from another, and therefore cannot be destroyed by another. If it cannot be destroyed by another, then if it is possible, it is actual.

Here, Scotus comes close to an outright endorsement of the notion of *causa sui* by resorting to a notion not unlike Aquinas' *virtus essendi*. The case is even more extreme in his *De primo principio*: 'By excluding *every cause other than itself*, both intrinsic and extrinsic, with respect to its being, from itself it is impossible not to be' (3. 19; my emphasis). This is because, Scotus tells us, that nothing that is from another has a more 'vehement and powerful being, than the uncausable has from itself' (ibid.). In this way, Scotus indicates that 'from itself' refers to something like a cause, indeed the only possible cause of this powerful and vehement being that the first cause gives itself. In a formula that sounds remarkably close to one that Descartes will use, Scotus seems here to say that the powerful and vehement being that the first cause has is what accounts for its existence and independence, i.e. its not needing any other cause to exist.

Since Aquinas' proof for the existence of God, and his rejection of the cogency of the notion of *causa sui*, operate without any reference to either the divine perfection or infinity, the notion of *virtus essendi*, that is, the way in which God is from Godself, formed no part of his proof. We saw, however, that when he comes to address those attributes, he did so by recourse to this power of being. Scotus, on the other hand, not only sets out to prove the existence of an infinite being, he does so by showing that there is a being that is the first efficient cause *and* the most eminent being. In combining the orders of causation and eminence, Scotus had to bring the discussion of God's

---

[28] See n. 1.

being 'from Godself' into the very heart of the proof. The result is that God's infinity takes on the characteristic of an 'intensity'.[29] Therefore, Scotus cannot avoid drawing together in his proof for the existence of God the notions of infinity, perfection, and power. It is in linking these three concepts that he is able to insert a cosmological argument within what is overall an ontological argument. The result is that for Scotus the 'vehement power' of the infinite being, and not God's effects, comes to function as a middle term in the demonstration of the existence of that being. While certainly that power belongs to God because of the kind of being God is, it is the power and not the essence of God that becomes a kind of middle term in Scotus' demonstration.

4. SUÁREZ ON ASEITY

Suárez's proof(s) for the existence of God appear as nothing more than shortened versions of Scotus'. Like Scotus, Suárez argues that infinite—finite is the first division of being. However, Suárez then goes on to show that this division is identical to several other divisions of being: from itself—from another, necessary—contingent, through essence—by participation. While we saw that Scotus made use of aseity in order to show the existence of a first efficient cause, Suárez draws the consequence of this: a being that is infinite is also *a se*. More accurately, Suárez argues that *a se* is another way of saying infinite.[30]

---

[29] This is argued in greater detail in Francis J. Catania, 'John Duns Scotus on "Ens Infinitum"', *American Catholic Philosophical Quarterly*, 67/1 (Winter 1993), 37–54. His conclusion is that ' "Infinite" does not change the meaning (*ratio*) of the perfection predicated of God; it expresses the manner in which that perfection is to be understood when applied to God: intensively realized and completely compossible with all other pure perfections' (p. 50). Catania shows that, for God, infinite means 'intensity of being', a notion that is quite similar to Aquinas' *virtus essendi*.

[30] Francisco Suárez, *Disputationes metaphysicae* [*DM*], disp. 28, sect. 1, art. 6, in *Opera omnia* [*Opera*], ed. D. M. André, xxv–xxvi (Paris, Vivès, 1856). This text will be referred to by disputation, section, and article number respectively. Jean-Robert Armogathe ('Caterus' Objections to God', in Roger Ariew and Marjorie Grene (eds.), *Descartes and his Contemporaries: Meditations, Objections, and Replies* (Chicago: University of Chicago Press, 1995), 21–33) rightly points to Suárez as a central antecedent to this discussion. He states that the textual reference for Descartes 'might be found in the treatise *De divina substantia et ejusque attributes*', where Suárez is reciting an opinion other than his own. He goes on to claim that for Suárez a thing which is *a se* is not necessarily infinite. Suarez, however, is merely

A se, however, adds 'nothing positive' to being, and therefore is not to be understood as *causa sui*, for 'nothing can be from itself through a positive origin and emanation' (*DM* 28. 1. 7). This formula, identical to one that Caterus will use, indicates merely a positive and simple perfection of being, namely, that it has *esse* without emanation from another, 'such that in itself and by its own essence it holds within (*claudit*) itself to exist, such that it receives being from no other, which perfection that being that does not have *esse* unless it receives it from another does not have' (ibid.). The division of being into *a se* and *ab alio*, like that into infinite and finite, arises not by adding something to being, but by recognizing the perfection of existing through its own essence—a perfection that has no origin outside the being that is *a se*.[31]

For Suárez, aseity seems to be defined both by reference to the essence of a thing and by relation to other things. In the first sense, he defines it, as we have seen, as 'existing through itself and through its own essence'. In the second sense, aseity refers to a lack of dependence on other things. The two senses together show that not only is infinite really the same as *a se*, but *a se* is also the same as necessary:

For that being that has being *a se*, and not from another, is not able not to be simply necessary, because it can neither deprive itself of its being (*esse*), as is self-evident, nor be deprived by another, since it does not depend on another; for what does not have *esse* from another is conserved in being by no other; and in this sense it is said to be from itself; and therefore it is entirely repugnant to it not to be. (*DM* 28. 1. 8)[32]

This shows that what is infinite must be *a se*, what is *a se* must be necessary, and what is necessary has being through its essence and not by participation. 'For that is called being through essence which,

---

arguing that these two attributes are not formally the same, but they obviously are really the same, since any divine attribute is identical with the divine essence. The discussion from the *Disputationes* shows their real identity (and, I might add, formal distinction) quite well. What is more, the discussion in the *Disputationes* is clearly Scotistic in its terms and conclusions.

[31] This is why *a se* and infinite, though really one and the same, and indeed demonstratively related, are not formally identical.

[32] Notice that Suárez here argues that an *a se* being cannot be deprived of being by another thing, because it is *conserved* in being by no other. Descartes equates causation and conservation, and therefore is able to think of aseity in terms of cause, namely as *causa sui*.

through itself and from the *power* of its essence, has being neither received nor participated by another' (ibid.; my emphasis).

Much like Scotus, and Aquinas before him, Suárez here shows a fundamental link being aseity and power. This power is both the power of its essence not to be through another *and* the power not to be deprived of its being by another. This power, furthermore, is that through which Suárez comes to understand what he calls 'perfections of being'. With reference to this power, i.e. entatative perfection, the concept of infinite can be explicated through an analogy to quantity. Just as we say one quantity is greater than another if it attains a further limit (*finitum*), we can talk of a kind of 'breadth' (*latitudo*) of the perfections of being in relation to entatative perfections and active power. So a finite being is finite because of its proper grade of perfection, perfection thought in relation to this active power. Yet each finite being participates in this perfection from a superior being in that it has only a certain grade of perfection in relation to the whole 'breadth' of being. Therefore,

a certain being is necessary in which the possible perfection of being of the breadth of being is in some mode contained, either formally or eminently; and this being we call simply infinite ... in the excellence of perfection. This infinity consists ... in such perfection of being, which, although it would be in itself one and indivisible, does not thus prevent other beings from possessing it, but rather contains in itself all possible perfections in some way, and thus not part of the perfection of being, but the whole eminence is in a certain way completed in itself. (ibid.)

Although aseity and infinity are not formally one and the same,[33] the proof of the existence of an infinite being requires that that being be *a se*. Aseity and infinity have a common term (i.e. a middle term), which turns out to be the active power of a thing. Therefore, while *a se* is merely a negation—*non ab alio*—it is a negation in reference only to extrinsic causes: '*a se* immediately negates only dependence on an extrinsic cause' (*DA* 46). Aseity does not, for Suárez, rule out dependence on something intrinsic and indeed seems to be dependent on the active power of the thing that is its perfection.

---

[33] Suárez, *Opera*, ii: *De attributis* [*DA*], 46.

5. DESCARTES: THE EXISTENCE OF GOD, POWER, AND CAUSATION

Descartes begins his proof of the existence of God with a division of ideas, i.e. of what he calls the 'images of things'. These ideas fall into three categories, categories that Descartes takes to be exhaustive in that there can be no other group of ideas. Ideas are either innate, adventitious, or invented by me. The division of ideas here is based on the ontological nature of the cause of the idea. Ideas that are adventitious will be caused by something that seems to be outside of me. Ideas that are invented are caused by myself. Innate ideas will be the realm in which the proof for the existence of God lives. The question is whether the idea of God is innate or adventitious and what its source might be.

Descartes proposes to investigate ideas only in so far as they are ideas. That is, even if an idea seems to have an index to something outside of myself, Descartes will begin by looking at its status as an idea. For Descartes, all ideas are 'modes of thought'. As he explains in the *Principles of Philosophy*, a mode is what scholastic philosophers meant when they spoke of attributes or qualities (AT viii. 26). The difference is that when we consider that some substance is affected or varied by them, we call them modes. When we consider the variation that is denominated by them, we call them qualities. When we more generally look at the substance in which they inhere, we call them attributes. So, a mode of thought is something that affects or varies a substance whose essence is thinking. In this way, an idea is not something that 'exists such that it needs nothing else for its existence', but is some affection or variation of that thing (AT viii. 24).[34] A mode, therefore, requires some substance for its existence. It is precisely because ideas are modes of thought, and that I am a thinking thing, that I might come to maintain that all ideas are caused by me, the substance of which they are affections.

But if we attend to a further difference among ideas, we can show that I cannot be the causal source of all my ideas. For ideas of substances, i.e. ideas that represent substances, by the mere fact that they represent substances, contain a kind of reality through that very

---

[34] Note already the influence of Suárez, at least in language.

representation. In other words, since a substance, as we saw above, is something that exists such that it needs no other for its existence, then an idea that represents a substance would also represent that independent existence. Descartes, following scholastic usage, calls the kind of reality that is present only in the representation 'objective reality'. So the idea of substance contains more objective reality than an idea of mode because the idea represents a greater reality. The idea of God, i.e. a supreme, eternal, infinite, omnipotent, omniscient creator, has more objective reality in it than the idea of a finite substance. So where do ideas get their objective reality?

It is here where Descartes enters into a discussion of the nature of causality, and the terms will be familiar from our discussion of Scotus and Suárez. Descartes begins by stating the Aristotelian–scholastic principle of causation: 'there must be as much reality in the efficient and total cause as in the effect of that cause' (AT vii. 40). Another version of this same principle is stated in the *Principles*: 'Nothing comes from nothing, nor is that which is more perfect from that which is less perfect as a total and efficient cause' (AT viii. 11–12).[35] This principle of causation applies equally whether we are considering formal reality or merely the representation or objective reality. That is, a stone must be caused by something equal to it in formal reality, and the idea of a stone must also be caused by something equal or greater. However, it must be the case that the cause of the objective reality of an idea must be something with as much formal reality as I conceive in the idea. Why is this the case? Because formal reality is more perfect than objective reality. Now the objective reality of the idea cannot come from nothing, so must come from something.

Descartes argues that while ideas can be caused by ideas, since one idea can have as much or more objective reality than another, our first and most important ideas must come from a cause that has as much formal reality as the idea has objective reality. The idea of a substance that is infinite, independent, supremely intelligent, supremely powerful, and creator of all contains much more objective reality than I contain formal reality. Therefore, this idea could not

---

[35] I take these as two versions of *the same principle*, because if the cause were not as perfect as the effect, then whatever it is that makes the effect more perfect would not come from the cause, and therefore would come from nothing.

have come from me. For the same reason, it could not have come from another being besides God, therefore God necessarily exists.

In Descartes's reply to the objections of Caterus, he argues that his argument hinges on the notion that, since I recognize that I am finite, imperfect, etc., I cannot be the source of my idea of God.[36] It is in this part of the argument that he further develops his notion of causation such that he begins to trouble the scholastic rejection of *causa sui*. He says that if 'I derived my existence from myself, then I would not doubt or lack anything at all, for I would have given myself all the perfections of which I have an idea, and thus I should myself be God' (AT vii. 48). This leads Descartes to go on to say that God has the power of existing through Godself. Thus, Descartes seems to maintain that God gives existence to Godself because God has the power to give to Godself all perfections. Descartes links here the notion of causation with power and uses power as a middle term in his demonstration of the existence of God. This link is intensified when the 'theologian' (Caterus) accuses Descartes of maintaining that God is *causa sui*, a position, he asserts, that can only be understood 'negatively'.[37]

The theologian smells immediately that Descartes might be proposing that God is *causa sui*:

From itself is accepted in two ways, first, positively, namely from itself as from a cause; and thus that it would be from itself and would give to itself its being ... Second it is accepted negatively that it would be by itself or not from another, and in this way, as far as I know, it is accepted by all. (AT vii. 95)

The theologian raises the standard scholastic arguments again *causa sui* and even points to one possible way to understand Scotus' concept of 'from itself'. His argument is quite simple: no one accepts the idea that something gives itself being. Descartes, however, mobilizes the other element of 'from itself', the one related, I have argued, to Aquinas' notion of *virtus essendi*.

---

[36] '... sed aliud quid ommitimus quod praecipue est considerandum, et a quo tota vis et lux hujus argumenti dependet' (*Meditations*, AT vii. 105).

[37] For a more detailed treatment of Caterus, see Armogathe, 'Caterus' Objections to God'.

Descartes begins with a shocking admission: 'I have not said that it is impossible for something to be the cause of itself' (AT vii. 108). He goes on to say that neither temporal succession nor diversity belongs to the notion of causation. Rather, he says, 'there is no thing such that we cannot ask why it exists, or rather inquire into the efficient cause of it, or, if it has none, why it needs none'. So far, this is simply an application of the principle of sufficient reason. But then Descartes continues:

Therefore, if I would suppose that no thing in any way is able to be towards itself that it is the efficient cause towards the effect, then I am so far from concluding that there is some first cause since, on the contrary, I would inquire into the cause of it itself that is called first, and thus would never come to any first of all. But I clearly admit that something can be in which there would be so great an inexhaustible power that it would need no other power that it would exist, nor also would it need now that it be conserved, and this therefore would be in a certain way cause of itself. (ibid.)

At this point Descartes has only pointed out two things. First, the principle of sufficient reason demands that we say that the first cause is caused by itself. Since the notion of cause, even efficient cause, does not demand that the cause be temporally prior to the effect, we can demand the cause of even an eternal being. Second, the notion of causation is bound up with the notion of power, and thus a being of infinite power would have to be cause of itself, otherwise it would be, to a certain extent, impotent. The cause we discover when we ask why God exists is God's inexhaustible power. But he has yet to say how this being is cause of itself.

This is where the connection to power comes into play. In response to Caterus, he says that surely we can understand that God is 'from itself', in the merely negative sense of not being from some cause. But once we attend to the immense and incomprehensible power that is contained in the idea of God, then we have to say that God is from itself not merely negatively, but also positively. This simply draws out the conclusion that we saw Scotus making in joining the order of efficient causation with that of eminence, and Suárez making when he links power to perfection and perfection to eminence. For where Scotus claimed that existence comes from the nature of the first efficient cause and most eminent being, Descartes completes this by saying that God is not from a cause different from God, nor from nothing, 'but from the real immensity of God's power'. Because of this, we are allowed to think God in a certain way with respect to Godself as an efficient cause with respect to itself, and thus to be from itself positively (AT vii. 110–11).

Arnauld is not satisfied with Descartes's explanation of the term *causa sui*, and calls it a hard and false idea (AT vii. 208). Descartes's response to Arnauld begins by reasserting what he claimed against Caterus: God is *in a certain way* like the efficient cause of God. What this 'certain way' might be is the heart of the issue.[38] Descartes goes on to say that *causa sui* 'can in no way be understood of efficient cause, but only that the inexhausted potency of God is the cause or rather reason on account of which God does not need a cause' (AT vii. 236). Since this power of God is a positive thing, we can say in a positive way that God is cause of Godself. But this positive thing that is the cause of God not needing an efficient cause should not be confused with an efficient cause, if efficient cause is taken to mean 'some positive influx' (ibid.).[39] In other words, we can ask why God does not need a cause, and the proper answer to that is not Arnauld's 'because God is God', but rather 'on account of the immensity of God's power' (AT vii. 237).

The need for arguing that God is *causa sui* arises from the demonstration of God's existence. 'Through this middle the existence of God can be concluded ...' (AT vii. 238). So the power of God stands between the essence of God and the existence of God and can be used to demonstrate that the latter belongs necessarily to the former. Without this middle, the existence of God cannot be demonstrated at all. This issue of the middle term that could be used in a demonstration

---

[38] I do not take it that Descartes was injudicious in his response to Caterus; nor did he alter his opinion in response to Arnauld. See Daniel E. Flage and Clarence A. Bonnen, *Descartes and Method: A Search for a Method in Meditations*, Routledge Studies in Seventeenth-Century Philosophy, i (London: Routledge, 1999) for the opposite claim. It should also be noted that Descartes often engages in strategic responses, particularly to Arnauld. In his letter of 18 March 1641, Descartes asks Mersenne to make some changes to his text 'so that it can be known that I have deferred to his judgment, so that others seeing how ready I am to take council, may tell me more frankly the reasons they have against me, and be less stubborn in opposing me with reasons' (AT iii. 334).

[39] This definition of cause is found also in Suárez's discussion of causation in the *Disputationes*.

of God's existence was precisely the issue that motivated Scotus' proof and is implicit in Suárez's discussion. The formal distinction between two attributes is what allows one to be used as a middle term in relation to others.

We should not ignore the phrase Descartes repeats often: God's immense power is the cause of God not needing an efficient cause. This is somewhat more than the negative sense of 'from itself' (not needing another cause) and somewhat less than saying that God is the efficient cause of Godself.

> I think it necessary to show that between *efficient cause*, properly called, and *no cause*, there is something intermediate, namely the *positive essence of the thing*, to which the concept of efficient cause can be extended in the same way in which we are accustomed in geometry to extending the concept of an arc of an indefinite circle to the concept of a straight line ... (AT vii. 239)

If we link the positive essence of a thing to its active power, as Aquinas, Scotus, and Suárez do, then Descartes (who also links these) merely draws a further conclusion from a long tradition. How can we extend efficient cause to God such that God is in some way the efficient cause of God? Because in God essence and existence are not distinct. We seek an efficient cause for the existence of, for example, this triangle, but point to the essence or form of the triangle as the cause of its having three lines. Since in God essence and existence are not distinct, we can extend the term 'efficient cause' to point to the essence of God as the reason why God needs no cause for existence (AT vii. 243). The entire demonstration of God's existence relies on deploying God's power as the middle term, and that power must be related to God in some way like an efficient cause is related to its effect. This journey into scholastic discussions of aseity has shown that the use of God's power as a middle term is already implicit (and often explicit) in those discussions.

Thus we have, for Descartes, the notion of perfection linked to power and forming the *medium* of a demonstration of God's existence. Here, he recalls Aquinas' concept of *virtus essendi* and Scotus' concept of noble being possessing 'vehement' power, and Suárez's linking of power, perfection, and aseity to infinity. Descartes, however, realizes that this appeal requires that efficient causation be thought in terms of power. If a being is perfect, it must possess infinite power, and if it possesses infinite power, then it must be cause of itself. Therefore, Descartes can reply to Arnauld and Caterus that if they pay careful attention to the scholastic tradition that they cite, they would not be so horrified by his claim that God is *causa sui.*

DePaul University

5

Hobbesian Mechanics

DOUG JESSEPH

The concept of motion lies at the very centre of Hobbes's philosophical system. In his scheme of things motion is the only cause, and because all of philosophy involves reasoning about causes, he is committed to the thesis that motion is the ultimate explanatory concept. Indeed, Frithiof Brandt noted that 'Whenever we sift the subject to the bottom we come across motion in Hobbes,' and he concluded that instead of being characterized as a materialist 'Hobbes should more properly be called a motionalist, if we may be permitted to coin such a word.'[1]

Notwithstanding the absolute centrality of motion in Hobbes's philosophy, there is nevertheless some difficulty involved in understanding how an evidently physical concept like motion can properly play a central role in first philosophy.[2] Hobbes himself insisted on a firm distinction between the absolute demonstrative certainty of first philosophy and the ineradicably conjectural and hypothetical nature of physics. Yet the part of his treatise *De corpore* that bears the title 'First

---

[1] Frithiof Brandt, *Thomas Hobbes' Mechanical Conception of Nature* [*Mechanical Conception*] (Copenhagen: Levin & Munksgaard; London: Librairie Hachette, 1928), 379.

[2] In discussing Hobbes I generally use the term 'first philosophy' for what usually goes by the name 'metaphysics'. This is the expression Hobbes preferred, since he regarded metaphysics as an unintelligible exercise in Aristotelian obscurantism. In Hobbes's words: 'There is a certain *Philosophia prima* on which all other Philosophy ought to depend; and consisteth principally, in right limiting of the significations of such Appellations, or Names, as are of all others the most Universall. ... The Explication (that is, the settling of the meaning) of which, and the like Terms, is commonly in the Schools called *Metaphysiques*; as being a part of the Philosophy of Aristotle, which hath that for title. ... And indeed that which is there written, is for the most part so far from the possibility of being understood, and so repugnant to naturall Reason, that whosoever thinketh there is anything to bee understood by it, must needs think it supernaturall' (*Leviathan*, ch. 46; *EW* iii. 672). On first philosophy or metaphysics in Hobbes, see Pierre Magnard, 'Philosophie première ou métaphysique', in Yves-Charles Zarka and Jean Bernhard (eds.), *Thomas Hobbes: Philosophie première, théorie de la science et politique* (Paris: PUF, 1990), 29–37.

Philosophy' contains what appear to be substantive physical principles, including laws of motion and collision. One might therefore wonder whether the Hobbesian system is grounded in a fundamental confusion of physics with first philosophy, in which empirical concepts like space and motion intrude into the realm of abstract first principles governing all of philosophy.

My purpose here is to explain how Hobbes could claim that the basic principles of motion can be a priori, necessary, and fundamental to first philosophy while regarding physics or natural philosophy as uncertain, fallible, and based upon hypotheses. To do this, I will begin with an account of the structure of Hobbes's programme for philosophy as it is set out in *De corpore*, after which I will contrast Hobbes's view of the proper development of the science of mechanics with the *Mechanica* of his nemesis, John Wallis. Several significant points will emerge from this investigation. First, that Hobbes regarded the laws of motion as a priori principles belonging to first philosophy rather than physics proper. Second, that much of his disaffection for Wallis's *Mechanica* is grounded in his own conviction that a true science of mechanics must take the form of a deductive system which proceeds from first principles that specify the causes of things. Finally, it should become clear that Hobbes's grand dream of establishing an a priori science of mechanics and philosophy came to grief, at least in part, because his treatment of motion does not provide an adequate basis for understanding concepts like force, acceleration, or collision.

I. PHYSICS AND FIRST PHILOSOPHY IN HOBBES'S *DE CORPORE*

Hobbes reserved the terms 'philosophy' or 'science' for demonstrative knowledge, which he characterized as 'knowledge of Consequences, and dependence of one fact upon another' (*Leviathan*, ch. 5; *EW* iii. 35). The advancement of such knowledge requires systematic organization, and in *De corpore* Hobbes announced his intention to 'lay open the few and first Elements of Philosophy in generall, as so many Seeds, from which pure and true Philosophy may hereafter spring up by little and little' (*DCo* I. i. 1; *EW* i. 2). He envisioned a grand tripartite system of treatises, *De corpore*, *De homine*, and *De cive*, that he intended to contain all the philosophy worth knowing. This order reflects Hobbes's ideal arrangement of the subject: beginning with a treatise on the nature of body, he intended to proceed next to a study of the nature of man (i.e. an animated, rational body), and thence to the doctrine of the commonwealth, an artificial body formed by the covenants that bind men together. As a matter of historical accident, *De corpore* was not published until 1655, some thirteen years after *De cive*. Although these treatises made their public appearance out of their intended order, Hobbes was nevertheless committed to the principle that all philosophy ultimately takes its principles from the nature of body.

The starting point for philosophy thus conceived is a small collection of definitions. Indeed, Hobbes characterized first philosophy as nothing more than setting out definitions, and he insisted that 'the making of Definitions, in whatsoever Science they are to be used, is that which we call *Philosophia prima*'.[3] Hobbesian method demands that syllogisms are then to be constructed from these definitions, thereby establishing conclusions as firmly as the definitions themselves; these conclusions can then serve to construct further syllogisms, with the result that ever more remote consequences of the initial definitions are established with absolute certainty.[4] Hobbes also defined philosophy as an inherently causal investigation or, in his words, 'the Knowledge acquired by Reasoning, from the Manner of the Generation of any thing, to the Properties; or from the Properties, to some possible Way of generation of the same' (*Leviathan*, ch. 46; *EW* iii. 664). Despite appearances, there is no real tension between these two characterizations of philosophy, because the investigation of causes and the construction of syllogisms are two essentially similar activities. Hobbes held that all reasoning is a kind of calculation involving the addition and subtraction of mental contents, or as he famously put it, 'REASON ... is nothing but *Reckoning* (that is, Adding and Subtracting) of the Consequences of generall

---

[3] Hobbes, *Six Lessons to the Professors of the Mathematiques, one of Geometry, the other of Astronomy* [*Six Lessons*] (London, 1656), 13; *EW* vii. 222.

[4] Thus, Hobbes was convinced that his exposition of the elements of philosophy in the first three parts of *De corpore* included 'nothing (saving the Definitions themselves) which hath not good coherence with the Definitions I have given; that is to say, which is not sufficiently demonstrated to all those that agree with me in the use of Words and Appellations, for whose sake onely I have written the same' (*DCo* iv. xxv. 1; *EW* i. 388).

names agreed upon' (*Leviathan*, ch. 5; *EW* iii. 9). A Hobbesian syllogism is consequently 'nothing but a Collection of the summe, of two
Propositions, joyned together by a common Term, which is called
the *Middle Terme*. And as Proposition is the addition of two Names,
so Syllogisme is the adding together of three' (*DCo* I. iv. 6; *EW* i. 48).
This sort of mental arithmetic also applies to the formation of concepts
and the investigation of causes. To form the complex concept *man*,
the more general concepts *body, animated*, and *rational* are summed
together and applied to the same thing (*DCo* I. i. 3; *EW* i. 4). Likewise,
the investigation of causes involves a search for the conditions which,
taken together, suffice for a given effect.[5] The point here is that, when
combined, causal factors necessitate their effects, just as the premisses
of a syllogism, when drawn together in a 'sum', necessitate their conclusions. Furthermore, Hobbes demanded that the definitions forming
the basis for the syllogisms of the true *philosophia prima* be such as
to express the causal generation of the things defined: 'where there
is place for Demonstration, if the first Principles, that is to say, the
Definitions contain not the Generation of the Subject; there can be
nothing demonstrated as it ought to be' (*Six Lessons*, Epistle; *EW* vii.
184). The result is that all of philosophy is an investigation into causes.

The four-part structure of *De corpore* mirrors this picture of the
method and structure of philosophy. Its first part (encompassing
chapters i–vi) is entitled 'Computation or Logique' and sets out
Hobbes's theory of reasoning as calculation, together with his treatment of names, syllogisms, and general methodology. The second part
(chapters vii–xiv) bears the title 'The First Grounds of Philosophy'
and contains the fundamental definitions and categories of being,
all of which are ultimately concerned with body and motion. As
Hobbes explained, 'words understood are but the seed, and no part
of the harvest of Philosophy', and his fundamental definitions in *De
corpore* are set out in accord with 'the Method I have used, defining
Place, Magnitude, and other most generall Appellations in that part
[of *De corpore*] which I intitle *Philosophia Prima*' (*Six Lessons*, 15; *EW*
vii. 226). The third part of *De corpore* (chapters xv–xxiv) is devoted

---

[5] In Hobbes's definition: 'A Cause is the Summe or Aggregate of all such Accidents both
in the Agents and the Patient, as concurre to the producing of the Effect propounded; all
which existing together, it cannot be understood but that the Effect existeth with them; or
that it cannot possibly exist if any one of them be absent' (*DCo* I. vi. 10; *EW* i. 77).

to 'Proportions of Motions and Magnitudes'. It develops a highly kinematic treatment of geometry, whose foundations were laid in the account of 'First Philosophy' in Part II. The fourth and final part of *De corpore* (chapters xxv–xxx) is called 'Physiques, or the *Phænomena of Nature*'. In it Hobbes explicates natural phenomena by advancing causal hypotheses which suffice to explain them, even if the hypotheses themselves must remain conjectural. The essential difference in method between Part IV and the rest of *De corpore* is this dependence upon causal hypotheses: the other branches of philosophy rest upon transparently true first principles and known causes, while the detailed treatment of nature can only be undertaken hypothetically. In Hobbes's formulation of the matter at the beginning of the fourth part of *De corpore*:

There are therefore two Methods of Philosophy, One from the Generation of the things to their possible Effects, and the other from their Effects or Appearances to some possible Generation of the same. In the former of these, the Truth of the first Principles of our ratiocination (namely Definitions) is made and constituted by our selves, whilest we consent and agree about the Appellations of things. And this part I have finished in the foregoing Chapters. ... I now enter upon the other part, which is the finding out by the Appearances of Effects of Nature which we know by Sense, some wayes and means by which they may be (I do not say, they are) generated. The Principles therefore, upon which the following discourse depends, are not such as we our selves make and pronounce in general terms, as Definitions; but such, as being placed in the things themselves by the Author of Nature, are by us observed in them, and we make use of them in single and particular, not universal propositions. Nor do they impose upon us any necessity of constituting Theoremes, their use being onely (though not without such general Propositions as have been already demonstrated) to shew us the possibility of some production or generation. (*DCo* IV. xxv. 1; *EW* i. 387–8)[6]

---

[6] Hobbes makes essentially the same point at the close of *De corpore*, when he announces that 'In the first, second, and third Parts [of *De corpore*], where the Principles of Ratiocination consist in our own Understanding, that is to say, in the legitimate use of such Words as we our selves constitute, all the Theoremes (if I be not deceived) are rightly demonstrated. The fourth Part depends upon *Hypotheses*; which unless we know them to be true, it is impossible for us to demonstrate that those Causes which I have there explicated, are the true Causes of the things whose productions I have derived from them' (*DCo* IV. xxx. 15; *EW* i. 531). On Hobbes and the necessity of hypotheses in physics, see Frank Horstmann, 'Hobbes on Hypotheses in Natural Philosophy', *Monist*, 84 (2001), 487–501.

This point will be of significance later, but the distinction between these two sorts of method is worth pointing out here.

The procedure by which causes are uncovered in Hobbesian first philosophy is 'resolution' or 'analysis' that begins with an object or event and proceeds to its causal antecedents. When applied at the most general level in the search for universal causal principles, this analytic procedure terminates with the concept of motion, because motion is the ultimate cause of everything. As Hobbes explains: 'the Causes of Universall things (of those at least that have any Cause) are manifest of themselves; or (as they say commonly) known to Nature; so that they need no Method at all; for they have all but one Universall Cause, which is Motion' (*DCo* I. vi. 5; *EW* i. 69). Elsewhere, he remarked that one salient cause of erroneous reasoning is 'not knowing what motion and its properties are; that is, not knowing the immediate natural cause of everything'.[7]

Because motion is the ultimate causal principle in Hobbes's system, the whole of his philosophy becomes a study of the consequences of motion. The development of this philosophy proceeds synthetically (or 'compositively') from causes to effects, beginning with the most basic definitions which do not so much identify causes as set out 'the explication of our Simple Conceptions' (*DCo* I. vi. 6; *EW* i. 70). These simplest definitions are of such concepts as place and motion, to which Hobbes then adds definitions of 'their Generations or Descriptions; as (for example,) that *a Line is made by the Motion of a Point, Superficies by the Motion of Line*, and *one Motion by another Motion, &c.*' (ibid.). The things thus generated or described are geometrical objects, and Hobbes thereby makes geometry one of the fundamental branches of philosophy. Pursuing the synthetic development further Hobbes comes to

the consideration of what Effects one Body moved worketh upon another; and because there may be Motion in all the severall parts of a Body, yet so as that the whole Body remain still in the same place, we must enquire, first, what Motion causeth such and such Motion in the whole, that is, when one Body invades another body which is either at Rest, or in Motion, what way, and with what swiftnesse the invaded Body shall move; and again, what Motion this second Body will generate in a third, and so forwards. From

---

[7] Hobbes, *Principia et problemata aliquot geometrica, ante desperata, nunc breviter explicata et demonstrata* [*Principia et problemata*] (London, 1674), 38; *LW* v. 206.

which Contemplation shall be drawn that part of Philosophy which treats of Motion. (*DCo* I. vi. 6; *EW* i. 71–2)

Instead of characterizing this part of first philosophy as that which 'treats of Motion', it might more aptly be called mechanics.[8] Hobbes's doctrines imply that all philosophy 'treats of Motion' at some level, but what is distinctive about this part of philosophy is that it yields the basic laws of motion and impact.

From the account sketched so far it is evident that Hobbes saw a tight link between first philosophy and natural philosophy. Geometry mediates between these two, as Hobbes explains:

because all Appearance of things to sense is determined, and made to be of such and such Quality and Quantity by Compounded Motions, every one of which has a certaine degree of Velocity, and a certaine and determined way; therefore in the first place we are to search out the wayes of Motion simply, (in which Geometry consists;) next the wayes of such generated Motions as are manifest; and lastly the wayes of internal and invisible Motions, (which is the Enquiry of Naturall Philosophers.) And therefore they that study Naturall Philosophy, study in vaine, except they begin at Geometry; and such Writers or Disputers thereof, as are ignorant of Geometry, do but make their Readers and Hearers lose their time. (*DCo* I. vi. 6; *EW* i. 73)

This close connection between geometry and natural philosophy also implies that there is no fundamental distinction between first philosophy and natural philosophy. Indeed, it would be fair to say that Hobbes's first philosophy is founded on concepts traditionally assigned to natural philosophy.

Hobbes proposed that the best way to begin his inquiry into first philosophy is, in his words,

from *Privation*; that is, from feigning the World to be annihilated. But if such annihilation of all things be supposed, it may perhaps be asked, what would

---

[8] The term 'mechanics' (or its Latin equivalent, *mechanica*) underwent a substantial change in meaning during Hobbes's lifetime, as I will discuss in Section 3. Hobbes himself rarely used the term, except in his polemical *Censura brevis* directed against Wallis's treatise *Mechanica*. Nevertheless, it makes sense to see this part of Hobbes's *De corpore* as his system of mechanics because it contains many principles traditionally associated with the science of mechanics: laws of motion and collision (*DCo* III. viii, xv, xxii), an analysis of angles of incidence and reflection (*DCo* III. xix, xxiv), the determination of centres of gravity (*DCo* III. xxiii), the study of static equilibrium (*DCo* III. xxiii), and an account of accelerated motion (*DCo* III. xvi).

remain for any Man (whom onely I except from this Universal annihilation
of things) to consider as the Subject of Philosophy, or at all to reason upon; or
what to give Names unto for Ratiocinations sake. (*DCo* II. vii. 1; *EW* i. 91)

Hobbes concluded from this thought experiment of an annihilated
world that such a person could still think, and indeed remember
previous experiences. The imagined solitary thinker would thereby
have such concepts as space, body, motion, and cause, as well as
having a language in which to describe these concepts. However,
one concept he would lack is that of an immaterial self or soul.
On Hobbes's principles, no such thing could have been perceived
when the world of external bodies was in existence, and the supposed
annihilation of the world does nothing to bring such a concept into
introspective focus.

Although the thought experiment of the 'annihilated world' bears
some resemblance to the *cogito* of Descartes, it proceeds from an
entirely different set of assumptions and is directed towards a very
different goal. The Cartesian *cogito* places the existence of the entire
material world in doubt in order to establish the fundamentally immaterial nature of the mind; Descartes then proceeds to take the mind's
knowledge of itself as the means to investigate other principles of
first philosophy. In contrast, Hobbes simply assumes that the solitary
thinker exempted from otherwise universal annihilation is a material
being and that his thoughts are motions taking place in his (material)
sensory apparatus.[9] The announced goal of Hobbes's thought experiment is to show that 'though all things be still remaining in the
world, yet we compute nothing but our own Phantasmes' (*DCo* II.
vii. 1; *EW* i. 92). The hypothesis of an annihilated world is therefore

[9] Hobbes's account of sensation as 'nothing else but motion in some of the internal parts
of the Sentient' (*DCo* IV. xxv. 2; *EW* i. 390) appears explicitly only in the fourth part of *De
corpore* as the most likely hypothesis for the phenomenon of sense, but it is clearly assumed
in the opening chapters of that work and it could not be contradicted by any supposition
at the outset of the treatise. Hobbes's assumption that the solitary thinker is a material
being is likewise implicit, but his commitment to a thoroughgoing materialism is evident
even in his definition of the subject of philosophy as 'every Body, of whose Generation or
Properties we can have any knowledge' (*DCo* I. i. 8; *EW* i. 10). The result is that the only
things about which we can philosophize are bodies, and the hypothesis of the annihilated
world cannot suppose the existence of immaterial minds or souls. On the methodological
role of Hobbes's argument from the 'annihilated world', see Michel Malherbe, 'Hobbes et
la fondation de la philosophie première', in Michel Malherbe and Martin Bertman (eds.),
Thomas Hobbes: De la métaphysique à la politique (Paris: J. Vrin, 1989), 17–32.

intended to show that all reasoning (which Hobbes identifies with computation) takes as its object certain 'phantasms' or sensory experiences. The result is that in Hobbes's account of the mind there can be no non-sensory, purely intellectual faculty of the sort Descartes held to be the locus of genuine knowledge. In the Cartesian scheme, such knowledge must be attained by withdrawing the mind from the senses and turning the intellect to the contemplation of such abstract concepts as God, the soul, or the geometric notion of extension. In stark contrast, Hobbes famously declared that 'the Originall of [all ideas] is that we call SENSE; (For there is no conception in a mans mind, which hath not at first, totally, or by parts, been begotten upon the organs of Sense). The rest are derived from that originall' (*Leviathan*, ch. 1; *EW* iii. 2). This restriction of all concepts to those derived from sensation, together with Hobbes's doctrine that sensory experience is nothing more than motion in the human sensory apparatus, therefore requires that the foundations of first philosophy be sought in concepts that are accessible to the senses and presuppose nothing further than the elementary notions of body, motion, and impact.

Chapters vii–xi of the second part of *De corpore* contain Hobbes's definitions of the key concepts in first philosophy, which concepts he takes to be available to anyone who engages in the thought experiment of the 'annihilated world'. The list includes the paired concepts of space–time, body–accident, cause–effect, power–act, and identity–difference. Such a list could well be found in any scholastic or Cartesian catalogue of the principles of first philosophy, but Hobbes systematically interpreted them in purely physical terms.[10] The concept of cause, for example, is reduced to that of efficient or material cause, the 'principle of individuation' is rendered as a principle of bodily continuity, and the traditional substance–accident dichotomy is reinterpreted as body–accident, which is the same as declaring substance and body to be convertible terms.

One might very well expect that a philosopher who identifies substance with body should offer something like a reason for accepting this quite radical identification, but Hobbes nowhere mounts anything

---

[10] This point has also been made by Yves-Charles Zarka, 'First Philosophy and the Foundation of Knowledge', in Tom Sorell (ed.), *The Cambridge Companion to Hobbes* (Cambridge: Cambridge University Press, 1996), 62–85, at 65–7.

like a sustained argument for his materialism. Rather than construct a case for materialism, a project which would require appeal to premisses an opponent might well reject, Hobbes structured his first philosophy in a way that systematically excludes the possibility of an immaterial substance. As we saw, the 'annihilation experiment' and the fundamental concepts that Hobbes derives from it presuppose an epistemology in which all legitimate concepts are constructed from antecedent sense experience. This epistemology in turn rules out such insensible, immaterial notions as a Cartesian soul; a materialistic treatment of sense perception then closes the circle by identifying sensation with motions in the brain and sensory organs. The result, as Hobbes intended it, is that all concepts in the one true philosophy are rendered explicable in terms of the motion and impact of material bodies. To some degree, Hobbes's procedures can be seen as appealing to a sort of principle of parsimony: by undertaking to show that matter and motion account for all of the relevant phenomena, he can motivate his materialism by making immaterial substances superfluous. At a somewhat deeper level, however, the Hobbesian project makes the concept of body so basic that it cannot be 'thought away', and reflection is supposed to show that the concept of body is essential to an account of anything at all that exists or might exist.

We can see this sort of procedure at work in Hobbes's objections to Descartes's Second Meditation. In response to the Cartesian *cogito*, Hobbes first identifies thought with the having of 'phantasms' when he reasons that 'from the fact that I think, or have phantasms, whether I am awake or dreaming, it follows that I am thinking' (AT vii. 172). He then argues that thoughts or phantasms require a subject in which they inhere, and this subject may well be something corporeal.[11] Hobbes then infers that matter must, in fact, be understood as the underlying subject in which thought inheres. In his words:

It seems to follow from this that a thinking thing is something corporeal. For it seems that the subject of any act can be understood only in terms of something corporeal or in terms of matter, as the author himself shows later in his example of the wax: the wax, despite the changes in its color, hardness,

---

[11] '... all philosophers distinguish a subject from its faculties and acts, that is, from its properties and essences; for an entity is one thing, and its essence is another. Hence it may be that the thinking thing is the subject of mind, reason, or intellect, and this subject may be something corporeal. The contrary is assumed, not proved' (AT vii. 172).

shape, and other acts, is still understood to be the same thing, that is the same matter that is the subject of all these changes. (AT vii. 173)

Hobbes's point is that the only model we have for a persisting subject that underlies qualitative change is that of bodies enduring even as their sensible properties alter. He takes this to be exemplified by the example of the notorious piece of wax in the Second Meditation, as well as something presumed in the Aristotelian ontology of matter and form. He then concludes that matter must be the underlying subject that endures through change, regardless of the qualities that change, be they shapes, colours, motion, or thoughts. As he puts it: 'knowledge of the proposition "I exist" depends on knowledge of the proposition "I think"; and knowledge of this depends on the fact that we cannot separate thought from the matter that thinks; so it seems that it would be better to infer that the thinking thing is material rather than immaterial' (AT vii. 173–4). Furthermore, Hobbes holds that the only way in which material bodies can be changed or initiate change is through motion and impact, and this has the consequence that the laws of motion must occupy an especially privileged place in his philosophy.

2. HOBBES AND THE LAWS OF MOTION

We have seen that Hobbes's philosophical system is founded on concepts that would traditionally be assigned to natural philosophy rather than first philosophy. This interpretation can be further illustrated by considering Hobbes's statement and justification of the laws of motion. As I have argued, Hobbes regarded the fundamental principles of motion as part of first philosophy, and this means that what appear to be substantive physical principles (such as laws of motion) appear in those sections of *De corpore* concerned with first philosophy. There is no anomaly here, however, because Hobbes conceived of motion as the most basic explanatory concept in all of philosophy, so his account of first philosophy must be framed in terms of motion and its principles. I want now to focus on two principles of motion and their justifications, because by examining them we can get a better picture of the relationship between Hobbesian natural philosophy and first philosophy. The first of these is a version of the law of inertia set out in chapter viii of *De corpore*, while the second is the mechanistic principle of action by contact set out in chapter ix.

Although it makes sense to speak of Hobbes as setting out laws of motion, these should not be thought of in close analogy with the 'Axioms, or Laws of Motion' in Newton's *Principia*.[12] In the Newtonian presentation, the axiomatic status of the laws of motion means that they are incapable of proof and must be accepted without further justification, presumably because they are either evident to reason, or at least because they are useful for making systematic predictions. Hobbes, however, took his laws of motion to be capable of proof, and he even offered proofs of them. In fact, he was convinced that his own first philosophy would enable the proof of such traditionally indemonstrable principles as the eighth axiom from book 1 of Euclid's *Elements*, which asserts that the whole is greater than the part.[13] Hobbes's proofs of such geometrical axioms or laws of motion proceed by analysing the concepts contained in them, until the analysis reaches fundamental definitions whose truth depends only upon the meanings of the terms employed. Such geometric and mechanical principles therefore have the status of purely semantic or conceptual truths, the apprehension of which requires nothing more complex than the grasp of definitions, which themselves are essentially made true by stipulation.

---

[12] On Newton's conception of laws of motion and force, see I. Bernard Cohen, 'A Guide to Newton's *Principia*', in Sir Isaac Newton, *The Principia: Mathematical Principles of Natural Philosophy*, tr. I. Bernard Cohen and Anne Whitman, assisted by Julia Budenz (Berkeley: University of California Press, 1999), 1–370, at ch. 5; Alan Gabbey, 'Force and Inertia in the Seventeenth Century: Descartes and Newton' ['Force and Inertia'], in Stephen Gaukroger (ed.), *Descartes: Philosophy, Mathematics and Physics* (Brighton: Harvester; Totowa, NJ: Barnes & Noble, 1980), 230–320; and Richard S. Westfall, *Force in Newton's Physics: The Science of Dynamics in the Seventeenth Century* (London: Macdonald; New York: American Elsevier, 1971).

[13] As he puts it: 'From what has been said, those Axiomes may be demonstrated which are assumed by *Euclide* in the beginning of his first Element about the Equality and Inequality of Magnitudes; of which (omitting the rest) I will here demonstrate onely this one, *the Whole is greater then any Part thereof*; to the end that the Reader may know that those Axioms are not indemonstrable, & therefore not Principles of Demonstration; and from hence learn to be wary how he admits any thing for a Principle, which is not at least as evident as these are. *Greater* is defined to be that, whose Part is Equal to the Whole of another. Now if we suppose any Whole to be A, and a Part of it to be B; seeing the Whole B is Equal to itself, and the same B is a Part of A; therefore a Part of A will be Equal to the Whole B. Wherefore by the Definition above, A is Greater then B, which was to be proved' (*DCo* II. viii. 25; *EW* i. 119).

Before investigating Hobbes's account of the laws of motion, it is worth pointing out that his epistemology requires something beyond the simple verbal exercise of propounding definitions. Although his account of first philosophy puts a great deal of stress on the importance of proper definitions, Hobbes also holds that the inferential connection between concepts can be grasped with a level of intuitive certainty that places them beyond doubt. Moreover, he does not scruple to call some principles 'evident to reason' or 'known by the natural light', thereby employing standard locutions to be found in an epistemology locating criteria for knowledge in an intellectual act of comprehension that is self-ratifying or otherwise unchallengeable.[14] The point here is that Hobbes entertains no serious sceptical doubts about the reliability of our basic grasp of definitions or the drawing of simple consequences from them; nor does his philosophy reduce to a crude empiricism that denies any role to intellectual faculties.[15]

Hobbes's statement and proof of his version of the inertial principle are contained in section 19 of chapter viii of *De corpore*. To avoid possible confusions that might result between this principle and more familiar (i.e. Newtonian) laws of motion, I will call it the 'persistence principle' rather than the law of inertia, for reasons that should become clear.[16] The chapter containing the persistence principle is

---

[14] This tendency is particularly evident in Hobbes's writings on mathematical methodology. For instance, he speaks of axioms as 'known by the natural light and not found out by teachers of arithmetic, but grasped by boys with the understanding of the words themselves' (*Examinatio et emendatio mathematicæ hodiernæ* (London, 1660), 61; *LW* iv. 95). Faulty or absurd principles are characterized as 'most horribly flawed and contrary to the immediate light of nature' (*Lux mathematica* (London, 1672), 38; *LW* v. 148).

[15] Brandt (*Mechanical Conception*, 227) makes this point in the context of distinguishing between what he terms 'rationalist' and 'sensualist' elements in Hobbes's philosophy, concluding that 'Hobbes was a rationalist in so far as he clearly saw that there is a kind of knowledge, purely deductive, which arrives at new knowledge syllogistically by means of concepts and propositions. ... Hobbes therefore acknowledges a province of knowledge which is distinct from mere empirical knowledge by its absolute, formal certainty, and this province of knowledge is science. But, on the other hand, he must be called a sensualist in so far as he is of the opinion that ultimately it is perception that furnishes us with the material for knowledge, also the material for scientific knowledge.'

[16] It is worth mentioning that the term 'inertia' meant something quite different at the time than it came to mean after Newton. In Hobbes's day, inertia was conceived of as the tendency of a body to come to rest, which is rather far from the import of Hobbes's persistence principle. My terminology is close to that used by Daniel Garber, *Descartes' Metaphysical Physics* [*Descartes' Physics*] (Chicago: University of Chicago Press, 1992), who terms Descartes's version of the law the 'principle of persistence'.

part of Hobbes's exposition of first philosophy and bears the title 'Of Body and Accident'. Hobbes is concerned in this chapter with the distinction between body (or substance) and its accidents; the most important accident of body is motion, which he defines as 'a continual relinquishing of one Place, and acquiring of another' (*DCo* II. viii. 10; *EW* i. 109). The persistence principle governs the manner in which this accident of body is generated or destroyed, and therefore has two parts. The first part concerns the generation of motion and asserts: 'Whatsoever is at Rest, will always be at Rest, unless there be some other body besides it, which, by endeavouring to get into its Place by motion, suffers it no longer to remain at Rest' (*DCo* II. viii. 19; *EW* i. 115). The second part of the principle concerns the destruction of the accident of motion. It reads: 'Whatsoever is Moved, will always be Moved, except there be some other body besides it, which causeth it to Rest' (*DCo* II. viii. 19; EW i. 115).[17]

More significant than the statement of the persistence principle is Hobbes's justification for it. He appeals to something like a principle of sufficient reason to show that a resting (or moving) body cannot bring itself out of its state of rest (or motion). As he puts it:

For suppose that some Finite Body exist, and be at Rest, and that all Space besides be Empty; if now this Body begin to be Moved, it will certainly be Moved some way; Seeing therefore there was nothing in that Body which did not dispose it to Rest, the reason why it is Moved this way is in something out of it; and in like manner, if it had been Moved any other way, the reason of Motion that way had also been in something out of it; but seeing it was

---

[17] The 1656 English version differs from the 1655 Latin original here, which asserts only that 'Whatever is at rest is understood always to be at rest, unless there is some other body outside of it, by whose action it is supposed that it can no longer remain at rest. ... Similarly, whatever is moved is understood always to move, unless there is something outside of it because of which it comes to rest' (*DCo* II. viii. 19; *LW* i. 102–3). The alteration in the English version helps clarify the first part of the persistence principle by adding that a body at rest can be brought into motion only by being pushed by another body, rather than the vague and indeterminate language of the Latin original, which states only that some external body must be supposed to bring a resting body out of its state of rest. This modification foreshadows the principle of action by contact, which I will consider shortly. More interesting is the fact that Hobbes's language in the 1656 English version goes beyond what his definition of motion permits. Motion as defined by Hobbes is simply change of location, but he finds himself needing to speak of a moving body exercising power by 'endeavouring' to occupy the place of a second body so that it 'suffers it no longer to remain at Rest'. Whether Hobbes's system can accommodate this sort of language is a matter I will take up in the concluding section.

supposed that Nothing is out of it, the reason of its Motion one way would be the same with the reason of its Motion every other way; wherefore it would be Moved alike all wayes at once, which is impossible. (*DCo* II. viii. 19; *EW* i. 115)

The proof of the second half of the persistence principle follows essentially the same line of argument: if a body is in motion and we suppose nothing else to exist, then there is no reason for it to come to rest at one time rather than another, so it would have to come to rest at every point, which is absurd. One might note in passing the methodological similarity between this argument and Hobbes's 'annihilation experiment' which introduces his first philosophy. Both proceed from the assumption of a world lacking anything other than a solitary object whose properties are investigated; then from the examination of a single case he derives principles of unlimited scope.

There is obviously a great deal in this argument that might meet objection from one who does not share Hobbes's assumptions. In particular, an Aristotelian might conceive of motion as dictated by an internal principle or form, through which a body's potentiality to be at different places is actualized. In such a case, the fact that nothing 'outside' of a moving body could determine it to motion or rest does not imply that there is literally nothing to determine it.[18] Further, it seems just plain crazy to think that such a principle is some sort of conceptual truth following from the very definition of motion. We surely *seem* to have the capacity to imagine worlds in which material bodies spontaneously initiate motion in themselves or grind to a halt with no outside interference. Indeed, Aristotelian physics assumes that (sublunar) bodies can remain in motion only as long as an external force is applied, since their natural state is one of rest. But if Hobbes is right, such things are as unimaginable as round squares or married bachelors.

---

[18] Seth Ward, in his long and detailed polemic against the Hobbesian philosophy, raised precisely this point: 'What an assertion! Let us see the argument. "If a body is at rest", (he says) "the cause of motion" (or, if it moves, the cause of its resting) "is outside of it, but it was supposed that there was nothing outside of it." That is, because no body is supposed, then nothing is supposed, which fits so well with his principles. But we can say that there is nothing supposed outside of the body (for indeed we have learned from Hobbes himself to say this), and yet God could either set it in motion and determine its direction, or destroy it absolutely; nor would anyone judge our words to be empty' (Ward, *In Thomæ Hobii philosophiam exercitatio epistolica* (Oxford, 1656), 81).

In point of fact, Hobbes granted that, although we may 'feign in our Mind' that an accident such as motion could be initiated without an external cause, or that 'we may imagine something to arise where before was Nothing, and Nothing to be there where before was something', nevertheless 'we cannot comprehend in our Minde how this may possibly be done in Nature' (*DCo* II. viii. 20; *EW* i. 116). I take Hobbes to be claiming that philosophically untutored common sense is simply mistaken about what is metaphysically possible. We might reason that, because we think we can form an image of a body spontaneously setting itself in motion or coming to rest, such things are at least possible. I suggest, however, that Hobbes would hold that what we imagine in such a case is radically incomplete and in fact not capable of being made coherent. To succeed in fully imagining a body being set in motion one must imagine some cause that necessitates the motion, which in Hobbes's scheme of things means imagining some body or bodies that collide with it. If we think we can imagine the motion initiating without imagining such an external cause, we are simply mistaken about what we can conceive. This, I take it, is what lies behind Hobbes's declaration that 'Philosophers, who tie themselves to natural reason', recognize that it is inconceivable that a body should initiate its own motion or spontaneously bring itself to a halt (*DCo* II. viii. 20; *EW* i. 116).[19]

The second Hobbesian law of motion which I wish to consider is what I call the principle of action by contact. It is intimately connected with the persistence principle, but fills in Hobbes's mechanistic picture of the world by stating that a body can only be set in motion through contact with a contiguous body. Hobbes's statement of the principle and his argument for it appear in section 7 of chapter ix of *De corpore*, which bears the title 'Of Cause'. Hobbes writes:

There can be no Cause of Motion, except in a Body Contiguous, and Moved. For let there be any two Bodies which are not contiguous, and betwixt which the intermediate Space is empty, or if filled, filled with another body which is at Rest; and let one of the propounded Bodies be supposed to be at Rest, I say it shall always be at Rest. For if it shall be Moved, the Cause of that

---

[19] For a fuller account of Hobbes's treatment of explanation and understanding, see Ioli Patellis, 'Hobbes on Explanation and Understanding', *Journal of the History of Ideas*, 62 (2001), 445–62.

Motion (by the 8th. Chapter 19th. Article) [i.e. the persistence principle]
will be some external body; and therefore if between it and that external
Body there be nothing but empty Space, then whatsoever the disposition be
of that external Body, or of the Patient it selfe, yet if it be supposed to be
now at Rest, we may conceive it will continue so til it be touched by some
other Body; but seeing Cause (by the Definition) is the Aggregate. Of all
such Accidents, which being supposed to be present it cannot be conceived
but that the Effect will follow, those Accidents which are either in external
Bodies, or in the Patient itself, cannot be the Cause of future Motion; and in
like manner, seeing we may conceive, that whatsoever is at Rest, will still be
at Rest, though it be touched by some other body, except that other Body
be moved, therefore in a contiguous Body which is at rest, there can be
no Cause of Motion. Wherefore there is no Cause of Motion in any Body,
except it be Contiguous and Moved. (*DCo* ii. ix. 7; *EW* i. 124–5)

The argument here is compressed and needlessly baffling, but the
general line of reasoning is clear enough. By the persistence principle,
a body at rest cannot initiate its own motion. Furthermore, Hobbes
has available his definition of cause as the aggregate of all accidents in
the agent and patient such that, having supposed them, the effect must
be understood to follow (*DCo* ii. ix. 3; *EW* i. 121). These together
imply that any cause of motion in a resting body must lie outside of
it and be of such nature that the cause necessitates motion in it. But
a body at rest and surrounded by empty space can be understood to
remain motionless, so empty space lacks the requisite causal power
to initiate motion in a body at rest. If, however, the motionless
body is in contact with another motionless body, the collection of
motionless bodies can likewise be understood to remain motionless,
since an adjacent body at rest has no motion to contribute to the
original motionless body. Thus, a body at rest and surrounded either
by a vacuum or by other motionless bodies can never initiate motion;
which is equivalent to saying that the only cause of motion in a body
is a contiguous moving body.

Again, there is much in this reasoning that might draw criticism, and
I will not attempt to defend it. At a minimum, Hobbes's procedure
begs the central question because he rules out things like action
at a distance or a self-moving body as incoherent or conceptually
impossible. The upshot is that if Hobbes is right, a violation of the
principle of action by contact is not just empirically false but downright

unthinkable. Of course, many have proposed physical or metaphysical theories that deny the principle of action by contact—Cartesian mind–body dualism, or Aristotelian theories of change and motion come to mind as instances where the principle is denied. Hobbes is evidently committed to the claim that such doctrines are not even worth discussing, since they amount to nothing more than empty words that can convey no real content.

Another interesting feature of Hobbes's treatment of the action by contact principle is that his discussion of it contains a criticism of Descartes's laws of impact. After stating his argument for the action by contact principle, Hobbes continues:

> The same reason may serve to prove, that whatsoever is Moved, will always be Moved on in the same way and with the same Velocity, except it be hindered by some other Contiguous and Moved Body, and consequently that no Bodies either when they are at Rest, or when there is an interposition of *Vacuum*, can generate or extinguish or lessen Motion in other Bodies. There is one that has written, that things Moved are more resisted by things at Rest, then by things contrarily Moved, for this reason, that he conceived Motion not to be so contrary to Motion as Rest. That which deceived him was, that the words *Rest* and *Motion* are but contradictory Names; whereas Motion indeed is not resisted by Rest, but by contrary Motion. (*DCo* II. ix. 7; *EW* i. 125)

The reference here is to Descartes's fourth rule of impact set out in section 49 of Part II of his *Principles of Philosophy*. This rule, one of the great embarrassments of Cartesian physics, asserts that a quiescent body cannot be set in motion by impact with a smaller body, irrespective of the relative sizes or velocities of the two bodies. The ultimate source of this error is, as Hobbes noted, the Cartesian principle that 'rest is contrary to motion, and nothing can be led by its own nature to its own destruction' (*Principles of Philosophy*, II. 37; AT viii. 63).[20] Evidently, Hobbes took Descartes to be a philosopher so confused about the nature of motion that he elevated an incoherent principle to the status of a divinely sanctioned law of impact.

---

[20] On Descartes and the laws of impact, see Gabbey, 'Force and Inertia', 245–72; Garber, *Descartes' Physics*, ch. 8; and Stephen Gaukroger, *Descartes' System of Natural Philosophy* (Cambridge: Cambridge University Press, 2002), 125–30. Descartes's principle that motion is fundamentally opposed to rest is contradicted by Hobbes at *DCo* III. xv. 3: 'it is therefore manifest, that Rest does nothing at all, nor is it of any efficacy; and that nothing but Motion gives Motion to such things as be at Rest, and takes it from things moved' (*EW* i. 213).

In addition to these two laws of motion, Hobbes introduced the concepts of *conatus* (or 'endeavour' in English)[21] and *impetus* into the foundations of his mechanics. Among other things, these play the basic role of accounting for the transmission of motion from one body to another in collision, as well as figuring in the account of phenomena such as equilibrium. As Hobbes defines it, *conatus* is essentially a point motion, or motion through an indefinitely small space: 'I define ENDEAVOUR *to be Motion made in less Space and Time then can be given*; that is, *less then can be determined or assigned by Exposition or Number*; that is, *Motion made through the length of a Point, and in an Instant or Point of Time*' (*DCo* III. xv. 2; *EW* i. 206). Impetus is defined as '*the Swiftness or Velocity of the body moved, but considered in the several points of that time in which it is moved; In which sense Impetus is nothing else but the quantity or velocity of Endeavour*' (*DCo* III. xv. 2; *EW* i. 207). Impetus therefore amounts to a measure of the *conatus* exercised by a moving body over the course of time, and it provides a means of comparing the relative forces exerted by moving bodies.[22] The concepts of *conatus* and impetus give Hobbes the means to study simple mechanical concepts such as static equilibrium or laws of impact for inelastic bodies.

Having briefly considered the foundations of Hobbes's mechanics, I would like to return for a moment to the issue of the demarcation between first philosophy and natural philosophy in Hobbes's system. From the account assembled thus far it is evident that Hobbes took mechanics, or the doctrine of motion, to be an a priori science whose truths are both necessary and demonstrable. This much explains why

[21] The term *conatus* derives from the Latin verb *conor*, meaning to strive or attempt. Hobbes's English equivalent is the term 'endeavour', but (except when directly quoting Hobbes's English) I will retain the Latin term, since it has gained wide currency in the secondary literature. For studies of this doctrine, see Jeffrey Barnouw, 'Le Vocabulaire du *conatus*', in Yves-Charles Zarka (ed.), *Hobbes et son vocabulaire: Études de lexicographie philosophique* (Paris: J. Vrin, 1992), 103–24; Martin Bertman, '*Conatus* in Hobbes's *De Corpore*', *Hobbes Studies*, 14 (2001), 25–39; Brandt, *Mechanical Conception*, ch. 9; and Kurd Lasswitz, *Die Geschichte der Atomistik von Mittelalter bis Newton*, 2 vols. (Hamburg: 1890), ii. 214–24. Howard R. Bernstein, '*Conatus*, Hobbes, and the Young Leibniz', *Studies in History and Philosophy of Science*, 11 (1980), 167–81, studies Hobbes's conception of *conatus* in connection with Leibniz's early doctrines of motion.

[22] So, for instance, having defined resistance in terms of the *conatus* of one body contrary to the *conatus* of one that comes in contact with it, Hobbes defines 'FORCE to be the *Impetus* or Quickness of Motion multiplyed either into it self, or into the Magnitude of the Movent, by means whereof the said Movent works more or less upon the other body that resists it' (*DCo* III. xv. 2; *EW* i. 212).

the persistence principle and the action by contact principle are granted the status of conceptual truths whose negations are supposed to be incoherent and literally unimaginable. But there is more to natural philosophy than mechanics, and Hobbes used the term 'physics' for that part of natural philosophy which could not be deductively established from transparently true definitions. This distinction is brought out in the famous declaration in the Epistle to Hobbes's *Six Lessons*:

Of Arts, some are demonstrable, others indemonstrable; and demonstrable are those the construction of the Subject whereof is in the power of the Artist himself; who in his demonstration does no more but deduce the Consequences of his own operation. The reason whereof is this, that the Science of every Subject is derived from a præcognition of the Causes, Generation, and Construction of the same; and consequently where the Causes are known, there is place for Demonstration; but not where the Causes are to seek for. Geometry therefore is demonstrable; for the Lines and Figures from which we reason are drawn and described by our selves; and Civill Philosophy is demonstrable because, we make the Commonwealth our selves. But because of Naturall Bodies we know not the Construction, but seek it from the Effects, there lyes no demonstration of what the Causes be we seek for, but onely of what they may be. (*Six Lessons*, Epistle; *EW* vii. 193–4)

The result is that natural philosophy must have two parts. One is the doctrine of motion or mechanics, which is at best conceptually distinct from geometry or first philosophy: it is grounded in definitions which express true causes while its conclusions are both necessary and a priori. The remainder of natural philosophy (for which Hobbes more or less consistently reserves the term 'physics') will be grounded in hypotheses which express the possible causes of natural phenomena. This undertaking is ineradicably conjectural and it therefore cannot attain the epistemic status of mechanics. As Hobbes expressed the distinction between these two parts of natural philosophy:

Since one cannot proceed in reasoning from the effects to the causes of natural things produced by motion without a knowledge of those things that follow from every kind of motion; and since one also cannot proceed to the consequences of motions without a knowledge of quantity (which is geometry); nothing can be explained by physics without something being demonstrated *a priori*.[23]

Similar remarks can be found at the beginning of Part IV of *De corpore*, when Hobbes announces that his investigation into 'Physiques, or the Phænomena of Nature' must proceed without the 'synthetic' method of demonstration from known causes and undertake an 'analytic' approach in which causes are hypothesized, and the results compared to experience.

Nevertheless, the fundamental properties of motion are known a priori, and it is also a priori certain that the phenomena of nature are produced by the motion and impact of bodies. Explanations in terms of non-mechanical causes such as substantial forms or other accoutrements of scholastic natural philosophy can thus be ruled out from the beginning. The result is that the science of motion belongs to first philosophy, and indeed the concept of motion is the fundamental concept in all of philosophy. In contrast, the explanation of specific natural phenomena belongs to physics or natural philosophy, and the detailed development of physics requires the application of the principles taken from first philosophy. This application, however, proceeds hypothetically and therefore lacks the absolute certainty characteristic of geometry and mechanics. The principles of Hobbesian mechanics will, however, encompass a good deal. The geometric or mechanical sections of Hobbes's *De corpore* include the study of uniformly accelerated motion, collision, centres of gravity, and an analysis of the statics of the beam balance. This much follows from definitions that specify the causes of the phenomena studied, and is certain and necessary. On the other hand, the explanation of such things as 'sense or animal motion', the freezing of water, or the attractive power of the magnet remain hypothetical and uncertain. Further, the source of the uncertainty in physics is the fact that the principles on which it depends are 'placed in the things themselves by the Author of Nature' (*DCo* IV. xxv. 1; *EW* i. 388), and thus cannot be known with certainty by humans, who lack 'makers knowledge' of the material world.

---

[23] Hobbes, *Elementorum philosophiae sectio secunda de homine* (London, 1656), ch. 10, sect. 5, p. 60; *LW* ii. 93.

3. HOBBES VERSUS WALLIS ON THE SCIENCE OF MECHANICS

My account of Hobbes and his science of mechanics can be put in a somewhat different light when we attend to his criticisms of John Wallis's treatise *Mechanica*, a work published in three parts between 1669 and 1671.[24] As part of his long and bitter controversy with Wallis, Hobbes appended a critique of the first part of the *Mechanica* to his 1671 treatise *Rosetum Geometricum*.[25] This polemical piece, which bears the title *Primae partis doctrinae Wallisianae de motu censura brevis*, was Hobbes's attempt to show the superiority of his treatment of mechanics over that of his great antagonist. As such, it has the obvious limitations of a piece produced in the course of a controversy, in that it frequently aims to score cheap rhetorical points without actually offering much in the way of substantive or thoughtful criticism. Nevertheless, there are some interesting and significant theoretical points that emerge in the course of Hobbes's *Censura*, and I will be concerned with them here.

Mechanics as understood in Aristotelian and scholastic science incorporated the principle that constant application of force is required to keep a body in motion, and it distinguished between natural and violent motions—the former being those dictated by an internal principle of motion or rest and directed towards a body's natural place, while the latter depart from the ordinary course of nature and arise from an externally applied force. The study of simple machines in this science was undertaken as a means of *intervening* in nature to produce motions that would otherwise be hindered. Mechanics, thus understood, is a way of producing literally unnatural results to serve human purposes. In the course of the seventeenth century, this notion lost its centrality and the term 'mechanics' became synonymous with

[24] The work in question is Wallis, *Mechanica, sive, De motu, tractatus geometricus* [*Mechanica*], 3 pts. (London, 1699–71). I use the version in Wallis, *Johannis Wallis S.T.D .... Opera Mathematica* [*OM*], 3 vols. (Oxford, 1693–9). References are to part, chapter, and definition or proposition number, with a volume and page citation to *OM*.

[25] On the nasty, brutish, and long mathematical controversy between Hobbes and Wallis, see Douglas Jesseph, *Squaring the Circle: The War between Hobbes and Wallis* (Chicago: University of Chicago Press, 1999). Hobbes's *Primae partis doctrinae Wallisianae de motu censura brevis* [*Censura*] (London, 1671) is his critique of Wallis's *Mechanica* and was published as a separately paginated appendix to Hobbes, *Rosetum geometricum* (London, 1671).

the theory of motion itself, and indeed all motions eventually came to be seen as equally natural.[26] By the time Wallis published his treatise on mechanics, the very title of the work reflected this change: he called it *Mechanica, sive Tractatus geometricus de motu*. In its first definition he declared 'I call *mechanics* the geometry of motion,' explaining that he opposed the traditional relegation of mechanics to the 'illiberal' arts as well as the characterization of non-constructive geometric solutions as merely 'mechanical' (*Mechanica*, I. i, def. 1; *OM* i. 575). Instead, Wallis declared, 'We take *mechanics* in neither of these two senses, but understand it as the part of geometry which considers motion and investigates by means of reasons and demonstrations the force by which any motion is propagated' (*Mechanica*, I. i, def. 1; *OM* i. 575). The result of this methodological orientation is that the *Mechanica* takes the form of a treatise in the Euclidean style, with definitions, propositions, and scholia.[27]

Part I of Wallis's *Mechanica* is a very general and foundational treatment dealing with the basic laws of motion, the descent of heavy bodies, and the theory of statics developed through a study of the beam balance.[28] Notwithstanding his antipathy to Wallis and seemingly everything associated with him, Hobbes held that the general method employed in the *Mechanica* was not merely correct, but in fact the only way to develop a true science of motion. And indeed, by casting his treatise in Euclidean form and beginning with definitions, Wallis followed the Hobbesian model for a proper science. Of course, Hobbes found Wallis's actual implementation of this model deficient in many crucial respects. As he remarked, Wallis 'uses the right method, proceeding from definitions, but these are

---

[26] On the development of the understanding of mechanics in the 17th century, see Alan Gabbey, 'The Case of Mechanics: One Revolution or Many?', in David C. Lindberg and Robert S. Westman (eds.), *Reappraisals of the Scientific Revolution* (Cambridge: Cambridge University Press, 1990), 493–528; and Alan Gabbey, 'Mechanics', in J. L. Heilbron (ed.), *The Oxford Companion to the History of Modern Science* (Oxford: Oxford University Press, 2003), 502–5. See Daniel Garber, 'Descartes, Mechanics, and the Mechanical Philosophy', *Midwest Studies in Philosophy*, 26 (2002), 185–204, for an account of the issues in the context of Cartesian mechanics.

[27] One point worth mentioning here is that Wallis has no specifically mechanical axioms; instead he uses definitions and then develops the material by applying geometry to the definitions.

[28] The three chapters of part I bear the titles 'De motu generalia', 'De gravium descensu, et motuum declivitate', and 'De libra'.

flawed and some of them cannot be used to demonstrate anything, which is the worst flaw' (*Censura*, 1; *LW* v. 51). Many of Hobbes's criticisms are sufficiently petty and beside the point that they do not merit extended consideration.[29] Nevertheless, he also raised some substantive objections, and a consideration of them can be of use in understanding his conception of mechanics and its place in his philosophy.

One complaint that Hobbes raised time and again was that his own *De corpore* had delivered a superior treatment of the subject. He thus argued that, in the odd cases where Wallis's *Mechanica* actually gets something right, the relevant truth had already been revealed in parts II and III of *De corpore*, and Wallis had either failed to acknowledge the prior (and superior) presentation of it or he might in fact have plagiarized from it. So, for instance, when Wallis defined 'resistance or force of resisting' to be 'a contrary power of motion, or that which resists motion' (*Mechanica*, I. i, def. 7; *OM* i. 576), Hobbes remarked,

This is flawed. The powers of an act, that is of motion cannot be contrary, nor can the word 'resist' appear in the definition of 'resistance' in order not to define a thing by itself.

Resistance is where there are two contiguous mobile bodies and the *conatus* of one is contrary to the *conatus* of the other, either in whole or in part. This is what [Wallis] intended, for he read this definition in my book *De Corpore* at Chapter 15, article 2. But not wanting to seem to use something of mine, which he had earlier dared to contradict, when he took the pains to change it and make his own definition, he corrupted mine. (*Censura*, 3; *LW* v. 53–4)

This sort of criticism reflects more of Hobbes's disdain for Wallis than any essential difference in their respective approaches to mechanics, but it does highlight the principle (which we saw applied against Descartes) that motion only resists motion. Here, instead of arguing that rest is not contrary to motion, Hobbes uses the principle to claim that a body cannot have two contrary motions and therefore one body can only be resisted by *another* body whose motion is contrary. This is a point to which Hobbes frequently returns, charging that Wallis

---

[29] For instance, when to Wallis's definition of the term 'momentum' as 'that which conduces to the production of motion', Hobbes retorted, 'and so, a hand, a lever, a bow, and any instrument which we use to move something is a momentum' (*Mechanica*, I. i, def. 3, *OM* i. 576; *Censura*, 2; *LW* v. 52).

falsely attributes motion to things at rest and generally fails to give a proper explication of resistance and momentum.[30]

Hobbes's most fundamental differences with Wallis's *Mechanica* can be summarized in two distinct objections. First, that Wallis self-consciously avoided offering a causal explanation of the central phenomena to be studied, and second that he based his mechanics on a mathematical theory that departs in significant ways from the geometric paradigm that Hobbes took to be fundamental to all science.

Wallis made clear his reluctance to consider the causes of mechanical phenomena in the twelfth definition of the first chapter of the *Mechanica*, where he defined gravity as 'a motive force [directed] downward, or toward the center of the Earth'. In explicating this definition he remarked that 'We shall not investigate what the principle of gravitation might be, considered physically, nor whether it should be called a quality or affection of body, or go by some other name.' After a brief list of various proposals that had been put forth as to the nature of gravity, Wallis remarked, 'It is enough that by the name *gravity* we understand that force of moving downward which we perceive by sense, both in the heavy body itself and in the less efficacious obstacles which impede it' (*Mechanica*, I. i, def. 12; *OM* i. 576). This sort of approach obviously fails to satisfy Hobbes's criteria for a genuine science of motion, since it refuses to take up the question of what causes gravitation. Hobbes poured scorn on the definition with the remark that 'knowledge (*scientia*) of the causes of gravity or

---

[30] To take one instance among several, Hobbes objects to proposition 10 of the first chapter in Part I of Wallis's *Mechanica*, which analyses the case where the joint effect of a momentum (i.e. that which conduces to the generation of motion) and an impediment (that which impedes or opposes motion) is determined. The proposition reads, 'Where momentum and impediment are conjoined, if the momentum is more powerful (*praepollet*), they are to be taken together as a momentum; but if the impediment is more powerful, they are to be taken together as an impediment; and in both cases in the amount of the excess of the more powerful over the less; but if they are of equal strength, they are to be taken together as neither momentum nor impediment. And if many momenta or impediments are conjoined: the total momentum or impediment is to be taken as the sum of all of them' (*Mechanica*, I. i, prop. 10; *OM* i. 585). Hobbes retorts that 'He takes the demonstration from the fact that momentum and impediment are contraries: the one bringing motion about, the other destroying it (*causa ut sit, causa ut non sit*). But this is false. Two motions coming together from different termini of the same right line are contraries: for motion and rest are not opposed contrarily, but rather privatively (*Motus & Quies non opponuntur contrarie, sed privative*)' (*Censura*, 18; *LW* v. 72).

the motion of heavy bodies does not seem to our Savilian professor to contribute anything to the doctrine of weight. It is enough for him that heavy bodies admit of $+, -, =$: that is greater, less, and equal, so that if the cause of gravity were other than what it is, all the phenomena concerning weight would still appear the same as they now do' (*Censura*, 5; *LW* v. 55).

Hobbes voiced a similar complaint against the fifteenth definition of Part I, where Wallis defined 'the direction of force or of the moving body' to be 'the right line along which the motive force tends' (*Mechanica*, I. i, def. 15; *OM* i. 578). Hobbes objected that 'in applying this to the descent of a heavy body, [Wallis] assumes that heavy bodies are born downward of their own accord (*sua sponte*), that is that they are moved by themselves without an efficient cause, which is both a Scholastic way of speaking, and false' (*Censura*, 6; *LW* v. 58).

The point of these objections and their connection to Hobbes's first philosophy and methodology should be clear enough: he demands more from a science of mechanics than an accurate description or quantitative treatment of motion, and in fact he requires that the true causes of mechanical phenomena be set out in the definitions and first principles upon which such a science is founded. By failing to account for motion through its causes, Wallis is led to embrace a theory which is both incomplete (because it fails to specify the causes that bring things about) and absurd (because it erroneously attributes self-motion to bodies). In the specific case of gravitation, Hobbes himself did not think he had sure and certain knowledge of its cause—he treated it hypothetically in the thirtieth (and final) chapter of *De corpore* as part of physics proper, attributing the descent of heavy bodies to a complex communication of circular motion arising from the diurnal rotation of the earth.[31] But Wallis's refusal even to take up the question of the

---

[31] Hobbes's account of gravitation in *DCo* IV. xxx is complex enough to deserve separate treatment and cannot be investigated in detail here. It proceeds from the assumption that the world is a plenum. Thus, if a body (a stone, say) is thrown upwards, the spaces successively vacated by the stone will be successively filled by displaced air. Hobbes then supposes, 'Seeing aire is by the diurnal revolution of the Earth more easily thrust away, then the Stone, the aire which is in the Orbe that contains the Stone will be forced further upwards then the Stone. But this, without the admission of *Vacuum*, cannot be, unless so much aire descend … from the place next above; which being done, the Stone will be thrust downwards. By this means therefore the Stone now receives the beginning of its Descent, that is to say, of

cause of gravitation was, according to Hobbes, a serious shortcoming in his *Mechanica*.

Hobbes's objections to the mathematics employed in Wallis's *Mechanica* derive from his conception of geometry as the fundamental mathematical science and his denigration of algebraic and analytic methods. In Hobbes's view, the application of algebra to geometry yields no new results, and instead introduces a 'scab of symbols' which clutter the otherwise clear and convincing 'synthetic' demonstrations set out in the style of the ancients.[32] Wallis was an enthusiastic proponent of algebraic techniques, and much of his *Mechanica* is given over to the algebraic statement and solution of physical problems. Hobbes took such an approach as symptomatic of Wallis's atrophied or underdeveloped intellectual powers and declared it 'manifest' that Wallis 'understood absolutely nothing about the nature of motion beyond what is commonly known, but when he transcribed what he had read into symbols, he not only did not demonstrate these things, but through his ignorance of the rule of subtraction in the arithmetic of species, he corrupted them' (*Censura*, 25; *LW* v. 82).[33]

---

its Gravity. Furthermore, whatsoever is once moved, will be moved continually (as hath been shewn in the 19th Article of the 8th Chapter [i.e. the persistence principle]) in the same way, and with the same celerity, except it be retarded or accelerated by some external Movent. Now the aire (which is the onely Body that is interposed between the Earth A and the stone above it E) will have the same action in every point of the straight line EA, which it hath in E. But it depressed the stone in E; and therefore also it will depress it equally in every point of the straight line EA. Wherefore the stone will descend from E to A with accelerated motion. The possible cause therefore of the Descent of Heavy Bodies under the Æquator, is the Diurnal motion of the Earth' (*DCo* IV. xxx. 4; *EW* i. 512–13). The difficulties facing this account are obviously huge, not the least being its implication that gravitational acceleration will vary with longitude, owing to the differential rotational velocity of the parts of the earth.

[32] Hobbes dismissed Wallis's *De sectionibus conicis tractatus* (Oxford, 1655) as 'so covered over with the scab of Symboles, that I had not the patience to examine whether it be well or ill demonstrated' (*Six Lessons*, 49; *EW* vii. 316). On Hobbes's rejection of analytic geometry, see Jesseph, *Squaring the Circle*, ch. 5.

[33] The 'arithmetic of species' is Hobbes's term for algebra, with the idea that algebra is concerned with arithmetical operations on variables which represent kinds or species of magnitude. His complaint that Wallis is ignorant of the proper rule for subtracting species reprises his objection to proposition 8 of the first chapter of Part I of *Mechanica*. Wallis proposed that 'The aggregate of contrary magnitudes (*contrarium*), insofar as they are contraries, is equal to the excess of the greater; but the aggregate of magnitudes of the same sign (*congruentium*) is their sum' (*Mechanica*, I. i, prop. 8; *OM* i. 584). Hobbes objects that the difference, for instance, between the magnitudes A and −A is equal to 2A, while their aggregate is 0. The basis of Hobbes's objection is the ambiguity of the Latin term *aggregatum*

This sort of criticism is connected with Hobbes's demand for a science of motion that deals with causes. Hobbes took synthetic geometric demonstrations to be proper demonstrations by way of causes, particularly when the foundations of geometry had been rewritten in his style, where geometry is a generalized science of body whose first principles express the motions by which geometric objects are generated. Algebraic treatments of motion, such as that offered by Wallis, fail to be truly scientific, first by disregarding the genuine causes of motion and second by employing a mathematics that manipulates symbols without attending to true causes. Hobbes raised another line of objection to the mathematics of Wallis's *Mechanica*, namely that it illegitimately relied upon infinitary considerations by employing the method of indivisibles.[34] Fascinating as this line of inquiry is, I will avoid addressing it specifically, since I think it ultimately reduces to the same basic contention, namely that Wallis's 'analysis by indivisibles' does not proceed from causes.

4. CONCLUSIONS

The results of this foray into Hobbes's science of mechanics can be summarized fairly readily. In Hobbes's estimation, 'this saying of Aristotle is true, "to know is to know through causes"' (*Principia et problemata*, 1; *LW* v. 156). Consequently, both first philosophy and natural philosophy are concerned with the investigation of causes. As it happens, motion is the ultimate cause of everything, and to the extent that philosophy is a demonstrative body of knowledge, it must include motion and the laws of motion among its first principles. Small wonder, then, that the persistence principle and the principle of action by contact make their appearance in that part of *De corpore* entitled 'Philosophia prima'. The Hobbesian science of mechanics is a priori, strictly necessary, and turns out to be only

---

contrarium, which could be taken to mean the arithmetical sum, but could also refer to the sum of their absolute values. That is, Wallis interprets the aggregate of A and −3A as −2A, where Hobbes points out that they differ by a total of 4A, and the aggregate could be taken as |A| + |−3A| (*Censura*, 16; *LW* v. 70).

[34] In essence, Hobbes argues that Wallis's use of infinitesimal magnitudes is unrigorous because it falsely assumes that a continuous magnitude can be composed of an infinity of infinitesimal parts. His criticisms are contained in the Postscript to the *Censura* (*Censura*, 26–9; *LW* v. 84–8).

conceptually distinct from pure geometry. It is therefore no accident that Hobbes included such mechanical material as centre of
gravity determinations and a study of the beam balance in the third
(or geometric) part of *De corpore*. The rest of natural philosophy,
which consists in the detailed construction of mechanical explanations of natural phenomena, fails to have this level of certainty. It
is not demonstrative, but rather hypothetical, although the hypotheses upon which it is based must be mechanical in the sense that
they concern only local motion and impact. Hobbes's account of
the shortcomings of Wallis's treatment of mechanics highlights his
concern with developing a science that proceeds demonstratively
from definitions expressing the true causes of things. Wallis was
right to think that mechanics is the 'geometry of motion', but (at
least according to Hobbes) he used the wrong sort of geometry and
forgot to concern himself with the causes of motion. Had Wallis
done so, his *Mechanica* would have turned out to be a recapitula-
tion of parts II and III of *De corpore*. Or so Hobbes would have us
believe.

We can close this study by considering the fate of Hobbes's
programme for a science of mechanics. In stark contrast to the
case of his political philosophy, Hobbes's writings on mechanics had
essentially no influence on the subsequent development of the subject.
This includes instances of the sort of 'hidden influence' detailed by G.
A. J. Rogers, in which Hobbes's ideas were either assimilated without
explicit acknowledgement or provided a theoretical position against
which later thinkers reacted.[35] The failure of Hobbes's programme for
mechanics is evident in the fact that in his *History of Mechanics* René
Dugas made no mention whatever of Hobbes,[36] while Wallis (who
seldom passed up the opportunity to rebuke Hobbes) never once
bothered to address the criticisms of his *Mechanica* set out in Hobbes's
Censura, even as he replied ad nauseam to the mathematical criticisms
in Hobbes's writings from the same period. In light of Hobbes's
status as a respected and active participant in scientific discussions in
Paris in the 1640s (where his theories of motion, optics, and other

[35] See G. A. J. Rogers, 'Hobbes's Hidden Influence', in G. A. J. Rogers and Alan Ryan
(eds.), *Perspectives on Thomas Hobbes* (Oxford: Oxford University Press, 1988), 189–205.

[36] See René Dugas, *A History of Mechanics*, tr. J. R. Maddox (Neuchâtel: Éditions du
Griffon, 1955; repr. New York: Dover, 1988).

scientific contributions were taken seriously[37]), it may seem odd that his approach to mechanics went essentially nowhere.

The spectacular failure of Hobbes's ambitions in this regard is partially explained by the fact that his scientific reputation has been demolished as a result of his many failed attempts to square the circle and solve other famous geometrical problems. The third part of *De corpore*, which contains Hobbes's geometry and the foundations of his mechanics, also features several botched attempts to square the circle. These (along with other aspects of Hobbesian mathematics) were the object of Wallis's withering criticism in *Elenchus geometriae Hobbianae*,[38] and in the ensuing exchange of polemics Hobbes saw his once considerable reputation as a mathematical savant thoroughly devastated. The damage done to his intellectual standing by these mathematical misadventures is illustrated by Christian Huygens's 1662 remark that Hobbes had 'so diminished his credit with everyone, that almost as soon as they see a new problem propounded by Hobbes, they declare that a new *pseudographēma* [false figure] has appeared'.[39]

A fuller explanation for why Hobbes's programme for mechanics sparked so little interest can be discerned by considering both the strengths and weaknesses of his approach. Hobbes's assimilation of mechanics to first philosophy has the virtue of taking the principles of mechanics as truths whose absolute necessity guarantees that they will hold regardless of the arrangement or contents of the actual world. There is no need, in Hobbes's view, to fear that the basic laws of motion and collision might face empirical disconfirmation, since they have the kind of necessity traditionally associated with the principles of pure geometry. Hobbesian mechanics is therefore a *scientia* in the strictest classical sense: a deductively organized body of knowledge whose first principles identify causes.

[37] For an account of Hobbes's scientific reputation on the European continent, see Noel Malcolm, 'Hobbes and the European Republic of Letters' ['Republic of Letters'], in Malcolm, *Aspects of Hobbes* (Oxford: Oxford University Press, 2002), 457–545. Some measure of the standing accorded Hobbes's scientific works by French savants can be taken from the fact that Marin Mersenne included extracts from Hobbes's writings in the Preface to his *Ballistica*, which appeared as part of his *Cogitata physico-mathematica* [*Cogitata*] (Paris, 1644).

[38] Wallis, *Elenchus geometriae Hobbianae* [*Elenchus*] (Oxford, 1656).

[39] Christian Huygens to Sir Robert Moray for Hobbes, 10/20 Dec. 1622, in Noel Malcolm (ed.), *The Correspondence of Thomas Hobbes*, 2 vols. (Oxford: Oxford University Press, 1994), ii. 537.

Such virtues are, however, offset by serious drawbacks in Hobbes's approach. In the first place, the organization of Hobbes's mechanics (especially in its canonical formulation in *De corpore*) seems haphazard, with elements developed out of their order of logical dependence and a general structure that is more a random walk through topics in physics than a reasoned exposition of the subject matter.[40] A second and related flaw is that Hobbes offers little in the way of rigorous demonstrations from first principles, notwithstanding his many claims to have pursued precisely that method in his mechanics. As we saw in the case of the 'proofs' for the persistence principle and the principle of action by contact, Hobbes's level of argumentation falls well short of the strict deductions he advertised in his grand programmatic statements. The remainder of his geometry and mechanics rarely achieves a significantly higher level of rigour. Indeed, Hobbes's treatment of motion and its principles in *De corpore* contrasts unfavourably with that in Wallis's *Mechanica*, where a structure of definitions, axioms, and theorems is matched by a generally high level of rigour in the argumentation (although Wallis's treatment is far from flawless). A third defect in Hobbes's mechanics is the fact that it contains little or nothing new or ground-breaking. Hobbes spent more than a decade putting *De corpore* in order, and the mechanical material included many topics he discussed with Parisian savants in the 1640s during his self-imposed exile in France. But what had seemed cutting-edge when Mersenne was preparing his *Cogitata* in the early 1640s was rather more stale than novel by the time *De corpore* was published in 1655.[41] Hobbes's treatment of such topics as static equilibrium or centres of gravity added nothing to the science of mechanics, and

---

[40] To take a few salient examples, the treatment of accelerated motion in *De corpore* (taken almost straight out of Galileo's *Two New Sciences*) appears in the third, or geometric, part at chapter xvi, while the account of gravitation is postponed to the fourth part, in chapter xxx. The equality of angles of incidence and reflection is assumed in chapter xix and used to derive results concerning bodies in collision, but is not proved until chapter xxiv. The persistence principle and the principle of action by contact are stated and justified in chapters viii and ix, then reprised in the account of *conatus* and collision in chapter xv, where they appear with other principles. The scattershot nature of Hobbes's physics is apparent in the title of chapter xxviii: 'Of Cold, Wind, Hard, Ice, Restitution of Bodies bent, Diaphanous, Lightning and Thunder, and of the Heads of Rivers'.

[41] As Malcolm puts the matter: 'The world-view [*De corpore*] presented, which might have seemed adventurous and challenging had it appeared in the 1640s, was much less novel in the mid-1650s' ('Republic of Letters', 498).

Wallis gleefully declared that whatever *De corpore* might have gotten right in matters of mechanics had been published earlier elsewhere, particularly by Mersenne, and he charged Hobbes with plagiarizing from his French associates.[42]

All of the shortcomings mentioned thus far certainly contributed to the failure of Hobbes's mechanics to exercise a significant influence on the subsequent development of the subject. However, they are all to one degree or another 'cosmetic' problems that could, at least in principle, be remedied by alterations in Hobbes's presentation. A far more serious, and I believe ultimately fatal, problem confronts Hobbesian mechanics, and this is the inability of the concept of motion to do the explanatory work Hobbes requires of it. In his definition, motion is 'the continual relinquishing of one Place, and acquiring of another' (*DCo* II. viii. 10; *EW* i. 109).[43] Thus understood, motion involves no more than transition from place to place, and there is nothing in the definition to account for the fact that a moving body's collision with a resting body of equal magnitude will set the second body in motion. Indeed, Hobbes's scheme does not even permit the introduction of the concept of force, if by the term *force* we understand something like the power to initiate motion. Hobbes does indeed offer definitions of the terms '*conatus*', 'impetus', 'force', and 'resistance', but they all reduce back to the concept of motion: *conatus* is motion through an indefinitely small space, impetus is the quantity or velocity of *conatus* over time, force is the product of impetus and magnitude of a body, and resistance is a *conatus* of one body directed against that of another (*DCo* II. xv. 2; *EW* i. 206–12).

The point can be brought home by considering Hobbes's objection to Wallis's definition of *gravity* as 'A motive force [directed] downward, or toward the center of the Earth' (*Mechanica*, I. i, def. 12; *OM* i. 576). Hobbes objects:

Gravity is a quality or accident of a body moved downward; but *motive force* is a quality or accident of a body moving downward. Yet nobody except a

[42] In his *Elenchus* (pp. 132–4) Wallis assembled a catalogue of results from *De corpore* which he claimed could be found in the writings of Mersenne, and particularly in the *Tractatus mechanicus, theoricus et Practicus*, which appeared as part of the *Cogitata*.

[43] Essentially the same definition appears in *Leviathan*: 'Motion is change of Place' (ch. 46; *EW* iii. 676).

schoolboy (*praeter Scholarem*) will doubt that the thing moving and the thing moved are different subjects. Both of them, *gravity* as well as *motive force*, are a certain *conatus*, that is the beginning of a motion; but the one is in a body moving, and the other in the body that has moved; and *conatus* is the same thing to motion that a point is to a line. (*Censura*, 5; *LW* v. 55–6)

Thus, the motive force by which a body descends is nothing more than a *conatus* or point motion in the direction of its descent. One could paraphrase this by saying that the force responsible for a body's motion is nothing other than the body's motion itself, so that the explanation of why a body is set in motion is the fact that it moves. The inadequacy of this approach is made all the clearer when we recall Hobbes's dismissal of scholastic accounts of gravitation in *Leviathan*, where he declared:

the Schools will tell you out of Aristotle, that the bodies that sink downwards, are *Heavy*; and that this Heavinesse is it that causes them to descend: But if you ask what they mean by *Heavinese*, they will define it to bee an endeavour to goe to the center of the Earth: so that the cause why things sink downward, is an Endeavour to be below; which is as much as to say, that bodies descend, or ascend, because they doe. (*Leviathan*, ch. 46; *EW* iii. 678)

It would thus be reasonable to infer that there is something fundamentally mistaken about Hobbes's whole project for a science of mechanics. As Alan Gabbey has put the matter, 'we discover that forces in general have evaporated completely from [Hobbes's] system, leaving only a collection of names defined in terms of each other and, ultimately, in terms of motion and body, the sole explanatory principles admissible in natural (and indeed civil) philosophy'; this leads him to conclude that 'the extremism of just such a mechanistic programme explains in large measure why the Hobbesian approach proved unfruitful for the development of the mechanical sciences'.[44]

I think Gabbey's analysis is essentially correct, and it highlights a fundamental problem for Hobbes's philosophical system, at least as it is set out in *De corpore*. Hobbes defines philosophy as an investigation into causes, and he holds that motion is the one universal cause of everything. But he defines motion purely in terms of change of place, without reference to any power or agency through which a body

---

[44] Gabbey, 'Force and Inertia', 233–4.

changes its location or by which it might bring about any effect at all. A contrast with the Cartesian system is instructive here. Descartes grounded his laws of motion in the immutability of God's nature; this guarantees that when the deity exercises the power by which he sustains the world, the sum total of motion will remain constant. As a result, bodies in motion or collision will acquire or lose the requisite motion necessary to conserve the total quantity throughout the world as a whole. In such a system, causal power can be attributed to moving bodies, even if the ultimate ground of such power lies with God's activity. In Hobbes's system, however, there is no mention of God (or any other agent) in the formulation and justification of the basic laws of motion. The result is that the foundations of Hobbes's grand mechanical philosophy remain essentially mysterious, for if we ask why a body in motion remains in motion, or why motion should be transmitted from one body to another in collision, we discover nothing that even approaches an answer. Hobbes thought that he could show the persistence principle and the principle of action by contact to be necessary truths on which an entire science of motion could be based. As we have seen, his attempted proofs of these principles encounter serious difficulty, and I think the underlying problem has now been identified: Hobbes's own concept of motion, from which all else is supposed to flow, is bereft of any notion of causal power or agency and consequently incapable of delivering the desired results.[45]

[45] Earlier versions of this chapter were presented at the University of Chicago and the University of Minnesota. My thanks to the audiences for helpful comments and discussion.

6

Locks, Schlocks, and Poisoned Peas: Boyle on Actual and Dispositive Qualities

DAN KAUFMAN

A piece of gold dissolves when it is immersed in aqua regis: gold is dissolvable in aqua regis; *dissolvability in aqua regis* is one of the qualities of gold. Now, imagine a world with the same natural laws as the actual world. In that world, a piece of gold exists, but aqua regis does not. In that world, does gold actually have the quality *dissolvability in aqua regis*? According to Robert Boyle, the answer to this question is 'no'. In that world, is it true that *if* there were some aqua regis and a piece of gold were immersed in it, the gold would dissolve? According to Boyle, the answer is 'yes'. This seems like a strange thing to say, given Boyle's answer to the first question and his common-sense view that qualities (e.g. dissolvability) are not to be confused with their manifestations (e.g. dissolving). In this chapter, I hope to show why Boyle gives these answers. More importantly, I hope to show how Boyle can *consistently* give these answers.

It is safe to say that Boyle was obsessed with the topic of qualities. He wrote forty-two published works, and twenty-seven of them explicitly treat the qualities of bodies, both the mechanical production of qualities *in general* and the production of *particular* qualities.[1] Boyle's examination of qualities was, of course, not restricted to theoretical investigation, but included seemingly endless experiments to support the corpuscularian hypothesis and the theory of qualities Boyle understood it to entail. And given what Boyle says in the Preface to *The Origine of Formes and Qualities (According to the Corpuscular Philosophy)* (henceforth *OFQ*) about the importance of qualities, it is not surprising that he devoted so much energy to their investigation:

---

[1] Peter Anstey, *The Philosophy of Robert Boyle* [*Boyle*] (London: Routledge, 2000), 19.

The Origine ... and Nature of the Qualities of Bodies, is a Subject, that I have long lookt upon, as one of the most Important and Usefull that the Naturalist can pitch upon for his Contemplation. For the Knowledge we have of the Bodies without Us, being for the Most part, fetched from the Informations the Mind receives by the Senses, we scarce know anything else in Bodies, upon whose account they can worke upon our Senses, save their Qualities ... And as 'tis by their Qualities, that Bodies act Immediately upon our Senses, so 'tis by vertue of those Attributes likewise, that they act upon Other bodies. (*Works*, v. 298)

Despite Boyle's obsession with qualities, he is surprisingly shy about giving a general definition of 'quality'. Rather, he thinks that it is sufficient, not to mention easier, to provide examples than to give a definition.[2] Among the properties Boyle claims are qualities are heat, cold, firmness, flexibility, brittleness, astringency, inflammability, volatility, fixity, colour, corrosiveness, poisonousness, magnetism, and electricity. His examples of qualities include certain 'manifest' qualities, 'chemical' qualities (a species of manifest), 'medical' qualities (species of manifest), sensible qualities, and occult qualities.[3] Boyle's reluctance to give a general definition of what qualities are, however, has led to interpretative difficulties. For instance, Peter Anstey and Edwin Curley—two scholars I believe to have done the most philosophically interesting work on Boyle[4]—have claimed that the likelihood of coming up with an interpretation of Boyle on qualities that is both internally consistent and accommodates all of the relevant texts is low, to say the very least. I wish to show that there is an interpretation that perhaps will not solve *every* interpretative problem associated with Boyle's theory of qualities, but it will go some way towards solving what I take to be one of the most problematic aspects of Boyle's theory, namely reconciling his

---

[2] See *Works*, v. 314–15 and vi. 267–8. Boyle does admit, however, that to give a general definition of "quality" 'be probably a much easier Task, then to define many Qualities, that may be nam'd in particular, as Saltness, Sowrness, Green, Bluw, and many others, which when we hear nam'd, every man know what is meant by them, though no man (that I know of) hath been able to give accurate Definitions of them' (*Works*, v. 315).

[3] See also *Works*, v. 360–1, and Anstey, *Boyle*.

[4] See Anstey, *Boyle*, ch. 4; Anstey, 'Robert Boyle and the Heuristic Value of Mechanism', *Studies in History and Philosophy of Science*, 33 (2002), 161–74, at 165; Edwin Curley, 'Locke, Boyle and the Distinction between Primary and Secondary Qualities' ['Distinction'], *Philosophical Review*, 81 (1972), 438–64.

"relative" view of qualities (i.e. his view that qualities consist partly in actual relations between bodies and other things, either other bodies or perceivers) with his view that bodies can have "dispositive qualities" (i.e. bodies can have qualities dispositively, even in the absence of any actual relations that bodies may have to other things).

Before I get into the thick of things, I wish to mention something I will *not* do in this chapter: I will not talk about "primary and secondary qualities" in Boyle. More precisely, I will not use these terms. The influence of Locke on the study of Boyle has resulted in the phenomenon of 'Locke-ing' Boyle;[5] that is, recognizing Boyle's influence on Locke, and then reading Locke's views back onto Boyle. Scholars of Boyle recognize that, contrary to what most philosophers may think, he *never* in fact uses the term "primary quality" and only uses "secondary quality" twice. Moreover, in half of these cases (i.e. *one* case), Boyle uses the term "secondary quality" to refer to a medical quality, i.e. the purgative (i.e. laxative) quality of rhubarb.[6] However, perhaps because of familiarity or convenience, scholars proceed to use these terms when discussing Boyle. And, unlike Locke, Boyle explicitly refuses to call size, shape, texture, and motion "qualities" at all, let alone "primary qualities".[7] If we philosophers are going to take Boyle seriously in his own right, and not merely as a precursor and influence on Locke, then we need to be careful with his own technical vocabulary.

I. MECHANICAL AFFECTIONS AND QUALITIES

1.1. *What Are qualities?*

Although Boyle does not give an informative definition of what qualities are, he repeatedly tells us what qualities *do*. He states that the 'severall powers to act on other Bodies or dispositions to be wrought on by them; which (Attributes) do as well deserve the name

---

[5] This is, as far as I know, Laura Keating's term in Keating, 'Un-Locke-ing Boyle: Boyle on Primary and Secondary Qualities', *History of Philosophy Quarterly*, 10 (1993), 305–23.

[6] See Anstey, *Boyle*, 39, and Keating, 'Un-Locke-ing Boyle'. Boyle uses the term "sensible quality", however. See *Works*, ii. 98.

[7] For instance, in *Cosmical Qualities*, Boyle states: 'I consider that the Qualities of particular Bodies (for I speak not here of Magnitude, Shape, and Motion, which are the Primitive Moods and Catholick Affections of Matter itself) ...' (*Works*, vi. 287).

of Qualities, as diverse other Attributes to which it is allow'd' (*Works*, vi. 268). Qualities are those features of bodies in virtue of which bodies cause both changes in other bodies and perceptions in perceivers, and are acted upon by other bodies. In so far as they are one of the relata of any causal relation,[8] they are explanatory, in accounts both of perception and of purely physical phenomena (see *Works*, v. 324). As such, the knowledge of qualities makes up 'the most fundamental and useful part of Natural Philosophy' (*Works*, v. 288). Not only are qualities explanatory (i.e. in the sense that they explain why some *past* phenomenon happened), they also have predictive power; that is, knowledge of a body's qualities will allow the natural philosopher to predict future phenomena. Boyle thinks that a feature of an 'excellent hypothesis' is that it will 'enable a skillfull Naturalist to Foretell Future *Phænomena*'.[9] Boyle certainly considers the corpuscularian hypothesis to be excellent, and, as we'll see, he believes his theory of qualities to be entailed by the corpuscularian hypothesis. Presumably, the fact that knowledge of qualities aids knowledge of what a body will do in certain conditions is another reason why Boyle thinks that knowledge of qualities is crucial to natural philosophy.

One of the more difficult aspects of Boyle's view of qualities to make sense of is his view that qualities are *in* bodies (see e.g. *Works*, v. 298, vi. 283). As we'll soon see, Boyle thinks that for a body to have a quality it must stand in some actual relation to another body or perceiver, and as such qualities are not wholly intrinsic properties of an individual body.[10] However, this does not mean that the quality is not *in* that body. For example, a piece of gold has the quality of *dissolvability in aqua regis* only if there is some aqua regis; nevertheless, the dissolvability is a quality of the piece of gold not of the aqua regis, nor of the gold *plus* the aqua regis. Presumably, this is one of the reasons why Boyle writes separately about corrosiveness and

---

[8] For example, aqua regis dissolves gold because of a quality of the aqua regis and because of a quality of the gold. In this case, we might say that aqua regis has an active quality, and the gold has a passive quality.

[9] 'Notes on a Good and an Excellent Hypothesis' (untitled by Boyle), in *Selected Philosophical Papers of Robert Boyle*, ed. M. A. Stewart (Indianapolis: Hackett, 1991), 119.

[10] It is notoriously difficult to give an account of an intrinsic property. However, on both the "intuitive" account (an intrinsic property of *x* is a property that *x* could have even if were lonely) and David Lewis's account (an intrinsic property of *x* is one that would be shared by any duplicate of *x*), Boylean qualities are not intrinsic properties.

corrosibility and the aperitive and "aperitable" qualities. This is not that strange if we recognize Boyle's qualities as asymmetric relational properties. An asymmetric relational property of an individual *x*, such as *being taller than*, is had by *x* only if there is some *y* shorter than *x*; but this property is a property of *x*, not *y*.

1.2. *A brief overview of Boyle's corpuscularian ontology*

An exhaustive examination of Boyle's ontology is far beyond the scope of this chapter. However, I wish to give a brief overview for the purposes of distinguishing qualities from 'mechanical affections'.

Boyle is careful to present his corpuscularianism in terms neutral with respect to the ultimate structure of matter; that is, he doesn't wish to formulate his theory in a way that would require that matter be atomistic, nor that it would require that matter be infinitely divisible (*Works*, viii. 103–4). Yet it is fairly clear that he accepts the existence of very small, *naturally* indivisible bodies.[11] These bodies have proper parts, but are indivisible by any natural means (or the likelihood of natural division is so negligible as to be almost non-existent), although they could be divided by God or by our minds (i.e. by a *distinctio rationis*).[12] Boyle sometimes refers to these naturally indivisible bodies as 'corpuscles', but when he is being precise, he calls them 'minima naturalia' to distinguish them from the teeny-weeny aggregates of *minima*, which Boyle also calls 'corpuscles'. These

[11] See Thomas Holden, *The Architecture of Matter from Galileo to Kant* (Oxford: Oxford University Press, 2004), ch. 1, for a helpful catalogue of the various types of divisibility discussed in the 17th century. On Holden's account of the types of divisibility, Boyle's *minima* are physically indivisible, metaphysically divisible, formally divisible, and intellectually divisible.

[12] 'That there are in the World great store of Particles of Matter, each of which is too small to be, whilst single, Sensible; and, being Entire, or Undivided, must needs both have its Determinate Shape, and be very Solid. Insomuch, that though it be *mentally*, and by Divine Omnipotence divisible, yet by reason of its Smalness and Solidity, Nature doth scarce ever actually divide it; and these may in this sense be call'd *Minima* or *Prima Naturalia*' (*Works*, v. 325–6). See also 'Of the Atomicall Philosophy', an early manuscript (1651–3), where Boyle claims that material "atoms" are not 'indivisible or Mathematicall points which are so void of quantity that the subtle rasor of Imagination it selfe cannot dissect them, but minima Naturalia or the smallest particles of bodyes, which [atomists] call Atomes not because they cannot be suppos'd to be divided into yet smaller parts … but because tho they may be further subdivided by the Imagination yet they cannot by Nature, which not being able in her resolutions of Naturall bodyes to procceed ad infinitum must necessarily stop somewhere' (*Works*, xiii. 227).

minima have only three properties:[13] size, shape, and motion or rest. Boyle tries to establish the properties of *minima* in at least three ways. First, there is Boyle's use of *transdictive inference*, a common form of inference among natural philosophers of the seventeenth and eighteenth centuries. Transdictive inference has roughly the following form (subject, of course, to specifying appropriate Fs): All observable or observed Fs have property *p*; therefore, unobservable Fs have *p*.[14] Boyle is employing transdictive inference when he states: 'And since Experience shews us ... that this division of Matter is frequently made into insensible Corpuscles or Particles, we may conclude, that the minutest fragments, as well as the biggest Masses of the Universal Matter are likewise endowed each with its peculiar Bulk and Shape' (*Works*, v. 307).[15] Because all sensible bodies have a determinate size and shape (and implicitly, Boyle is assuming that division of a body results merely in more bodies), he infers that the smallest bodies or *minima* will have a determinate size and shape.

Second, in one of the only clear-cut cases of a priori, "metaphysical" reasoning,[16] Boyle argues for the properties of *minima* from the very

[13] See Antonio Clericuzio, *Elements, Principles, and Corpuscles: A Study of Atomism and Chemistry in the Seventeenth Century* [*Elements*] (Dordrecht: Kluwer, 2000), chs. 1 and 4. Clericuzio claims that there are reasons to think that Boyle—at least *sometimes*—holds that *minima* have properties other than just the mechanical affections, and Clericuzio takes this to indicate the influence of the alchemical–chymical tradition on Boyle. Obviously, these issues are too large and complex to address adequately in the present chapter. I will point out, however, that in *OFQ* (Boyle's most detailed theoretical discussion of qualities and mechanical affections) there is no clear evidence that he holds that *minima* have anything other than mechanical affections. In my view, the fact that Boyle thinks that *minima* have only mechanical affections indicates a break with the alchemical–chymical tradition in so far as that tradition held that *minima* are the smallest particles of elements. The additional properties of *minima* in that tradition are included in Boyle's category of "manifest qualities", and there is no indication that Boyle thinks that those qualities are had by *minima*. See *Works*, vi. 267–8. Thanks to Dan Garber for making me think more about this. Presently, I use 'property' in a neutral manner to refer to qualities, mechanical affections, and anything else we attribute to something. Later it will be used in a more technical sense, a sense that will be explicitly indicated.

[14] See Andrew Pyle, *Atomism and its Critics: Problem Areas Associated with the Development of Atomic Theory of Matter from Democritus to Newton* [*Atomism*] (Bristol: Thoemmes Press, 1995), 528–39.

[15] Other famous instances of transdictive inference are found in Descartes (in the French version of *Principles of Philosophy*, IV. 201) and Newton (his '3rd rule of Reasoning' in the *Principia*). See Robert Wilson, 'Locke's Primary Qualities', *Journal of the History of Philosophy*, 40 (2002), 201–28. A related notion is what Anstey calls "the familiarity condition", which states that we explain the unfamiliar in terms of the more familiar.

[16] Another is the case of the lonely corpuscle.

concept of *body*: 'For being a finite Body, its Dimensions must be terminated and measurable: and though it may change its Figure, yet for the same reason it must necessarily have *some Figure* or other' (*Works*, v. 307). The concept of *body* is such that, although an individual body can change with respect to its determinate shape, the determinable *shape* is essential to it—it simply wouldn't be a body otherwise. The same goes for the other mechanical affections, size and motion or rest.

Third, there is *the Case of the Lonely Corpuscle*.[17] In this thought experiment, Boyle considers which properties a single *minimum* would have if it were 'lonely', i.e. if it were the only material thing in existence. Boyle thinks that a lonely corpuscle would have only the mechanical affections: size, shape, and motion or rest. As he states: 'if we should conceive that all the rest of the Universe were annihilated, except any of these entire and undivided Corpuscles ... it is hard to say what could be attributed to it, besides Matter, Motion (or Rest), Bulk, and Shape' (*Works*, v. 315). And 'these three, namely *Bulk, Figure*, and either *Motion* or *Rest*, (there being no Mean between these two) are the three *Primary* and most *Catholick Moods* or Affections of the *insensible* parts of Matter, <u>consider'd *each* of them *apart*</u> (*Works*, v. 333; my emphasis).[18] As we will see, a lonely corpuscle would have no *qualities* at all.

Boyle, however, thinks that aggregates of *minima* have an additional and extremely important mechanical affection: texture. Texture is the structure or arrangement ('disposition', as Boyle sometimes calls it) of aggregates of *minima*. Given the work that textures do in Boyle's corpuscularianism, however, texture cannot be merely the arrangement of *minima*, if arrangement is only the *spatial* arrangement of *minima*, i.e. the spatial relations among the *minima* in the aggregate. Rather texture also includes the mechanical affections of the individual *minima* composing the aggregate; and in the case of a larger body, its

---

[17] As far as I know, 'lonely corpuscle' is Peter Alexander's term in Alexander, *Ideas, Qualities and Corpuscles: Locke and Boyle on the External World* [*Ideas*] (Cambridge: Cambridge University Press, 1985). See also Pyle, *Atomism*, 539–44.

[18] See also *Works*, v. 334. In *Ideas*, Alexander thinks that texture is not a mechanical affection for Boyle (although Alexander uses the term "primary quality"), nor is it a primary quality for Locke. The reason: texture is not a feature of a lonely corpuscle. This shows, according to Alexander, that texture is not *inseparable* from all bodies and hence fails one of the tests for being a Lockean primary quality or Boylean mechanical affection. See Wilson, 'Locke's Primary Qualities', and Anstey, *Boyle*, for reason to think that texture is a primary quality for Locke and a mechanical affection for Boyle.

texture will include the textures of the smaller aggregates of *minima* composing the larger body. For Boyle, the shape (for instance) of the *minima* that compose the aggregate is going to be relevant to the qualities that the body's texture will produce (see e.g. *Works*, VI. 529). As such, we need to include the mechanical affections of the *minima* in the arrangement as a feature of the texture of a body.

Boyle calls size, shape, motion or rest, and texture the *mechanical affections*, and they are the only wholly intrinsic properties of any composite body; and, as I have mentioned, all but texture will be properties of all bodies, whether a single *minimum* or an aggregate of *minima*.

From even a superficial reading of Boyle, we can see that there is a very important relationship between the mechanical affections of a body and its qualities. Boyle says that qualities are 'derived from', 'can be deduced from', and 'depend on' the mechanical affections. A case could be made—and has been made by Peter Alexander among others—that qualities are numerically identical to textures or other mechanical affections. It has been rightly pointed out by several scholars (e.g. Anstey, Curley, Keating, and O'Toole), however, that things are not that simple. In fact, there are overwhelming reasons to think that identifying qualities with the mechanical affections of a body is greatly mistaken. In Boyle's most explicit pronouncements about qualities, he absolutely denies this view. There are texts, however, in which Boyle appears to say that qualities are identical to mechanical affections. I will say something towards the end of the chapter about these texts.

2. BOYLE'S 'EXCURSION' AND RELATIVE QUALITIES

The problem on which I will focus concerns the tension arising from Boyle's relative theory of qualities *and* his acceptance of so-called dispositive qualities. In order to see how this tension arises, we first must look at Boyle's theory of qualities, presented most fully in '*An EXCURSION about the* Relative Nature *of* Physical Qualities' in *OFQ* (henceforth, the 'Excursion'). In the 'Excursion', Boyle presents several examples to show that two things are true. First, scholastic philosophers who believe in *qualitates reales* are greatly mistaken about the nature of qualities. Boyle thinks, contra those philosophers, that the attribution of a multiplicity of qualities to a body does not require attributing a multiplicity of distinct real entities to a body. In fact, Boyle calls the scholastic view 'the Grand Mistake' (*Works*, v. 309). For the sake of this discussion—which will not suppose that Boyle has gotten the subtleties of the scholastic position right—the scholastic view is simply the view that for every quality we attribute to a body, there is some distinct (i.e. separable) entity in that body.[19] So, the more attributes a body has, the more real entities there are in that body,[20] and if a body gains a new quality, something intrinsic to the body must be added. Second, the corpuscularian account of qualities is true and perfectly adequate to explain the origin, nature, and multiplicity of qualities. I must point out that the first goal (the attack on the Grand Mistake) depends almost wholly on the success of the second goal. That is, Boyle's examples show the scholastics' Grand Mistake only if the positive corpuscularian account of qualities is successful. Boyle explicitly states that '*unless we admit the Doctrine I have been Proposing* [i.e. the corpuscularian view of qualities as Boyle has just presented it], we must Admit, that a Body may have an almost Infinite Number of New Real Entities accruing to it, without the Intervention of any Physical Change in the Body its self' (*Works*, v. 311; my emphasis). The implication is clear: if Boyle's theory of qualities is false, then his attack on scholastic real qualities fails. I mention this now because a problem will arise from this later.

The most famous example in the 'Excursion' used for these two purposes is the example of the lock and key. Though this passage is well known, I quote it at length:

We may consider, then, that when *Tubal-Cain*, or whoever else were the Smith, that Invented *Locks* and *Keys*, had made his first Lock, (for we may Reasonably suppose him to have made that before the *Key*, though the Comparison may be made use of without that Supposition,) That was onely a Piece of Iron contriv'd into such a Shape; and when afterwards he made a Key to that Lock, That also in itself Consider'd, was nothing but a Piece of Iron of such a Determinate Figure: but in Regard that these two Pieces of Iron might now be Applied to one another after a Certain manner, and

---

[19] See Pyle, *Atomism*, 508–28.

[20] Boyle thinks that his theory avoids, and his scholastic opponents face, an issue of qualities "overcrowding" in a body (*Works*, v. 311).

that there was a Congruitie betwixt the Wards of the Lock and those of the Key, the Lock and the Key did each of them now Obtain a new Capacity and it became a Main part of the Notion and Description of a Lock, that it was capable of being made to Lock or Unlock by that other Piece of Iron we call a Key, and it was Lookd upon as a Peculiar Faculty and Power in the Key, that it was Fitted to Open and Shut the Lock, and yet by these new Attributes there was not added any Real or Physical Entity, either to the Lock, or to the Key, each of them remaining indeed nothing, but the same Piece of Iron, just so Shap'd as it was before. (*Works*, v. 309–10)

Before we examine this passage and what it tells us about qualities, we should notice that the 'clear implication is that the point made about the lock and key is illustrative of other qualities.'[21] In fact, the very title of the 'Excursion' concerns 'the Relative Nature of *Physical* Qualities'.[22] The example of the lock and key is intended to support a *general* corpuscularian theory of the qualities of bodies.

In order to get clear about what is going on in the example, let us spell it out in detail. Call the 'Piece of Iron contriv'd into such a Shape', existing before there is a key, a 'schlock'. Call the time at which there was a schlock but no key, t_1, and the time at which there was a schlock and a key, t_2. There are several points to recognize in this passage:

(1) At t_1, the only (relevant)[23] features of the schlock are its mechanical affections.

(2) At t_1, the schlock does not have an aperitable[24] quality (i.e. the openable quality).

(3) At t_2, the schlock acquires the aperitable quality.

(4) Absolutely nothing intrinsic about the schlock changes from t_1 to t_2. It retains all and only the same determinate mechanical affections.

(5) It is in virtue of its mechanical affections *plus* its *actual relation* to the newly existing key that the schlock acquires a new ability,

---

[21] Anstey, *Boyle*, 87.

[22] Note that Boyle states that *physical* qualities have a relative nature. He is therefore not limiting his account to strictly "sensible" qualities. *All* qualities of bodies have a relative nature.

[23] The schlock has *some* qualities (e.g. colour), but it lacks the quality under discussion.

[24] I think I have invented this word. In *A Free Enquiry*, Boyle refers to the ability of a key to open a lock as an "aperitive" quality. A body has an aperitable quality when there is a body with a corresponding aperitive quality. See *Works*, x. 561.

a new quality. This is precisely the thrust of the attack on scholastic *qualitates reales*: there is no new *real* quality, despite the fact that there *is* a *new* quality in the lock.[25]

In *Men's Great Ignorance*, Boyle again presents the lock and the key example for the same positive purpose (minus an explicit attack on *qualitates reales*):

I consider in the second place, That the Faculties and Qualities of Things being (for the most part) but certain Relations, either to one another (as between a Lock and a Key;) or to Men, as the Qualities of External things referr'd to our Bodies, (and especially the Organs of Sense,) when other Things, whereto These may be related, are better known, many of These with which we are now more acquainted, may appear to have useful Qualities not yet taken notice of ... To our present purpose it may suffice to adumbrate my Meaning by the newly hinted Example of a Lock and a Key, where, *as* that which we consider in a Key, as the power or facultie of Opening or Shutting supposes and depends upon the Lock whereto it corresponds; *so* most of those Powers & other Attributes that we call Qualities in Bodies, depend so much upon the Structure or Constitution of other Bodies that are dispos'd or indispos'd to be acted on by them ... (*Works*, vi. 521–2)

This passage and the 'Excursion' make it clear that Boyle thinks that the qualities of a body are not fully reducible to (a fortiori, not identical to) any intrinsic property or mechanical affection of that body. If they were, then it would be impossible for a body to acquire new qualities without some change of mechanical affection.[26] But Boyle's examples explicitly deny this suggestion.[27] This should come as no surprise. Whereas mechanical affections are wholly intrinsic feature of bodies, qualities are not.[28]

The relative theory of qualities is reiterated throughout Boyle's works. For instance, in 'An Introduction to the History of Particular

---

[25] See *Works*, vi. 287, and the discussion of corrosiveness and corrosibility in viii. 337, 472–3.

[26] See Curley, 'Distinction', and Reginald Jackson, 'Locke's Distinction between Primary and Secondary Qualities', *Mind*, 38 (1929), 56–76.

[27] Boyle does believe that bodies *can* change qualities in virtue of a change in their mechanical affections. He does not, however, think that a change in mechanical affections is either necessary or sufficient for a change of qualities. See, for instance, *Works*, iv. 26.

[28] See Clericuzio, *Elements*, 137.

Qualities', in the example of the distilled putrefied urine[29] (*Works*, vi. 282–3): 'the same body ... may, by vertue of its Shape and other mechanicall Affections ... have such differing respects to different Sensories, and to the Pores, &c., of divers other Bodies, as to display severall differing Qualities' (*Works*, vi. 282). According to Boyle, distilled putrefied urine has all of the following relative qualities: pungent taste, offensive smell, white colour, causticity, lachrymatory quality, sneeze-producing quality, sedative-to-hysterical-women quality, diaphoreticity, diureticalness, a quality that causes brass filings to turn blue, a quality that causes some plant juices to turn green, and a quality enabling it to dissolve copper. At the end of this list, Boyle repeats: 'the same Particles applyd to severall other Bodies, to which they have differing Relations, have such distinct operations on them as may intitle these saline spirits to other Qualities. But to enumerate them in this place were tedious, especially haveing already nam'd so many Qualities residing in this spirituous Salt' (p. 283). This, Boyle says, illustrates the relative nature of qualities, that 'this or that Relation to other Bodies, divers of which Relations we stile Qualities' (p. 280).

Boyle does not, however, think that different relations automatically entail a diversity of qualities.[30] Boyle mentions 'how great the power may be, which a Body may exercise by virtue of a single Quality, may appear by the Various and oftentimes Prodigious Effects, which Fire produces by its Heat, when thereby it melts Mettals, calcines Stones, destroyes whole Woods and Cities, &c.' (*Works*, v. 324–5). Prima facie this passage seems to be in stark contrast to the putrefied urine example. In the latter, Boyle seems to think that each of the various relations establishes a distinct quality in the urine, but in the former, Boyle thinks that the quality which enables fire to produce various effects is but a single quality, namely heat. I don't think the views expressed here are incompatible. It is clear to me as it is to Boyle that the particular effects of fire listed by Boyle (i.e. melting, calcining, destroying wood) *are* the effects of its heat. However, fire's

---

[29] 'Spirit of urine', a solution of ammonia and ammonium carbonate (Hunter and Davis's Glossary in Boyle's *Works*).

[30] Boyle's strange example of the "father" in *OFQ* (*Works*, v. 309) illustrates this. Of course, when a man has a child, he becomes a father in virtue of this new relation; however, having more than one child, while producing another relation, does not endow the man with another "quality".

ability to cause the sensation of colour in me is due not to its heat but rather to its colour. The qualities of the urine listed by Boyle and their effects seem to be very unlike the effects of a fire's heat. Of course, if Boyle's corpuscularian natural philosophy is to be as 'excellent' as he thinks, there will need to be some way of distinguishing when a single quality is responsible for different effects and when a plurality of qualities is responsible. The fact that in many cases Boyle refrains from naming the quality but instead simply cites its effect(s) indicates that perhaps we do not have names for such qualities. In any case, it seems absolutely right for Boyle to say that the power that urine has to calm down hysterical women is a different quality from its pungent taste. In the case of the fire, it seems absolutely right for Boyle to say that each of the effects listed results from the same quality (heat).[31]

Finally, the necessity of actual relations for a body to have qualities is illustrated by a thought experiment repeated in several of Boyle's works. For instance, in *Cosmical Qualities*—a work that Boyle characterizes as a sequel to *OFQ*[32]—Boyle says:

> So that although if divers Bodies that I could name were placed together *in vacuo*, or removed together into some of those imaginary spaces, which divers of the Schoolmen fancie to be beyond the Bounds of our Universe, they would retaine *many* of the Qualities they are now endowed with; yet they would not have them All: but by being restored to their former place in this World, would regain a new *Set* of Faculties (or Powers) and Dispositions. (*Works*, vi. 287–8)[33]

If qualities were intrinsic properties of bodies, this thought experiment would fall flat on its face: A body in an *in vacuo* world or an 'imaginary space'[34] surely would have the same intrinsic properties as it has in

---

[31] This is supported by Boyle's words in *Works*, v. 313, where he says that diverse effects do not necessarily come from a diversity of qualities. Not surprisingly, the example used to illustrate this is *heat*! The sun can harden, soften, melt, thaw, vaporize, blanch, yellow, ripen, etc. But 'these are not distinct Powers or Faculties in the Sun, but onely the Productions of its Heat ... diversify'd by the differing Textures of the Body that it chances to work upon'.

[32] See *Works*, vi. 288, and John Henry, 'Boyle and Cosmical Qualities', in Michael Hunter (ed.), *Robert Boyle Reconsidered* (Cambridge: Cambridge University Press, 1994), 119–38.

[33] This thought experiment is also found in *Works*, v. 318 and vi. 272, 275.

[34] "Imaginary space" was a technical term used by philosophers, largely in reaction to the Condemnation of 1277 in Paris, in which the denial of a vacuum was condemned, to refer to a possible empty space "beyond the world". See Daniel Garber, *Descartes'*

our world. The fact that Boyle discusses this thought experiment in several works should indicate the importance of the existence of other bodies and relations between them, and that he believes that qualities are not intrinsic properties.

3. THE ACTUAL-RELATION REQUIREMENT

We have seen so far that Boyle holds what I call the "Actual-Relation Requirement" (ARR) concerning qualities. Stated briefly, ARR is the view that a body has qualities only if it stands in an actual relation to another existent body or perceiver. Of course, most scholars recognize that Boyle holds ARR. As Peter Anstey says, 'In the *Forms and Qualities* and elsewhere Boyle speaks of the necessity of the existence of other bodies for the presence of a power. That is, both relata must be present and standing in some kind of relation for there to be a power in the agent.'[35] It isn't clear, however, what exactly it is for the relata to be *present*, nor in what kind of relation agent and patient must stand. Unfortunately, Boyle does not explicitly address these issues. Fortunately, throughout his works, he leaves hints as to how ARR is to be spelled out in more detail.

There are passages in which Boyle characterizes ARR in a 'loose' way, and there are passages in which ARR is character-ized 'strictly'—though he does not characterize qualities both strictly and loosely concerning the same features of ARR.

3.1. *Looseness of ARR*

In 'Of Man's Great Ignorance of the Knowledge of Natural Things', Boyle says the following, first emphasizing ARR, and then indicating the looseness of this requirement:

Metaphysical Physics (Chicago: University of Chicago Press, 1992), 127; Edward Grant, *Much Ado about Nothing: Theories of Space and Vacuum from the Middle Ages to the Scientific Revolution* (Cambridge: Cambridge University Press, 1981); Edith Dudley Sylla, 'Creation and Nature', in A. S. McGrade (ed.), *Cambridge Companion to Medieval Philosophy* (Cambridge: Cambridge University Press, 2003), 184–7; Dennis Des Chene, *Physiologia: Natural Philosophy in Late Aristotelian and Cartesian Thought* (Ithaca, NY: Cornell University Press, 1996), 385–90; Pyle, *Atomism*, 232–43.

[35] Anstey, *Boyle*, 102.

As if there were no Lock in the World, a Key would be but a piece of Iron of such a determinate Size and Shape ... For *as* if some barbarous *American* should among other pieces of Shipwrack, thrown by the Sea upon the Shore, light upon a Key of a Cabinet, he would probably look on it as a piece of Iron, fit onely for the inconsiderable Uses of any other piece of Iron made much broader at each end than in the middle; but, having never seen a Lock, would never dream that this piece of Iron had a faculty to secure or give access to all that is contain'd in some well furnisht Chest or rich Cabinet. (*Works*, vi. 522)

Although Boyle does not indicate much about the spatial distance between the key and the lock, let us suppose (something that is supported by and/or consistent with many other texts) that the cabinet with its lock are not to be found in the shipwrecked items; for all we know the lock could be hundreds of miles away. Nevertheless Boyle thinks that the barbarous American would be ignorant of the *fact* that the piece of metal (i.e. the key) has a certain quality. ARR, then, is pretty loose: whereas the lock and key both need to exist, they need not be in the same room or on the same beach together. Boyle also discusses quality-constituting relations between a body and 'an Innumerable company of other Bodies, whereof some are near it and others very remote' (*Works*, vi. 275). Spatial proximity then does not appear relevant when it comes to the relations that constitute qualities.[36] In fact, he seems to think that the mere existence of a new menstruum would endow gold with a new quality:

And if one should Invent another Menstruum (as possibly I may Think my self Master of such a one), that will but in part dissolve pure Gold, and change some part of it into another Metalline Body, there will then arise another new Property, whereby to distinguish That from other Mettals; and yet the Nature of Gold is not a whit other now, then it was before this last Menstruum was first made. (*Works*, v. 311)

The looseness of ARR is also indicated by the fact that Boyle thinks that the existence of an 'accidental' agent or patient (e.g. an accidental key, i.e. a piece of metal not specifically made for the lock but which

---

[36] I am merely pointing out that spatial proximity and 'current engagement' (i.e. when the key is actually in use, opening the lock) are irrelevant to ARR. However, as I will point out shortly, Boyle does not think that the existence of just-any-key is relevant to ARR: the aperitable quality of the lock depends on the existence of a particular key—one that would in fact unlock the lock. Thanks to Steve Nadler for bringing the need to clarify this to my attention.

nevertheless would open it) is enough to endow the relevant bodies
with a particular quality. As Boyle states:

> Nature her self doth, sometimes otherwise, and sometimes by Chance, pro-
> duce so many things, that have new Relations unto others: And Art, especially
> assisted by Chymistry, may, by variously dissipating Natural Bodies, or Com-
> pounding either them, or their Constituent Parts with one another, make
> such an Innumerable Company of new Productions, that will each of Them
> have new operations, either immediately upon our Sensories, or upon other
> Bodies whose Changes we are able to perceive, that no man can know,
> but that the most Familiar Bodies may have Multitudes of Qualities, that he
> dreams not of. (*Works*, v. 311; see also vi. 521, viii. 545)

Boyle thinks that the mere existence of something, whether spatially
close to a body or not, which would act on or be acted upon by that
body in certain ways, endows that body with a quality. Even if all the
gold were located in Sydney and all the aqua regis were located in
Denver, gold would still be dissolvable in aqua regis. For Boyle, actual
qualities are clearly not to be confused with their manifestations; as
long as the relevant relata exist, the relevant quality exists, no matter if it is never manifested. Boyle's qualities are superabundant and
come cheap.

  Boyle also thinks that there may be all sorts of 'unheeded' relations
that we don't know about, but which result in qualities of which
we are ignorant (see also *Works*, iii. 229, 262; vi. 287–9). In the
'Excursion', he states that his view, unlike the scholastic view of
qualities, can accommodate 'an almost Infinite Number' of qualities.
Given that a body may stand in a huge number of quality-endowing
relations to other bodies or to perceivers, and that there is a huge
number of 'unheeded' relations, a body may have a correspondingly
huge number of qualities arising from these relations. As Boyle says,
there may be a 'much vaster multitude of *Phænomena*, and among them
of Qualities, then one that does not consider the matter attentively
would imagine' (*Works*, vi. 275; see also v. 311, quoted above). This
passage, and others like it, indicate something very important, namely
that Boyle thinks that whether a body actually has a quality is not an
epistemic matter of whether someone knows that a body has a quality
or whether a quality has been manifested (see also *Works*, viii. 545).
Gold would still be dissolvable in aqua regis even if no one ever knew

about this quality of gold; but gold would not have this quality if there were no aqua regis in the world.

3.2. *Strictness of ARR*

We have seen so far that ARR is fairly loose in what it requires for there to be a quality-endowing relation. However, in other respects, Boyle characterizes ARR more strictly. For instance, he thinks that the aperitable quality of the lock not only requires the existence of a key but a key that would in fact lock or unlock that lock if it were 'duly apply'd' to it; that is, every *actual* quality depends on a particular agent or patient. The example of the poisoned peas in the 'Excursion' illustrates this point. In this example, Boyle relates a story of three nuns who were poisoned when ground glass was mixed with their peas. Boyle thinks that the 'Deleterious Faculty' or poisonous quality of the peas is present in them only in relation to the three nuns who were poisoned by the peas; the peas did not have a poisonous quality in relation to 'diverse others of the Sisters (who yet escap'd unharm'd)' (*Works*, v. 311). Do we then want to say that the peas were poisonous *simpliciter*, yet the nuns other than the three were not poisoned by them? I don't think Boyle is saying that. Qualities are those properties that, among other things, tell us what a body would do in certain circumstances (i.e. the manifestation conditions). To say that the peas are poisonous is to say that there is a relevant patient, and if she ate the peas, she would be poisoned. But, as Boyle says: 'though the three Nuns we have been speaking of were Poison'd by the Glass, yet many others who eat of the other Portions of the same mingled Pease, receiv'd no mischief thereby' (*Works*, v. 312). Just as the qualities of a particular lock depend on the existence of a particular key (and not just *any* key), likewise, the existence of the poisonous quality of the peas depends on having particular patients (e.g. the three nuns), such that *those* patients would be poisoned by the peas if they were to eat the peas. In the same vein, Boyle says that certain animals whose stomachs are 'Lin'd or Stuff'd with Gross and Slimy Matter', would be able to eat the peas without being harmed.[37]

---

[37] *Works*, v. 312, and Jennifer McKitrick, 'A Case for Extrinsic Dispositions' ['Extrinsic Dispositions'], *Australasian Journal of Philosophy*, 81 (2003), 155–74.

In other words, the peas are not poisonous to those animals; so, if the peas were in a world in which the only animals were the animals with slimy stomachs, the peas would not have a poisonous quality at all. We have already seen something like this, when Boyle characterizes gold not as dissolvable *simpliciter*, but as dissolvable *in aqua regis*. In fact, in the following passages Boyle seems to gloss *Q is a relative quality* precisely as *Q is a quality only relative to a particular x*:[38]

This *Corrosibility* of Bodies, is as well as their Corrosiveness a Relative thing; as we see, that Gold, for instance, will not be dissolved by *Aqua fortis*, but will by *Aqua Regis*; whereas Silver is not soluble by the latter of these Menstruums, but is by the former. ... the Quality, that disposes the body it affects to be dissolv'd by Corrosive and other Menstruums, does (as hath been declared) in many cases depend upon the Mechanical Texture and Affections of the body *in reference to the Menstruum that is to work upon it* ... (*Works*, viii. 472–3; see also iii. 344)

[Qualities are those things] upon whose account one Body is fitted to act upon others, or disposed to be acted on by them, and receive Impressions from them; as Quicksilver has a Quality or Power ... to dissolve Gold and Silver, and a Capacity or Disposition to be dissolved by *Aqua fortis*, and (though lesse readily) by *Aqua Regis*. (*Works*, viii. 287)

And in *A Free Enquiry into the Vulgarly Receiv'd Notion of Nature*, he says:

And so a Key may either acquire or lose its Power of opening a Door (which, perhaps, some School-Men would call its *aperitive Faculty*,) by a Change, not made in itself, but in the Locks it is apply'd to, or in the Motion of the Hand, that manages It. (*Works*, x. 561–2)

Beyond the point about a particular agent or patient, there are two important further points being made about ARR in the passage from *A Free Enquiry*: (1) By changing the locks that a key previously fitted, the key, despite no change in its mechanical affections, may lose a quality.[39] Therefore, qualities are not identical to mechanical

---

[38] It is acceptable to say that a body B_1 has Q in virtue of the existence of bodies of kind K, where each of the K-bodies are individuals whose existence (without other members of K) would be sufficient to endow B_1 with Q. Also, for Boyle, kinds are dependent (at least for their initial formation) on individuals.

[39] Sydney Shoemaker calls dispositional properties that can be lost or gained merely by altering other bodies 'mere-Cambridge powers' and claims that Boyle's qualities are examples of these: 'A particular key on my key chain has the power of opening locks of a certain design. It also has the power of opening my front door. It could lose the former

affections, nor are they wholly intrinsic properties of bodies. (2) The inability to apply the key to the lock eliminates the aperitive quality of the key. Many contemporary philosophers, myself included, think that it makes sense to say that a body has a disposition, even if it is not going to be manifested. Boyle, however, in the passage above, presents a case in which a key is appropriately shaped, a suitable lock exists, the laws of nature are constant (I'm supposing), and yet the key may lose its aperitive quality in virtue of 'the Motion of the Hand, that manages It'. This is a very strange thing to say. Does Boyle really mean that, say, an awkward person who mismanages the key—the way Ted Striker from the classic motion picture *Airplane* has a "drinking problem": he can hold the drink, but when he attempts to drink it, he misses his mouth—causes that key to lose its aperitive quality? Does the key lose its aperitive quality only when in the possession of that person?

Unfortunately, Boyle does not go into detail here. Frankly, the only way for me to make sense of Boyle's suggestion is to consider something like a world in which *everyone* is stricken with a shaking palsy; everyone in that world shakes so much that, just as a matter of fact, no one ever manages (or will ever manage) to insert the key into the lock and turn it. In the shaking world the manifestation conditions for the aperitive quality are metaphysically and nomologically possible, but are never actually going to obtain. The case of the shaking world is a case in which two worlds (say, our world and the shaking world) are indistinguishable with respect to the two-place relation between the key and the lock (or the *n*-place relation between the key, the lock, the laws of nature, 'unheeded agents', etc.), but the key doesn't have the aperitive quality in the shaking world. This seems to indicate that the likelihood of manifestation is relevant to the existence of a quality *within a world*; while I claimed earlier that the mere existence of the relevant relata is sufficient for the existence of a quality, it now

power only by undergoing what we would regard as a real change, for example, a change in its shape. But it could lose the latter without undergoing such a change; it could do so in virtue of the lock on my door being replaced by one of a different design. Let us say that the former is an intrinsic power and the latter is a mere-Cambridge power' (Sydney Shoemaker, 'Causality and Properties', in Shoemaker, *Identity, Cause, and Mind* (Cambridge: Cambridge University Press, 1984), 221). See also McKitrick, 'Extrinsic Dispositions', and Curley, 'Distinction'.

appears that Boyle is claiming the contrary. We can make some sense of this, though unfortunately not perfect sense, if we acknowledge that, for Boyle, *quality-endowing relations are never two-place relations*.[40] The laws of nature and 'unheeded agents' are going to be a relatum of any quality-constituting relation, even in relatively straightforward cases. For instance, in *A Free Enquiry*, Boyle says:

> For an Individual Body, being but a Part of the World, and incompass'd with other Parts of the same great *Automaton*, needs the Assistance, or Concourse, of other Bodies, (which are external Agents) to perform divers of its operations, and exhibit several *Phænomena's*, that belong to it ... For, whatever the Structures of these living Engines [i.e. animals and plants] be, they would as little, without the Co-operations of external Agents; such as the *Sun, Æther, Air, &c.* be able to exercise their Functions ... (*Works*, x. 469)

Following this passage Boyle also includes 'the *laws of motion* freely established and still maintained by God' as a relatum in any quality-constituting relation. In other places, he explicitly contrasts the treatment of qualities found in *OFQ* (in which he emphasizes the relative nature of qualities illustrated by *noticeable* relations) with the emphasis found in *Cosmical Qualities*:

> I have in the *Origine or Formes* touched upon this subject already, but otherwise than I am now about to doe. For whereas that which I doe *there* principally, (and yet but Transiently) take notice of, is *That one Body being surrounded with other Bodies, is manifestly wrought on by many of those among whome 'tis placed:* that which I chiefly in *This Discourse* consider is, the Impressions that a Body may receive, or the power it may acquire, from those vulgarly unknown, or at least vnheeded Agents, by which it is thus affected, not only upon the account of its owne peculiar Texture or Disposition, but by vertue of the generall Fabrick of the World. (*Works*, vi. 288)

---

[40] In the shaking world, one of the relevant relata is a person capable of inserting the key into the lock. So, this shaking world is simply a bizarre instance of the absence of one of the relata required for the presence of a quality. However, I don't think that this suggestion completely helps this case. Even if everyone has the shaking palsy, it is both metaphysically and nomologically possible that a shaking key-holder simply gets lucky and manages to insert the key and open the lock. Or that a wind blows the key into the lock and it is opened. These possibilities are especially troubling when we consider the abundance of "accidental" or "lucky" congruities in nature. I honestly do not know what to say about these cases.

And in *OFQ*, Boyle explicitly mentions that the quality of whiteness is present in crushed ice 'by reason of the Fabrick of the World, and of our Eyes' (*Works*, v. 320). In a world with different laws, crushed ice may cause the sensation of redness; in a world with different laws, a force field may be generated when the key is brought closer to the lock, which prevents insertion; etc.

Finally, ARR requires that the bodies in question (as well as the other relevant relata) are contemporaries, i.e. a body has a quality at *t* only if all of the relata required for that quality exist at *t*. Whereas spatial proximity seems to be irrelevant to ARR, contemporaneousness is required by ARR. This is illustrated, once again, by Boyle's example of the lock and key and the example of the gold and the newly invented menstruum: it is only when the key comes into existence that the lock acquires its aperitable quality, and once the menstruum is invented, the gold acquires a new quality. Conversely, the lock and key can lose the quality through a subsequent change in the other.

We have now spelled out in more detail the requirements of Boyle's ARR for the existence of a quality. It is apparent just how far his thinking about qualities diverges from contemporary views of qualities as dispositions or powers. In contemporary discussions of dispositions and powers, two ideas have widespread acceptance: That dispositions are reducible to their bases (i.e. the categorical properties which endow the body with dispositions),[41] and that intrinsic duplicates will share all and only the same dispositions.[42] For the sake of discussing Boyle, let us characterize intrinsic duplicates as individuals having qualitatively identical mechanical affections.[43] Boyle, as we have seen, disagrees with both of these widespread views: he thinks that qualities are not reducible to their bases, in his case, the mechanical affections; and he thinks that *it is possible that intrinsic duplicates differ in their qualities at different times in the same world* and *it is possible that intrinsic duplicates*

---

[41] A notable exception is McKitrick, who argues that at least some dispositions are not intrinsic properties ('Extrinsic Dispositions').

[42] For instance, Mark Johnston, 'How to Speak of the Colors', *Philosophical Studies*, 68 (1992), 221–63; David Lewis, 'Finkish Dispositions', *Philosophical Quarterly*, 47 (1997), 143–58; George Molnar, *Powers: A Study in Metaphysics* (Oxford: Oxford University Press, 2003).

[43] By characterizing intrinsic duplicates in this way, if $x = y$, then x and y (at the same time) are intrinsic duplicates.

differ in their qualities at the same time in different worlds.[44] The former
can happen in several ways, perhaps because the body required for the
existence of a quality begins or ceases to exist, or because an 'unheeded'
relation required for the existence of a quality begins or ceases to
obtain, or because the laws of nature change. The schlock–lock–key
case explicitly illustrates that intrinsic duplicates can have different
qualities in the same world at different times. Moreover, Boyle thinks
that the natural laws are what I call 'ultra-contingent', obtaining only
because God wills them to obtain, and to have the content they do
only because God wills them to. I say that they are 'ultra-contingent'
because unlike many other philosophers who believe that the natural
laws are contingent in so far as they are willed by God, Boyle parts
company with these philosophers and holds a more radical position:
whereas many philosophers hold that God creates the natural laws,
once he has done so, he is 'bound' to uphold them, Boyle believes
that God creates the laws and can also *change* them: 'the most free and
powerful Author of those Laws of Nature, according to which all the
Phenomena of Qualities are regulated, may (as he thinks fit) introduce,
establish or change them in any assign'd portion of Matter' (*Works*,
viii. 312). And: 'laws of nature determin'd and bound up other Beings
to act accordingly to them, yet he has not bound up his own hands by
them, but can envigorate, suspend, over-rule; and reverse any of them
as he thinks fit'.[45] So, intrinsic duplicates in different worlds could
stand in the appropriate relation (i.e., say, the relation that the lock
and key stand in with respect to each other, the relation that endows
each with the relevant qualities) and yet lack those qualities owing to
different natural laws. And because Boyle thinks that God not only
created the natural laws but also could change them now, intrinsic
duplicates in the same world (the same things at different times) could
stand in a relation to each other at different times and have different
qualities from those they had before the laws were changed.

   Boyle also thinks that there can be a difference in qualities of
intrinsic duplicates at the same (or different) time(s) in different worlds

----

[44] See McKitrick, 'Extrinsic Dispositions', 159, and Anstey, *Boyle*, 104. For Boyle, qualities are "extrinsic dispositions", i.e. ones which have all of the "marks of dispositionality"
(e.g. manifestation conditions, etc.) but which are such that they could be had by one of a
pair of intrinsic duplicates and not the other.

[45] The Boyle Papers, Royal Society Archives, London, vol. vii, fo. 113.

(perhaps '*in vacuo* worlds' or 'imaginary spaces'). We have seen this illustrated (implicitly) by the case of the lock and key, the gold and aqua regis case, etc.: in a different world, a world in which there are no keys, a schlock would not have aperitable qualities; in a world without aqua regis, gold would not be dissolvable, etc.

It is uncontroversial that Boyle thinks that qualities necessarily involve relations. But what *are* relations according to Boyle? Frankly, I don't know, but in my defence, it is not my fault: Boyle simply never gives an explicit account of the ontological status of relations.[46] But what he does say, while not helping with the question of the ontological status of relations, does help when thinking about the relationship between mechanical affections, relations, and qualities. He says that a change in the mechanical affections of a body can bring about a change in the relations that that body will have: because qualities are 'Relative Attributes, one of these now-mentioned Alterations, though but mechanicall, may endow the Body it happens to, with new Relations both to the Organs of Sense, and also to some other Bodies, and consequently may endow it with additionall Qualities' (*Works*, vi. 282; see also vi. 529). And when Boyle discusses the corrosibility of certain metals, he explains what he means by saying that the '*Corrosibility* of Bodies is as well as their Corrosiveness a Relative thing ... And this relative Affection, on whose account a Body comes to be corrodible by a *Menstruum*, seems to consist in *three* things, which all of them depend upon Mechanical Principles' (*Works*, viii. 472). The three things mentioned by Boyle which produce a body's corrosibility are the size of 'pores' (which allows the menstruum to get in between the corpuscles of the gold), the size and solidity of the corpuscles, and the cohesion of the corpuscles (*Works*, viii. 472–3). The mechanical affections of a body determine the *possible* relations it can stand in, and the existence of another body to which it actually stands in relation determines in which of the possible relations it *actually* stands. In the lock and key example from the 'Excursion', Boyle says that the aperitable quality 'was nothing new in the Lock, or distinct from the Figure it had before those Keyes were made' (*Works*, v. 310). And every other example in the 'Excursion' seems to reduce qualities to mechanical affections: the dissolvability of gold in aqua regis is 'not

---

[46] See Anstey, *Boyle*, ch. 4.

in the Gold any thing distinct from its peculiar Texture' (p. 310); the poisonousness of the peas 'is really nothing distinct from the Glass its self ... as it is furnish'd with that determinate Bigness, and Figure of Parts, which have been acquir'd by Comminution' (pp. 311–12); and the 'echo-quality' of a cave 'is in It nothing else but the Hollowness of its Figure' (p. 319). And in general, Boyle says that '[Qualities] are not in the Bodies that are Endow'd with them any Real or Distinct Entities, or differing from the Matter its self, furnish'd with such a Determinate Bigness, Shape, or other Mechanical Modifications' (*Works*, v. 310). Moreover, because qualities depend on relations, and the variety of relations (both actual and merely possible) depend on the mechanical affections, we get an explanation of the texts in which Boyle seems to be claiming that a body's qualities are identical to its mechanical affections. The reductivist and identity passages are only stating that mechanical affections will play a major role (in fact, they will play the *only* role on the part of the individual body itself!) in determining in which relations that body will stand to other bodies.

4. THE 'CHIEFEST DIFFICULTY': DISPOSITIVE QUALITIES

Although the 'Excursion' (and its title) supports the view that qualities are not intrinsic features of bodies, that qualities arise in virtue of actual relations between bodies or between bodies and perceivers, Boyle seems to undermine this view in a passage in *OFQ* in which he addresses a difficulty for his relative notion of qualities—which *importantly* he thinks is not a problem *simply* for his relative view of qualities; rather the difficulty is 'the chiefest, that we shall meet with against the Corpuscular Hypothesis' (*Works*, v. 317). The implication is that Boyle believes that his relative theory of qualities is entailed by corpuscularianism. It is not clear that corpuscularianism entails the relative view of qualities (for instance, it seems that a corpuscularian could hold that qualities are identical to mechanical affections; and as such, bodies could have qualities even in the absence of actual relations[47]). In any case, because we are interested in a problem that

[47] Perhaps this is not an option, given Boyle's explicit characterization of corpuscularianism (discussed below).

arises for Boyle, what is important is that *Boyle* thinks that the relative view of qualities is entailed by corpuscularianism.

Here is the objection Boyle proposes to himself:

whereas we explicate Colours, Odours, and the like Sensible qualities, by a *relation to our Senses*, it seems evident, that they have an *absolute* Being irrelative to *Us*; for, Snow (for instance) would be white, and a glowing Coal would be hot, though there were no Man or any other Animal in the World: and 'tis plain, that Bodies do not onely by their Qualities work upon *Our senses*, but upon *other*, and those, Inanimate *Bodies*; as the Coal will not onely heat or burn a *Man's hand* if he touch it, but would likewise heat Wax, (even so much as to melt it, and make it flow) and thaw Ice into Water, though all the Men and sensitive Beings in the World were annihilated. (*Works*, v. 317)

The relative view of qualities given by Boyle in the 'Excursion' entails that if there were no perceivers or other bodies[48] in the world, a body would not have any qualities. The objection is perfectly general, and does not concern only sensible qualities: if Boyle's relative view of qualities is right, then in the absence of the relatum, nothing would be white, cold, fragile, dissolvable in aqua regis, and so on for any other putative quality.

In an initially surprising move, Boyle does not bite the bullet and simply say, what should be expected, given both the theory of relative qualities and the case of the lonely corpuscle: 'That is right: without actual relations a body would not have any qualities but only mechanical affections. Didn't you read later on in *OFQ* (*Works*, v. 334), where I say that the mechanical affections are "the [only] Affections that belong to a Body, as it is consider'd in it self, without relation to *sensitive* Beings, or to other Natural Bodies"?' Instead he agrees with the hypothetical objector: 'I do not deny, but that Bodies may be said, *in a very favourable sense*, to have those Qualities we call Sensible, though there were no Animals in the World' (*Works*, v. 318–19; my emphasis).[49] He then introduces something that seems

---

[48] See Frederick O'Toole, 'Qualities and Powers in the Corpuscular Philosophy of Robert Boyle', *Journal of the History of Philosophy*, 12 (1974), 295–315, at n. 23, and *Works*, v. 334.

[49] A lot would seem to rest on the meaning of 'favourable' here. According to the *OED*, in this context, it means "allowable". However, the text cited as a use of the term in this sense is the very text from Boyle we are presently considering! Not very helpful.

to undermine much of what he has said before about qualities: the notion of a body having a quality *dispositively*:

so, if there were no Sensitive Beings, those Bodies that are now the Objects of our Senses, would be but *dispositively*, if I may so speak, endow'd with Colours, Tasts, and the like; and *actually* but onely with those more Catholick Affections of Bodies, Figure, Motion, Texture, &c. (*Works*, v. 319)

What does Boyle mean by having a quality dispositively? He says that a body has a quality dispositively 'in its having such a disposition of its Constituent Corpuscles that, *in case it were duely apply'd* to the Sensory of an Animal, *it would produce* such a sensible Quality, which a Body of another Texture would not' (*Works*, v. 319; my emphasis).[50] And in *Men's Great Ignorance*, Boyle gives a similar account, while explicitly not restricting it to the sensible qualities he discusses in *OFQ*. In fact, he even uses the example of the lock and key again: 'if there were no such Objects in the World, those Qualities, in the Bodies that are said to be endow'd with them, would be but Aptitudes to work such Effects, in case convenient Objects were not wanting' (*Works*, vi. 521–2).

Dispositive qualities appear to be had by a body when two conditions are met: first, when a relatum, which would endow the body with an actual quality, does not exist; second, when certain counterfactuals are true of the body. But then dispositive qualities are consistent with the improbability (impossibility?) of the manifestation conditions for that quality. A piece of gold would have the dispositive quality of *dissolvability in aqua regis* even if there were no aqua regis in the world. And Boyle claims that dispositive qualities are qualities 'in a very favourable sense'. How can he possibly say this? Moreover, in addition to undermining Boyle's theory of relative qualities, other problems arise. First, for Boyle (actual) qualities have both explanatory and predictive power in corpuscularian natural philosophy. But it seems that dispositive qualities—if they tell us what a body would do, if it were to act upon or to be acted upon by another body—would do all of the same work in an explanatorily adequate natural philosophy.

---

[50] As Peter Anstey correctly points out, Boyle uses the term "disposition", as was common in the 17th century, in two different ways. He uses it most often to refer to the manner in which a body is arranged (i.e. its "texture") (e.g. *Works*, ii. 100, 108; iv. 26; vi. 288; viii. 449); and he uses it to refer to an ability, capacity, power that a body has in virtue of its mechanical affections (*Works*, ii. 24, 102; iv. 33; vi. 526; viii. 337, 449). In the passage just quoted, Boyle is using it in the former sense.

And if that were the case, then corpuscularian natural philosophy doesn't need actual qualities. Boyle himself states that among the conditions of any excellent hypothesis is the following: 'That it be the Simplest of all the Good ones we are able to frame, at lest Containing nothing tht is Superfluous or Impertinent.'[51] But if actual qualities were superfluous, then the corpuscularian philosophy would not be excellent. Second, Boyle's attack on the Grand Mistake of the scholastics depends on the truth of the relative theory of qualities. If qualities can be had *in a very favourable sense*, in the absence of relations, then it is unclear how the 'Excursion' would constitute an argument against the scholastic real qualities. Finally, Boyle thinks that the relative view of qualities is *entailed* by corpuscularianism. If the relative view of qualities is expendable, then corpuscularianism entails an expendable theory of qualities! All three of these consequences would be bad for Boyle. If Boyle is going to make so much rest upon his relative theory of qualities and ARR, then it seems that the admission of dispositive qualities is detrimental to his project.[52]

5. EXPERIMENTALISM AND ANTI-APRIORISM

Boyle says very little about dispositive qualities, and even less about how their admission does not undermine his theory of relative qualities. In fact, we've seen that one of his responses to the 'chiefest difficulty' is a simple admission that there are dispositive qualities. Boyle apparently does not think that dispositive qualities are incompatible with the theory of relative qualities. Surely there are reasons for Boyle's calm confidence in the face of the 'chiefest difficulty'. Boyle mentions several considerations concerning the 'chiefest difficulty', some of which seem irrelevant to the issue. The third consideration concerns the "situatedness" of bodies with actual qualities. He says:

the actions of particular Bodies upon one another must not be barely æstimated, as if two Portions of Matter of their Bulk and Figure were plac'd

---

[51] 'Notes on a Good and an Excellent Hypothesis', 119.

[52] Of course, both actual qualities and dispositive qualities are *specified relatively*: talk of both will involve reference to a relatum. The difference between the two is that the relatum specified in an attribution of an actual quality must *exist*, whereas the relatum in an attribution of a dispositive quality does *not* exist. So, *specifying* a property by appeal to a relatum does not guarantee that it is an *actual* quality.

in some imaginary Space beyond the World, but as being scituated in the World, constituted as it now is, and consequently as having their action upon each other liable to be promoted, or hindered, or modify'd by the Actions of other Bodies besides them. (*Works*, v. 318)

The situatedness of bodies comes up in many other texts. For instance:

I shall observe that when we are considering how numerous and various Phænomena may be exhibited by mixt bodies, we are not to look upon them precisely in themselves, that is, as they are portions of Matter, of such a determinate nature, or Texture; but as they are parts of a World so constituted as ours is, and consequently as portions of Matter which are plac'd among many other Bodies. (*Works*, vi. 272; see v. 321; vi. 272, 275, 281)

Why is the situatedness of bodies relevant to our issue? I believe that the importance placed on situatedness illustrates Boyle's well-known commitment to natural philosophy, where this is understood, among other things, as an attempt to explain (and predict) the behaviour of bodies in *this* world, a world in which bodies are not in an "imaginary space" or an "*in vacuo* world", but rather a world in which bodies in fact have quality-endowing relations, and in which it is the business of the natural philosopher to discover these qualities. Unfortunately, Boyle does not seem to be addressing the issue of dispositive qualities: this consideration only explains why Boyle would appeal to situatedness to explain why bodies in fact have the actual qualities they do, but it does not explain why Boyle thinks that dispositive qualities would be had by bodies, in a very favourable sense, even in *in vacuo* worlds. We would think that if Boyle appeals to situatedness to explain the having of qualities, then dispositive qualities would not be qualities at all (and ultimately this is Boyle's view). But if so, it remains peculiar that Boyle says that dispositive qualities are qualities in a favourable sense. *By itself* the situatedness of bodies does not help address the worries arising from dispositive qualities. However, as we will see shortly, situatedness is a necessary feature of corpuscularianism as Boyle thinks of it, and the latter helps address our present concerns.

The key to reconciling Boyle's relative qualities with his acceptance of dispositive qualities and to see how situatedness is relevant is to recognize the uncontroversial fact that Boyle is first and foremost a natural philosopher whose conclusions about qualities are grounded in experiments not in a priori metaphysical philosophizing (see *Works*, vi. 407, viii. 322).[53] Boyle's endorsement of an experimental method, his desire to compile a Baconian "natural history" of qualities, and his opposition to a priori "system builders" is expressed throughout his writings. For instance:

And truly, *Pyrophilus*, if men could be perswaded to mind more the Advancement of Natural Philosophy than that of their own Reputations, 'twere not methinks very uneasie to make them sensible, that one of the considerablest services that they could do Mankind, were to set themselves diligently and industriously to make Experiments, and collect Observations, without being over-forward to establish Principles and Axioms, believing it uneasie to erect such Theories as are capable to explicate all the Phænomena of Nature, before they have been able to take notice of the tenth part of those Phænomena that are to be explicated ... That then that I wish for, as to Systems, is this, That men in the first would forbear to establish any Theory, till they have consulted with (though not a fully competent number of Experiments, such as may afford them all the Phænomena to be explicated by that Theory, yet) a considerable number of Experiments in proportion to the comprehensiveness of the Theory to be erected on them. (*Works*, ii. 13–14)

The experimental natural philosopher will discover the qualities of bodies and how bodies behave, 'such as without the diligent Examination of particular Bodies would, I fear, never have been found out *à priori* ev'n by the most profound Contemplators' (*Works*, ii. 24). And Boyle wishes 'chiefly to keep my Judgment as unprepossess'd as

---

[53] It should be noted that recently the relationship between Boyle's corpuscularianism and his experimentalism has been questioned in Alan Chalmers, 'The Lack of Excellency of Boyle's Mechanical Philosophy', *Studies in History and Philosophy of Science*, 24 (1993), 541–64. Chalmers argues both that Boyle's success as an experimental scientist was not aided by his corpuscularianism and that his corpuscularianism was not supported by his experiments. An adequate response to these claims deserves more space than I have here and would take us too far away from our topic. For some responses to Chalmers, see Andrew Pyle, 'Boyle on Science and the Mechanical Philosophy: A Reply to Chalmers' ['Boyle on Science'], *Studies in History and Philosophy of Science*, 33 (2002), 175–90; Anstey, *Boyle*; and Anstey, 'Robert Boyle and the Heuristic Value of Mechanism' ['Heuristic Value'], *Studies in History and Philosophy of Science*, 33 (2002), 161–74. What is important for *my* purposes is the fact that Boyle himself thinks that there is an intimate dependence-relation between experimentalism and corpuscularianism.

It has been pointed out by Anstey ('Heuristic Value'), however, that Boyle's corpuscularianism places certain non-experimental restrictions on the range of *possible* results from experimentation. For instance, Boyle would never entertain that an experimental result came from *qualitates reales* or scholastic substantial forms.

might be with any of the Modern Theories of Philosophy, till I were provided of Experiments to help me to judge of them' (*Works*, ii. 86).[54]

At times Boyle demonstrates his famous mild agnosticism and at other times his disparaging antagonism towards metaphysical issues and a priori reasoning in natural philosophy.[55] His well-known agnosticism concerning the nature of body and the origin of motion stems from his interest in the experimental fruitfulness of both Atomistic and Cartesian natural philosophy. In a famous passage from the Preface to *Some Specimens of an Attempt to Make Chymical Experiments Useful to Illustrate the Notions of the Corpuscular Philosophy*, Boyle states that the

> Atomical and Cartesian Hypotheses ... might be look'd upon as one Philo-
> sophy ... I know that these two sects of Modern Naturalists disagree about
> the Notion of Body in general, and consequently about the Possibility of a
> true Vacuum, as also about the Origine of Motion, the indefinite Divisible-
> ness of Matter, and some other points of less Importance than these: But in
> regard that some of them seem to be rather Metaphysical than Physiological
> Notions, and that some others seem rather to be requisite to the Explication
> of the first Origine of the Universe, than of the Phænomena of it in the
> state wherein we now find it; in regard of these, I say, and some other
> Considerations, and especially for this Reason, That both parties agree in
> deducing all the Phænomena of Nature from Matter and local Motion.
> (*Works*, ii. 87)

Here Boyle states something repeated elsewhere (e.g. *Works*, v. 292), namely that he is much less interested in the metaphysical differences dividing the sects of mechanical philosophers than in what they have in common, namely a rejection of scholastic substantial forms, *qualitates reales*, and teleological natural explanations, and their appeal to the mechanical features of small bits of matter to explain all natural phenomena.[56]

---

[54] See also *Works*, v. 288, 292, 299, and Rose-Mary Sargent, 'Learning from Experience: Boyle's Construction of an Experimental Philosophy', in Hunter (ed.), *Robert Boyle
Reconsidered*, 58–9.

[55] See Richard Arthur, 'The Enigma of Leibniz's Atomism', *Oxford Studies in Early
Modern Philosophy*, 1 (2003), 183–227; Marie Boas, 'The Establishment of the Mechanical
Philosophy' ['Establishment'], *Osiris*, 10 (1952), 412–541; Pyle, 'Boyle on Science'; Anstey,
Boyle; Steven Shapin and Simon Schaffer, *Leviathan and the Air-Pump: Hobbes, Boyle and the
Experimental Life* [*Air-Pump*] (Princeton: Princeton University Press, 1985).

[56] See also *Works*, v. 354; Anstey, *Boyle*, 92; Sargent, 'Learning from Experience', 69.

Most important for present purposes is Boyle's own explicit characterization of the corpuscular philosophy:

> when I speak of the *Corpuscular* or *Mechanical* Philosophy ... I plead only for such a Philosophy, as reaches but to things purely Corporeal, and distinguishing between the first *original of things*; and the subsequent *course of Nature*, teaches, concerning the *former*, not onely that God gave Motion to Matter, but that in the beginning He so guided the various Motions of the parts of it, as to contrive them into the World he design'd they should compose ... and established those *Rules of Motion*, and that order amongst things Corporeal, which we are wont to call the *Laws of Nature*. And having told this as to the *former*, it may be allowed as to the *latter* to teach, That the Universe being once fram'd by God, and the Laws of Motion being settled and all upheld by His incessant concourse and general Providence; the Phænomena of the World thus constituted, are Physically produc'd by the Mechanical affections of the parts of Matter, and what they operate upon one another according to Mechanical Laws. (*Works*, viii. 103–4)

Boyle's characterization of corpuscularianism wears on its face its anti-a priori method,[57] the importance of situatedness, the importance of discovering how actual things actually behave,[58] and its concern only with *our* corporeal world. He is concerned with how *our world* works, not how any possible world works (see *Works*, v. 318, 321; vi. 272, 275), and our world is one in which bodies are in fact situated and which has its own contingent natural laws. The natural philosopher should concern himself with explanation of how *those* bodies behave: 'all whom [i.e. atomists and naturalists in general] I wish, that though men cannot perhaps in all things, yet at least as far as they can, they would accustom themselves to speak and think as Nature does really and sensibly appear to work' (*Works*, ii. 108). And in the unpublished 'Of Naturall Philosophie',[59] Boyle lists two 'Principles of naturall Philosophie', the second of which is 'That it is requisite

---

[57] See Boas, 'Establishment', 487–8, 492; Sargent, 'Learning from Experience', 69; Keating, 'Un-Locke-ing Boyle', 321.

[58] See *Works*, iii. 256: 'For it is one thing to be able to shew it possible for such and such Effects to proceed from the Various Magnitudes, Shapes, Motions, and Concretions of Atoms, and another thing to be able to declare what precise, and determinate Figures, Sizes, and Motions of Atoms, will suffice to make out the propos'd *Phænomena*, without incongruity to any others to be met with in Nature.'

[59] Boyle papers, vol. xxxvi, fos. 65–6.

to be furnished with observations at [*sic*] Experiments'. And among the list of 'Reasons of which take these Observations' are '(1) That we consult nature to make her Instruct us what to beleeve not to confirme what we have beleeved,' and '(5) That therefore Reason is not to be much trusted when she wanders far from Experiments & Systematicall Bodyes of naturall Philosophie are not for a while to be attempted.'

Boyle's experimental method and his opposition to apriorism in natural philosophy is, of course, well known,[60] and perhaps accounts both for his relative neglect by contemporary historians of philosophy and for the overwhelming amount written on Boyle by historians of science. Given that this is well-explored territory, I will not dwell on it any longer. I wish only to emphasize its importance to Boyle's theory of qualities and its relevance to the issue of dispositive qualities. Even in *OFQ*—the most 'metaphysical' of his treatment of qualities—Boyle's views about the qualities of bodies are intended to be supported by his experimental work.[61]

Boyle thinks that the natural philosopher knows how things in the corporeal world behave by knowing as many qualities of bodies as he can; and given the prominent role of experiment and Boyle's disparaging remarks about the a priori speculation of 'systematic' philosophers, the qualities of bodies are not known except by observation. Moreover, because Boyle thinks that we may be ignorant of indefinitely many qualities a body has, in order to know that a body has a particular quality, we must observe the *manifestation* of that quality. Proper observation of a quality just is the observation of its manifestation along with recognition of the relevant manifestation conditions. For example, we cannot know that gold has the quality of *dissolvability in aqua regis* unless we have observed some gold actually

[60] For instance, John Henry, 'Occult Qualities and the Experimental Philosophy: Active Principles in Pre-Newtonian Matter Theory', *History of Science*, 24 (1986), 335–81; Shapin and Schaffer, *Air-Pump*; Boas, 'Establishment'; Sargent, 'Learning from Experience'; Michael Hunter, 'How Boyle Became a Scientist', *History of Science*, 33 (1995), 59–103; Clericuzio, *Elements*.

[61] In fact, the Second Part of *OFQ* (*Works*, v. 356–442) is devoted to the discussion of experiments supporting the theory of qualities discussion in the First, or 'Theoretical', Part. When talking about qualities, Boyle is talking about qualities, 'whose Existence I can manifest, not only by considerations not absurd, but also by real Experiments and Physicall Phænomena' (*Works*, vi. 289).

dissolving in aqua regis. So, in our present world, a world in which gold is actually dissolvable in aqua regis, we cannot know what the gold *would* do if immersed in aqua regis unless we have observed an instance of gold dissolving in aqua regis.

Because Boyle thinks that only situated bodies have actual qualities, it then follows that knowledge of a body's actual qualities requires that that body is situated. Now, for Boyle, the difference between whether a body at a time has an actual quality or a dispositive quality consists primarily in whether the body in question stands in a quality-constituting relation. But whether a body stands in such a relation at *t* shouldn't affect the manner in which we *know* what that body at *t* *would* do in certain circumstances. In *any* case, to know what a body would do, we must have observed a manifestation of an actual quality.

We are now in a position to see that actual qualities, which can only be had when certain relations obtain, are completely indispensable to the attribution of dispositive qualities to bodies. That is, not only do dispositive qualities *not* make actual qualities dispensable, their attribution in fact makes actual qualities indispensable. First, however, we need to spell out in more detail what dispositive qualities are, and we must recognize the situations in which Boyle thinks that the issue of dispositive qualities arises; that is, the situations which would lead us even to think about a body's dispositive qualities. Here is what Boyle says:

> it seems evident, that they [i.e. sensible qualities] have an *absolute* Being irrelative to *Us*; for, Snow (for instance) would be white, and a glowing Coal would be hot, though there were no Man or any other Animal in the World ... the Coal will not onely heat or burn a *Man's hand* if he touch it, but would likewise heat Wax ... and thaw Ice into Water, though all the Men, and sensitive Being in the World were annihilated. (*Works*, v. 317)[62]

As this and other texts make clear, dispositive qualities become an issue in (roughly) two kinds of situation: (1) when a relevant relatum ceases to exist;[63] (2) when we imagine counterfactual situations in

---

[62] The explicit discussion of dispositive qualities in *OFQ* mainly concerns *sensible* qualities. But as I have already mentioned, this phenomenon is not peculiar to sensible qualities, but relates to all qualities. In the case of many sensible qualities, the quality-constituting relatum must be a perceiver, or 'sensitive Being'.

[63] Indicated by the example of the pin and the corpse (*Works*, v. 319–20), as well as implicitly by the discussions of the lock and key: if we altered a key that previously had an aperitive quality in relation to the lock, then the lock dispositively has the aperitable quality.

which the quality-constituting relation is absent (see e.g. *Works*, v. 317, 319). In these sorts of situation, however, there are constraints imposed by Boyle's theory of relative qualities: we are presently in an epistemic situation in which we know, for instance, that gold is actually dissolvable in aqua regis, but we are imagining what gold would be like in case aqua regis (which, if it were to exist, would endow the body with an actual quality) were not to exist. Now consider six worlds, each of which contains some gold and is the same as our world with respect to laws of nature and other relevant considerations except when specified:

(W_1) Never any aqua regis.

(W_2) No aqua regis at t_1; some aqua regis at t_2; gold immersed in aqua regis at t_2; immersion and dissolving observed; no aqua regis at t_3.

(W_3) No aqua regis at t_1; some aqua regis at t_2; gold never immersed in aqua regis; no aqua regis at t_3.

(W_4) No aqua regis at t_1; some aqua regis at t_2; gold immersed in aqua regis at t_2; immersion and dissolving *not* observed; no aqua regis at t_3.

(W_5) Aqua regis all the time; no immersion of gold.

(W_6) Aqua regis all the time; immersion and dissolving of gold observed at t_2.

We can say the following about Boyle's *actual* qualities in these worlds: According to ARR, the bare minimum required for the existence of an actual quality is the existence of all of the relata of a quality-constituting relation. So, in W_1 there is no actual quality: if there never is any aqua regis, then gold is never dissolvable in aqua regis. And again considering ARR, according to which contemporaneousness is both necessary (and sufficient in this case, given my stipulation about the transworld constancy of laws and other relevant relata) for a quality-constituting relation, in W_2-W_4 there is no actual quality at t_1; there is at t_2; and there is not again at t_3. If there was some aqua regis at one time but no longer any, then gold had the quality at one time but lacks it now. The situations in W_5 and W_6 are as straightforward as in W_1: if the relevant relatum is always present, then the quality is always present. Remember that Boyle does not think that having a quality requires a manifestation of that quality; also, recalling a point

I made earlier, Boyle thinks that a body can have a huge number of qualities of which we are totally ignorant.

So much for the ontological situation in these worlds, but now consider the epistemic situation. Obviously, we cannot know that a body has a quality in a world in which it does not have that quality; so in W_1 we don't know that gold is dissolvable in aqua regis. Given that both manifestation of a quality and observation of the manifestation are necessary in order to know that a body has a certain quality, in W_3, W_4, and W_5 we are ignorant of the gold's dissolvability, despite the fact that gold actually has that quality at least some of the time. W_6 is a world in which we know that gold is dissolvable owing to the manifestation and observation of the manifestation of that quality. But what about W_2, the most interesting world for our purposes? As we have already seen, gold lacks the actual quality at t_1 (because it fails to satisfy ARR's contemporaneousness condition); gold has the actual quality at t_2 (because it satisfies ARR at t_2); but gold again lacks the actual quality at t_3 (because it fails to satisfy the contemporaneousness condition). But at t_3 we know, in virtue of manifestation and observation, that gold actually had that quality at t_2. We know at t_3 what gold *would* do if there were some aqua regis and the gold were immersed in it. What we say, then, is that gold is *dispositively* dissolvable in aqua regis at t_3.

Now consider these intrinsic duplicates, these pieces of gold, at t_4, a time after t_3. Do the pieces of gold differ in their dispositive qualities at t_4? I believe that Boyle thinks so: of the three pieces of gold, only the piece in W_2 has *dispositive* dissolvability at t_4, and at t_4 in W_3, W_4, W_5, and W_6, the gold lacks dispositive dissolvability. (The gold in W_6 lacks dispositive dissolvability because dispositive qualities require the *absence* of the relevant relatum; otherwise it is unclear how dispositive qualities would differ from *actual qualities*, and it is stipulated that the relevant relatum is always present in W_6.)

Before I defend this claim about Boyle's dispositive qualities, let me address an initial objection with significant prima facie weight against my interpretation:

> Listen, Boyle characterizes dispositive qualities solely in terms of counterfactuals and the absence of relevant relata. Let me refresh your memory: Boyle says that dispositive qualities are 'such a

disposition of its Constituent Corpuscles, that *in case it were duely apply'd* to the Sensory of an Animal, *it would produce* such a sensible Quality, which a Body of another Texture would not'. And 'if there were no such Objects in the World, those Qualities, in the Bodies that are said to be endow'd with them, would be but Aptitudes to work such Effects, in case convenient Objects were not wanting' (*Works*, vi. 521–2). Boyle even compares dispositive qualities to a lute's being in tune: 'we say that a Lute is in tune, whether it be actually plaid upon or no, if the Strings be all so duly stretcht, as that it would appear to be in Tune, if it were play'd upon' (*Works*, v. 319).[64] But, like the in-tune lute, certainly the pieces of gold in those worlds (at times when it is lacking actual dissolvability in virtue of the non-existence of aqua regis) have 'Aptitudes to work such Effect, in case convenient Objects were not wanting.' And pieces of gold have 'such a disposition of [their] Constituent Corpuscles' that, 'in case [they] we duely apply'd' to aqua regis, they *would* dissolve, whereas 'a Body of another Texture would not'. That is, they are such that *were* they immersed in aqua regis, they would dissolve. They are simply in the unfortunate situation of being in a world without aqua regis. But lack of aqua regis *plus* having the relevant true counterfactuals is sufficient, according to Boyle, for having *dispositive dissolvability in aqua regis*. So, how can you say that one of these pieces of gold has a dispositive quality (dispositive dissolvability in aqua regis) that the others lack? Either all the pieces have this dispositive quality or none of them do.

At first glance, there is some weight to this objection. Boyle, after all, *does* say the things quoted above, and it is true that the relevant counterfactuals are equally true of the pieces of gold in each of the worlds. Ultimately, however, I don't think this worry is detrimental to my interpretation of Boyle. I suggest that Boyle holds both that dispositive qualities are identical *in re* to a body's determinate mechanical affections—and in this "inappropriate" sense, both pieces

---

[64] In order to make the lute example relevant here, and not to attribute to Boyle an obvious confusion between having a quality and the manifestation of that quality, let us imagine that the lute is in a world in which there are no things that could play it. In this case, as with the other cases of dispositive qualities, the lute lacks *actual* in-tune-ness.

of gold will be dispositively dissolvable—*and* that (keeping the laws fixed) intrinsic duplicates can differ with respect to their dispositive qualities. Showing that Boyle holds the latter thesis and *how* he holds it will solve the problems stated earlier that dispositive qualities seem to pose for him.

Remember that Boyle thinks that there is a difference between a body actually having a quality and someone knowing that it has that quality. This can be due to many things, one of which is our ignorance of 'unheeded' or unknown relations. In the case of dispositive qualities, however, there are no such relations of which we could be ignorant. I want to suggest that in the case of dispositive qualities, there is not much of a difference between a body's having a dispositive quality and our knowing that it has that dispositive quality. That is, for Boyle dispositive qualities are simply mechanical affections known to behave in such-and-such a way in certain circumstances. Boyle says that a body has a dispositive quality when a relevant *relatum* is absent but when the body has 'such a disposition of its Constituent Corpuscles' such that it *would have* an actual quality if the relevant *relatum* existed. In this context, 'disposition' can only mean 'texture',[65] and texture is one of the mechanical affections of composite bodies. Given this, Boyle clearly thinks that dispositive qualities are identical *in re* to mechanical affections. But if that is right, then aren't dispositive qualities simply a body's determinate mechanical affections? Moreover, mechanical affections are both independent of and more fundamental than actual qualities.[66] So, isn't there a sense in which dispositive qualities would be more fundamental than and independent of actual qualities? Yes, in a sense, dispositive qualities are mechanical affections; but, no, they are not more fundamental than actual qualities even supposing that mechanical affections are more fundamental than actual qualities. Boyle, in a sense, identifies dispositive qualities with the mechanical affections, in particular the *texture* of a body (or a subset

---

[65] This is vindicated when Boyle says that 'a Body of another Texture would not' produce the same effect. But mostly noticeable is a passage we have already seen in which Boyle says that bodies with dispositive qualities are '*actually* [endowed] onely with those more Catholick Affections of Bodies, Figure, Motion, Texture, &c.'.

[66] They would be independent in the sense that it is possible for a body to have mechanical affections but no qualities; whereas it is impossible for a body to have qualities without mechanical affections. They would be more fundamental in the sense that, as Boyle repeatedly says, qualities 'flow from' and 'are deriv'd from' mechanical affections.

of the texture). As we have already seen, Boyle thinks that in the absence of relations, bodies would have only 'those more Catholick Affections of Bodies, Figure, Motion, Texture, &c.' (*Works*, v. 319). The mechanical affections are 'the Affections that belong to a Body, as it is consider'd in it self, without relation to *sensitive* Beings, or to other Natural Bodies' (*Works*, v. 334). Because dispositive qualities are had in the absence of a quality-constituting relation, they *could* be nothing else *in re* other than mechanical affections. Wouldn't we then say that a body, in virtue of the possibility of its having its mechanical affections prior to (or in the absence of) any actual relations, has all of its dispositive qualities? No. I suggest that, for Boyle, dispositive qualities are similar to *entia rationis*, i.e. they are identical *in re* to the mechanical affections, but prior to the observation of actual qualities, we cannot understand them to exist at all. Only in virtue of the observation of actual qualities of bodies can we understand what a body would do if the appropriate relation obtained. And, as we have seen, what a body would do in virtue of its mechanical affections if a certain relation obtained, *but which doesn't*, is just what we are talking about when we attribute a dispositive quality to it. Dispositive qualities and mechanical affections are thus identical *in re*; *in bodies*, the "ground" of dispositive qualities is the mechanical affections. Conceding this point, however, does not entail that *all there is* to dispositive qualities is mechanical affections. Boyle's dispositive qualities are, among other things, mechanical affections *known to behave in such-and-such a manner*. But because there are worlds in which this knowledge is absent or is present only after a certain time, but in which the relevant mechanical affections are present, dispositive qualities are not identical *simpliciter* to mechanical affections. Dispositive qualities are not a distinct *ontological or metaphysical* category. Dispositive qualities are, if you will forgive the scholastic language, *entia rationis* with a *fundamentum in re*, and their *fundamentum* is the mechanical affections.

If my interpretation is correct, then sense can be made of the pervasiveness of "reductive" passages in Boyle. For instance, Boyle says that the aperitive quality of the key is not 'distinct from the Figure'; the sensible qualities do not differ 'from the Matter its self, furnish'd with such a Determinate Bigness, Shape, or other Mechanical Affections' and 'there is in the Body, to which these Sensible Qualities are attributed, nothing of Real and Physical, but the Size, Shape, and Motion, or Rest of its component Particles, together with that Texture of the whole'; gold's dissolvability in aqua regis is 'not in the Gold any thing distinct from its peculiar Texture'; the poisonousness of the ground glass in the nuns' peas 'is really nothing distinct from the Glass its self ... as it is furnish'd with that determinate Bigness, and Figure of Parts, which have been acquir'd by Comminution'; the echo-producing quality of the cave 'is in It nothing else but the Hollowness of its Figure'.[67] These texts certainly make it appear as though *actual* qualities are nothing more than mechanical affections. We have seen, however, that Boyle clearly denies this. Taking a cue from O'Toole, I think that all that Boyle is saying here is that *in the body*, there *is* nothing more to a quality other than its mechanical affections. That does not mean that mechanical affections are all there is to qualities: a body's mechanical affections plus other bodies or perceivers, as we have seen, determine which actual relations it stands in, and only when it stands in an actual relation do qualities come to be. The same goes for dispositive qualities: because, by definition, dispositive qualities are had only in the absence of a relatum that would endow a body with an actual quality, they can be 'nothing in the body' other than its mechanical affections. But as with actual qualities, there is more to the story than just mechanical affections. The rest of the actual-qualities story (i.e. existence of a relevant relatum) cannot, however, be the rest of the story with dispositive qualities. Nevertheless, because of Boyle's "reductive" remarks about actual qualities, despite there being more to an actual quality than just what there is *in* the body, the fact that Boyle claims that dispositive qualities are identical *in re* to mechanical affections, it doesn't follow that dispositive qualities are nothing more than mechanical affections. It follows, just as it does with actual qualities, that the "something more" must be *extrinsic* to the body. In the case of actual qualities, the extrinsic feature is the relatum external to the body's mechanical affections; in the case of dispositive qualities, the extrinsic feature is our manner of thinking about the body's mechanical affections.

[67] The fact that Boyle sometimes says that these qualities are nothing 'real' in bodies other than mechanical affections, clearly indicates that they are not *qualitates reales*, as Anstey (*Boyle*) has pointed out. Nevertheless, these passages do seem to indicate a form of reductionism in Boyle.

I realize that Boyle never explicitly says that dispositive qualities are *entia rationis*. But he *does* explicitly hold that (*a*) dispositive qualities are identical *in re* to mechanical affections; (*b*) knowledge of qualities is the most important thing for natural philosophers; (*c*) this knowledge is had only when there is an observation of a manifestation of an actual quality. Dispositive qualities, therefore, carry more conceptual baggage than the mechanical affections. To see that Boyle believes that it is possible for *x* to involve a conceptual component that *y* lacks, even though *x* is identical *in re* to *y*, consider a precedent for this way of thinking in Boyle. Boyle, and Locke after him, hold a conventionalist account of essences, kinds, or species. I will discuss Boyle's theory of kinds shortly, but for now, we need only recognize one aspect of his theory. More often than not, both Boyle and Locke use the term "property" as a technical term from the Aristotelian five predicables: a property is a 'proprium', an attribute that is not part of the essence or definition of a species, but which is entailed by that essence or definition.[68] Boyle and Locke use this term in a slightly different manner to refer to any quality that is essential to a kind of thing or, derivatively, is essential to an individual in so far as it is a member of a certain kind. Boyle and Locke think that, for any kind or species, *we* decide, on the basis of observable similarities between individuals, which qualities will be included in the set of qualities necessary for inclusion in that kind or species.[69] A certain colour,[70] for instance, can be a quality at one time and a property at another; or it can be a quality of individuals of one kind and a property of individuals of another kind. Yellowness is a *quality* of some horses, but it is a *property* of gold.[71] Properties,

---

[68] Porphyry's *Isagoge* (in Paul Vincent Spade (tr. and ed.), *Five Texts on the Mediaeval Problem of Universals* (Indianapolis: Hackett, 1994), 10): a *proprium* is 'what occurs in the whole species, in it only, and always, as the capacity to laugh in man'. See also D. P. Henry, 'Predicables and Categories', in Norman Kretzmann, Anthony Kenny, and Jan Pinborg (eds.), *Cambridge History of Later Medieval Philosophy* (Cambridge: Cambridge University Press, 1982), 128–42.

[69] For detailed discussion of this issue in Locke, see Dan Kaufman, 'Locke on Individuation and the Corpuscular Basis of Kinds' ['Locke on Individuation'], *Philosophy and Phenomenological Research* (forthcoming).

[70] Colour is perhaps not the best example because there are scholars who think that colour is not a quality at all for Boyle or Locke. I believe they are right about Locke. However, the textual evidence that Boyle thinks that colours are qualities is overwhelming.

[71] '... and though an Accident can be but accidental to Matter, as it is a Substantial thing, yet it may be essential to this or that particular Body ... though Roundness is but

however, are *not* a new ontological category: they are simply *qualities-considered-in-a-certain-way*, namely as being essential to a kind. I think that Boyle's dispositive qualities are like Boylean–Lockean *propria*, in this respect: They are *mechanical-affections-considered-in-a-certain-way*. Of course, there are dissimilarities between the case of *propria* and the case of dispositive qualities. I merely wish to call attention to the fact that there are other aspects of Boyle's thought in which he embraces things that are identical *in re* despite being conceptually (and temporally) distinct. Just as a quality can be a property at one time but not at another time, so too can something be a mechanical affection at one time but a dispositive quality at another.[72]

Boyle is not, however, drawing metaphysical conclusions from epistemic considerations; he is not claiming that there is another genuine kind of qualities (dispositive qualities) based on what we know about actual qualities. Rather, dispositive qualities are simply the mechanical affections *considered in a certain way*. And because the way in which the mechanical affections must be considered in order to count as dispositive qualities requires observation of the manifestation of an actual quality, this conceptual component enters the scene *after* both the mechanical affections and the actual qualities which depend on the mechanical affections.

Direct evidence for my interpretation of Boyle is admittedly scarce, partly because Boyle doesn't discuss *what* dispositive qualities *are* in any great detail, and partly because my interpretation is based on inferences from his general method to a particular application of that method—an application that he does not explicitly make. However, in Boyle's own response to the chiefest difficulty, he says the following: 'if there were no Sensitive Beings, those Bodies that are *now* the Objects of our Senses, would be but *dispositively*, if I may so

Accidental to Brass, yet 'tis Essential to a Brasen Sphære; because, though the Brasse were devoid of Roundnesse, (as if it were Cubical, or of any other figure,) it would still be a Corporeal Substance, yet without that Roundness it could not be a Sphære' (*Works*, v. 324). Sometimes Boyle calls properties 'essential modifications': 'a *Modification*, because 'tis indeed but a Determinate *manner of Existence* of the Matter, and yet an *Essential Modification*, because that though the concurrent Qualities be but Accidental to Matter, (which with others instead of Them, would be Matter still,) yet they are *essentially necessary* to the Particular *Body*, which without those Accidents would not be a Body of that Denomination, as a *Mettal* or a *Stone*, but of some other' (*Works*, v. 334).

[72] This, of course, is not to say that a quality (or mechanical affection) ceases to be a quality (or mechanical affection) once it "becomes" a property (or dispositive quality).

speak, endow'd with Colours, Tasts, and the like' (*Works*, v. 319; first emphasis mine).[73] I take the reference to the bodies that are *now* the objects of our senses to indicate that Boyle thought that dispositive qualities are attributed on the basis of what is actually the case *now*. That is, given the way the world is now, a world in which snow is actually white and gold is actually dissolvable in aqua regis, we may, imagining perceivers and aqua regis to disappear, attribute dispositive qualities to snow and gold. In cases both of imagined counterfactual situations and of a no-longer-existing relatum, dispositive qualities are attributed on the basis of what is actually known to be the case in our world at the present time. Because snow has previously caused the sensation of whiteness in a perceiver, and because coal has previously melted wax, we are now in a position to say what *would* be the case if perceivers and wax ceased to exist *and* if (keeping the laws fixed) there never were perceivers or wax. In other words, we are now in a position to attribute a dispositive quality.

We have already seen that Boyle's theory of kinds provides a precedent for things that are conceptually distinct yet identical *in re* in his ontology. His theory of kinds, furthermore, provides additional evidence, *powerful* evidence, for my interpretation of the relationship between actual and dispositive qualities in Boyle. A close reading of Boyle's discussion of dispositive qualities reveals something quite important: he only mentions dispositive qualities as belonging to *kinds* of things or to individual members of a kind. (This is true even in the 'Excursion', as we will see.) When addressing the chiefest difficulty and explicitly discussing dispositive qualities, he speaks of the dispositive qualities of *snow*, *coal*, *soot*, and *pins* (*Works*, v. 317, 319). This may seem like a small matter, but it is important to our discussion because these are kinds, and Boyle is a conventionalist about kinds in much the same way as Locke after him.[74] The following passages are representative of Boyle's view of kinds:

---

[73] See *Works*, v. 321, where Boyle also emphasizes the importance of 'a World constituted as ours *now* is' (my emphasis).

[74] I cannot go into detail here, so the following will have to suffice for now: when I say that Boyle is a conventionalist about kinds I mean that he rejects both Aristotelian essences and qualitatively identical corpuscular arrangements in each member of a kind, and that he thinks that it is *we* who decide which of the many objective similarities between individuals are *properties* of a kind. For a detailed examination of Locke's account of kinds,

observing many Bodies to agree in being Fusible, Malleable, Heavy, and the like, they gave to that sort of Body the name of *Mettal*, which is a *Genus* in reference to Gold, Silver, Lead, and but a *Species* in reference to that sort of mixt Bodies they call *Fossilia* ... I observe that if (for Instance) You ask a Man, what Gold is, if he cannot shew you a piece of Gold, and tell You, This is Gold, he will describe it to You as a Body, that is extremely Ponderous, very Malleable and Ductile, Fusible and yet Fixt in the Fire, and of a Yellowish colour: and if You offer to put off to him a piece of Brass for a piece of Gold, he will presently refuse it, and (if he understand Mettals) tell You, that though Your Brass be coloured like it, 'tis not so heavy, nor so malleable, neither will it like Gold resist the utmost brunt of the Fire, or resist *Aqua Fortis*: And if You ask Men what they mean by a Ruby, or Niter, or a Pearl, they will still make You such Answers, that You may clearly perceive, that whatever Men talk in Theory of Substantial Forms, yet That, upon whose account they really distinguish any one Body from others, and refer it to this or that *Species* of Bodies, is nothing but an Aggregate or Convention of such Accidents, as most men do by a kind of Agreement (for the Thing is more Arbitrary than we are aware of) think necessary or sufficient to make a Portion of the Universal Matter belong to this or that Determinate *Genus* or *Species* or Natural Bodies. (*Works*, v. 322-3)

... an Aggregate or Convention of Qualities is enough to make the portion of Matter 'tis found in, what it is, and denominate it of this or that Determinate sort of Bodies ... For such a Convention of Accidents is sufficient to perform the Offices that are necessarily requir'd in what Men call a Forme, since it makes the Body such as it is, making it appertain to this or that Determinate Species of Bodies, and discriminating it from all other Species of Bodies whatsoever: as for Instance, Ponderousness, Ductility, Fixtness, Yellowness, and some other Qualities, concurring in a portion of Matter, do with it constitute Gold, and making it belong to that Species we call Mettals, and to that sort of Mettals we call Gold, do both denominate and discriminate it from Stones, Salts, Marchasites, and all other sorts of Bodies that are not

see Kaufman, 'Locke on Individuation'. It must also be noted that Boyle does sometimes talk about the *nature* of certain bodies apart from the collection of qualities we use to distinguish kinds. This may seem to indicate that he was more of a realist than he seems to be. However, in those passages, he uses the term "nature" to refer to its collection of mechanical affections, its "corpuscular microstructure", or *texture*, *not* to the kind or species to which an individual belongs. This is especially noticeable in 'An Introduction to the History of Particular Qualities', where Boyle mentions 'portions of Matter, of such a determinate nature or Texture' (*Works*, vi. 272). So, when he discusses the *nature* of a body, irrespective of the kind of which it is a member, he should be taken to mean its texture and nothing more.

Mettals, and from Silver, Brass, Copper, and all Metals except Gold. (*Works*, v. 324; see also v. 328, 332, 334–5; vi. 279)

On the basis of observable similarity of qualities between individuals, we pick out certain of the similar qualities as essential to the kind or species of thing to which individuals similar with respect to *those* qualities belong. After that the qualities (now *properties* with respect to the species) that belong to a kind is largely a matter of convention or 'a kind of Agreement'.[75]

Boyle's theory of kinds is lurking even in the lock and key example in the 'Excursion'. He carefully avoids calling the schlock a 'lock'; instead he says it 'was onely a Piece of Iron, contriv'd into such a Shape', and the key too 'was nothing but a Piece of Iron of such a Determinate Figure' (*Works*, v. 310).[76] But once the lock gains the aperitable quality, 'it became a Main part of the Notion and Description of a Lock'. The aperitable quality is now a *property* of the kind *Lock*. Likewise, when discussing the invention of a new menstruum that will partially dissolve and partially transmute gold, Boyle says, 'there will then arise another new Property, whereby to distinguish [gold] from other Mettals' (*Works*, v. 311). The use of the term "property" is very telling: here, as elsewhere, collections of properties are what distinguish individuals of one kind from individuals of another kind, and properties are qualities that are considered essential to a particular kind.

How does Boyle's theory of kinds support my interpretation of the relationship between actual and dispositive qualities and mechanical affections? Boyle attributes dispositive qualities only to *kinds* (or individual members of kinds), and kinds are formed by picking among similar actual qualities (and not merely actual qualities, because Boyle thinks that there are a huge number of *unobserved* qualities a body may have, but *observed* actual qualities), and then kinds are perpetuated by convention. It follows that nothing could be a member of a kind without having (or having had at some

[75] For a recent discussion of Boyle's theory of kinds, see Jan-Erik Jones, 'Boyle, Classification and the Workmanship of the Understanding Thesis', *Journal of the History of Philosophy*, 43 (2005), 171–83.

[76] Of course, *iron* is a kind, but it is not a kind that has the aperitable quality as a property. Boyle thinks that a quality of *x* can be merely a quality in so far as *x* is an F, but can be a property in so far as *x* is a G; see the quotation in n. 71.

time) actual qualities. And if dispositive qualities are had only by kinds or members of kinds, as Boyle's discussion of the chiefest difficulty indicates, then there are no dispositive qualities without there having been actual qualities. Once again, we see that, in Boyle, there is an asymmetrical dependence of dispositive qualities on actual qualities: something could have actual qualities without being a member of a kind at all; therefore, something could have actual qualities without dispositive qualities, whereas something could not have dispositive qualities without having or having had actual qualities.

CONCLUSION: ADDRESSING THE PROBLEMS

My interpretation of Boyle allows us to see that the three 'problems' presented earlier are not genuine problems for him. To say that dispositive qualities can do the work of actual qualities in natural philosophy is to say something that Boyle explicitly rules out, namely a priori reasoning in natural philosophy. Think about how we could possibly say that a body is dispositively F, given Boyle's method. We could only attribute dispositively-F on the basis of the observation of the manifestation of actually-F. Thus, there is no a priori attribution of dispositive qualities. The attribution of a dispositive quality depends on the prior observation of a manifestation of an actual quality. Actual qualities, then, are indispensable for dispositive qualities, but dispositive qualities are dispensable for actual qualities (see W_6). Therefore, dispositive qualities cannot render actual qualities dispensable to natural philosophy. Moreover, according to Boyle, an actual quality is had only when ARR is satisfied. If actual qualities are required for dispositive qualities, then Boyle's theory of relative qualities is unaffected and the attack on the scholastics' *qualitates reales* can go forward. Finally, given the dependence of dispositive qualities on actual qualities, the corpuscularian philosophy, which entails the relative nature of qualities, is unaffected.

I have attempted to show that Boyle can allow attributions of dispositive qualities without damage to his theory of relative qualities. Boyle's method rejects a priori reasoning in natural philosophy, and an attribution of dispositive whiteness to snow or dispositive heat to coal in the absence of observation of the manifestation of actual whiteness and actual heat would constitute the worst kind of a priori speculation a natural philosopher could embrace. Dispositive qualities are attributed only to kinds or members of kinds, and according to Boyle's theory of kinds, kinds cannot be formed without observation of the manifestation of actual qualities. I have also attempted to say something about *what* dispositive qualities are. Given that they cannot be anything *in re* other than mechanical affections, but that they are mechanical affections *known* to have behaved in certain ways, dispositive qualities are similar to *entia rationis* grounded in a body's mechanical affections. They are mechanical affections *considered* in a certain way. And the way they are considered depends on there being or having been actual qualities, and actual qualities have a relative nature—they must satisfy ARR. Therefore, Boyle's theory of relative qualities survives the admission of dispositive qualities.[77]

University of Colorado, Boulder

[77] An earlier and much shorter version of this chapter was given at the New England Colloquium in Early Modern Philosophy at Harvard. I wish to thank members of that audience, especially Justin Broackes, Don Garrett, Anja Jauernig, Martin Lin, and Alison Simmons, for their helpful comments. Thanks also to my colleagues Bob Pasnau and Rob Rupert, and to past students Andrew Alwood, Bryan Hall, and Derek Kern, for discussing the issues in this chapter with me. Thanks to the editors of *OSEMP*, Dan Garber and Steve Nadler, for their comments and suggestions. For miscellaneous help, I thank Michael Ben-Chaim and Jennifer McKitrick. Finally, thanks to Amy Weller and Sophie Charlotte Lovetron for creating an environment in which it was easy to devote so much time to Boyle.

7

Atomism, Monism, and Causation in the Natural Philosophy of Margaret Cavendish

KAREN DETLEFSEN

I. INTRODUCTION

In 1653 Margaret Cavendish published her first book, a book of poems (*Poems, and Fancies*), the first fifty pages of which are devoted to expounding an atomic theory of nature.

> Small *Atomes* of themselves a *World* may make,
> As being subtle, and of every shape:
> And as they dance about, fit places finde,
> Such *Formes* as best agree, make every kinde. ...
> Severall *Figur'd Atomes* well agreeing,
> When joyn'd, do give another *Figure* being.
> For as those *Figures* joyned, severall waies,
> The *Fabrick* of each severall *Creature* raise.[1]

Two years later, among the prefatory materials to the first edition of her more traditionally written *Philosophical and Physical Opinions* (hereafter *Opinions*) she includes a 'Condemning Treatise of Atomes' in which she abandons this earlier position. 'I have considered that if onely matter were atoms, and that every atome is of the same degree, and the same quantity, as well as of the same matter; then every atom must

---

[1] Margaret Cavendish, *Poems, and Fancies* [*PF*] (London, 1653; facs. repr. Menston: Scolar Press, 1972), 5, 9. Other abbreviations of frequently cited primary texts from Cavendish are as follows. *GNP*: *Grounds of Natural Philosophy* (London, 1668; facs. repr. West Cornwall, Conn.: Locust Hill Press, 1996); *NBW*: *New Blazing World*, 2nd edn. (1668), in Susan James (ed.), *Political Writings* (Cambridge: Cambridge University Press, 2003), 1–109; *ODS*: *Orations of a Divers Sort*, 2nd edn. (1668), in James (ed.), *Political Writings*, 111–292; *OEP*: *Observations upon Experimental Philosophy*, ed. Eileen O'Neill, 2nd edn. [based on the 1668 edn.] (Cambridge: Cambridge University Press, 2001); *PL*: *Philosophical Letters; or, Modest Reflections upon some Opinions in Natural Philosophy* (London, 1664); *PPO*: *Philosophical and Physical Opinions*, 2nd edn. (London, 1663).

be of a living substance ... for else they could not move, but would be an infinite dull and immoving body.' Furthermore, if atomism were the true account of the nature of matter, then 'there would be an infinite and eternal disorder' (I consider reasons for this latter belief in Sections 4 and 5).[2] From 1655 onwards, Cavendish's theory of matter would remain a theory of material plenism, the view that the world is everywhere and only matter which is extended infinitely and which can be internally divided without end. Cavendish rejects the existence of anything immaterial in the natural world (including souls); she believes that matter is ubiquitously sensing, rational, and self-moving (though there are many forms—both human and non-human—of sense and reason given the variety of nature's kinds; GNP 18); and she claims that nature's parts are completely interrelated into a single whole. For these reasons, her mature matter theory has, reasonably, been called 'organicist materialism',[3] and one essential feature of it is the fact that human and non-human nature are essentially the same sort of thing because composed of matter. Her rejection of atomism in favour of this latter account of material nature would be repeated with regularity throughout her mature work.

Despite Cavendish's own protestations against an atomic theory of matter, some commentators believe that she did not—or, more significantly for her philosophy, could not—drop atomism as the true account of the material world. Stephen Clucas, for example, believes that what Cavendish rejected was merely 'the simple mechanism of "classical mechanism"', according to which inert bits of matter interact by way of a few simple laws. She does not thereby reject all forms of atomism. Jay Stevenson thinks that she must be disingenuous in her rejections of atomism because one of her own arguments against atomism (Sections 3 to 5) rests upon the premiss of natural harmony,

---

[2] Margaret Cavendish, 'A Condemning Treatise of Atomes' *Philosophical and Physical Opinions*, ['Condemning Treatise'], in 1st edn. (London, 1655), A3ᵛ. This treatise was excised from the second edition of the *Opinions*, from which I usually quote in this chapter (see n. 1).

[3] Eileen O'Neill, 'Cavendish, Margaret Lucas', in *The Routledge Encyclopedia of Philosophy* (New York: Routledge, 1998), 260–4, at 260; and Eileen O'Neill, Introduction ['Introduction'], in *OEP*, pp. x–xxxvi, at p. xvi. For an account of why Cavendish believes all matter must have perceptive states, see my 'Reason and Freedom: Margaret Cavendish on the Order and Disorder of Nature' ['Reason and Freedom'], *Archiv für Geschichte der Philosophie* (forthcoming).

and yet Cavendish elsewhere repeatedly acknowledges examples of disharmony obtaining in the natural world (specifically in human psychology)—disharmony that one might argue is best explained by atomism.[4]

I think Cavendish's anti-atomistic account of the natural world can be vindicated against both Clucas's and Stevenson's positions. Cavendish has two main arguments against atomism which I call the 'logico-mathematical' argument and the 'normative' argument. While the former, grounded in the unending divisibility of matter, is the stronger of the two for establishing material plenism, the latter is clearly Cavendish's signature argument, and it is the most interesting for us given what it tells us about her overall philosophy of nature. According to the normative argument against atomism, atoms, as freely acting beings, would produce disorder in nature, and yet we experience nature as orderly, and this seems to preclude atomism as the correct theory of matter.

I deal first (Section 2) with the logico-mathematical argument in order to refute Clucas's claim that Cavendish actually does retain atomism beyond her early years. The logico-mathematical argument is all she needs to establish material plenism and to reject atomism as a theory of matter. I deal then (Sections 3 to 5) with the normative

---

[4] Stephen Clucas, 'The Atomism of the Cavendish Circle: A Reappraisal' ['Reappraisal'], *The Seventeenth Century*, 9/2 (1994), 260. Clucas seems slightly more swayed by Cavendish's anti-atomism in her *Observations* given her repudiation of a vacuum and her endorsement of the non-atomic nature of matter's parts in that book. But even here, he notes how material parts' interrelations 'recall atomic interactions' (p. 262). Jay Stevenson, 'The Mechanist–Vitalist Soul of Margaret Cavendish' ['Mechanist–Vitalist'], *Studies in English Literature*, 36 (1996), 536. Stevenson's concerns and approach are very different from my own. He believes that the persisting atomism in Cavendish's work is a reflection of Cavendish's conception of psychology, and that his disingenuous attempts to disguise her enduring atomism are in themselves informative of her psychological theories. I appeal to his article because he has identified what I take to be a real difficulty with Cavendish's atomism that (I believe) requires treatment if we are to make sense of her natural philosophy. Moreover, resolving this difficulty is also helpful in dealing with her monism and theory of occasional causation. So, while Stevenson's focus is on human psychology, mine is on her broader natural philosophy, though my conclusions have consequences for any part of nature, including her theory of psychology. In offering the following account of Cavendish's natural philosophy, I start from the assumption that Cavendish's philosophy is internally coherent, and I try to find that coherence. I take that guiding assumption to be anathema to Stevenson's overall project. Robert Hugh Kargon also thinks Cavendish is an atomist, but he seems to hold this belief because he focuses exclusively upon the *Poems*, the only book in which it is clear that Cavendish endorses atomism. Robert Hugh Kargon, *Atomism in England from Hariot to Newton* (Oxford: Clarendon Press, 1966), 73–6.

argument in order to refute Stevenson's claim that Cavendish would like to abandon atomism in her mature thought but cannot do so for reasons internal to her philosophy. The normative argument, I contend, is not directly about matter at all. Rather, it is about the free causal agency of individuals, and the argument is meant to establish prescriptions about normatively good behaviour among these individuals. They ought not to behave atomistically, distinct from all others as if not bound together by common norms.[5] Disorders, then, arise from free actions of individuals, whether those individuals belong to a material world composed of atoms or a plenum. An atomistic theory of *matter* is not necessary in order to account for disorders, *pace* Stevenson's claim. Yet, while the normative argument does not lead directly to a conclusion about the nature of matter, Cavendish clearly links this argument with a non-atomistic matter theory. So I show how she might use this argument to reach indirectly the conclusion that matter is a plenum and not atomistic. This leads us to a distinctive feature of her overall philosophy—that she often conceives of the non-human natural world in terms of the human, social world, which is explanatorily primary for her.

Understanding Cavendish's normative argument against atomism in this way also allows us to contrast her general philosophy of nature with that of Spinoza (Section 6), a valuable contrast to draw since her system resembles his in many striking ways.[6] Cavendish endorses a monistic conception of nature, but this is prima facie at odds with

[5] Anna Battigelli also notes this element of Cavendish's ideas on atomism: 'Cavendish's interest in atomism was less an interest in physical theories of matter than a fascination with a metaphor that served to explain political and psychological conflict ...' (Anna Battigelli, *Margaret Cavendish and the Exiles of the Mind* [*Exiles*], (Lexington: University Press of Kentucky, 1998), 49). See also, Emma L. E. Rees, *Margaret Cavendish: Gender, Genre, Exile* [*Gender*] (Manchester: Manchester University Press, 2003), 57. I agree with Battigelli and Rees on the normative element of Cavendish's concern with atomism, but she is also, I shall argue, interested in matter theory and the relation between matter and politics.

[6] I am not making a historical claim here. Cavendish and Spinoza were rough contemporaries, but Cavendish would not have been familiar with any of his work as she read only English, and none of his texts were translated into English during her lifetime. Rather, there are many points of conceptual affinity between the two, an insight made by Susan James. See 'The Philosophical Innovations of Margaret Cavendish' ['Innovations'], *British Journal for the History of Philosophy*, 7/2 (1999), 219. There are crucial differences between the two, and perhaps the principal one is the fact that Cavendish, but not Spinoza, believes that a transcendent, immaterial God exists. While she claims to bracket discussions of God in natural philosophy, leaving considerations of him to the theologians (e.g. *PL* 3, 142; *OEP* 217), she does occasionally appeal to God in order to make sense of the natural world; see

her theory of occasional causation. On the one hand, according to an especially robust conception (Spinoza's, for example), monism amounts to a belief that there is just one natural substance—the whole of infinitely extended nature—and this substance acts as the sole principal (and necessitating) cause of all effects. On the other hand, Cavendish's occasional theory of causation seems to require multiple finite individuals, each acting freely as a self-determining principal cause. Understanding the precise character of her normative argument against atomism allows us to see the limits of her monism such that her theory of occasional causation is preserved, and this shows that her philosophy of nature is unique in the seventeenth century, mimicking not even that of Spinoza, conceptually one of her closest contemporaries.

2. CAVENDISH'S LOGICO–MATHEMATICAL ARGUMENT AGAINST ATOMISM

Cavendish provides two key arguments against atomism in her corpus: what I call the normative argument (to be dealt with in the next three sections) and the logico-mathematical argument. The logico-mathematical argument against atomism depends upon Cavendish's

n. 37 below. For work on Cavendish's relations with others of her contemporaries, see the growing body of secondary literature on this, including Neil Ankers, 'Paradigms and Politics: Hobbes and Cavendish Contrasted', in Stephen Clucas (ed.), *A Princely Brave Woman: Essays on Margaret Cavendish, Duchess of Newcastle* (Aldershot: Ashgate, 2003), 242–54; Battigelli, *Exiles*; Jacqueline Broad, *Women Philosophers of the Seventeenth Century* [*Women Philosophers*] (Cambridge: Cambridge University Press, 2002), ch. 2; Sarah Hutton, 'In Dialogue with Thomas Hobbes', *Women's Writing*, 4/3 (1997), 421–32; Sarah Hutton, 'Anne Conway, Margaret Cavendish and Seventeenth-Century Scientific Thought', in Lynette Hunter and Sarah Hutton (eds.), *Women, Science and Medicine, 1500–1700: Mothers and Sisters of the Royal Society* (Phoenix Mill: Sutton, 1997), 218–34; Sarah Hutton, 'Margaret Cavendish and Henry More', in Clucas (ed.), *A Princely Brave Woman*, 185–98; James, 'Innovations', 219–44; Eve Keller, 'Producing Petty Gods: Margaret Cavendish's Critique of Experimental Science', *English Literary History*, 64 (1997), 447–71; O'Neill, 'Introduction', pp. x–xlvii; Lisa T. Sarasohn, '*Leviathan* and the Lady: Cavendish's Critique of Hobbes in the *Philosophical Letters*' ['*Leviathan* and the Lady'], in Line Cottegnies and Nancy Weitz (eds.), *Authorial Conquests: Essays on Genre in the Writings of Margaret Cavendish* (Madison, Wis.: Fairleigh Dickinson University Press, 2003), 40–58; Elisabeth Strauss, 'Organismus versus Maschine. Margaret Cavendish' Kritik am mechanistischen Naturmodell', in J. F. Maas (ed.), *Das Sichtbare Denken. Modelle und Modelhaftigkeit in der Philosophie und den Wissenschaften* (Amsterdam: Rodopi, 1993), 31–43; and Jo Wallwork, 'Old Worlds and New: Margaret Cavendish's Response to Robert Hooke's *Micrographia*', *Women's Writing 1550–1750*, 18/1 (2001), 191–200.

rejection of a vacuum or empty space as logically inconceivable—what is not anything cannot exist (e.g. *PL* 452)—together with her implicit mathematical belief in the infinite divisibility of matter. For example: 'there can be no atom, that is, an indivisible body in nature; because whatsoever has body, or is material, has quantity; and what has quantity, is divisible' (*OEP* 125; cf. 263); the 'Nature of a Body ... is, to be divisible. ... it is impossible for a Body ... to be indivisible' (*GNP* 239). There cannot exist natural minima, therefore, because no part of matter is physically distinct from the rest of nature owing to empty space separating that part from all others. Furthermore, Cavendish rejects empty space *beyond* nature too (*OEP* 130–1). Nature as a whole is not an atom either, therefore, because it is not a material minimum; it is spatially infinite. And within the infinitely extended material plenum, no single part is indivisible, and so no single part is a minimum unit. In spite of the strength of this argument, based on the mathematical premiss that matter always has quantity and so is always divisible, Clucas maintains that we cannot interpret Cavendish as rejecting atomism. He challenges the anti-atomism interpretation of her later philosophy along at least two fronts. First, Cavendish actually 'accepts, for example, that matter is not infinitely divisible', thus allowing for natural minima, or atoms. Second, atomism in the seventeenth century is not a single category, and it is really only 'the simple mechanism of "classical atomism"' that Cavendish rejects.[7]

It is true that Cavendish occasionally denies the infinite divisibility of matter: 'one part cannot be either infinitely composed, or infinitely divided' (*PL* 158). Two things can be said in the face of such passages. First, there are at least as many passages (such as the two cited above) in which Cavendish asserts the divisibility of matter as long as it is extended. This fact, together with the fact that matter is partly defined by quantity of extension, means matter will be divisible no matter how small it gets, and this is tantamount to infinite divisibility. Cavendish herself recognizes that she is not always unequivocal in her writings, but her equivocations seem to be partly due to her actively working through and developing her thoughts on paper.

---

[7] Clucas, 'Reappraisal', 259 ff. For a historical account of atomism that displays the complexity of the doctrine, see Andrew Pyle, *Atomism and its Critics: Problem Areas Associated with the Development of Atomic Theory of Matter from Democritus to Newton* (Bristol: Thoemmes Press, 1995).

'An Argumental Discourse' in her *Observations upon Experimental Philosophy* (*OEP* 23–42; hereafter *Observations*), and the weighing of opposing positions against each other in *Orations of Divers Sorts*, are just two obvious examples of this process transparently at work in her corpus. Most often, however, a settled position on a given topic can be found in Cavendish, often when she herself offers elucidations and corrections of past views in light of more careful thought. 'An Explanation of Some obscure and doubtful passages occurring in the Philosophical Works, hitherto published by the Authoresse' included in the early pages of the first edition of the *Observations* (though excised from the later) is a classic example.[8] If we take her philosophy to be maturing, then we should take the infinite divisibility of matter to be her settled position since the passage against this position that Clucas cites, and the only others that I have found, are from her 1664 *Philosophical Letters* (hereafter *Letters*) or earlier, while those favouring infinite divisibility appear in 1666 and later.

Second, more substantially, a close study of the passages in the *Letters* that seem to deny matter's infinite divisibility shows that it is not clear that this is what Cavendish is actually doing in those passages. Rather, she seems to be doing two different things. First, she seems to be denying that an *actual* infinite division can occur if a body also happens to be compounded into a finite unity: 'the Compositions hinder the Divisions in Nature, and the Divisions the Compositions' (*PL* 51; cf. 158). This seems to be a point about what is actual rather than possible, and the tendency of matter to compound into finite beings hinders the tendency of matter to divide without limit, but this does not preclude the infinite divisibility of matter. Second, she is comparing the parts of nature to nature as a whole, and she says that the whole of nature, as infinite, is infinitely divisible, but the parts of nature, as finite, cannot be infinitely divisible. '... for infinite composition and division belong onely to the Infinite body of Nature, which being infinite in substance may also be infinitely divided, but ... a finite and single part' cannot be infinitely divided (*PL* 158). How so? Cavendish seems to think that a body that is infinitely divisible has infinitely many parts, and that this, in turn, means that the body itself is infinitely large. This can be said of nature as a whole only, but not of a finite part within nature. She

[8] Margaret Cavendish, *Observations upon Experimental Philosophy* (London, 1666), 45–68.

is wrong, of course, that a body with infinite parts must be infinitely large. As the infinitesimal calculus would eventually prove, as long as the infinite parts are infinitely small, the composition will be finite. But Clucas is wrong to believe that what Cavendish denies in these passages is that matter can be divided without end. I think Cavendish *does* believe that matter is divisible without end, and this is in accord with her later claims that 'whatsoever … is material, has quantity; and what has quantity, is divisible' (*OEP* 125), together with her belief that 'Nature … is material; and if material, it has a body; and if a body, it must needs have a bodily dimension; and so every part will be an extended part' (*PL* 158). And so every part, no matter how small, is divisible.

The second reason Clucas gives for endorsing the atomistic interpretation of Cavendish's later philosophy—that Cavendish rejects only mechanical atomism and not all forms of atomism—also has some textual support. After all, in the 'Condemning Treatise' from which I quoted at the outset of this chapter, Cavendish does seem to imply that if every atom were 'a living substance', at least some of the difficulty with (classical, mechanical) atomism would be alleviated. Thus, Clucas believes that Cavendish

retains a residual attachment to the broad principle of atomic structure. Her objections, it seems, are to the idea of *mechanical* atomism. She cannot accept that the collision and chance motion of atoms 'fleeing about as dust and ashes, that are blown about with winde' can account for the orderly composition of the material fabric of nature, with its 'undissolvable Laws' and 'fixt decrees'. Chance collisions, she felt, could only produce 'wandring and confused figures' and 'eternal disorder'.[9]

Clucas here takes the fact that nature is orderly and harmonious to establish that Cavendish may need a 'vitalist' conception of nature to explain this fact, with vitalism understood as a theory that attributes life, sense, and reason to matter. It seems especially crucial that nature be supposed to possess such features given that Cavendish also believes we can make no appeals to God in our natural investigations, and so one obvious source of order is precluded from natural explanations (*PL* 3, 201–11). Thus, while Cavendish rejects the non-teleological, chance-based mechanical atomism, Clucas believes that she is still an

---

[9] Clucas, 'Reappraisal', 261. Clucas here quotes Cavendish, 'Condemning Treatise', A3ᵛ.

atomist, and 'Cavendish's atomism is a synthesis of materialism and vitalism.'[10] Still, given what I believe is a necessary commitment to the infinite divisibility of matter, Cavendish's arguments against atomism must be at least rejections of material units as *minima naturalia*.[11] But since this is a sufficient condition for atomism, her logico-mathematical argument is decisive in establishing the impossibility of any form of material atomism whatsoever. Thus, we can reasonably conclude that Cavendish's matter theory is one of a living, sensing, reasoning material plenum, rather than perceptive atoms.

It seems that the job is done and that the non-atomistic conclusion is reached. But while Cavendish certainly appeals to the logico-mathematical refutation of atomism, she clearly favours the normative argument which appears with notable frequency. Given this, and given that I think this latter argument tells us a great deal about her philosophy of nature in general, I now consider that argument in order to determine just what role it plays in Cavendish's philosophy.

3. CAVENDISH'S NORMATIVE ARGUMENT AGAINST ATOMISM

I call Cavendish's second argument against atomism her normative argument because it is based on the assumption of norms or standards in nature. Specifically, it is premised on the beliefs that there is a standard of order or harmony, and that perversions from this standard cause true disorders and can rightly be denounced.[12] There are two crucial assumptions in this argument that must be borne in mind throughout this discussion. First, there are objective norms, distinct from human convention and from our subjective beliefs that there are norms.[13]

[10] Clucas, 'Reappraisal', 261–2.

[11] For further scepticism (in light of Cavendish's own texts) about Clucas's claim that she retains atomism, see also Broad, *Women Philosophers*, 43.

[12] My full reasons for calling this a 'normative' argument will come clear in Sections 4 and 5 below.

[13] I argue elsewhere for how Cavendish might convincingly attribute objective norms and standards to the natural world such that we might consider some events (e.g. civil war, disease) to be true perversions and not just apparent perversions, erroneously believed to be true perversions by humans with a particular, subjective, and finite perspective. For the purposes of this chapter, I simply grant that Cavendish is entitled to this assumption. See my 'Reason and Freedom'.

Second, Cavendish thus recognizes that there are true perversions from these norms. There are real disorders and disharmonies in nature. These are not merely our finite way of perceiving events in the natural world that are, from an infinite perspective, perfectly orderly. So, for example, she says that there is an overall law of peace and order that nature as a single, principal cause imposes upon her parts: 'I say Nature hath but One Law, which is a wise Law, *viz.* to keep Infinite matter in order, and to keep so much Peace, as not to disturb the Foundation of her Government: for though Natures actions are various ... yet those active Parts, being united in one Infinite body, cannot break Natures general Peace' (*PL* 146).[14] While this is rather vague, we may reasonably take it as a claim about nature's overall plan to impose order through, for example, laws (or, at least, through regularities). Another example of nature's norms is that nature as a whole dictates what natural kinds or species will be found among her natural parts—natural kinds that are defined by their figure or shape and that (as universals) are eternal (*OEP* 197, 202–3; *GNP* 234–5). Perversions from nature's kinds are monsters (*OEP* 240), natural beings behaving in an 'irregular' fashion leads to diseases (*PL* 408–9), and individuals can sin thus rightfully incurring God's punishment (*PL* 348–50). These examples presuppose the existence of norms independent of human conventions, and they indicate that finite individuals can diverge from these norms.

Here is one textual example of the normative argument: 'were there a vacuum ... a piece of the world would become a single particular world, not joining to any part besides itself; which would make a horrid confusion in nature, contrary to all sense and reason' (*OEP* 129; cf. 169, 207–8; *GNP* 4).[15] Taking a piece of the world that becomes 'a single particular world' as an atom, this argument can, for now,

---

[14] This is a troublesome passage for Cavendish, and for reasons that become clear in Section 4 below. See n. 23.

[15] Cavendish here notes the natural confusion that would be spawned not just if atomism were true, but also if there were vacua. On this point, she is in accord with several late medieval and Renaissance commentators on and promulgators of Aristotle, many of whom believe that the existence of vacua would sunder the love and union found among material bodies in a plenum. Toletus and the Coimbrans are notable examples. See e.g. Charles Schmitt, 'Experimental Evidence for and against a Void: The Sixteenth-Century Arguments', *Isis*, 58 (1967), 352–66; and Edward Grant, *Much Ado about Nothing: Theories of Space and Vacuum from the Middle Ages to the Scientific Revolution* (Cambridge: Cambridge University Press, 1981).

be concisely stated thus: if atomism were true, then there would be only disorder in the natural world; but experience makes clear that the natural world is orderly; and so atomism cannot be true.

The assumption that atomism would result in disorder is unfounded, and it is especially suspect in light of the atomism of some of those in her immediate intellectual circle. Gassendi, for example, locates the ultimate source of the motion of atoms in God, thus ensuring order and harmony against the disorder that Cavendish assumes will befall the atomist's picture of nature (*Opera*, i. 337A).[16] Indeed, questioning the first premiss is precisely the second point I attribute to Clucas: Cavendish might refute her own normative argument against atomism simply by recognizing the viability of forms of atomism *other than* mechanical atomism together with its premiss of the chance encounter of passive, non-perceptive minimum material units. That is, it is not atomism that causes problems. Rather, the concern is with the chance-ladenness of bits of matter moving through space and aimlessly colliding. Moreover, Cavendish herself seems to concur, for she occasionally seems to believe that atomism would be acceptable as long as the atoms are perceptive: 'there can be no regular motion, without knowledge, sense and reason: and therefore those who are for atoms, had best to believe them to be self-moving, living and knowing bodies, for else their opinion is very irrational' (*OEP* 129). We get a similar suggestion when she challenges Epicurus' natural explanations: 'nor is this visible world, or any part of her, made by chance, or a casual concourse of *senseless and irrational* atoms' (*OEP* 264; my emphasis; cf. *OEP* 168–9). Thus, the normative argument would need to be more specific, with the first premiss reflecting Clucas's claim that only certain forms of atomism are inadequate for explaining nature's harmony and order: if nature were comprised of *non-rational, non-sensing* atoms, then there would be only disorder in the natural world; but experience makes clear that the natural world is orderly; and so *this specific form* of atomism cannot be true. But then the normative argument does not preclude all forms of atomism.

Cavendish, however, also goes further, rejecting even a form of atomism like the one that Clucas suggests. Even on the supposition

---

[16] Cavendish would reject Gassendi's account on the basis of our ignorance of God's nature and the precise relation between him and the world (e.g. *PL* 139, 141, 186–7; *OEP* 17), and this might account for the underlying assumption in her argument.

of 'self-moving, living and knowing' atoms, order would be wanting. Seemingly on any atomist thesis, nature would not

> be able to rule those wandering and straggling atoms, because they are not parts of her body, but each is a single body by itself, having no dependence upon each other. Wherefore, if there should be a composition of atoms, it would not be a body made of parts, but of so many whole and entire single bodies, meeting together as a swarm of bees. The truth is, every atom being single, must be an absolute body by itself, and *have an absolute power and knowledge*, by which it would become a kind of deity; and the concourse of them would rather cause a confusion, than a conformity in nature; because, all atoms being absolute, they would all be governors, but none would be governed. (*OEP* 129; my emphasis)[17]

As this passage makes clear, there is something about atomism *per se* that invites disorder. Even a form of atomism in which the atoms have 'power and knowledge'—atoms that are *not* inert and irrational—cannot avoid this outcome.

This brings us to Stevenson's reason for believing Cavendish must be an atomist. He writes:

> She ... disguise[s] her philosophy, claiming disingenuously to have revised her old views. ... Her retraction [of atomism] should not be taken at face value because the problem of [*absolute individuals*] hardly agreeing [in their actions—which Cavendish recognizes actually happens] is precisely what Cavendish's atomistic philosophy explains so well. In spite of her promise to theorize a more stable cosmic order. ... [the] essential features of her philosophy—the physicality, *autonomy*, and reflexivity of thinking things ... are preserved.[18]

According to Stevenson, the second premiss of the normative anti-atomism argument as presented above is denied by Cavendish herself elsewhere in her writings. Cavendish clearly allows that the world seems to be at least partly comprised of absolute individuals acting autonomously and therefore not in accord with stable cosmic norms. Cavendish herself frequently discusses cases of disorders which she

---

[17] It is unfortunate that Cavendish here chose a swarm of bees as the simile for a material world composed of atoms since a hive of bees when governed by a queen is an ideal natural model of a hierarchically organized society. See e.g. Thomas D. Seeley, *The Wisdom of the Hive: The Social Physiology of Honey Bee Colonies* (Cambridge, Mass.: Harvard University Press, 1995); and Charles D. Michener, *The Social Organization of Bees: A Comparative Study* (Cambridge, Mass.: Harvard University Press, 1974).

[18] Stevenson, 'Mechanist–Vitalist', 536; my emphases.

takes to be true perversions from objective, human-independent norms: humans' disorderly behaviour in, for example, civil wars (*NBW* 75; *ODS* 135–6) and the disharmonious behaviour of various organic parts leading to diseases in living bodies (e.g. *PPO* 43–4; *PL* 408–9; *GNP* 157–8) are two of her favourite examples. The natural world (both human and non-human) is *not* orderly and harmonious, or at least, it is not ubiquitously so. But since atomic individuals will, according to Cavendish, act in a disorderly fashion, then it is possible that the disorders that we do experience (and that she acknowledges are true of the world) are a result of the fact that atomism obtains. This conclusion holds on either version of atomism currently under consideration: disorder could arise either from non-perceptive atoms moving without an intelligent guide, or from rational atoms moving autonomously according to their own reasons that do not accord with the reasons of other atoms.

In sum, we can represent Cavendish's normative argument as follows: (1) if any form of atomism were a true account of matter, even a form according to which atoms are perceptive and self-moving, then disorder in the natural world would ensue; (2) the natural world is orderly; (3) therefore, no form of atomism is a true account of matter. In the spirit of Clucas's general approach, we can ask why we should accept the first premiss. That is, why would a form of atomism in which atoms have sense and reason result in disorder, while a material plenum of sensing, reasoning, and infinitely divisible matter would not result in disorder? Stevenson explicitly reminds us that the second premiss is denied by Cavendish herself. We can ask how, if at all, Cavendish might account for the fact that not all natural events are orderly and harmonious while still rejecting atomism as a theory of matter (and thus as a plausible explanation for the disharmony). To make sense of Cavendish's normative argument in the face of these serious criticisms, we need to revisit precisely what it is that she is trying to establish with the normative argument.

4. REINTERPRETING THE NORMATIVE ANTI-ATOMISM ARGUMENT: THE SECOND PREMISS

I believe that Cavendish's normative argument against atomism is considerably more sophisticated and interesting than presented in the previous section, and, in its sophisticated form, it avoids the criticisms sketched above. I offer an interpretation of this sophisticated argument in this and the following section. Crucially, the following interpretation is not systematically laid out in Cavendish's work itself, but there is textual evidence for many aspects of it, and it makes sense to interpret her philosophy in this light given that it brings disparate parts of her thought together into a conceptually coherent whole. So the following should be taken in the spirit of creative reconstruction of a position that we may fairly attribute to Cavendish (and, moreover, which I believe Cavendish would accept).

Cavendish's normative argument against atomism is based upon a specific method. She starts by observing effects, and she then speculates about the causes of them. Specifically, she starts with the observation that the natural world is orderly (these are the empirically known effects), and so the cause that gives rise to that order cannot be atomism (for reasons soon to be made clear). Yet as her own discussion of wars and diseases (for example) indicates, the effects we observe in nature are *not* all orderly, but there are disorderly perversions of norms, so we must find a cause that is capable of explaining both the fact that nature is, by and large, harmonious and the fact that it is sometimes not so. To identify this cause of both orderly and disorderly natural effects, we must first consider both Cavendish's account of freedom and her account of natural individuals.

Cavendish endorses a libertarian account of freedom, according to which finite material parts of the natural world, having both self-motion and reason, are capable of determining their own actions conforming to their own reasons, rather than being determined to act in a specific way by something extrinsic to them. At the same time, finite material parts do not thereby necessarily act without reference to other material parts, precisely because they are rational. Finite parts may consent to the rational suggestions made to them by other parts to behave in certain ways. A great deal can be said about Cavendish's theory of freedom and its relation to her theory of rational matter, especially in light of the debate between Hobbes and John Bramhall on necessity and freedom of the will. Indeed, the initial discussion between Hobbes and Bramhall occurred in the Cavendish household the year Margaret wed William Cavendish (1645), and it is likely that Cavendish knew the general positions of that debate.

For our purposes, however, we need only recognize that she does attribute such freedom to material parts: 'if man (who is but a single part of nature) hath given him by God the power and a free will of moving himself, why should not God give it to Nature?' (*PL* 95). Notice, that while Cavendish assimilates the human and nature (*OEP* 49), she does not thereby believe that the human is causally necessitated in the way that we generally think nature is, and, on this point, she disengages materialism and determinism, endorsing the former while still rejecting the latter. And so, the converse holds: we assimilate nature to how we think of humans, and no part of nature is necessitated (*OEP* 109).[19] Cavendish's belief that all parts of nature in and of themselves are free implies that nature *as a whole* does not causally determine its parts, and Cavendish says explicitly that nature therefore does not have knowledge of the future actions of its parts: 'That by reason every Part [of nature] had Self-motion, and natural Free-will, Nature [as a whole] could not foreknow how they would move ...' (GNP 102). This implies that the freedom she attributes to finite parts is a freedom that permits of the ability to act differently from how they actually will act; it implies, to reiterate, a libertarian conception of freedom. This is why nature as a whole with infinite wisdom cannot foreknow the actions of its parts.[20]

But what are these finite individuals that can act as libertarian free agents on Cavendish's account? Cavendish indicates that finite individuals obtain in nature when a portion of infinite matter takes on a specific figure or material shape, maintains that shape by its parts having a special natural affinity or sympathy for one another (e.g. *PL* 292), and thus becomes a natural individual within the whole of active matter, an individual whose parts conspire together towards

[19] Lisa T. Sarasohn notes the parity between Cavendish and Hobbes on their likening of human nature to the rest of nature, and Sarasohn also notes Cavendish's exalting of animals in contrasted with Hobbes's lowering of the human. Sarasohn, '*Leviathan* and the Lady', 49–50. It should be noted that it is not just animals that Cavendish 'exalts' but all of non-human nature. This is because, as Sarasohn points out, Cavendish asserts 'a principle of freedom in its [the universe's] very constitution' (p. 45). Sarasohn's article is informative on Cavendish's theory of freedom, though Sarasohn's primary interest is with a comparison and contrast between Cavendish's and Hobbes's political views as opposed to my interest with Cavendish's matter theory and natural philosophy, together with the political background to these aspects of her thought.

[20] I deal with Cavendish's position on freedom and how this relates to her theory of rational matter in my 'Reason and Nature'.

the common goal of remaining unified and rationally reacting to other beings in its environment. Each finite individual has its own capacity to move itself owing to the fact that it has its own share of moving matter, and it moves itself according to its own sense and reason (e.g. *OEP* 207). There is really only one whole—all of infinite nature—and what we think are finite wholes within nature are actually just temporarily stable figures, causally contributing at least in part to their own endurance, unity, and stability. Finite individuals are temporary centres of sense, reason, and self-motion. She writes:

for as there is infinite nature, which may be called general nature, or nature in general, which includes and comprehends all the effects and creatures that lie within her, and belong to her, as being parts of her own self-moving body; so there are also particular natures in every creature, which are the innate, proper and inherent interior and substantial forms and figures of every creature, according to their own kind or species. ... and these particular natures are nothing else but a change of corporeal figurative motions, which make this diversity of figures. (*OEP* 197)

Precisely because these finite individuals are centres of reason and self-motion, they can freely choose to respond rightly to the rational suggestion of other finite parts to behave in accordance with nature's overarching order—thus explaining natural order—or they may freely choose to respond in a way that disrupts this order—thus explaining natural disorder.

A difficulty comes about when we try to reconcile Cavendish's belief in radically free, finite parts that have the power to act in a disorderly, irregular fashion with passages such as this:

it is more easier, in my opinion, to know the various effects in Nature by studying the Prime cause, then by the uncertain study of the inconstant effects to arrive to the true knowledge of the prime cause; truly it is much easier to walk in a Labyrinth without a Guide, then to gain a certain knowledge in any one art or natural effect, without Nature her self be the guide, for Nature is the onely Mistress and *cause of all*. (*PL* 284; my emphasis)

That is, precisely because nature is the one, single whole individual, how does Cavendish preserve the freedom of finite parts against the causal necessitarianism of, for example, Spinoza's account of nature?

Help in easing this difficulty can be found by probing further the issue of freedom, and we can turn to the Hobbes–Bramhall debate for this help. I do not mean to indicate that Cavendish was directly influenced by specific elements of that debate (though she might well have been—after all, the debate took place in her husband's household around the time he and Cavendish wed), and so I am not making a historical claim.[21] Rather, I think that a solution implicit in Cavendish's system is explicit in the Hobbes–Bramhall debate, and examining that solution first in its explicit form is helpful for then locating it in Cavendish's philosophy. In his response to Bramhall's *Discourse of Liberty and Necessity*, Hobbes confesses a lack of understanding of Bramhall's distinction between moral and natural efficacy (*EW* iv. 247) when it comes to God's acting upon the human will. Bramhall clarifies:

> the will is determined naturally when God Almighty ... does ... concur by a special influence, and infuse[s] something into the will ... whereby the will is moved and excited and applied to will or choose this or that. Then the will is determined morally when some object is proposed to it with persuasive reasons and arguments to induce it to will. Where the determination is natural, the liberty to suspend its act is taken away from the will; but not so where the determination is moral. In the former case, the will is determined extrinsically, in the latter intrinsically.[22]

Adjusting this picture to Cavendish's theory of nature, we can think of the causal relation between nature as a whole (as opposed to God, as for Bramhall) and all of nature's sensing, rational parts (as opposed to just human wills, as for Bramhall) as potentially having two aspects: the whole of nature might have natural efficacy with respect to its

---

[21] Nonetheless, Cavendish had unusual access to the thought of Hobbes, even given the fact that she could not read any of his work not written in English. She did meet him while they were both in exile in Paris, and her husband and his brother Charles were tutored by Hobbes in the early 1630s. Margaret herself discussed metaphysics and natural philosophy extensively with her husband and brother-in-law—the conversations with her brother-in-law taking place primarily while the two were in England during several months in 1651–2 attempting to secure family property. Between her first-hand acquaintance with Hobbes and his work and second-hand knowledge through conversations with those friendly to her philosophical ambitions, she may well have been knowledgeable about his ideas on freedom. For details on Cavendish's life and acquaintances, see recent intellectual biographies by Anna Battigelli, Emma Rees, and Katie Whitaker: Battigelli, *Exiles*; Rees, *Gender*; and Katie Whitaker, *Mad Madge: The Extraordinary Life of Margaret Cavendish, Duchess of Newcastle, the First Woman to Live by her Pen* (New York: Basic Books, 2002).

[22] John Bramhall, *A Defence of True Liberty from Antecedent and Extrinsecall Necessity* (London, 1655); facs. repr. with introd. G. A. J. Rogers (London: Thoemmes, 1996), 171, 57–8.

parts, and nature might have moral efficacy with respect to its parts. Now, according to a necessitarian interpretation of nature, nature as a single whole exercises both natural and moral efficacy over its parts which are, to recall, merely effects of the principal cause that is all of nature. To be naturally or physically efficacious over its parts, nature as a whole presumably determines, from the top down, the precise quantity, direction, and so forth, of motion, thus determining each part's individual actions which would be mere effects and not causes. This sort of determination is precisely the source of Cavendish's problem because, if this were true of nature's relationship to its parts, then the libertarian account of freedom would be impossible, and yet she clearly wants such freedom for finite natural parts.

To preserve this freedom, we need to deny that nature is sole principal cause in this natural, physical sense. Rather, we must take finite individuals to be principal causes in the sense of being naturally or physically efficacious of their own actions. Cavendish certainly allows for this given her conception of finite individuals as rational centres of self-motion—stable, material figures that have consolidated their own motive power and share of reason so as to do physically the bidding of reasons they give to themselves for their action. So, nature as a whole is not the principal natural or physical cause of individual's free actions. There is a second possible way that it can act efficaciously towards its parts: it can act as morally efficacious cause. In exercising moral efficacy over its parts, nature simply proposes 'persuasive reasons' to induce the parts to move themselves in specific ways. Indeed, Cavendish does seem to attribute this sort of efficacy to nature as a whole. Nature has infinite wisdom (*GNP* 11) by which she knows and orders her parts (*PL* 8–9), and this order takes the form of a single, overall law of peace (*PL* 146), as well as the form of prescribing that certain natural kinds obtain (*OEP* 197). But, again learning from Bramhall, nature as a whole, acting as morally efficacious cause, does not necessitate nature's parts. It simply tries to persuade natural parts to respond in a specific way. Furthermore, nature's finite parts also act as morally efficacious causes (in addition to being physically or naturally efficacious) because they are self-motivated (intrinsically motivated) to act according to their own rational response to the rational suggestion given to them by nature as a whole (or by other parts within nature as a whole) to act in a specific fashion.

Making this distinction between natural (physical) and moral efficacy, attributing moral efficacy to the whole of nature, and attributing
both moral and natural efficacy to nature's finite parts, thus preserves
libertarian freedom and provides an explanation for the brute, experienced facts of disorder amid a general orderliness of nature. Making
this distinction accounts for libertarian freedom by allowing that finite
parts' actions are intrinsically generated and follow from reasons that
those finite parts give to themselves, and these reasons may or may
not accord with the rational suggestion to act in specific ways made to
them by other finite parts or the whole of nature. And the distinction
between natural and moral efficacy permits an explanation of disorders
by saying that they are the result of finite parts refusing to abide by
proper reasons given to them to act in an orderly fashion. Thus (as
suggested by Stevenson's concern), Cavendish says repeatedly that
nature in general may be orderly and harmonious, but there are still
some disorders in nature that come from the parts refusing to abide
by nature's overarching order.

... some [various motions in Nature] are Regular, some Irregular: I mean
Irregular as to particular Creatures, not as to Nature her self, for Nature
cannot be disturbed or discomposed, or else all would run into confusion;
Wherefore Irregularities do onely concern particular Creatures, not Infinite
Nature; and the Irregularities of some parts may cause the Irregularities of
other Parts. ... And thus according as Regularities and Irregularities have
power, they cause either Peace or War, Sickness or Health ... to particular
Creatures or parts of Nature ... (*PL* 238–9; cf. 279–80, 344–5; *OEP* 13,
33–4)[23]

---

[23] There is a tension between the implication here that there are irregularities in nature
due to the power or actions of parts, and the passage cited near the start of Section 3 which
says that the 'active Parts, being united in one Infinite body, cannot break Natures general
Peace' (*PL* 146). The former indicates that the parts can cause irregularities that violate
nature's peace while the latter indicates otherwise. One way of easing the tension is to say
that parts may well be irregular and may therefore cause less than peaceful actions within
nature, but this does not undermine nature's general order, which, prescriptively, remains
the same and which nature as a whole continues to suggest to its parts. Moral efficacy works
from the top down with nature suggesting a correct course of action to the parts, and it
works from part to part with one finite part suggesting a course of action to another finite
part. But the parts do not determine the whole *morally*, for nature as a whole continues to
prescribe the same general peace to all its parts, orderly and unruly alike.

Jacqueline Broad discusses the teleological character of Cavendish's philosophy, and by
this, Broad seems to mean an approach that takes the world to be orderly and harmonious

So Stevenson's concerns about the second premiss of the argument can be put to rest without forcing an atomistic account of matter onto Cavendish. Finite individuals as stable figures within a material plenum can be the source of both nature's general order and particular disorders. It is not necessary to call upon atomism to explain the latter. Indeed, when denying the truth of the second premiss in the normative argument (that is, when denying nature's ubiquitous harmony), this merely opens the possibility of atomism. It does not necessitate its truth. And indeed, as just presented, there is another way of accounting for these disorders within a non-atomistic account of matter.

Nonetheless, continuing to bracket the decisiveness of the logico-mathematical argument, atomism is still possible. Moreover, as is implicit in the first premiss of the normative argument, Cavendish herself associates the normative argument with a conclusion about matter theory. So we should probe further by focusing now on that first premiss. Why should we believe that if any form of atomism were a true account of matter, even a form according to which atoms are perceptive and self-moving, disorder in the natural world would ensue? Why would this form of atomism result in disorder, while a material plenum of sensing, reasoning, and infinitely divisible matter would not result in disorder?

5. REINTERPRETING THE NORMATIVE ANTI-ATOMISM ARGUMENT: THE FIRST PREMISS

In order to answer this question, we need to see Cavendish's normative anti-atomism as, in fact, much more significantly normative, indeed

---

(Broad, *Women Philosophers*, 43). But this does not seem enough to secure a teleological account of nature, for a material world moving in accordance with inviolable laws will also be orderly and harmonious, yet (witness Hobbes's natural philosophy) not one characterized by teleology. Even a thoroughly perceptive, self-moving natural world would not necessarily be an irreducibly teleological one (witness Spinoza's natural philosophy, especially his appendix following book 1 of the *Ethics*). This is the point at issue with the tension noted here. If, as the quote at *PL* 146 indicates, active parts of matter are *necessitated* to do what they do by the power of nature's 'general Peace', then the world can be one way, and one way only, and it is not clear how Cavendish's philosophy can escape Spinoza's arguments against finality in nature in the face of such necessitarianism. My interpretation of Cavendish—that nature exhibits irregularities due to the free choice of its parts, and also exhibits order due to the same free choice—both explains the source of Cavendish's teleology and alerts us to her divergence from the non-teleological, yet still orderly, nature of Spinoza's philosophy. Cavendish's teleology derives from nature's freedom, not its order.

prescriptively and not merely *descriptively* normative. That is, above I said that this argument is normative in the sense that it is based on the assumption of norms or standards in nature, but this is merely descriptive of nature. But perhaps the normative argument might actually be understood as follows: given that nature as a whole is infinitely wise and prescribes, from the top down, norms and standards of orderly and harmonious behaviour (nature as *morally* efficacious), an individual acting as if it were an atom—isolated from all others and bound by no overarching norms—would lead to disorder in its immediate environs at least. Because this violation of norms and standards of order would be bad, one ought not to behave as if one were such a being, even though our freedom permits exactly this sort of disorderly behaviour. This freedom comes about precisely because nature as a whole does not physically determine its parts. Rather, parts can determine their own physical movements. Individuals *ought not* to behave as if they were atomistic beings distinct from the whole of nature—beings with absolute power (including the power to set one's own norms of behaviour) that need not refer their actions to other individuals—because this will be potentially harmful to those other individuals.

A slightly different way of phrasing the argument is to say that if atomism were true, and if individuals could reasonably behave as if they were free from the constraints of other parts and of the whole of nature, then there would be no sense in saying that it is better to be healthy than to be sick, or to have sight than to lack it, to behave virtuously than to behave sinfully. But it is bad to be sick, to lack sight, or to sin (*GNP* 157–8, 85; *PL* 348–50).[24] And so natural parts *ought not* to behave with absolute freedom or without regard for others and for the whole of nature, since this leads precisely to such perversions. Yet another way of phrasing the argument is to acknowledge (as Cavendish does when employing the normative argument regarding atomism) that atoms are like deities, their behaviour in no way constrained, not even by norms (*PL* 431; *OEP* 129), for God produces norms, after all. He does not abide by extrinsically existing norms. But natural beings are neither like atoms nor like God. They are constrained by norms,

---

[24] It is crucial to bear in mind the content of n. 13. I note there that I assume that, for Cavendish, there are true norms in nature and, thus, true deviations from norms. While I merely assume it here, I do believe that she has a convincing argument for the assumption, and I deal with this elsewhere.

and they do not set norms for themselves by simply acting as they wish. Individuals within nature may act freely, but, in doing so, they may well violate norms, thus proving that they cannot rightly (even if they can literally) behave as if they were not defined in terms of their communities and ultimately in terms of all of nature.

Notice that, thus stated, Cavendish's normative anti-atomism says nothing about matter. This is an anti-atomism with atomism conceived of in a quasi-social way: one ought not to behave as if one were not part of a normatively guided community with other individuals. But this is still perfectly compatible with atomism as a theory about matter. Nature *could be* comprised of material atoms, but as long as there are overarching norms and standards guiding their behaviour, and as long as they abide by these standards, the prescriptions laid down by this new interpretation of the normative anti-atomism argument are satisfied. The first premiss as a statement about matter theory is still not established.

Two options arise at this juncture. First, we may completely disengage the two arguments found in Cavendish's corpus, laying the entire burden upon the logico-mathematical argument to establish the conclusion that matter is a plenum and not comprised of atoms. Accordingly, the normative argument (now in its normatively stronger form) is *not* an argument about matter theory at all. It is an argument concerned solely with establishing a conclusion about moral causal agency, most specifically the morally efficacious causal behaviour of finite beings. The normative argument establishes both prescriptive conclusions about how finite individuals with causal agency ought to conduct themselves as parts within the whole, and a descriptive conclusion about how most parts of the natural world seem actually to conduct themselves given that the world is, for the most part, orderly and harmonious.

The second option is to say that, while the normative argument surely leads to these prescriptive conclusions about the proper behaviours of finite beings, it can also lead to a conclusion about matter theory. Trying to show how it might do so has the triple virtues of (*a*) corresponding with Cavendish's own implicit belief that the normative argument tells us something about matter theory; (*b*) alerting us to the explanatory use to which Cavendish puts our experience of the sorts of social interactions we find among humans: Cavendish 'reads',

one might argue, the lessons learned from our experience of social relations into how she explains relations among natural material parts; and
(c) showing how she differs from Spinoza in her philosophy of nature.

Cavendish was aware of Hobbes's *De corpore*, the first English
translation of which appeared in 1656.[25] And so she would have been
aware of his division of philosophy:

The principal parts of philosophy are two. For two chief kinds of bodies, and
very different from one another, offer themselves to such as search after their
generation and properties; one whereof being the work of nature, is called a
natural body, the other is called a *commonwealth*, and is made by the wills and
agreement of men. And from these spring the two parts of philosophy called
natural and *civil*. (*EW* i. 11)

She was also clearly aware of the 'body politic' analogy that appeared
in Western philosophy from at least Plato and continued to appear
through to the seventeenth century if not beyond.[26] According to
the analogy, political systems (Hobbes's second part of philosophy,
with the second kind of body as its subject) behave functionally as
does the human body (Hobbes's first part of philosophy, with the
first kind of body as its subject). Just as the human body necessarily
has specific structures to allow healthy actions and functions, so too
political systems necessarily must have specific structures to function
appropriately, and both systems tend to be hierarchically organized.
So, for example, in the *Laws*, Plato likens a state that is in peace

---

[25] As Cavendish herself is not shy about admitting, she could read only English (*PF*
A6^r; *PL* C1^v). For various accounts of the relationship between Hobbes's and Cavendish's
thought, see some of the sources in n. 6 above.

[26] For a sustained account of Cavendish's use of the body politic analogy, see Oddvar
Holmesland, 'Margaret Cavendish's *The Blazing World*: Natural Art and the Body Politic',
Studies in Philology, 96/4 (1999), 457–79. Catherine Wilson addresses the contrast between
nature's orderly hierarchy and society's failure to exhibit the same degree of order ('Two
Opponents of Material Atomism: Cavendish and Leibniz' ['Two Opponents'], in Pauline
Phemister and Stuart Brown (eds.), *Leibniz and the English-Speaking World* (forthcoming)).
For a helpful summary of the main tenets and historical moments of the body politic analogy,
see David G. Hale, 'Analogy of the Body Politic' ['Analogy'], in Philip P. Weiner (ed.),
Dictionary of the History of Ideas (New York: Scribner's, 1973–4), i. 67–70. For uses of the
body politic analogy in Renaissance medicine, see Josep Lluís Barona, 'The Body Republic:
Social Order and Human Body in Renaissance Medical Thought', *History and Philosophy
of the Life Sciences*, 15 (1993), 165–80. It would be fruitful to pursue an investigation into
the historical and conceptual relation between Cavendish's philosophy and Renaissance
thought in general.

and friendship (rather than in war) to a healthy body,[27] and in the *Politics*, not only does Aristotle liken the state to a living body, but he follows through with the hierarchical implications of this: 'the state is by nature clearly prior to the family and to the individual, since the whole is of necessity prior to the part; for example, if the whole body be destroyed, there would be no foot or hand'.[28] Here is one example that shows Cavendish's use of the analogy: 'the truth is that a pure democracy is all body and no head, and an absolute monarchy is all head and no body, whereas aristocracy is both head and body, it is a select and proportional number for a good government, which number being united, represents and acts as one man' (*ODS* 276; cf. *NBW* 18).[29] Otto Mayr argues that the Renaissance saw the rise of the 'clockwork state' metaphor to join the analogy of the body politic. Whatever sense one makes of it, Hobbes himself seems to draw a parallel between the natural living body and the commonwealth by likening both to a clock or other such human-made (non-natural) mechanisms in both *De cive* (*EW*, vol. ii, p. xiv) and the *Leviathan* (*EW*, vol. iii, p. ix).[30] Cavendish, however, remains firmly committed to the body politic analogy, believing that both political and material bodies have the capacity to be natural, well-functioning wholes on the model of living organic

[27] Plato, *Laws* 628c ff., in John M. Cooper and D. S. Hutchinson (eds.), *Plato: Complete Works* (Indianapolis: Hackett, 1997), 1318–1616, at 1323 ff.

[28] Aristotle, *Politics* 1253ᵃ19–21, in Jonathan Barnes (ed.), *The Complete Works of Aristotle* (Princeton: Princeton University Press, 1984), ii. 1986–2129, at 1988.

[29] This passage is from Cavendish's *Orations of a Divers Sort*, in which she presents many competing opinions on various topics. It is not, therefore, necessarily the case that she supports aristocracy. Rather, I cite this passage to show that she clearly conceives of political states on analogy with organic bodies.

[30] For competing interpretations of what Hobbes intends, methodologically, by these analogies, see J. W. N. Watkins, *Hobbes's System of Ideas: A Study in the Political Significance of Philosophical Theories* (New York: Barnes & Noble, 1965), chs. 3–4; M. M. Goldsmith, *Hobbes's Science of Politics* (New York: Columbia University Press, 1966), chs. 1 and 7; Tom Sorell, *Hobbes* (London: Routledge & Kegan Paul, 1986). Sorell argues against both Watkins and Goldsmith that Hobbes does not and cannot study both types of body—natural and civil—through parallel methods. Hobbes is not primarily interested, according to Sorell, in explaining how the (clockwork) body politic is functionally organized and dependent upon its parts; such a course of study is appropriate for physical bodies only, not political bodies (*Hobbes*, 16–19). For a discussion of the clockwork state metaphor, see Otto Mayr, *Authority, Liberty, and Automatic Machinery in Early Modern Europe* [*Authority and Liberty*] (Baltimore: Johns Hopkins University Press, 1986), ch. 4.

bodies.[31] (Political bodies, however, often end up in an artificial state when humans do not rightly recognize the proper relation among their parts (e.g. *PL* 47–8). The case of democracy is one clear example.)

While Cavendish does, I believe, make use of the body politic analogy, there are unique characteristics of her version of it.[32] First, her natural system is non-deterministic. Not only does she reject the clockwork metaphor with its implication of mechanical motion—externally imposed motion necessitating, through inviolable physical laws, specific movements—but she is also opposed to the idea of forcing natural individuals to consent to a natural, hierarchical social system. There may be a truth about the best social organization, just as there is a truth about the correct religious belief to hold, but liberty of conscience on such matters must be respected precisely because forcing 'consent' undermines our nature as rational, self-moving, and therefore free beings (e.g. *GNP* 248–9). We must freely consent to our social systems, even if it means we do not concede to the single best (and, for Cavendish, hierarchical) system. It is better to allow individual freedom and have an ill political body than to have a healthy state without individual freedom. In fact, she

---

[31] Georges Canguilhem remarks upon Descartes's 'Envisioning the body in terms of a clockwork mechanism' thereby replacing 'a political image of command and magical type of causality (involving words or signs) with a technological image of "control" ...' (Georges Canguilhem, *La Connaissance de la vie* (Paris: J. Vrin, 1992), 114). Cavendish is conversely compelled by the political image of the body, together (as we shall see in the concluding section of this chapter) with the form of causality Canguilhem associates with that image. The extraordinary ways in which Cavendish uses this political image is suggested in what follows.

[32] As Étienne Balibar notes with respect to Spinoza's use of the body politic analogy, 'This would seem to place Spinoza squarely in the line of Hobbes (the *Leviathan*) and, more generally, of a whole tradition which defines the State as an individual and which runs from the ancient Greeks to the present day. However, we must press this point further, since such an assimilation covers in reality a wide range of different views. The individuality of the State may be thought of as either metaphorical or real, and "natural" or "artificial", as a mechanistic or an organic solidarity, as a self-organising principle of the State or an effect of its supernatural finality' (Étienne Balibar, *Spinoza and Politics*, tr. Peter Snowdon (London: Verso, 1998), 64). Cavendish, too, is in this long tradition, and Balibar's urging that we pay heed to the exact details of a given thinker's use of the analogy is important in Cavendish's case no less than in others'. Locating Cavendish in this tradition, including relating her use of the body politic concept to her underlying metaphysical and physical commitments and to her guiding political concerns, is a large, and future, project for which the present sketch serves as a minimal preliminary.

believes that 'it is not impossible to conquer a world. ... but, for the most part, conquerors seldom enjoy their conquest, for they being more feared than loved, most commonly come to an untimely end' (*NBW* 71).[33]

Second, in drawing the parallel between state and living body, Cavendish sets up an interesting dialectic between the two. On the one hand, the hierarchy and predominantly orderly behaviour of organic bodies serve as a normative model for human societies. On the other hand, the freedom that humans have as social (rather than as natural) beings is extended to all of non-human nature as well. So while non-human nature is the normative starting point (e.g. *PPO* C2^{r-v}; *PL* 13), Cavendish seems to take human society as the physically explanatory starting point, making the elements of the state—human beings as social beings—the explanatory model for the elements of the living body. When writing about disease in organisms, she portrays the errors in blatantly sociopolitical terms. '... diseases are occasioned many several ways; for some are made by a home Rebellion, and others by forreign enemies, and some by natural and regular dissolutions, and their cures are as different; but the chief Magistrate or Governors of the animal body, which are the regular motions of the parts of the body, want most commonly the assistance of foreign Parts, which are Medicines, Diets, and the like' (*PL* 409; cf. *PPO* 307–8; *OEP* 81; *GNP* 157–8). But for Cavendish, this need not be—and nor do I think it is—a metaphor only. This is because all finite parts of nature have their own share of a specific form of sense, reason, and self-motion. Consequently, freedom belongs to all finite parts of the natural world. So all parts may freely disobey the prescribed good of the societies in which they find themselves, be they human societies or the society of the body.

Third, while Cavendish may not be explicit about this, the body politic analogy must apply to all finite individuals. It is not just the politic state and the living (human) body that are drawn into the analogy, but every and all finite beings must be as well. Once again, this

---

[33] See Hale, 'Analogy', Mayr, *Authority and Liberty*, and John Rogers, *The Matter of Revolution: Science, Poetry, and Politics in the Age of Milton* [*Matter*] (Ithaca, NY: Cornell University Press, 1996), chs. 1 and 6, for discussion of the authoritarian character of both the body politic analogy and the mechanical, clockwork metaphor. See especially Rogers for Cavendish's break from this tradition.

follows from the fact that every finite individual is sensing, knowing, self-moving—indeed, alive, according to Cavendish (e.g. *OEP* 38–9). Moreover, all finite individuals remain unified as individuals because of the special sympathy and love or desire that the parts feel for others within the unified body (e.g. *PPO* 75; *PL* 167), and because of the fact that each part thus contributes to the well-working of the whole. Every individual system continues to survive and endure as long as its parts function towards the persistence of the individual. Every finite individual being is analogous to a living body or a commonwealth in this way.[34]

These unique characteristics of Cavendish's use of the body politic idea may enable one to extract a theory of non-atomistic *matter* from Cavendish's normative argument regarding atomism. The argument for this conclusion goes beyond anything we actually find in Cavendish's work, though various elements of this argument are explicit in her work, and it also coheres with her broad philosophy of nature. So I present this as a Cavendishian proposal. In social systems, humans are not atomistic individuals but are functionally related to one another in a specific way for the well-running (health) of the society. When we behave as if we were atomistic, social disorder ensues. This is democracy's failing. Similarly, within nature, finite individuals, no matter how small, are not atomistic, and when they behave as if they were, disorder (disease in organisms, disintegration of other finite wholes) ensues. But this conclusion turns on finite bits of matter—visible and subvisible—belonging to normatively bound communities. Ultimately, all individuals must belong to a single, normatively bound community that is all of nature, for only this can explain the overall order of the natural world. And one might argue that *this* can obtain only on a theory of material plenism. How so?

The normative argument depends upon nature as a whole prescribing appropriate behaviour to its parts, but these standards of behaviour

---

[34] The normative portrayal of atomistic individuals presented here is not, of course, unique to Cavendish. It has become especially prevalent among current-day communitarians intent on exposing both the inaccurate conception of the individual supposedly put forth by liberalism and the danger posed to the thriving of communities by individuals attempting to behave as such beings by, for example, pursuing individual rights to the exclusion of recognition of social groups. See, for example, Charles Taylor, 'Atomism', in Alkis Kontos (ed.), *Powers, Possessions and Freedom* (Toronto: University of Toronto Press, 1979), 39–62.

come from nature's infinite wisdom, and its wisdom comes from
its being materially infinite. Since all matter is rational, an infinite
quantity of matter has infinite reason (*GNP* 11). But if finite material
atoms that are distinct and separate from one another are all that exist
in nature—if atomism as a theory of matter were true—then there
would be no possible way for overarching standards and norms to
obtain for two reasons. First, there would be no infinitely extended
matter with its infinite aggregated wisdom to provide those norms.
Material atoms, as finite portions of matter, would have a merely
finite share of reason. This leads to one of the main problems with
material atoms for Cavendish. Because there is no aggregated, infinite
wisdom in finite atoms, there can be no single, universal standard
of behaviour. Each atom would therefore have to prescribe its own
norms to itself—each would be like a deity in this way, with an
'absolute power and knowledge' (*OEP* 129). Second, in lieu of an
infinitely aggregated material wisdom, one might suggest an immaterial substance existing apart from nature as the source of overarching
order. But this is precluded too. A contrast with Leibniz is useful here,
for he believes in the existence of immaterial atomistic beings which
nonetheless behave harmoniously among each other only because
God establishes harmony.[35] But since Cavendish rejects a role for
God in natural explanations (e.g. *PL* 201–11), that potential source
of universal standards is precluded too. But, once again, Cavendish
believes there *are* such standards, independent of human convention.
Our ability meaningfully to condemn certain actions as disorderly
presupposes standards that, on Cavendish's theory of matter, require a
non-atomistic infinite plenum of infinitely rational wise matter as the
only possible source of those standards.

   This new interpretation of the normative argument regarding atomism vindicates the first premise of that argument. In challenging the
truth of that premise, one asks why Cavendish believes that any form
of atomism, even one in which atoms have reason, would result in
disorder while a theory of rational matter in a plenum would not
result in disorder. There are really two parts to this problem. First,
why would rational atoms result in disorder? One could answer this

---

[35] For an account of the differences between Cavendish and Leibniz (as well as their
similarities), see Wilson, 'Two Opponents'.

by saying that should it be established that the world is comprised of only atoms, each of which is like a deity unto itself with absolute power, including the power to set its own norms given that there is nothing else besides individual atoms dictating norms, then not even atoms with reason (as opposed to irrational, chance-governed atoms) could lead to orderly behaviour. This is because each atom would be setting its own distinct standard of behaviour and acting accordingly. And, moreover, we see exactly this case arising in our world when individual parts within the whole of nature act as if they can rightly set their own standards and norms of behaviour distinct from those of nature as a whole. That is, individuals that, as a matter of fact, behave as if they were atoms prove, by example, the disorder that would follow from atomism as a thoroughgoing account of matter.[36] The second part to the question asks why a plenist account of matter would *not* give rise to disorder, and there are two ways of answering this question. One answer has it that a plenist theory of matter implies that nature as a whole has infinite rationality and wisdom. So infinite nature acts as a principal, morally efficacious cause encouraging, by rational persuasion, its parts to behave in an orderly fashion, thus giving rise to greater order. A second way of answering this is simply to challenge Cavendish on this claim that a material plenum results in thoroughgoing order because she herself leaves room for disorder, even on her own matter theory. This, of course, is Cavendish's denial of the second premiss dealt with in the previous section in such a way as to allow for the anti-atomism of the plenist view of matter. That plenist conception of matter is decisively established by the logico-mathematical argument and might well follow from the normative argument in the manner just presented.

6. MONISM AND CAUSATION

As far as her conception of nature is concerned, Cavendish is a monist. Depending upon precisely what this means, she might also be read

---

[36] Strictly speaking, if thoroughgoing atomism were true, there would not be any disharmony because there would be no single norm setting standards of right and good against which behaviour could be measured to determine how orderly (or not) it is.

as espousing a broadly Spinozistic conception of the natural world.[37] Indeed, as I shall soon show, there is significant textual evidence to tempt one to this conclusion. It would be incorrect, however, to read Cavendish as holding an especially robust (Spinozistic) form of monism, for this would undermine a central plank of her metaphysics, her theory of occasional causation. In order to ease the tension between her monism and her theory of causation, we must turn to the lessons of her normative argument against atomism to understand the limits of her monism. In the process, we see Cavendish's unique position in the history of seventeenth-century conceptions of nature.

There are two compatible ways one might conceive of Cavendish's monism. First, it might amount to the belief that there is one type of matter. I call this 'type monism', and Cavendish is certainly a type monist. While it is true that there are three aspects of matter—inanimate, sensitive animate, and rational animate—every possible piece of matter is comprised of all three aspects. This is because of her theory of complete blending (or inseparable commixture) according to which infinitely divisible matter will always include each of the three aspects of matter, regardless of how small the piece of matter becomes. Indeed, the infinite divisibility of matter is what permits the *complete* blending of all aspects of matter. Thus, 'although I make a distinction betwixt

---

[37] In an unpublished paper ('The Vitalist Natural Philosophies of Margaret Cavendish and Henry More'), Leni Robinson correctly points out that, strictly speaking, Cavendish is not a monist because she allows for the existence of both nature and God. There are two aspects to Robinson's position that must be heeded. First, Cavendish's philosophy is one of 'radical dualism of matter and spirit', or of nature (the material) and God (the immaterial). I fully grant this, and so specify that my claims about her monism are claims about her theory of nature considered in and of itself. This first point alerts us to an essential difference between Cavendish and Spinoza—her, but not his, acknowledgement of a transcendent God (see n. 6 above). The fact that Cavendish claims to fully sideline God in a discussion of the natural world which is (like Spinoza's nature) infinitely extended, and both material and perceptive, lends some legitimacy to the likening of their treatments of nature. But, and this is the second and most crucial aspect of Robinson's claim, Cavendish occasionally slips into a more thoroughgoing monism 'where Cavendish adopts ... the doctrines of a Neoplatonic cosmic system based on emanation'. Robinson is also right about this, and it would be an interesting project to investigate Cavendish's suggestion that God creates by emanation, and to pursue the impact of this suggestion upon her conception of nature, individuals, and laws. When I speak of Cavendish's monism in this chapter, I refer solely to the natural world, acknowledging the less than strict usage to which I put the term. My gratitude to Paul Guyer for his very helpful line of questioning during a presentation of this chapter in early form which led to my closer consideration of Cavendish's monism.

animate and inanimate, rational and sensitive matter, yet I do not say that they are three distinct and several matters; for as they do make but one body of nature, so they are also but one matter' (*OEP* 206; cf. 23−4). Every part of matter has motive, sensing, and reasoning capacities, and is also limited in its ability to move by inanimate matter. This is the single *type* of matter that exists.

Second, Cavendish's monism might amount to the belief that there is just one token: there is one single whole—all of nature—with parts within it being merely specific figures within the whole. I call this 'token monism'. An especially robust form of token monism would include claims about both substance and cause. Taken as a thesis about substance, (Ai) it would maintain that there is only one substantial individual—namely all of nature itself—which is the only whole, albeit with many parts. This contrasts with (Bi) the belief that there are multiple substantial individuals within nature, such that nature is simply a collection of wholes. Taken as a thesis about cause, (Aii) token monism depends upon top-down causal determinism with the whole of nature acting as the principal cause for all effects, parts within nature being mere effects, and nature as a whole determining the character of the parts. This contrasts with (Bii) a bottom-up conception of causal relations according to which multiple natural individuals (wholes within nature) act as principal causes in their interactions with each other, and these interactions determine the nature of the whole. Taken together, (Ai) and (Aii) would seem to necessitate specific and inviolable interrelations among the parts of nature. Cavendish never carves up the conceptual terrain this carefully, but it is helpful to do so in order to see the precise nature of her monism.

There is much textual evidence in favour of token monism even in the very strong form presented here. Here is a passage that supports token monism as a thesis about substance (Ai): 'I conceive nature to be an infinite body, bulk or magnitude, which by its own self-motion, is divided into infinite parts; not single or indivisible parts, but parts of one continued body, only discernible from each other by their proper figures, caused by the changes of particular motions ...' (*OEP* 126; cf. 47−8; *PL* 26). The following passage also supports (Ai) and the implication that necessary and specific relations hold among the parts of the one, single whole that is all of nature:

the Infinite whole is Infinite in substance or bulk, but the parts are Infinite in number, and not in bulk, for each part is circumscribed, and finite in its exterior figure and substance. But mistake me not, when I speak of circumscribed and finite single parts, for I do not mean, that each part doth subsist single and by it self, there being no such thing as an absolute single part in Nature, but Infinite Matter being by self-motion divided into an infinite number of parts, all these parts have *so near a relation to each other*, and to the infinite whole, that one cannot subsist without the other; for the Infinite parts in number do make the Infinite whole, and the Infinite whole consists in the Infinite number of parts. (*PL* 157–8; my emphasis; cf. *PL* 243)

The following two passages suggest that nature as whole, but no part within nature, acts as cause (Aii):

Neither do natural bodies know many prime causes and beginnings, but there is but one onely chief and prime cause from which all effects and varieties proceed, which cause is corporeal Nature, or natural self-moving Matter, which forms and produces all natural things; and all the variety and difference of natural Creatures arises from her various actions, which are the various motions in Nature. (*PL* 238)

… I do not intend to make particular creatures or figures, the principle of all the infinite effects of nature, as some other philosophers do; for there is no such thing as a prime or principal figure of nature, all being but effects of one cause. (*OEP* 17–18; cf. *PPO* 8; *OEP* 16, 141)

There is also conceptual evidence that suggests token monism best captures Cavendish's philosophy of the natural world, specifically her arguments against atomism. The logico-mathematical argument against atomism encourages the theory of type monism because of the fact of the unending divisibility of matter coupled with Cavendish's theory of complete mixing. Moreover, one might argue that the unlimited divisibility of matter's parts 'all the way down' finds a similar infinite composition of matter's parts 'all the way up'. This leads to token monism taken as a theory of substance (Ai) because what appear to be distinct individuals are really just parts of larger and larger parts, and so on ad infinitum. There is only one substantial whole: all of infinite nature itself; all of matter makes 'but one body of nature' (*OEP* 206). Cavendish's normative argument against atomism might suggest that she accepts token monism as a theory of cause (Aii). Since we cannot accept the supposition that finite individuals 'have an absolute power and knowledge' (*OEP* 129)—since we cannot accept atomism—it is perhaps not unreasonable to interpret her rejection of atoms' absolute power as a rejection of whole individuals acting as principal causes of natural effects (Bii).

But problems arise for the theory of token monism with a consideration of Cavendish's theory of occasional causation.[38] It is crucial here to make a distinction between occasional causation and occasionalism, since the latter posits the utter impotence of the natural world and God's will as the sole efficacious cause in that world, and Cavendish denies both premises. This follows from her insistence that we eliminate theology and appeals to God from our natural investigations (*PL* 201–11). As Steven Nadler shows, occasional causation is a more general theory than occasionalism and does not specify God as the principal source of causal change.

In simple terms, a relationship of occasional causation exists when one thing or state of affairs brings about an effect by inducing (but *not* through efficient causation ...) another thing to exercise its own efficient causal power. ... Thus, the term denotes the entire process whereby one thing, *A*, occasions or elicits another thing, *B*, to cause *e*. Even though it is *B* that *A* occasions or incites to engage in the activity of efficient causation in producing *e*, the relation of occasional causation links *A* not just to *B*, but also (and especially) to the effect, *e*, produced by *B*.[39]

Cavendish's theory of causation is a theory of occasional causation in this more general sense.

In her *Letters*, Cavendish explains to her fictional interlocutor that her own theory of causation, and not, for example, a theory based on the transfer of motion from one body to another, is the appropriate way to understand many (though not all) instances of causal interaction.[40]

---

[38] For an outstanding account of Cavendish's theory of causation and its historical context, see O'Neill, 'Introduction', pp. xxix–xxxv. I deal much more extensively with Cavendish's theory of occasional causation and its relation to freedom and natural disorders in my 'Reason and Freedom'.

[39] Steven Nadler, 'Descartes and Occasional Causation', *British Journal of the History of Philosophy*, 2/1 (1994), 39.

[40] Susan James deals with other forms of causal interaction in Cavendish's work, noting specifically the contrast between alteration (often accomplished by occasional causation) and generation (accomplished by transfer of inherently motive matter, and thus never by occasional causation) (James, 'Innovations'). O'Neill also stresses that Cavendish allows for transeunt causation (which is distinct from occasional causation) in, for example, respiration ('Introduction', p. xxxv).

Madam, give me leave to ask you this question, whether it be the motion of the hand, or the Instrument, or both, that print or carve such or such a body? Perchance you will say, that the motion of the hand moves the Instrument, and the Instrument moves the Wood which is to be carved. ... But I pray, *Madam,* consider rationally, that though the Artificer or Workman be the occasion of the motions of the carved body, yet the motions of the body that is carved, are they which put themselves into such or such a figure, or give themselves such or such a print as the Artificer intended; for a Watch, although the Artist or Watch-maker be the occasional cause that the Watch moves in such or such an artificial figure, as the figure of a Watch, yet it is the Watches own motion by which it moves. (PL 77–9)

In another example, when a body falls upon the snow, it is not the body that leaves its impression behind in the snow, but rather, 'the snow ... patterns the figure of the body. ... [It] patterns or copies it out in its own substance, just as the sensitive motions in the eye do pattern out the figure of an object' that it sees or perceives (*PL* 104–5). To 'pattern out' means to frame figures 'according to the patterns of exterior objects' (*OEP* 169), and most often in her writings, Cavendish seems to mean this very literally. The physical figure of the body falling upon the snow is physically printed out into the snow's matter from within the snow itself; bodies 'put themselves into such or such a figure' as the occasional cause intended (*PL* 79; cf. 539–40). While the precise mechanism of the interaction between occasional and principal cause is never fully specified, the ubiquitous rationality of matter is essential to this interaction. The occasional cause rationally suggests a course of actions that the principal cause may then rationally respond to by patterning out an appropriate figure.

So, according to Cavendish, in changes brought about by occasional causation, there is an occasional cause—the body eliciting the effect in another body—and there is a principal cause—the affected body itself bringing forth from within itself (patterning out) the appropriate effect. Cavendish has a number of motivations for believing that at least some causal interactions occur through occasional causation. One of these is her belief that motion, as a mode, cannot transfer from body to body, and so the motion of the affected body must come from within the affected body itself (*PL* 77–8, 445; *OEP* 200). Another motivation stems from Cavendish's recognition that we often err in our sense perception, and occasional causation can explain such errors. Erroneous perceptions (*PPO* 66–7)—for example, hallucinations when the subject perceives an object as present when it is not—cannot have come about owing to the influence of an immediately present external stimulus; they must have been brought forth from within the subject of perception herself. An external cause is thus unnecessary: 'the Object is not the *cause* of Perception, but is only the *occasion*: for, the Sensitive Organs can make such like figurative actions, were there no Object present; which proves, that the Object is not the Cause of the Perception' (*GNP* 56). Similarly, the fact that we may not feel a pinch when distracted by intense thought, establishes that there can be no direct causal connection between the object of perception (which is clearly not sufficient) and the perception itself (*OEP* 150). The principal cause may or may not respond to the rational suggestion of the occasional cause.[41]

Occasional causation undermines token monism since, under occasional causation, individual bodies within nature act as principal causes and are not mere effects (Bii). In principle, as the examples of perceptual errors just cited show, the occasion is neither necessary nor sufficient for the principal cause to act, thus allowing natural individuals as principal causes a significant degree of independence from other natural individuals, a degree of independence that goes beyond what would be tolerated by token monism taken in an especially robust sense as a theory both about substance and about cause.[42] So it seems that Cavendish is in a bind. There is textual evidence suggesting she endorses token monism, taken as a theory about both cause and substance. There is also conceptual evidence for token monism taking the form of her arguments against atomism. On the other hand, however, occasional causation, which seems as central to her metaphysical system as

---

[41] Dreams are a special and interesting case for Cavendish, as she herself notes (*PPO* 67, 280 ff.). I shall not deal with this case here. Of course, there are alternative ways of explaining such perceptual phenomena, including by appeal to mechanical explanations such as Hobbes's of which Cavendish was aware, having read *Leviathan* (*EW* iii. 3 ff.). Her explanation through occasional causation for these perceptual phenomena is another possibility, and she has independent reasons for favouring her approach, mainly that mechanical causal interaction on the model of motion transferring from body to body cannot happen given that motion as a mode *cannot* transfer from body to body.

[42] O'Neill draws our attention to this notable degree of independence when she notes that: '... (1) the occasion has no intrinsic connection with the effect; (2) it is not necessary for the production of the effect ... (3) it has no direct influence on the production of the effect ...' ('Introduction', p. xxx).

does her monism, includes an endorsement of finite individuals acting as principal causes which subverts token monism taken as a theory about cause. She cannot, it seems, retain both token monism and anti-atomism on the one hand, and occasional causation on the other hand. To solve this impasse, we must now draw upon the lessons learned from reinterpreting her normative theory of atomism.

Cavendish links her theory of occasional causation with freedom: 'the action of self-figuring [patterning] is free' (*PL* 24; cf. 18). This is not surprising because the theory of occasional causation supports a view of nature in which natural parts themselves act as principal causes and are not necessitated to behave in a certain way. They are necessitated neither by nature as a whole imposing, from the top down, specific interrelations among the parts (which then become mere effects and not causes at all), nor by occasional causes necessitating that the principal cause act in a specific fashion. That is, they are free from extrinsic control. There are different degrees of freedom within natural actions. Some natural events are dubbed 'voluntary' while others are 'occasioned'. Voluntary actions, understood in this new way, are actions that are not dependent upon or constrained by an occasional cause encouraging the principal cause to act in a specific manner. The principal cause acts entirely on its own; these voluntary actions are called actions 'by rote' (*OEP* 19–20); and they are freer than occasioned events. Principal causes that are encouraged to act in a specific way by occasional causes are free, of course, for the following reasons: the constraint exercised is neither necessary nor sufficient for the action to occur; the principal cause is self-moved; and the principal cause acts in accordance with its own reasons. But the occasional cause exercises some constraining influence—a moral influence—over the actions of the principal cause.[43] Memories and dreams are examples of perceptions that fit into the class of rote actions (*OEP* 33, 97, 272; *PPO* 280). A hand tossing a bowl is an example of an occasioned action (*PL* 445).

Actions that are constrained by an occasional cause are more regular and less prone to disorder (*OEP* 33), even if they are less free than

---

[43] O'Neill also (see n. 42) draws our attention to the notable degree of interdependence between occasional and principal cause when she notes that '... (4) an occasion has an indirect influence on the production of the effect by inducing the primary cause to act, and (5) insofar as it exerts this sort of influence, it counts as a partial efficient *moral* cause of the effect ...' ('Introduction', p. xxx).

are rote actions. Radically free individual parts in nature—parts that are constrained by nothing, not even the rational persuasion of an occasional cause—tend to non-orderly behaviour. Above I noted that the fact of erroneous perceptions is one motivation for Cavendish's theory of occasional causation. One might wish to argue that we need not take such perceptions as erroneous at all, but rather that they merely appear so from our finite point of view. This line of reasoning would continue to the conclusion that there is, in fact, no occasional causation at all. Rather (according to this line of argument) nature as a whole causally determines from the top down (Aii) that precise and specific relations hold between so-called occasional and principal 'causes', causes which are, strictly speaking, just effects of the one true cause, namely, all of nature. Thus (the argument continues) all experienced relations among finite parts hold necessarily (including so-called 'errors' of perception), even if not directly but rather indirectly (with nature as a whole mediating those relations). This interpretation could then be used to resolve the tension in Cavendish between her monism and anti-atomism on the one hand, and her supposed adherence to occasional causation on the other hand, by simply denying that there is room for the theory of occasional causation in her philosophy. There are two facts taken together that tell against this interpretation of Cavendish. First, nature as a whole is infinitely wise. 'Nature having Infinite parts of Infinite degrees, must also have an Infinite natural wisdom to order her natural Infinite parts and actions...' (*PL* 8–9; cf. 144, 161; *OEP* 121, 138, 214). Second, there are true natural errors (and not just events that we interpret as errors), be these perceptual errors or civil wars or disease. If a strict form of token monism were true, and infinitely wise nature were to causally determine relations among its parts to be harmonious and orderly, then there would be no natural disorders because nature's wisdom would necessitate order. But there *are* true disorders. The fact that Cavendish takes some natural events to be objectively bad because they are opposed to the wise order of nature, and not just subjectively so from a finite human point of view, indicates that infinitely wise nature *cannot* be acting as the single, principal, ordering cause. If it were, it would not permit such deviations.

I have shown already the connection between Cavendish's anti-atomism and her embrace of both type and token monism. There is also, we can now see, a connection—though a much looser one—between her theory of occasional causation and atomism, for both are identified as the source of natural disorders. Finite individuals within nature, when they act as principal causes, can act as renegade bodies independently from all others, just as she envisions atoms would do if they existed. So we see the parallel between, on the one hand, Stevenson's belief that Cavendish cannot give up atomism although she wants to do so, and, on the other hand, the tension between monism and occasional causation. Monism and anti-atomism are compatible, and both seem to imply natural order. And occasional causation and atomism are compatible, and both imply disorder.

This parallel between Stevenson's concerns and the tension between monism and occasional causation allows us to solve that latter tension precisely by turning to the solution proposed to Stevenson's concern. Recall that token monism can be taken as a theory either about substance or about cause. As a theory about cause, it states that nature is sole principal cause and that finite parts within nature are mere effects of that cause. But, as we learned from the Hobbes–Bramhall debate adjusted to suit Cavendish's theory of nature, nature as a whole might act as principal moral or natural (physical) cause. An especially strong form of token monism would say that nature acts as both sorts of cause. Must Cavendish be forced to this conclusion, especially given the texts cited above in favour of token monism taken as a theory about cause?

I believe not, and to show this, we need to deny that nature is principal cause in a natural, physical sense. To do this, we need to reinterpret the passages that urge token monism taken as a theory about cause (Aii). Here they are again:

Neither do natural bodies know many prime causes and beginnings, but there is but one onely chief and prime cause from which all effects and varieties proceed, which cause is corporeal Nature, or natural self-moving Matter, which forms and produces all natural things; and all the variety and difference of natural Creatures arises from her various actions, which are the various motions in Nature. (*PL* 238)

… I do not intend to make particular creatures or figures, the principle of all the infinite effects of nature, as some other philosophers do; for there is no such thing as a prime or principal figure of nature, all being but effects of one cause. But my ground is sense and reason, that is, I make self-moving matter, which is sensitive and rational, the only cause and principle of all natural effects. (*OEP* 17–18).

Rather than read these passages as endorsing the view that there is a single substantial cause (namely, all of nature taken as the single principal cause), we could as easily read these passages as endorsing the view that there is a single type of cause (namely, rational and sensitive matter). All effects we experience in the world come about as the result of self-moving matter (rather than, for example, a finite or infinite incorporeal mind). But that does not mean that the effects we experience come about as the result of the one, single material whole. That is, these passages may be read as an endorsement of type, but not token, monism. This stills allows that nature as a whole acts as some sort of principal cause—specifically, as the principal moral cause, or the ultimate source of natural order. As the locus of infinite wisdom, nature imposes rational order from the top down, but it does so without necessitating that its parts abide by this order. This is because the parts within nature also act as principal causes, both as principal moral causes (giving reasons of their own to themselves) and as principal natural or physical causes (acting or not on those reasons). As principal causes, they can act differently from how they ought to act according to infinite nature's prescriptions.

While Cavendish never presents her theory of matter and cause exactly like this, it is a viable interpretation because it can best explain her belief in the freedom of nature's parts, with freedom defined as rational self-activity. There is some textual evidence, too, that this is her intention. In the *Grounds of Natural Philosophy* (hereafter *Grounds*), for example, she writes:

To treat Infinite Effects, produced from an Infinite Cause, is an endless Work, and impossible to be performed, or effected; only this may be said, That the Effects, though Infinite, are so united to the material Cause, as that not any single effect can be, nor no Effect can be annihilated; by reason all Effects are in the power of the Cause. But this is to be noted, *That some Effects producing other Effects, are, in some sort or manner, a Cause.* (*GNP* 15; my emphasis)

Until the last sentence, this passage supports strong token monism as a causal theory since finite creatures are taken as mere effects (Aii), but the last sentence allows for the parts to be causes themselves, thus moving her monism (as a thesis about cause) to a weaker form that can accommodate some independent causal activity of finite creatures (Bii). Of course, as principal moral and natural causes, parts within the whole of infinite nature can freely choose to act within or outside of the confines suggested by nature as an infinite whole, and this explains both the variety we see within natural kinds as well as full-out perversions from natural kinds (e.g. *PL* 173–4, 238–9).[44]

As a theory of substance, Cavendish's token monism can be as robust as (Ai): there is only one substantial individual—namely all of nature itself—which is the only whole, albeit with many parts. Indeed, the logical anti-atomism argument, together with the conceptual impossibility of empty space or a vacuum and Cavendish's theory of complete blending, necessitates this conclusion. But this does not result in specific inviolable relations among finite parts holding with necessity; these relations may be merely contingent. This is permitted by the weakening of monism as a causal theory. Precisely because natural individuals can act as free principal causes determining themselves, there are no specific and necessary relations among them, and so it is possible for natural parts to exhibit significant independence from one another. But this does not detract from the fact that individuals are nonetheless in some sort of relation with others, that they ought to recognize this fact of interdependence, and that they ought, therefore, to have specific and necessary relations with each other—namely, those that are normatively good because they are in line with the overall natural order. Indeed, when the parts gain greater unity, there is also greater recognition that there is one truth to be pursued, and this is due to the greater consolidation of wisdom; nature as a whole knows itself and its norms and standards with full clarity (*GNP* 11). While wholly harmonious unity is the ideal towards which parts ought to strive, even if the precise and specific normative relations among

---

[44] One might wonder where the line between normal and abnormal variety is drawn for Cavendish, and here the answer would likely be similar to her explanation for how we determine natural kinds. We make likely guesses as to the kinds that nature determines will exist from the infinite kinds that 'only matter' could produce, and we make these guesses owing to the figures and shapes we experience in the natural world. All our suppositions made about nature in this way are merely probable, never certain (*PL* 507; *OEP* 214). So too we would need to make likely guesses as to what forms of variety fall within the range of normal variety and what forms fall into the range of the 'monstrous' on the basis of the normal range of variety we experience in any given natural kind.

parts are attained, these would still be fully voluntary and therefore contingent in the sense that they could have been otherwise had the parts of nature freely chosen otherwise.

Cavendish's motivations for holding this form of monism are not entirely grounded in a conception of matter. This should be clear from her two arguments against atomism and their quite distinct primary conclusions. It is true that her rejection of a vacuum and her acceptance of the divisibility of whatever has quantity (implying the infinite divisibility of matter) give her good metaphysical reasons for endorsing monism. But her beliefs that there are norms, standards, and harmony in nature, that individuals (both humans and non-humans) are free, and that this freedom permits dissent from norms, thus leading to disorders, are not beliefs grounded in claims about the nature of matter, motion, and vacua. These are decidedly value-laden claims, and they reflect Cavendish's broader interests and concerns with her society. As a royalist in exile for a decade and a half, and as an opponent of democratically organized political states for the lack of harmony they would breed (*NBW* 95), Cavendish had sociopolitical reasons for taking seriously the capacity of free, rational individuals to disrupt hierarchically imposed order in order to produce disorder and suffering in its stead. What is remarkable about her philosophy is that she extends this depiction of the capacities of human individuals to absolutely all finite natural beings because they are all, in some way, rational. She works her social concerns into the very fabric of her metaphysics of matter.

This affords her a unique place in seventeenth-century natural philosophy. Like Spinoza, she is a substance monist in so far as the natural world is concerned, and, also like Spinoza, she believes that natural substance is infinitely extended and thoroughly perceptive. But, unlike Spinoza, the details of her monism do not lead to a necessitarian conception of all natural beings, including humans. The widespread order we witness in the natural world comes from the freely granted, rational obedience that finite beings give to the rational suggestion of other finite beings. In concert with this explanation for nature's widespread harmony, the occasional disorders we witness in both non-human and human nature arise from the rationality of natural beings that freely dissent from rational command to behave in a specific way. Nature is therefore irreducibly teleological and

normative, quite unlike Spinoza's conception of nature. But while we
may explain the metaphysics of the actions of non-human nature in
terms of human actions in our social relations (they are, after all, of
the same nature and thus bound by the same forms of interaction),
non-human nature, with its superior order and harmony, serves as
the normative model for humans in our social interactions. This
has significant implications for how Cavendish believes we ought to
conduct ourselves socially. But that is a story for another time.[45]

[45] I thank the audience at the University of Pennsylvania's colloquium series for questions
and discussion on this chapter in its earliest form, and I am especially grateful to Steven Gross
for his written comments. Likewise, the audience at the University of Toronto's Nature and
Necessity Conference was extremely helpful, especially questions posed by or discussion
with Donald Ainslie, Christia Mercer, Lisa Shapiro, Catherine Wilson (who has also been
very generous in sharing her own, forthcoming, work on Cavendish), and Susan James
(with whom I also enjoyed inspiring conversation in London). Thanks to Leni Robinson
for allowing me to read her wonderful work on Cavendish and More, to Michael Ryan at
the University of Pennsylvania's Van Pelt Library for so thoughtfully sending me literature
on Cavendish, to Tan Kok Chor for comments on a later version of this chapter, to Anna
Cremaldi for her exacting eye in proofreading the final version, and to an anonymous
referee of this volume for useful feedback. For more general discussion of Cavendish and
early modern women philosophers in general, and for providing a model to emulate in so
many ways, I am grateful to Eileen O'Neill.

8

Descartes, the First Cartesians, and Logic

ROGER ARIEW

I. CARTESIAN COLLEGIATE TEXTBOOKS IN THE SEVENTEENTH CENTURY

Descartes wrote the *Principles of Philosophy* as something of a rival to scholastic textbooks, although the latter usually had quadripartite arrangements—that is, logic, ethics, physics, and metaphysics—mirroring the structure of the collegiate curriculum.[1] But Descartes produced at best only a partial physics and what could be called a general metaphysics: he did not finish his physics[2] and did not write a particular metaphysics;[3] he did not produce an ethics or logic for his followers to use or to teach from. These things must have been perceived as glaring deficiencies in the Cartesian programme and in the aspiration to replace Aristotelian philosophy in the schools. So the Cartesians rushed in to fill the voids. One can talk about their attempts to complete the physics—Louis de la Forge's additions to the *Traité de l'homme*, for example—or to produce more conventional-looking metaphysics—such as Johann Clauberg's later editions of his

---

[1] For the collegiate curriculum in 17th-century France, see L. W. B. Brockliss, *French Higher Education in the Seventeenth and Eighteenth Centuries: A Cultural History* (Oxford: Clarendon Press, 1987).

[2] Knowing what a course in physics looks like, Descartes understood that he needed to produce two further parts of his *Principles of Philosophy*: 'a fifth part on living things, i.e. animals and plants, and a sixth part on man'; he did not do so, as he said, because 'I am not yet completely clear about all of the matters I would like to treat in these two last parts, and do not know whether I am likely to have sufficient leisure or be able to make the experiments necessary to complete them' (*Principles of Philosophy*, IV. 188).

[3] See Jean-Luc Marion, *Sur le prisme métaphysique de Descartes: Constitution et limites de l'onto-théo-logie* (Paris: PUF, 1986), 9–72, and Roger Ariew, 'Descartes and the Late Scholastics on the Order of the Sciences', in C. Blackwell and S. Kusukawa (eds.), *Philosophy in the Sixteenth and Seventeenth Centuries: Conversations with Aristotle* (Aldershot: Ashgate, 1999), 350–64.

Ontosophia[4] or Baruch Spinoza's *Cogitata metaphysica*. Perhaps the most interesting attempt at a Cartesian ethics is the Latin-language student manual on Descartes's ethical thought printed in 1685.[5] Descartes never wrote such a book, but the clever translator was able to put together a tripartite treatise out of Descartes's own words: Part I on the greatest good, happiness, and free will; Part II on passions; and Part III on love.[6] Apparently, this manual became part of the curriculum at Cambridge University since it was republished numerous times there during the first three or four decades of the eighteenth century and bound into a single volume together with the scholastic ethics of Eustachius a Sancto Paulo[7] and the Christian ethics of Étienne de Courcelles.[8] There were Cartesian-style logic texts as well, the most prominent being the *Port-Royal Logic* (Paris, 1662).

The attempt to publish a Cartesian textbook that would mirror what was taught in the schools culminated in the famous multi-volume works of Pierre-Sylvain Régis and of Antoine Le Grand. The Franciscan monk Le Grand initially published a popular version

---

[4] Descartes, of course, saw himself as presenting Cartesian metaphysics as well as physics, both the roots and trunk of his tree of philosophy. But from the point of view of school texts, the metaphysical elements of physics (general metaphysics) that Descartes discussed—such as the principles of bodies: matter, form, and privation; causation; motion: generation and corruption, growth and diminution; place, void, infinity, and time—were usually taught in a course on physics. The scholastic course on metaphysics (particular metaphysics) dealt with other topics, not discussed directly in the *Principles of Philosophy*, such as: being, existence, and essence; unity, quantity, and individuation; truth and falsity; good and evil. Such courses usually also ended up with questions about knowledge of God, names or attributes of God, God's will and power, and God's goodness. The *Principles of Philosophy* by itself was not sufficient as a text for the standard course in metaphysics. That is how Clauberg's *Ontosophia* can be thought to respond to this need. In the work, Clauberg discusses being in general, dividing it into its general and primary sense of 'intelligible' being, a secondary and lesser sense of 'something' to be distinguished from 'nothing', and a third, particular sense of 'real' being, being outside the intellect, or substance, contrasting it with accident and mode. He goes on to talk about essence, existence, and duration. His remaining chapters concern pairs of concepts such as: one and many; true and false; good and evil; perfect and imperfect; distinct and opposite; the same and another; exemplar and image.

[5] *Ethice: In methodum et compendium, gratiâ studiosae juventutis, concinnata* (London, 1685).

[6] Part I consisted of Latin translations from Descartes's letters to Elisabeth; Part II was an abridgement from the three parts of the Latin translation of *Passions of the Soul*; and Part III consisted of Latin translations from Descartes's letters to Chanut and Elisabeth.

[7] That is, Part II of his *Summa philosophiae quadripartita*.

[8] Eustachius a Sancto Paulo, Étienne de Courcelles, and René Descartes, *Ethica; sive, Summa moralis disciplinae, in tres partes divisa* (Cambridge, 1707). Eustachius' part is called *Ethica* and de Courcelle's *Synopsis ethices*.

of Descartes's philosophy in the form of a scholastic textbook,[9] expanding it in the 1670s and 1680s;[10] it was then translated into English and published as *An Entire Body of Philosophy according to the Principles of the famous Renate Descartes* (London, 1694). On the Continent, Régis issued his *Système général selon les principes de Descartes* at about the same time (Amsterdam, 1691), having had difficulties receiving permission to publish. The *Système général*, the great Cartesian textbook, is an odd work. Although billed as a general system of Cartesian philosophy, it does not seem very systematic. Its various portions embody Régis's adaptations of diverse Cartesian and non-Cartesian philosophies: Arnauld's Port-Royal logic (mostly excerpted, though with some changes); Robert Desgabet's metaphysics;[11] Jacques Rohault's physics;[12] and an amalgam of Gassendist and Hobbesian ethics. But Régis's work set the standard for Cartesian textbooks, with the *Port-Royal Logic* as the model of Cartesian logic.

There were other attempts at setting out a complete Cartesian system before those of Le Grand and Régis. The first such textbook I know of is Jacques Du Roure's *La Philosophie divisée en toutes ses parties* (Paris, 1654) and its successor, *Abrégé de la vraye philosophie* (Paris, 1665). Du Roure was one of the first followers of Descartes, belonging to the group around Descartes's literary executor, Claude Clerselier. In Du Roure's case, the parts of philosophy included natural theology plus the usual parts of the curriculum. Thus, Du Roure was also the first to have written a Cartesian ethics and natural theology. Du Roure

---

[9] *Philosophia veterum e mente Renati Descartes, more scholastica breviter digesta* (1671).

[10] *Institutio philosophiae, secundum principia Renati Descartes, nova methodo adornata et explicata ad usum juventutis academicae* (London, 1672, 1678, and 1680).

[11] For an account of the peculiarities of the Cartesian metaphysics of Desgabets and Régis, see Tad Schmaltz, *Radical Cartesians* (Cambridge: Cambridge University Press, 2002).

[12] See Foucher to Leibniz (GP i. 398–400): 'You know that I think Régis has given the public a great system of philosophy in 3 quarto volumes with several figures. This work contains many most important treatises, such as that on percussion by Mariotte, chemistry by l'Emeri, medicine by Vieuxsang and by d'Uvernai. He even speaks of my treatise on Hygrometers, although he does not name it. There is in it a good portion of the physics of Rohault and he refutes there Malbranche, Perraut, Varignon—the first concerning ideas, the second concerning weight, and the third, who has recently been received by the Académie royale des Sciences, also concerning weight. The Metheores of l'Ami also in part adorn this work, and the remainder is from Descartes. Régis conducted himself rather skillfully in his system, especially in his ethics.'

and Clauberg, whom Du Roure apparently met during the latter's trip to France in 1648, wrote the first Cartesian-style logic texts.[13]

I would like to outline the logic of the Cartesians in the second half of the seventeenth century. Thus I propose to look at the logic texts of Clauberg, Du Roure, Le Grand, and Régis, among others, to compare them with some standard scholastic logic texts from the time, and to ask whether and in what way they differ. But first I need to discuss Descartes's views on logic in general, including his positive and negative views on dialectics and syllogism, in order to determine what were the Cartesian doctrines on logic that the first Cartesians should have followed when they wanted to compete with scholastic textbooks—this especially so given that Descartes's unorthodox views on logic had already been voiced in some quarters.

2. DESCARTES'S LOGIC IN CONTEXT

There is a standard Renaissance complaint about logic: basically, formal logic, that is, syllogism, is useless; it may even be harmful. For example, we see Francis Bacon in his *New Organon* (London, 1620) arguing that method alone, distinct from logic, is worthwhile: 'The syllogism consists of propositions, propositions consist of words, words are symbols of notions. Therefore if the notions themselves (which is the root of the matter) are confused and over-hastily abstracted from the facts, there can be no firmness in the superstructure. Our only hope therefore lies in a true induction.'[14] Similarly, Francisco

---

[13] Clauberg, *Logica vetus et nova* (Amsterdam, 1654; 2nd edn., Amsterdam, 1658) and *logica contracta* in *Opera omnia philosophica* (Amsterdam, 1691).

[14] Francis Bacon, *New Organon* (London, 1620), book I, Aphorism 14; also Aphorism 13: 'The syllogism is not applied to the first principles of sciences, and is applied in vain to intermediate axioms; being no match for the subtlety of nature. It commands assent therefore to the proposition, but does not take hold of the thing,' and elsewhere. See also Michel de Montaigne, who reports in his *Essais* (Bordeaux, 1580) that logic has no practical use, that its inventors must have been playing a game: 'What good can we suppose that knowledge of so many things was to Varro and Aristotle? Did it exempt them from human discomforts? Were they immune to the accidents that afflict a porter? Did they derive from logic some consolation for the gout? Because they knew how that humor lodges in the joints, did they feel it any less? ... Chrysippus said that what Plato and Aristotle wrote on logic must have been written as a game and for practice, and he could not believe they had said anything serious on so frivolous a subject' (*Apology for Raymond Sebond*, tr. Roger Ariew and Marjorie Grene (Indianapolis: Hackett, 2003), 48, 70). A related complaint can be found in Pierre de la Ramée, who argues that only method, not dialectics, can usefully

Sanchez, in *Quod nihil scitur* (Lyon, 1581), attacks the barrenness of conventional uses of the syllogism and the emptiness of elaborate definitions. On standard accounts, knowledge is a disposition acquired by demonstration, but Sanchez says he does not understand what a disposition is and, worst of all, demonstration amounts to explaining something obscure by something even more obscure: 'How subtle, how long, and how difficult is the science of syllogism! In fact it is *futile*, long, and difficult, and there is *no* science of syllogism!'[15] Sanchez even argues that syllogism destroys and obscures the sciences:

So what use have all these syllogisms been? Why did Aristotle spend so much effort on teaching them? And why do all his successors still expend their labour on them? When it comes to writing, we do not make any use of syllogisms, nor did Aristotle. No knowledge has ever emerged from them; indeed, they have led many sciences into error and confusion. As for discussions and disputes, we make even less use of syllogisms; we are content with a simple inference from one point to the next. Otherwise, our disputes would never end, but we would have to struggle at every stage to reduce a syllogism to its correct mood and figure, or to convert it, and endless other games of this sort. (*Quod nihil scitur*, 11)

Descartes was sympathetic to this sort of criticism; he produced similar arguments in the *Regulae*. There he begins by asserting: 'I find of little use those bonds by which the dialecticians seek to rule human reason.'[16] He continues, 'as to the other operations of the mind, moreover, which dialectic struggles to direct with the aid of these prior ones, they are useless here—or rather they may be counted as obstructions, since nothing can be added to the pure light of reason

---

order known precepts: 'Let us suppose that all the definitions, distributions, and rules of grammar are discovered and each correctly judged, and that all of these teachings are written on different tablets, which are thrown together and jumbled up out of order and put in a jug, as in the game of blank. What branch of dialectic could teach me to deal with such confused precepts and restore them to order? No method of discovery is necessary, for everything is already discovered. Every particular proposition is judged and proved. We will need neither the first judgments of propositions nor the consequences of syllogisms. Method alone is left as a reliable way of putting things together' (Ramus, *La Dialectique* (Paris, 1555), 138–9).

[15] Francisco Sanchez, *Quod nihil scitur* (Lyon, 1581), 7.

[16] Rule 2, AT x. 365. There is, of course, another argument in Rule 2, one against probable syllogisms, 'those war engines of the schools', from which Descartes claims emancipation.

without in some way obscuring it' (Rule 4, AT x. 372–3). So he rejects syllogisms as contrary to his ends. According to Descartes,

Dialecticians can find by their art no syllogism that yields a true conclusion unless they first have the material for it, that is, unless they have already learned the truth itself they are deducing in their syllogism. Hence it is clear that they themselves learn nothing new from such a form, and that vulgar dialectic is therefore entirely useless for those who wish to investigate the truth of things. On the contrary, its only use is that now and then it can expound more easily to others arguments already known; hence it should be transferred from philosophy to rhetoric. (Rule 10, AT x. 406)

The only positive thing Descartes can say about syllogism or dialectics in the *Regulae* is that there is a distant resemblance between syllogism and his method, which, in the fashion of Bacon, is all that he thinks is useful; he asserts: 'This is the sole respect in which we imitate the dialecticians: when they expound the forms of the syllogisms, they presuppose that the terms or subject matter of the syllogisms are known; similarly, we are making it a prerequisite here that the problem under investigation is perfectly understood' (Rule 13, AT x. 430). And he continues by describing what he calls deduction as a procedure that finds something unknown from what is already known; he specifies that the procedure can be achieved through a simple comparison of two or more objects with one another by means of a common idea. He insists, however, that 'since the forms of the syllogisms are of no help in perceiving the truth of things, it will be of advantage to the reader, if, after he has completely rejected them, he grasps the fact that every cognition whatsoever which is not obtained by a simple and pure intuition of one isolated object, is obtained by the comparison of two or more objects with one another' (Rule 14, AT x. 439–40). So deduction, one of the basic elements of Descartes's method (along with intuition), has little to do with the application of the laws of logic.[17] What Descartes has in mind is the type of inference used in mathematics, when we somehow 'perceive' how different propositions relate to each other and how an unknown truth follows from truths already known. Thus Descartes proposes the cultivation

[17] That Descartes's notion of deduction (*deductio*) is not logical deduction is further corroborated by the fact that he also calls it *inductio*. See Rule 3, AT x. 368.

of our native powers for discerning truth and falsity (i.e. intuition and deduction) together with his method—ordering, enumeration, etc.[18]

The *Regulae* was not generally available in the seventeenth century, though some Cartesians had access to various portions of it, as was obvious in the fourth edition of the *Port-Royal Logic* (Paris, 1674);[19] the work itself was first published in Latin in Descartes's *Opuscula posthuma* only in 1701.[20] So we should ask: to what extent could Descartes's views on logic be discerned through the treatises published during his lifetime? The answer is that Descartes repeats many of the same negative arguments from the *Regulae* in the *Discourse on Method*, Part II, when he gives what he calls the rules of his method. He also refers to these passages from the *Discourse* in the Preface to the French translation of the *Principles*.[21] In the later texts, we find the two traditional negative points about dialectics and syllogism, but the discussion about method is considerably abbreviated and another slightly different positive view seems to emerge as well. Missing in these texts is the seemingly foundational Cartesian view about our native intelligence, intuition, and deduction.

We do encounter the two negative points about logic in the *Discourse*. There is the complaint that syllogisms are useless: 'they serve rather to explain to someone else the things one already knows, or even ... to speak without judgment on matters of which one is ignorant, rather than to learn them' (AT vi. 17). There is also the

---

[18] As Stephen Gaukroger puts it: 'Descartes's construal of inference in terms of an instantaneous grasp in accord with the natural light of reason precludes any attempt to provide a formal account of logical relations, since any such attempt would of necessity focus on inferential steps, and this is precisely what Descartes's account is designed to take us away from' (*Cartesian Logic: An Essay on Descartes's Conception of Inference* (Oxford: Clarendon Press, 1989), 72). But Gaukroger sees a distinction between deduction (inference) and mathematical reasoning for Descartes: 'Yet throughout his work Descartes thinks of true and effective reasoning in terms of mathematical reasoning and mathematical reasoning is, for him, algebraic reasoning. Algebraic reasoning is formal, indeed it is the paradigm of formal reasoning' (ibid.). For a different view of deduction and mathematical reasoning in Descartes, in which algebraic reasoning is not formal, see Danielle Macbeth, 'Viète, Descartes, and the Emergence of Modern Mathematics', *Graduate Faculty Philosophy Journal*, 25 (2004), 87–117.

[19] See Part IV, ch. 2.

[20] As was the *Recherche de la vérité*, which also deals with logic (AT x. 415 ff.), but which doesn't add much to the argument. A Dutch version of these two texts was published in 1684, but this fact does not appreciably change the history of their reception.

[21] Descartes had announced these themes in *Principles of Philosophy*, I. 10, published four years before the Preface.

worry that logic in general might be harmful: 'although it contains, in effect, very true and good precepts, nevertheless there are so many others, mixed up with them, which are either harmful or superfluous, that it is almost as hard to separate the one from the other as to draw a Diana or a Minerva from a block of marble'.[22] In the *Discourse*, Descartes also compares the possibly harmful or superfluous effects of logic with those of the analysis of the ancients and the algebra of the moderns. He claims that the latter two have defects as well: they both extend to extremely abstract matters which seemingly have no utility; the analysis of the ancients 'cannot exercise the understanding without fatiguing the imagination'; and the algebra of the moderns has been made into 'a confused and obscure art that bothers the mind, instead of a science that cultivates it' (AT vi. 18). This is why he sought *another method* 'which, having the advantages of these three, would be exempt from their faults' (AT vi. 18) and, towards this end, he exhibits his four rules of method: the rules of evidence, of the division of difficulties, of the order of inquiry, and of the completeness of enumerations (AT vi. 18–19). The rules of method now substitute for what we, readers of the *Regulae*, take to be Descartes's real method, exercising our native intelligence, intuiting and deducing, etc. To make the point clear: intuition and deduction do not occur anywhere in the *Discourse*. The four rules of method stand by themselves without further foundation.

Descartes refers to the *Discourse* in the Preface to the French translation of the *Principles*, as 'a Discourse on the Method of rightly conducting one's reason and seeking the truth in the sciences, *where I summarized the principal rules of logic*' (AT ixb. 15; my emphasis). Thus, by 1647, Descartes came to call his four rules of method the principal rules of *logic*. This is to be explained by another passage from the same Preface, in which Descartes talks about the order of teaching and the tree of philosophy. According to Descartes, before applying himself to true philosophy a person who has only common and imperfect knowledge should form a code of morals sufficient to regulate the actions of his life and should likewise study logic, but not the logic of the Schools:

---

[22] AT vi. 17–18. In *Principles of Philosophy*, I. 10, Descartes gives as an example of a harmful result attending to the use of the logic of the schools: '*That conceptions which are perfectly simple and clear of themselves are obscured by the definitions of the Schools.* . . . philosophers err in trying to explain by definitions logically constructed, things which were perfectly simple in themselves; they thereby render them but more obscure.'

for this is strictly speaking nothing but a dialectic which teaches ways of expounding to others what one already knows or even of holding forth without judgment about things one does not know. Such logic corrupts good sense rather than increasing it. I mean instead the kind of logic that teaches us to direct our reason with a view to discovering the truths of which we are ignorant. Since this depends to a great extent on practice, it is good for the student to work for a long time at practicing the rules on very easy and simple questions like those of mathematics. (AT ixb. 14–15)

So again, the logic of the Schools is a 'dialectic' that corrupts rather than improves good sense, but this time we also have Descartes's method as another logic recommended as a good practical exercise to improve one's mind. And now the critique of the syllogism is not explicitly mentioned and problems of mathematics are recommended indirectly as things that would exercise the mind.[23]

Before concluding this brief survey of Descartes's views on logic, I should mention one other text that seems a bit different from all the others, though it is not altogether inconsistent with them. The text, a portion of what is often called the *Conversation with Burman*, was not published in the seventeenth century and could have hardly affected anyone except Johann Clauberg, who had a role to play in its dissemination. Commenting to (Frans?) Burman on the *Discourse*

---

[23] Descartes's way of speaking—'ma logique', 'la vraie logique', 'as against la logique ordinaire', 'la logique de l'Ecole'—has other precedents in his works, though these seem to indicate that Descartes might have had another line of thought that there was a 'true logic' different from the logic of the Schools that might have been other than his method. In the *First Set of Replies* to Caterus, speaking of the idea of God Descartes said: 'in this idea is contained what God is, at least insofar as I am capable of understanding it; and according to the laws of true logic, we must never ask about the existence of anything until we first understand what it is' (AT vii. 108). Presumably Descartes had originally said 'selon les lois de ma logique', since, referring to this passage, Descartes told Mersenne in a 1640 letter, 'In the place where I put "in accordance with the laws of my logic," please put "in accordance with the laws of the true logic" … The reason why I add "my" or "the true" to "logic" is that I have read theologians who follow the ordinary logic and inquire what God is before inquiring whether God exists' (AT iii. 272–3). It is difficult to make very much sense of the passages from the Reply to Caterus and the letter to Mersenne: it is hard to see why the true logic or Descartes's method, as described in the four rules of method of *Discourse*, Part II, would forbid him to ask of something whether it exists without knowing what it is. And, according to Descartes, the four rules of method are sufficient to constitute his logic: 'in place of the large number of rules that make up logic, I would find the following four to be sufficient, provided that I made a strong and unswerving resolution never to fail to observe them' (AT vi. 18). Thus, either there is more to the 'true logic' or there is some unspecified argument that the four rules of the *Discourse* require one to know what something is before asking whether it exists, or more narrowly what God is before asking whether he exists.

passage about the harmful role of logic, Descartes allegedly limited the
range of these statements to dialectics alone; he said:

This really applies not so much to logic, which provides demonstrative proof
on all subjects, but to dialectic, which teaches us how to hold forth on all
subjects. In this way, it undermines good sense, rather than building on it.
For in diverting our attention and making us digress into the stock arguments
and headings, which are irrelevant to the thing under discussion, it diverts us
from the actual nature of the thing itself. (AT v. 175)

This might have been Descartes's view in 1648, but it would have
been an evolution from his more negative assertions about syllogism
in the 1620s and 1630s. Logic itself is now rehabilitated; only the
rhetorical misuse of logic—'dialectics'[24]—is considered harmful.

Thus there are at least three Descartes positions to be sketched:
(1) the Descartes of the *Regulae*, that is, the real Descartes according
to us, in which truth is grasped by means of our native intelligence,
using intuition and deduction, etc., together with the thought that
traditional logic takes us away from the truth; (2) the Descartes of
the *Discourse*, in which rules of method are given as another method,
instead of traditional logic, which is considered harmful; and (3) the
late Descartes, in which the rules of method are given as the principal
rules of logic, together with a generally positive view of logic,
criticisms of logic being limited to the portion of it called dialectics.

3. CARTESIAN LOGIC

The more positive view extended to all of logic is what François
Bayle[25] depicts in his brief chapter on logic in *The General Systeme
of the Cartesian Philosophy*. Bayle was a member of the Faculty of
Medicine at the University of Toulouse; he was an active participant
in the Société des lanternistes (a forum for discussing ideas and
reporting on new experiments), teaching alongside Régis and others.
His main philosophical work, *The General Systeme*, a synopsis of the
Cartesian system constructed out of Descartes's whole corpus, survives
only in a 1670 English translation. There are the usual words of caution

---

[24] Referring to a part of logic and not to logic as a whole.

[25] This Bayle should not be confused with the more famous Pierre Bayle, author of the
Dictionnaire historique et critique.

about logic in Bayle's chapter, but Bayle clearly wishes to extend what Descartes described as the salutary effect of practising his method to all of logic, including the logic taught in the schools:

It cannot be said, that the Precepts which are commonly taught in Schools, are to be altogether rejected or despised, since they are established upon very good Reasons; nor that a great number of Questions, which are treated therein, and which at first appear odd enough, are of no use. For although it be not valuable, to know the truths which they explain, yet the difficulty there is in examining them exerciseth the Mind, and renders it more able to penetrate and to clear up Difficulties which are met with in weighty matters; provided, Men use this Caution, that by too much applying the Mind to those things which subsist no otherwise than in an Idaea, they be not taken for real Beings, and such as do exist without the Understanding.

Thus *Geometricians* make themselves capable, promptly to explicate the most difficult Problems in those matters which are of use in the life of Man, by exercising themselves in the most knotty and the most abstract Questions of Algebra, and by making Magical Squares and other things, which are of no use in themselves.[26]

The chapter ends with Bayle declaring:

But, to speak precisely, no man of good sense, that acts candidly, and labours only to find out Truth, either alone or jointly with others, without any design of deceiving them, and without any ground of fearing to be deceived himself by any Sophism, needs any other Precepts of Logick, but these four ensuing.

And then Bayle recites the four rules of method from the *Discourse*, with slight variations.[27]

A similar positive slant is given to logic in Le Grand's 'Logick', Part I of *The Institution of Philosophy*, chapter 2, 'Of the true Use of Logick, shewing that Logick is useful and necessary to the Conduct of a Rational Life':

---

[26] François Bayle, *The General Systeme of the Cartesian Philosophy* (London, 1670), 'Of Logick', 78–81.

[27] 'The *first* is, never to receive any thing for true, which is not evidently known to be such, that is, never to take in more into our Judgments, than what presents it self so clearly and distinctly, that we cannot at all doubt thereof. The *second*, to divide each of the difficulties, which we discuss into as many small parts as is possible, and necessary for examining them the better. The *third*, orderly to conduct our Thoughts, by beginning with the most simple and the most easily knowable Objects, and so by degrees to ascend to the knowledge of the more compounded. The *fourth*, to make throughout such complete Enumerations, and such universal Reviews, that we be assured, we omit nothing.'

True it is, that *Logick* seems to have declined from its primitive Majesty, since it now chiefly considers *Forms*, and is in a manner wholly taken up with the Resolving of unprofitable *Questions:* Yet neither it is wholly to be undervalued upon that account, since those *Questions* exercise the Wit of Men, and are not a little conducive to the examining of the Difficulties we meet with in other Sciences. As *Geometricians*, by exercising themselves in the crabbed Questions of *Algebra*, which are altogether Abstracted, and of no use for the Conduct of Life, are nevertheless thereby disposed for the understanding of other difficult *Problems*, that are of great use in the Life of Man. In a word, which way soever we consider *Logick*, we shall find it to be of use, and in that regard not inferiour to the *Arts* or *Sciences*.[28]

An affirmative view of logic and syllogism is also clearly behind the observations of the Oratorian Nicolas-Joseph Poisson, in his commentary on the *Discourse on Method*, *Remarques sur la méthode de M. Descartes*. Poisson gives lengthy explanations of the four rules of method, but all he has to say about Descartes's critique of syllogism and logic is that

Descartes admits that he received much assistance from logic, the analysis of the ancients, and algebra, and at the same time he shows in what way those sciences are useful and in what way they are defective. I do not know what use he has made of the rules of logic he learned from his teachers, except perhaps that it is by their means that he has penetrated better the opinions of the schools, whether to retain them or to undo their influence on him.[29]

And Poisson proceeds in the same way to neglect Descartes's parallel criticism of the analysis of the ancients and algebra as too abstract and useless, confused and obscure, simply praising Descartes's own use of analysis and algebra:

As for analysis, we see a continual use of it in Descartes, not only in geometry, but also in the most common matters, where Descartes's arguments always seem to be imbued with this method, which has become natural to him. He has also used algebra frequently, and has even made it the key to his geometry. (p. 38)

---

[28] Antoine Le Grand, *An Entire Body of Philosophy* (London, 1694), i. 3.

[29] Nicolas-Joseph Poisson, *Commentaire; ou, Remarques sur la méthode de M. Descartes, où l'on établit plusieurs principes généraux nécessaires pour entendre toutes ses oeuvres* (Vandosme, 1670), 38.

However, not all commentators were as positive about logic as Bayle, Le Grand, and Poisson. In Du Roure's *Logique*, Part I of his *Abrégé de la vraye philosophie*, there is a discussion of 'Les Deffaux du Syllogisme', situated within a generally constructive and extended account of the matter, form, and principles of the syllogism:

Regarding the defects of syllogism, I say that it is a kind of reasoning particular to some people, necessary for no one, difficult for everyone. In the end, [it is] encumbered by a multitude of precepts, which are ridiculous, uncertain, and perhaps false. 1. Therefore syllogism hardly serves anyone except those who make of it a kind of commerce. 2. It is enough to reason by things without needing a plurality of words to signify them ... why is it necessary to use such a mass of superfluous words and propositions of which the syllogism is composed? 3. Some claim that the syllogism is a means for knowing the truth; but we must consider that it is a means more difficult than the truth itself.[30]

It is clear that the Cartesians were not themselves united in their criticisms of logic and did not all support Descartes's views about the value of logic, dialectics, and syllogism. So we may ask what made the logic of the Cartesians a Cartesian logic. The obvious answer lies in their emphasis on method. However, what they meant by method varied widely; again they did not fully agree among themselves and did not in general support Descartes's views about method. For example, Du Roure begins his logic text with method, by which he means primarily what he calls analysis and synthesis;[31] he continues

---

[30] Jacques Du Roure, *Abrégé de la vraye philosophie* (Paris, 1665), 'Logique', sect. 87.

[31] There are numerous methods called analysis and synthesis in early modern philosophy, most of which have nothing to do with the various things Descartes called analysis and synthesis—resolution and composition within the method of the *Regulae*, the two modes of demonstration of the *Second Replies*, or the analysis (and synthesis) of the ancients. Scipion Dupleix defines one of the standard scholastic notions in his *Logique* (1603) chapter on analysis and synthesis: 'Analytic (in the same way as *resolutive* in French) is a Greek word derived from *analysis*, that is to say, *resolution*; it is nothing more than a regress or return of a thing to its principles and (to speak more clearly) a dissolution of the pieces of which a thing is composed—so that it is the contrary of composition. For example, throw a bush into the fire: what will be fire in it will be turned into fire; air will be exhaled; water will be evaporated; but if the wood is green, the air and water will mix and a kind of foam will come out of the pores; the terrestrial will be resolved into ashes. And through this resolution we will judge that this wood was composed of the four elements. In the same way, in the analytic part, we see the whole structure and composition of the syllogism through the resolution of the three pieces of which it is composed—what we call the *subject, attribute,* and *intermediate* or *medium*' (Roger Ariew, John Cottingham, and Tom Sorell, *Descartes's Meditations: Background Source Materials* (Cambridge: Cambridge University Press, 1998), 99).

by discussing experience, including the following statements he takes
to be true: 'All our knowledge comes from experience [that is, the
senses]. ... And whoever makes use of reason more than experience
or reflections on experiences often falls into error' (*Abrégé de la vraye
philosophie*, sect. 20). Du Roure then deals with Reasoning, starting
with the reduced case of a single complex proposition and continuing
with enthymemes composed of two propositions; he then produces
a thorough discussion of syllogism, ending with a section on axioms.
Very little or none of this is in itself particularly Cartesian.

Nevertheless, it does clearly break from the customary order that
the scholastics gave to logic in their textbooks. Scholastics usually
followed an order of topics dictated by the various books of Aristotle's
*Organon: Categories, On Interpretation, Prior Analytics, Posterior Analytics,
Topics,* and *Sophistical Refutations.* For example, after two introduct-
ory books containing some preliminary questions,[32] Scipion Dupleix
writes six other books, corresponding to Aristotle's six logical works:
Dupleix's book III concerns categories, that is, substance, quantity,
quality, relations, and so forth; book IV is about nouns, verbs, and
statements; book V discusses syllogism; book VI is about science and
demonstration;[33] book VII deals with topics; and book VIII is about
paralogisms. One can say analogous things about the logic textbooks of
other early seventeenth-century French scholastics, such as Eustachius
a Sancto Paulo, Pierre du Moulin, and René de Cerisiers.

On the Cartesian side, Clauberg's *Logica contracta*[34] follows a similar
pattern, starting with the categories and continuing with attribute
and accident; cause and effect; subject and adjunct; relation; whole

(Dupleix's chapter, after all, is a commentary on Aristotle's *Posterior **Analytics*** as understood
in late scholasticism.) Du Roure's analysis and synthesis follow the same lines as Dupleix:
'Method is the order of the sciences and of their discourse: where one makes several things
out of one, which is called the analytic method, or from several one, which is called the
synthetic or compositional method' (sect. 2).

[32] On such issues as 'l'utilité de la Logique', 'Comment est-ce que la Logique peut estre
appellée science', 'Comment est-ce que la Logique peut estre dite Art', and 'De la definition
et division de la Logique', and genus, species, accidents, and universals.

[33] This is where one typically finds discussions of method and what is called analysis and
synthesis or resolution and composition.

[34] *Logica contracta*, as its title suggests, is a short treatise (pp. 911–36 of *Opera omnia*, ii,
as opposed to *Logica vetus et nova*, which takes up pp. 765–912 of the same volume). Little
is known about its genesis: see Theo Verbeek, 'Johannes Clauberg: A Biobibliographical
Sketch', in Theo Verbeek (ed.), *Johannes Clauberg (1622–1665) and Cartesian Philosophy in the
Seventeenth Century* (Dordrecht: Kluwer, 1999), 190.

and part; the same and other; universal and singular; definition; and division. Clauberg's second part of logic begins with the grades of judgement—qualitative statement; truth and falsity; opposition, conversion, and equivalence; and composite statement—and continues with argument and syllogism, both perfect and imperfect, and true and false. His third part of logic deals with the grades of memory and his fourth part concerns teaching and dialectics, order and fallacy. Again, very little of this seems Cartesian.[35]

In contrast, Clauberg's *Logica vetus et nova* begins with a Prolegomena arguing, along Descartes's line from the end of *Principles of Philosophy*, Part I, that the principal origin of error is to be found in the prejudices of childhood. Logic is the corrective for these mental imperfections; thus, in the first book of his logic, Clauberg devises a scheme that involves Descartes's rules of method and traditional logic, following the pattern of his *Logica contracta*, as three 'grades' or levels of logic. The first level has to do with accepting clear and distinct perceptions; it includes the rule of evidence and ends up with the rule about the division of difficulties, but it also discusses traditional topics such as substance, attribute, and mode; essence and existence; universal and singular; definition; and division. The second level concerns right judgement and involves the rule about the order of inquiry, ending with the rule of the completeness of enumerations; it also discusses induction and syllogism. Clauberg's third level concerns memory. Thus Descartes's subtle shift in position, especially his final stance in the Conversation with Burman with which Clauberg was familiar, allowed Clauberg to reinterpret Descartes's rules of method as part of logic, now integrated into a legitimate branch of learning that even included syllogisms.[36]

---

[35] Though this should not be overstated; there are in fact Cartesian elements in the work: logic is still the art of right thinking, which involves clear and distinct perceptions, right judgement, and these things being brought to memory (*Logica contracta*, 913).

[36] Clauberg was also helped in this by his general view of Descartes's works. Clauberg's second book, *Defensio cartesiana* (Amsterdam, 1652), was primarily a reply to *Consideratio theologica* (Leiden, 1648), a detailed commentary on Descartes's *Discourse on Method* from an orthodox theological point of view, by the Leiden professor Jacobus Revius. The *Defensio cartesiana* provoked a reply from Revius, which Clauberg answered with *Initiatio philosophi; sive, Dubitatio cartesiana* (Leiden, 1655). In his defence of Cartesianism, Clauberg distinguished between Descartes's popular and his esoteric works; according to Clauberg, the *Discourse on Method* belongs to the first category, while the *Meditations* and *Principles of Philosophy* belong to the second. Thus Clauberg could emphasize the view of logic

Clauberg interspersed Cartesian logic into the traditional framework and Du Roure inverted the scholastic order, discussing method and experience before demonstration and syllogism; other Cartesians found it more expedient and perhaps more intellectually satisfying, however, to follow more strictly the scholastic order in logic, grafting on Descartes's logic in a section about method at the end of their treatises. The *Port-Royal Logic*, which dominated in the second half of the seventeenth century (thus also Régis's *Logique*), and Le Grand's *Logick* are divided into four parts: (I) Ideas, including Aristotle's categories, universals, and names; (II) Propositions (or Judgements), truth and falsehood; (III) Reasoning (or Discourse), including syllogisms, topics, and sophisms; and (IV) Method. By method, however, these writers signify analysis and synthesis, which again does not have to be anything particularly Cartesian, though we do find Descartes's logic, that is, his rules of method, enumerated in the chapters on analysis. The *Port-Royal Logic* lists Descartes's four rules, saying that they are 'general to all sorts of methods and not particular to the method of analysis alone' (*Logique*, 375), but then moves on to give five rules of composition, focusing on these and enlarging them by chapter 10 to eight principal ones: 'The method of the sciences reduced to eight principal rules' (ibid. 428–31). Régis follows suit, of course. He also lists the four rules, but he adds a faint echo of the critique of syllogism: 'These four precepts can easily supplement what is missing from Aristotle's logic; we can even guarantee that they are more useful, because they can serve to discover the truth, something that those of the Philosophers cannot contribute to' (*Système général*, i. 48). Régis also adds a chapter on 'the advantages we draw from observing the four precepts of analysis' (ibid. i. 52–4) and abbreviates the lengthy *Port-Royal* discussion of synthesis into a single three-page chapter and just three brief rules: (1) to leave no term ambiguous; (2) to use clear and evident principles; and (3) to demonstrate all propositions (ibid. i. 56).

Le Grand does not formally list Descartes's four rules of method, though his logic seems to be the most Cartesian of the lot. His justification (taken up by Régis) for dividing logic into four parts

embodied in the *Principles* (and *Conversation with Burman*), that the Cartesian rules of method are the 'principal rules of logic'. For more on the relationship between these works and Clauberg's logic, see Massimiliano Savini, *Le Développement de la méthode cartésienne dans les Provinces-Unies (1643–65)* (Lecce: Conte Editore, 2004).

is that there are four operations of the mind, represented by ideas, by which we perceive, propositions, by which we judge, syllogisms, by which we reason or discourse, and method, by which we order. Given this organization, Part I of Le Grand's *Logick* discusses the clear and distinct perception of the mind, beginning with a chapter on the hindrances to science and how they are to be removed, basically recapitulating Descartes's discussion of the prejudices of childhood from the end of the *Sixth Replies* and the beginning of the *Principles*. Le Grand then sets out, in the remainder of Part I, ten rules for the attainment of truth, including: '1. We are to admit of nothing that involves any thing of Doubtfulness' (*Entire Body of Philosophy*, i. 5); '2. We are not to rely too much on our Senses' (ibid. i. 6); '3. Whatsoever we perceive, we perceive with our Minds' (ibid. i. 7); and '4. That is True which we know clearly and distinctly.'[37] The rules are interspersed within a Cartesian-style discussion of the modes of perception, that is, pure intellection, imagination, and sense, and a somewhat less Cartesian account of the five universals, or predicables. Chapters on substance and its modes follow, including 'How the Name of Substance agrees to God and the Creatures' (ibid. i. 17). Le Grand's answer to this question is that substance is not used univocally but equivocally between God and creatures.

Part II of Le Grand's *Logick* is about judgement, truth, and falsity, together with seven rules for judgement. Part III is about syllogism; it contains rules for simple and complex syllogisms and examples of imperfect arguments, topical and sophistical syllogisms. Finally, Part

---

[37] Le Grand, *Entire Body of Philosophy*, i. 8. The other rules are: '5. It avails much to the Clear and distinct perception of Truth, to retain in one's Mind an accurate Genealogy of Things and Modes, that with one cast of an Eye we may be able to take a view of the whole Universe of Things, beginning from the most General, and ending with the most Special' (i. 18); '6. The Idea or Perception of every thing is by so much the more clear and perfect, by how much the more Parts, Causes and Adjuncts of the thing it doth represent' (i. 22); '7. Those Things are to be looked upon as agreeing which agree in some common Idea or reason, or whereof the one is included in the Idea of the other; and they are said to disagree or to be diverse, which are the Objects of different Idea's and are apprehended after a diverse manner; or the one whereof is not included in the Idea of the other' (i. 22); '8. That Idea, or perception of a thing is clear and distinct, which represents the thing it self to the Mind, according to the foregoing Rules of Truth: And that obscure and confuse, which doth more or less depart from the same' (i. 23); '9. He whose Mind is furnished with most, and most perfect Ideas, is the most knowing and understanding Man' (i. 23); '10. The names of Things which we use in Philosophizing must be clear and determinate as to their Signification; not obscure or Ambiguous' (i. 25).

IV, 'Concerning Method, or the Orderly Disposition of Thoughts',
deals with the analytic and synthetic methods, resolution and composition. As we have said, Le Grand does not formally set out Descartes's
rules of method in the chapters on analysis. But as part of the analytic
method, he asserts that since this method is the art that guides reason
in the search for truth, we must determine the nature of the question
we wish to examine. He adds, in a Cartesian fashion, that what we are
to determine are questions because we cannot proceed to something
unknown except by means of something known, and questions are
propositions that include something known and something unknown
(ibid. i. 45). He then specifies that whenever the nature or cause of
anything is proposed, we must

in the first place accurately examine all the Conditions of the question
propounded, without minding things as are Extraneous, and do not belong
to the Question. Secondly, We are to separate those things which are certain
and manifest from those that include any thing of Confusion or Doubt.
... Thirdly, Every Difficulty we meet with is to be divided into Parts. ...
Fourthly, We are orderly to dispose of our Perceptions, and the Judgments
we frame thence; so that beginning from the most easie, we may proceed
by degrees to those that are more difficult. ... Fifthly, That the Thing in
question, be furnished with some Note or other that may determine it, and
make us judge it to be the same, whenever we meet with it. (ibid. i. 46)

This seems to be Le Grand's version of Descartes's four rules of
method, restricted to what is useful to analysis. Le Grand ends his
Logick with some chapters on composition, giving various rules of
definition, axiom, and demonstration similar to the ones given by the
Port-Royal Logic.

4. CONVERGENCE BETWEEN CARTESIAN AND SCHOLASTIC
LOGIC

It would appear that the Cartesians' greatest innovation was the
new form they gave to their logic. But in 1648 Louis de Lesclache
published a scholastic textbook, *La Philosophie divisée en cinq parties.*
Its first part was a scholastic logic, itself arranged into four parts,
the first three concerning 'les trois actions de l'entendement',
namely, 'la conception, le jugement, et la consequence', and the

fourth concerning 'la methode', that is, resolution and composition.[38] Lesclache even decided that the usual questions about whether logic is a science or an art belonged to the second part of philosophy, that is, science, and not in the first part, logic.[39] Lesclache saw himself as a teacher and defender of the scholastic viewpoint. In fact, his logic was even attacked in an anonymous treatise, Lesclache's critic claiming that there was nothing original in his logic: 'Truly, to satisfy his desire completely, if I did not find the origin of his tables in Abraham de Guise, Kekkermann, Eustachius a Sancto Paulo, Hallier, Hoeckelshoven, Timpler, Zuingger, and Crassot, I would have admitted that he is their author.'[40] Obviously the contents, if not the form, of Lesclache's logic were considered traditional.

So ultimately, in the second half of the seventeenth century, we have many Cartesians toning down Descartes's negative remarks about logic in order to write Cartesian logics that blend with the logic of the schools, in which Descartes's method is simply appended to the last part of the traditional logic and is considered at best only a portion of the section on analysis (that is, Le Grand's Descartes). This Descartes need not be thought of as a philosopher of Bacon's ilk, that is, someone who proposes his method instead of formal logic (the real Descartes according to us), nor even someone who proposes his method as the principal rules of logic (Clauberg's Descartes). At the same time we have a scholastic logician rearranging the order of logic, dropping the traditional preliminary questions about the status of logic, and adding a new final section on method, that is, analysis and synthesis. The convergence between the ultimate Cartesian logic and scholastic logic is striking.[41]

University of South Florida

---

[38] Lesclache's 'resolution' is just the scholastic notion: breaking down a whole into its parts or knowledge into its first principles; 'composition' is its opposite.

[39] Lesclache's main claim to fame, however, rested on the many tables he published in the work and published again in *La Philosophie expliquée en tables* (Paris, 1656).

[40] *La Philosophie particulière combattue par celle de l'escole; ou, L'On examine les Discours et les tables d'un philosophe de ce temps* (Paris, 1650), 7–8.

[41] I gave early versions of this chapter to a meeting of the Centre d'études cartésiennes, Paris-IV, the Haverford College Distinguished Visitor Lecture series and Department of Philosophy Senior Honors Seminar, and Daniel Garber's Princeton University Descartes Graduate Seminar. I am grateful to the various members of these groups for their critical discussions, which were useful to me in sorting out my thoughts, and especially to Jean-Luc Marion, Ettore Lojacono, Massimiliano Savini, Aryeh Kosman, Danielle Macbeth, and Daniel Garber.

9

On the Necessity and Nature of Simples: Leibniz, Wolff, Baumgarten, and the Pre-Critical Kant

ERIC WATKINS

Standard histories of modern philosophy suggest, at least by their practice, that the philosophical landscape in Germany between Leibniz's death in 1716 and the publication of Kant's *Critique of Pure Reason* in 1781 is of little significance, either intrinsically or for our understanding of those modern philosophers that are of interest. For example, Christian Wolff, whose comprehensive series of systematic textbooks was extremely influential at the time, is typically mentioned not for his own philosophical views, but rather for popularizing Leibniz's philosophy. Alexander Baumgarten is widely recognized for his early advocacy of aesthetics as an autonomous discipline, but not for his views in metaphysics and epistemology, since his primary contribution in theoretical philosophy was a Latin textbook whose most immediately noticeable departure from Wolff is its unusually terse mode of presentation. The pre-Critical Kant is often dismissed as well, in part owing to disparaging remarks that he later made about his early works, and in part owing to the judgement that his pre-Critical writings are an instance of precisely the kind of dogmatic metaphysics that his Critical philosophy is supposed to overcome. The same refrain is repeated with minor variations for many other figures at the time, such as Martin Knutzen, Moses Mendelssohn, and Johann Nicolas Tetens. The standard picture is thus that Leibniz is the master, while Wolff and Baumgarten endeavour simply to reproduce his philosophy in a more systematic form, and the pre-Critical Kant bides his time with fruitless metaphysical inquiries until his revolutionary meta-philosophical reflections bring about the Critical turn and an entirely new way of thinking. As a result, the standard view is committed to ascribing a more or less monolithic philosophical position to Leibniz and his immediate successors in Germany in so far as Wolff and Baumgarten are judged by the extent to which they capture (or distort) Leibniz's actual position, while the pre-Critical Kant is viewed as reacting to them in ways that are of no lasting interest because of the vast gulf that allegedly separates the pre-Critical from the Critical Kant. While differences between the views of these figures may be acknowledged regarding certain inessential details, the fundamental assumptions, arguments, and positions are, or at least ought to be, roughly the same.

Since the standard view gives rise to an expectation of considerable uniformity, it is quite striking to note how significant the difference is between Leibniz's fully *idealistic* monadology and the pre-Critical Kant's *physical* monadology. Leibniz, in his later years, explicitly holds that everything—including bodies—is ultimately composed entirely of mindlike entities, i.e. substances endowed with a representative power, whereas the pre-Critical Kant asserts that all bodies are composed of physical points that are endowed with mass (inertial force) and exercise attractive and repulsive forces. Obviously enough, these radical differences immediately entail that the standard view cannot be maintained. However, they also raise a question that is both more interesting and more important: How is this shift from Leibniz's idealistic monadology to the pre-Critical Kant's physical monadology to be explained?

The short answer is that, for philosophical and historical reasons to be described in detail below, Wolff, Baumgarten, and the pre-Critical Kant all reacted to their predecessor's views on a series of more limited points that, taken together, amounted to a much more radical shift. This answer is instructive on several counts. For one, not only does it set the historical record straight, but, more importantly, it can also do so in such a way that each figure can be represented as reacting in a fully intelligible way to the situation he encountered. For another, by allowing us to see Leibniz's philosophy—its assumptions, arguments, and aims—not from the perspective of a radically opposed position or even that of a sympathetic contemporary reader simply intent on understanding what Leibniz actually thought, but rather from perspectives that can seem to differ from it only slightly, one can come to appreciate a wealth of surprisingly rich possibilities that are implicitly contained in Leibnizian philosophy that Leibniz himself did not explicitly pursue. Finally, by adopting such a point of view, one can also have clearer insight into the significance of certain structural features of Leibniz's and the Critical Kant's philosophies that may not otherwise be immediately apparent.

More specifically, in the following I show that Wolff, Baumgarten, and the pre-Critical Kant attempt to develop novel arguments for the necessity of simple substances, or monads, and to articulate a range of positions regarding the nature of such substances, and that, when taken in context, the differences in their arguments and positions make good historical and philosophical sense. (1) I first present, as the requisite background, Leibniz's position on these topics and certain questions that naturally arise with regard to them. (2) I then explain two main components of Wolff's reaction. Though Wolff accepts Leibniz's main argument for the necessity of simples, he develops a second argument that is different from anything Leibniz formulates in print, though it is based on principles that Leibniz accepted (and mentions briefly in private correspondence). In fact, since this new argument is not tied to a criticism of Descartes's position, as Leibniz's primary argument is, it even represents an advance over Leibniz's in terms of its scope. Wolff is also agnostic about the nature of simples that compose bodies, given that Leibniz has, he thinks, never in fact proved that all simples must be endowed with the power to represent the world, and his agnosticism on this point has several important consequences for aspects of his broader view.

The next step (3) is to show how Baumgarten takes advantage of the space that Wolff's agnosticism about the nature of simples has created by suggesting that monads could be nothing more than physical points endowed with impenetrability, a view that Leibniz does not explicitly argue against and that he may not even have entertained in the form in which Baumgarten proposed it. I then explain (4) how the pre-Critical Kant embraces Baumgarten's suggestion that monads are physical and, owing to his interest in scientific issues and his early acceptance of Newtonian physics, develops a more robust physical monadology by ascribing inertia and attractive and repulsive forces to physical monads and having them play a foundational metaphysical role in his physics. Kant's understanding of how a physical monadology should be understood brings with it a significant revision of Leibniz's distinction between primitive and derivative forces, which allows him to respond in original ways to the questions that naturally arose for Leibniz and that remained problematic for Wolff and Baumgarten to varying degrees. In short, we get from Leibniz's idealistic monadology to the pre-Critical Kant's physical monadology by reflecting on what the strongest argumentative basis for the necessity of monads might be and by seeing (with Wolff's help) that monads do not have to be minds (or very much like minds), as Leibniz held, but could be physical in either a minimal sense (as Baumgarten suggested) or a much more robust sense (as Kant argued) by being an integral part of one's scientific view.

This depiction of the historical development from Leibniz's idealistic to the pre-Critical Kant's physical monadology illustrates in a very concrete way how distinctively Leibnizian positions could be developed in detail and with significant philosophical support in their favour. However, it also opens up a perspective (5) from which one can attain three further insights. First, it reveals the importance of activity not only for the unity that substances have intrinsically, but also for the unity that obtains between substances belonging to larger unities, such as that of the world as a whole. Second, it establishes the centrality of Leibniz's distinction between primitive and derivative forces, and also raises important questions about why he understands that doctrine exactly as he does. Finally, it gives us a better understanding of the context of the development of the Critical Kant's acceptance of idealism. To follow the path that leads from Leibniz to Kant and these further insights, however, it is necessary to begin by considering Leibniz's reaction to Descartes in the 1680s and 1690s.

I. LEIBNIZ

In 1686, in a short note published in the *Acta eruditorum*, Leibniz argued that Descartes's physics was based on a law of motion that is false.[1] Specifically, Leibniz attacked Descartes's law according to

---

[1] 'Brevis Demonstratio Erroris memorabilis Cartesii et aliorum circa legem naturae, secundum quam volunt a Deo eandem semper quantitatem motus conservari; qua et in re mechanica abutuntur. Communicata in litteris d. 6. Jan. 1686 datis' (*Acta Eruditorum* (1686); repr. in GM vi. 117–19).

which the quantity of motion, represented by the product of volume and motion, had to be conserved in the world. Leibniz suggested that when conjoined with certain other assumptions, Galileo's law of freely falling bodies is inconsistent with Descartes's law, and that what he called living force, as measured by mv^2, must be conserved throughout all changes in bodies instead. Though Leibniz's remarks spurred considerable debate in learned circles in Europe throughout the next half-century by initiating the so-called *vis viva* controversy, his initial critique of Descartes was limited to a *single* foundational issue in *physics*.

In 1695 Leibniz broadened considerably the scope of his public critique of Descartes with the publication of 'A New System of the Nature and Communication of Substances, and of the Union of the Soul and Body' in the *Journal des Savants*.[2] In this article, Leibniz attacked *several* of Descartes's fundamental *metaphysical* claims. Perhaps best known is his discussion of the mind–body relationship.[3] Specifically, in the latter half of the 'New System', Leibniz rejects both Descartes's interactionist position and Malebranche's occasionalist alternative. The mind and the body cannot act on each other, as Descartes seemed to hold, since it is a fundamental truth of metaphysics, Leibniz argues, that no two finite substances can act on each other causally.[4] (Elsewhere, Leibniz also contends that since the natures of mind and body are, according to Descartes, radically distinct, there can be no proportion and hence no intelligible connection between any state of the mind and any particular motion of the body, which thus rules out causal interaction between mind and body.[5]) And while Leibniz certainly grants that God creates everything that exists at every moment in time, he rejects the occasionalist gambit of interpreting God to be the *sole* cause of the (mental and bodily) states of finite substances. If one were to appeal solely to divine intervention

[2] While Leibniz published this article anonymously, it was well known that he was its author. In fact, it stimulated considerable discussion, with Foucher, de Beauval, Bayle, and others publishing criticisms of it, criticisms to which Leibniz responded in print.

[3] For simplicity's sake, I shall use the term 'mind' very broadly to refer to both rational and non-rational souls and to cover what Descartes, Leibniz, Wolff, Baumgarten, and Kant mean, despite their various significant doctrinal differences.

[4] As Leibniz remarks in the 'New System', 'the action of one substance on another is neither the emission nor the transplanting of an entity' (Gottfried Leibniz, *Philosophical Essays* [*Essays*], ed. and tr. R. Ariew and D. Garber (Indianapolis: Hackett, 1989), 141).

[5] See Leibniz's letter to Arnauld, 30 Apr. 1687, in Leibniz, *Essays*, 83.

to explain specific states of the world, and not to secondary causes as well (i.e. to the causal activity of finite substances), one would, he objects, be committed to perpetual miracles.[6]

Since Descartes's and Malebranche's ways of explaining the relation between the mind and the body are inadequate, Leibniz proposes a third: 'we must say that God originally created the soul (and any other real unity) in such a way that everything must arise for it from its own depths, through a perfect *spontaneity* relative to itself, and yet with a perfect *conformity* relative to external things'.[7] That is, according to Leibniz's 'new system', a finite substance can act only on itself so as to cause the progression of its own states, though God has set up all finite substances prior to creation so that their states appear harmonious despite the absence of any real causal interaction between them. Leibniz then goes on to point out that his 'new system' not only presents the sole possible account of the mind–body relation, but also fits well with several other orthodox metaphysical theses, such as the existence of God and the freedom of the soul. Thus, in the 'New System' Leibniz argues that by attending to difficulties inherent in Cartesian positions on the mind–body relationship, an interesting and, he thinks, more satisfying alternative can be developed.

Earlier in the 'New System', however, Leibniz had also presented an argument against another of Descartes's distinctive metaphysical theses, namely that bodies are nothing more than extended substances. According to Descartes, bodies do not consist of substantial forms and primary matter, as scholastic Aristotelians had thought; nor, as Leibniz understands him, are they the seats of active causal powers by means of which they could cause changes of motion in each other; rather, as purely geometrical figures, they are simply extended in space.[8] Leibniz

---

[6] Leibniz, *Essays*, 143.   [7] Ibid.

[8] Descartes's actual views on this point are a matter of dispute. On the one hand, Descartes consistently emphasizes that bodies are simply extension, which would seem to be exhausted by their geometric and kinematic properties of size, shape, position, motion, rest, number, and duration. In the *Principles of Philosophy* (Part II, principle 11), Descartes explicitly argues that there is no real distinction between space and body (or corporeal substance). This view has been defended by Daniel Garber (*Descartes' Metaphysical Physics* (Chicago: University of Chicago Press, 1989)), Gary Hatfield ('Force (God) in Descartes' Physics', *Studies in History and Philosophy of Science*, 10 (1979), 113–40), and Peter Machamer ('Causality and Explanation in Descartes's Natural Philosophy', in P. Machamer and R. G. Turnbill (eds.), *Motion and Time* (Columbus: Ohio State University Press, 1976)). On the other hand, Descartes's argument for the existence of the external world in Meditation

explains how he came to think about bodies, or matter, in a very different way as follows:

> In the beginning, when I had freed myself from the yoke of Aristotle, I accepted the void and atoms, for they best satisfy the imagination. But on recovering from that, after much reflection, I perceived that it is impossible to find the *principles of a true unity* in matter alone, or in what is only passive, since everything in it is only a collection or aggregation of parts to infinity. Now, a multitude can derive its reality only from *true unities*, which have some other origin and are considerably different from [[mathematical]] points [[which are only the extremities and modifications of extension,]] which all agree cannot make up the *continuum*. Therefore, in order to find these *real entities* I was forced to have recourse to a formal atom, since a material thing cannot be both material and, at the same time, perfectly indivisible, that is, endowed with a true unity.[9]

Leibniz thus clearly rejects Descartes's account of matter. His reasoning in this passage, however, is perhaps not made fully explicit, as the argument can be developed in (at least) two different versions. The first version, for which the *infinite divisibility* of matter is crucial, proceeds as follows. If matter is simply extension, as Descartes held, and if extension is infinitely divisible, then matter is infinitely divisible. However, if matter is infinitely divisible, then everything in it is only a collection or aggregation of parts to infinity. Therefore, matter, on Descartes's conception, is only a collection or aggregation of parts to infinity. However, if matter is only a collection of parts to infinity, then it has no ultimate parts, but since the reality of a whole depends on the reality of its parts, matter, lacking ultimate parts, must also lack reality, given that 'what is not truly *one* being is not truly one being'.[10] However, a second version, which depends essentially on

6 seems to require the causal efficacy of bodies. Attributing causal efficacy to bodies has been developed in different ways by Alan Gabbey ('Force and Inertia in the Seventeenth Century: Descartes and Newton', in S. Gaukroger (ed.), *Descartes: Philosophy, Mathematics, and Physics* (Brighton: Harvester, 1980), 230–320) and Michael Della Rocca (' "If a Body Meets a Body": Descartes on Body–Body Causation', in R. J. Gennaro and C. Huenemann (eds.), *New Essays on the Rationalists* (New York: Oxford University Press), 48–81).

[9] Leibniz, *Essays*, 139. Text enclosed in brackets is thought to be later additions Leibniz made to his own manuscript, which were not included in the published version.

[10] This quotation is from Leibniz's correspondence with Arnauld, 30 Apr. 1687, in Leibniz, *Essays*, 86. Leibniz repeats essentially the same argument in 'On Nature Itself' (ibid. 162).

the contrast between the *continuity* of matter and the *discreteness* of reality, can be articulated as follows.[11] For Leibniz's problem with Descartes's conception of matter could be not that matter cannot consist of ultimate parts (given that the infinite divisibility of matter precludes such parts), but rather that whatever parts one arrives at through division must be continuous, which is inconsistent with Leibniz's view that reality (or any whole that is to be real) must consist of discrete parts.[12] In short, since real entities must be discrete, but matter, considered as consisting in extension alone, is not, matter cannot be real.[13] On either version of Leibniz's argument, however, it follows that matter, as Descartes understood it, lacks true unities and thus reality.

If matter can thus be real only if 'true unities' exist, what, according to Leibniz, must such simple entities be like? In the passage quoted above, Leibniz argues that the true unities that are required for the reality of matter can be neither material atoms nor (mathematical) points. If the true unities were material atoms, then they would be spatially extended and thus divisible, i.e. not truly unities or simple. If they were (mathematical) points, then they would be unities, but they could not, in that case, constitute the continuous nature of extended matter (as Descartes conceived of it), since (i) even an infinite number of unextended points cannot constitute a continuous magnitude (such as a line) and (ii) (mathematical) points are merely limitations or modifications *of* extension and thus cannot constitute extension itself. Leibniz's arguments thus show that matter can consist neither in extension alone, as Descartes held, nor in material atoms, as Democritus and Newton thought, nor in (mathematical) points.

---

[11] That Leibniz characterizes Descartes's position as positing the nature of matter in what is merely passive could suggest yet a third version of the argument. For Leibniz could be objecting that matter, considered merely as extension, cannot be real since it is not active and only what is active can be real. We shall return to the importance of activity to Leibniz's metaphysics below. It is immediately clear, however, that the textual basis for this last version of the argument is the slimmest of the three.

[12] For discussion of Leibniz's views on the relationship between mathematics and metaphysics in Leibniz's middle and later years, see Samuel Levey, 'Leibniz on Mathematics and the Actually Infinite Division of Matter', *Philosophical Review*, 107 (1998), 49–96.

[13] The second version of this argument may not ultimately be distinct from the first, since it is possible that the reason that only discrete entities can be real is that only they possess the requisite kind of unity. Leibniz's mention of continuity may thus simply be a remark hinting at an intermediary step in the argument.

Instead, one must accept indivisible unities of some other kind to make sense of the reality of extended bodies.

Later in the 'New System', Leibniz repeats several elements of his argument against Descartes and then describes his positive conception of the simples that are required by his argument as follows:

In addition, by means of the soul or form there is a true unity corresponding to what is called the *self* (*moy*) in us. Such a unity could not occur in the machines made by a craftsman or in a simple mass of matter, however organized it may be; such a mass can only be considered as an army or a herd, or a pond full of fish, or like a watch composed of springs and wheels. Yet if there were no true *substantial unities*, there would be nothing substantial or real in the collection. That was what forced Cordemoy to abandon Descartes and to embrace the Democritean doctrine of atoms in order to find a true unity. But *atoms of matter* are contrary to reason. Furthermore, they are still composed of parts, since the invincible attachment of one part to another (if we can reasonably conceive or assume this) would not eliminate diversity of those parts. There are only *atoms of substance*, that is, real unities absolutely destitute of parts, which are the source of actions, the first absolute principles of the composition of things, and, as it were, the final elements in the analysis of substantial things. We could call them *metaphysical points*: they have *something vital*, a kind of *perception*, and *mathematical points* are the *points of view* from which they express the universe. But when corporeal substances are contracted, all their organs together constitute only a *physical point* relative to us. Thus physical points are indivisible only in appearance; mathematical points are exact, but they are merely modalities. Only metaphysical points or points of substance (constituted by forms or souls) are exact and real, and without them there would be nothing real, since without true unities there would be no multitude.[14]

In this passage, the true unities or formal atoms that Leibniz had argued for previously are referred to as metaphysical points, which are contrasted with mathematical and physical points, and are likened to our mind or soul. He defines a metaphysical point as a substantial unity destitute of parts, but also describes it further—without explicit argument—as what has a representative power or force of perception, as what is alive, as what contains the source of its actions within itself, and as what serves as the fundamental principle of composition. The

similarities between metaphysical points and Aristotelian substantial
forms are not accidental; in an earlier passage, Leibniz indicates that
he is happy to rehabilitate certain aspects of Aristotelian substantial
forms in describing his true unities or formal atoms.[15]

If one follows Leibniz in accepting the idea that the true unities that
are required for the reality of extended bodies are metaphysical points
endowed with representational force, how exactly does a metaphysical
point serve as the fundamental principle of composition and thus allow
him to avoid the objection that he raised for Descartes's account?
That is, how is the unity that one entity possesses—mind—relevant
to bestowing reality on another entity—extended body—that lacks
such a unity? To understand Leibniz's reply, one must first attend to
a distinction he draws between being *per se* and being *per accidens*. To
be an entity that can exist independently of others, a substance must
be able to exist entirely through itself and thus must have being *per
se*. A collection, composite, or aggregate, by contrast, is not capable
of independent existence, since it can exist only if a certain accidental
relation holds among its members, for which reason it is said to have
being only *per accidens*. Accordingly, it is clear that extended bodies,
which, in virtue of their infinite divisibility, are simply a certain kind of
aggregate, cannot have being *per se*, but rather only being *per accidens*.[16]

With this distinction in hand, we can turn to a passage from
Leibniz's *New Essays on Human Understanding* (written in 1704–5,

[15] Unfortunately, Leibniz does not adequately clarify in that passage the precise role
that substantial forms are supposed to play in his ontology. Borrowing on distinctions that
have been drawn in the literature, especially by Robert Adams (*Leibniz: Determinist, Theist,
Idealist* [*Idealist*] (New York: Oxford University Press, 1994)) and Daniel Garber (most
recently in 'Leibniz and Fardella', in P. Lodge (ed.), *Leibniz and his Correspondents* (New
York: Cambridge University Press, 2004), 123–40), Leibniz's position can be interpreted in
very different ways. For example, this passage leaves open whether a metaphysical point is
an independently existing substance in its own right, or whether it is simply one constituent
principle of substances that also stand in need of a second, namely matter. It also leaves
open the question of whether there are two kinds of substances (simple and composite,
i.e. corporeal, substances) or only one, and if the latter, whether the matter to which a
substantial form added is an organic body or simply an element of passivity (that would
contrast with the activity of the substantial form). While Leibniz does clearly accept this
latter view (and also a fully idealist version of it) in *The Monadology*, his view in the so-called
middle period (in the mid-1680s) is less clear.

[16] In fact, in the passage quoted above, Leibniz seems to be drawing a contrast between
these different kinds of unity when he insists that 'a simple mass of matter, however
organized it may be', can 'only be considered as an army or a herd or a pond full of fish',
not a 'true unity' like our soul.

though published only much later in 1765), where he describes the
sense in which aggregates have unity and thus reality as follows:

> This unity of the idea of an aggregate is a very genuine one; but fundamentally
> we have to admit that this unity that collections have is merely a respect
> or a relation, whose foundation lies in what is the case with each of the
> individual substances taken alone. So the only perfect unity that these 'entities
> by aggregation' have is a mental one, and consequently, their very being is
> also in a way mental, or phenomenal, like that of the rainbow.[17]

That is, Leibniz maintains that aggregates do not have unity intrinsically or being *per se* because their unity is not the unity that substances
have as such. However, he insists that they do still have a unity and
it is 'very genuine'. Instead of being a substantial unity, this unity is
a relation among a plurality of entities that obtains, in part, on the
basis of features of each of the individual entities 'taken alone'. For
an aggregate has a unity only if its members possess properties in
virtue of which they stand in a certain relation to each other. But
Leibniz seems to think that the properties of such entities do not
stand in this relation when 'taken alone'. If a relation is to obtain
between the properties of distinct entities, they must be *taken together*;
a mind, Leibniz thinks, must actively represent each entity as standing
in relation to others that are to be members of the aggregate. For
example, an army possesses no unity on its own and is not an entity
in its own right; instead, it exists only if there is a plurality of soldiers
whom, say, a general thinks of as standing in certain relations to each
other.[18] Similarly, a body, as a collection that is infinitely divisible
into smaller spatially extended parts, is not an entity existing in its
own right, but rather derives its reality from a relation among the
properties of its parts (or constituent entities) that a mind grasps as
related (e.g. spatially). Thus, it is legitimate to speak of the reality of
a collection or aggregate but only because a mind actively imposes
an accidental unity on a plurality of entities on the basis of relations

---

[17] Leibniz, *New Essays on Human Understanding*, ed. P. Remnant and J. Bennett (New
York: Cambridge University Press, 1996), 146. For discussions of this issue, see Donald
Rutherford, *Leibniz and the Rational Order of Nature* (New York: Cambridge University
Press, 1995), 136, 271–2, and Paul Lodge, 'Leibniz's Notion of an Aggregate', *British Journal
for the History of Philosophy*, 9 (2001), 467–86.

[18] Leibniz's own example illustrates this point as well, since the 'springs and wheels' of a
clock are united by our perceiving them as being related so as to tell time.

it perceives among their properties.[19] Leibniz can attribute unity and thus reality to bodies in this way, but it is important to note that he can do so only by requiring that minds actively *take* a plurality of entities *together* and represent them as related and hence united in virtue of their intrinsic properties.[20] It is for this reason that he explicitly characterizes the unity and reality of aggregates or collections as *mental* or *phenomenal*; a collection is an ideal rather than a real entity.

Leibniz discusses the relationship between metaphysical unities and physical bodies further in the 'Specimen dynamicum', Part I of which appeared in the *Acta eruditorum* in the same year as the 'New System' was published. In the course of articulating a dynamical physics that was designed to complement his distinctive metaphysics, Leibniz distinguishes between primitive and derivative forces and then further between active and passive instances of each. Primitive active forces are described as substantial forms, which thus function as the true unities required by his objection to Descartes's position. Primitive passive forces, by contrast, are identified with prime matter, though he notes that this term is to be conceived of not in exactly the same sense as the scholastics had, but rather as the power to resist change. Since both kinds of primitive force are enduring first principles of things, they are, Leibniz claims, only 'general causes' and cannot be used to explain particular phenomena. In Leibniz's mature metaphysics (e.g. in *The Principles of Philosophy; or, The Monadology*, written in 1714, but not published until 1720), primitive active force is identified with appetition, while primitive passive force is associated with the lack of clarity and distinctness in our perceptions.

Derivative forces, by contrast, are invoked to explain the specific properties of bodies.[21] Derivative active force is said to constitute a body's impetus as well as its dead and living forces, while derivative

---

[19] I do not mean to suggest that Leibniz requires that the mind that represents entities as standing in relations is distinct in kind from the entities so represented. Indeed, the contrary is the case, since Leibniz holds that every monad represents every other.

[20] It is important to note that the mind need neither be conscious of this nor form an intention to do so, for it to occur. Also, sense perception also contains an element of passivity, in addition to the activity being emphasized here.

[21] Derivative forces are not specific to physical properties; they can be invoked in explanations of specific mental states as well.

passive forces are responsible for its impenetrability and resistance, or inertia. In this context, a derivative force is a particular state at one moment in time that is the cause of a physical state of a body at the next moment in time. What is supposed to make a derivative force derivative is the fact that it is a 'limitation', 'modification', or 'accidental variation' of primitive force. On occasion, Leibniz seems to think of a thing's primitive force as containing the enduring law of the series of its states, in which case a derivative force is an aspect of its present state that forms one member of that series. By understanding forces and laws in this way, Leibniz attempts to develop a physics of derivative forces that is compatible with his metaphysics of true unities.

One dimension of Leibniz's public philosophical position can thus be summarized as follows: By reflecting on Descartes's philosophy and raising objections to certain aspects of it, Leibniz is led to a novel position in metaphysics and physics. Rather than accepting Descartes's view that bodies are merely extension, Leibniz argues that bodies can be real only if true unities or metaphysical points exist. He articulates his conception of true unities further by arguing that they cannot be either material atoms or (mathematical) points, but rather are to be understood as minds, i.e. unities endowed with representational forces. Understanding true unities in this way then gives Leibniz the ability to explain how they can bestow unity on something that does not have it on its own, because minds can actively impose an accidental unity on a plurality of entities on the basis of some relation that minds represent their properties as standing in. Leibniz fills out this conception by advancing a dynamical physics according to which the active and passive forces that are the specific causes of the states of bodies are derivative from the more general, primitive mental forces of the true unities he had originally posited in response to Descartes's view.

However, even if Leibniz has raised several objections to Descartes's position and presented a novel alternative to it, a number of questions naturally arise regarding the precise details of his own account. The first question derives from noting that Leibniz's argument was designed to show merely that extended bodies could be real, despite their infinite divisibility, only if indivisible metaphysical points exist. However, since Leibniz conceives of these metaphysical points as mindlike, and holds that minds can bestow unity and thus reality on bodies only if the latter are understood as merely phenomenal or ideal, he ends up having to deny the reality of bodies in attempting to save their reality. Is there no way of avoiding such a paradoxical-sounding conclusion?[22]

Second, if *primitive* force is perceptual or *mental*, how exactly are any of the derivative forces that cause the *physical* states of bodies to be derived from it? That is, how does Leibniz overcome a slightly different version of the problem concerning the heterogeneity of the mind and the body that he had raised against Descartes? Granted, Leibniz does not explicitly characterize the relationship between primitive mental forces and derivative physical forces as a *causal* relationship between heterogeneous *substances*, but the physical forces are supposed to be *derivative* from mental forces, and the lack of proportionality between these forces could seem to threaten the intelligibility of the derivation relationship just as Leibniz thought it did that of the causal relation in Descartes's case.[23]

Third, if the derivative forces of bodies are essentially *relational* and the primitive forces of minds necessarily *intrinsic*, then how exactly do the latter give rise to the former, especially if the primitive forces of minds are supposed to serve only as general causes and thus are not to be appealed to in explaining specific changes in bodies?[24] It is true that Leibniz can appeal to the representational activity of minds

---

[22] The paradoxical ring here arises not simply from the fact that bodies, understood merely as extended beings, cannot, according to Leibniz's argument, be substances as such (and thus fundamentally real), but must rather be derivative, which can seem to contrast with what Descartes might naturally have meant by saying that something is real. One could remove that paradox simply by distinguishing, as Leibniz does, between different kinds of reality: fundamental reality (which is reserved for substances) and derivative reality (which applies to extension and the other accidents of substances). The paradox also arises from the fact that the ultimate ontological status of bodies is mental rather than physical, according to (the later) Leibniz's position. Using the term 'paradox' is meant here to indicate not any contradiction in the resultant position, but rather that there is a way of stating how the dynamics of Leibniz's argument leads the Cartesian to a position that is quite distant (e.g. at least two steps removed) from the original point at which it starts, since his argument requires denying that one can attribute to extension the privileged ontological and explanatory roles that were important to Descartes. In short, despite Leibniz's way of stating his objection, very little of Descartes's position can be saved if it is correct.

[23] In short, the problem here is that it is difficult to make sense of how (and why) physical bodies are to reduce to mental entities, given their different properties and laws.

[24] For discussion of this question about Leibniz's account of the relation of primitive and derivative forces, see Adams, *Idealist*, 378–99. Especially relevant is Adams's remark: 'There

to explain how relations between distinct entities are represented, for, as we saw above, a mind can relate several different things by taking them together and relating them to each other on the basis of their intrinsic properties. However, even granting Leibniz this point, it is still the case that such relations are intrinsic to each monad, because appealing to the activity of monads in this way explains only how a mind *represents* relations, and not how such relations could actually exist between distinct things. As a result, actual relations between distinct entities could seem to remain unaccounted for on Leibniz's account.

These three lines of inquiry can be combined into one densely packed question: How do the unchanging unities that represent the world by means of activities that are intrinsic to them ground (or render intelligible) changing physical relations between extended bodies? Unfortunately, Leibniz does not provide an explicit answer to the various aspects of this question—at least not to the wider reading public at the time.[25]

2. WOLFF

Christian Wolff, who corresponded with Leibniz for over a decade (from 1704 to 1716), is often credited with popularizing Leibniz's position in the first half of the eighteenth century in Germany, but he is also frequently blamed—or at least looked down upon—for not having a proper or full appreciation of Leibniz's views. In this section, I argue that investigating Wolff's discussion of the necessity and nature of simples is quite instructive in a number of ways, giving us a far more accurate and also interesting insight into Wolff's actual contributions.

may well be serious problems here, but there is little evidence that they troubled Leibniz' (p. 381).

[25] It is undeniably true that the reception of Leibniz's thought in Germany throughout the 18th century was heavily influenced by restrictions on which of his writings were publicly available. However, these restrictions did not, or so I shall argue below, prevent his successors from lodging well-motivated criticisms of his views and from developing alternative positions, especially concerning those points that come up for discussion in the concluding section. This is not to say that their criticisms are ultimately successful or that their alternative views are preferable to Leibniz's, but rather merely that they understand certain aspects of his position well enough that their remarks are worthy of serious consideration.

For one, Wolff both articulates Leibniz's argument for the necessity of simples in greater detail and develops a novel and more powerful argument for the same conclusion on the basis of premisses that Leibniz explicitly accepted. For another, Wolff decides not to follow Leibniz in thinking that all simple substances must be monads, i.e. endowed with the force of representation, for a complex set of plausible reasons. Not only does Wolff think that Leibniz has not produced an argument that would actually support such a counter-intuitive claim, but he can also use the consequences that follow from being agnostic about the nature of simple substances to his advantage in addressing two of the questions that naturally arose for Leibniz's position.

Wolff first presents an argument for the necessity of true unities, or simples, near the beginning of his systematic metaphysics in his *Rational Thoughts on God, the World and the Soul of Human Beings, Also All Things in General* (which was published in 1719–20), only a few sections after his infamous attempt to derive the principle of sufficient reason from the principle of non-contradiction. Moreover, Wolff's argument is closely related to Leibniz's. In §76 of *Rational Thoughts*, Wolff presents the argument as follows:

If there are composite things, there must also be simple beings. For if no simple beings were present, then all parts—they can be taken to be as small as you might ever like, even inconceivably small parts—would have to consist of other parts. But then, since one could provide no reason where the composite parts would ultimately come from (*keinen Grund anzeigen könte, woher denn die zusammengesetzten Theile endlich herkämen*), just as little as one could comprehend where a composite number would arise from if it contained no unities in itself, and yet nothing can be without a sufficient reason (§30), one must ultimately admit simple things from which the composites arise.[26]

Formalized, Wolff's argument for simples runs as follows.

P1: Either there are simples or everything is composite.
C1: If there were no simples, then everything would be composite. (from P1)

---

[26] Christian Wolff, *Vernünftige Gedancken von Gott, der Welt und der Seele des Menschen, auch allen Dingen überhaupt* [*Vernünftige Gedancken*] ([Halle], 1724); repr. of the 11th edn. in Wolff, *Gesammelte Werke*, division 1, vol. ii (Hildesheim:Georg Olms, 1983), §76, p. 36.

P2: If everything were composite, then all parts of a composite would in turn be composite and therefore divisible into further parts.

P3: If all parts of a composite were divisible into further parts, there would be no ultimate reason for the (existence of the) parts.

P4: There must be an ultimate reason for the (existence of the) parts. (principle of sufficient reason)

C2: There are simples. (via an extended *modus tollens* from C1, P2, P3, and P4)

Wolff's argument clearly sides with the version of Leibniz's argument in the 'New System' that stressed the infinite divisibility of matter rather than the distinction between the continuity of matter and the discreteness of reality. His argument might seem to differ from this version of Leibniz's argument in so far as Wolff appeals to the principle of sufficient reason, whereas Leibniz invokes the idea that the reality of a collection depends on the existence of simples (and, in turn, on the idea that only what is truly *one* being is truly one *being*). However, this difference is, I think, ultimately merely apparent. For as we saw in Leibniz's explanation of the distinction between being *per se* and being *per accidens*, the true unities required by Leibniz's argument end up providing the *reason* for the accidental being of the collection. Granted, Wolff's way of putting the point (in terms of 'where parts come from') may not be particularly clear, but I see no fundamental difference here that is of importance.

Moreover, later, in *Philosophia prima; sive, Ontologia*—his more detailed Latin treatment of ontology, published in 1728—Wolff continues to endorse the argument Leibniz had introduced against Descartes, for in §686 of that work he asserts:

If there are composite beings, then there must also be simple beings, or, *without simple beings composite [beings] cannot exist.* For composite beings are composed of parts that are distinct from each other mutually (§531). But if those parts were composed once more of parts that are distinct from each other mutually, then they, too, would be composite beings (§531). Therefore, as long as other, smaller parts are admitted from which larger parts are composed, the question continuously arises, whence they are composed, consequently, it is not yet intelligible, whence, in the end, the smallest composite beings result that make up the composition of the other composites. Because, in this way, the sufficient reason is not contained in the notion of the composite, why it is composed (§56), yet a composite being cannot exist (§70) without a sufficient reason why it is a composite being rather than not a composite being, the sufficient reason of a composite being is to be sought outside the composite being, and therefore in a simple being (§665). If, therefore, composite beings should exist, simple beings must exist as well, or, without simple beings, a composite being can neither be conceived nor exist.[27]

However, Wolff's way of stating the argument has an important advantage over earlier formulations in so far as it reveals a serious weakness in the argument, namely, that it ignores the possibility that composition itself might contain the reason for a composite being.

Fortunately, in other passages in the *Philosophia prima; sive, Ontologia*, Wolff can be read as addressing this weakness. In §533 Wolff asserts: '*The essence of a composite being consists in the way in which such parts are combined with each other.*'[28] Then, in a later series of paragraphs from a section titled 'On the Modifications of Things, Especially Simples', he argues as follows:

§789 *The essence of a composite being consists in mere accidents.* ...

§791 *Accidents cannot exist without substances.* ...

§792 *There is nothing substantial in a composite being other than simple beings.* For the essence of a composite [being] consists in mere accidents (§789), consequently because nothing can pertain to a composite [being] unless the reason of it is contained in its essence (§168), everything else that pertains to the same [composite being] is an accident (§785). Because nevertheless accidents cannot exist without substance (§791), there must be something substantial beyond the essence. Wherefore because composite [beings] cannot exist without simple beings (§686), simple beings are what is substantial in them, and therefore there is not anything substantial in a composite being other than simple beings.

---

[27] Christian Wolff, *Philosophia prima; sive, Ontologia* [*Ontologia*] ([Frankfurt and Leipzig], 1736); repr. in Wolff, *Gesammelte Werke*, division 2, vol. iii (Hildesheim: Georg Olms, 2001), 517–18.

[28] Ibid. 416.

§793 *There are no substances other than simple substances & composite beings are aggregates of substances.*[29]

Wolff's argument here can be formalized as follows.

P1: The essence of a composite being consists in the way in which its parts are combined.

P2: The way in which the parts of a composite being are combined is an accident.

C1: The essence of a composite being consists in an accident. (from P1 and P2)

P3: Accidents cannot exist without substance.

C2: The essence of a composite being cannot exist without substance. (from C1 and P3)

P4: The substance required for the essence of a composite being is either composite or simple.

P5: If the substance required for the essence of a composite being were composite, its essence would consist in an accident, which would therefore not in fact be a substance.

C3: The essence of a composite being cannot exist without a simple substance. (from C2, P4, and P5)

P6: A composite being (and its essence) exist(s).

C4: A simple substance exists. (from C3 and P6)

This argument excludes the possibility that *composition alone* could contain the reason for a composite being, which allows Wolff to infer that the reason for a composite being must lie, at least in part, in the *simple beings* that make it up. And the key ideas that allow him to draw this conclusion are that composition is a relation and that relations—at least composition relations—are accidental and thus require something substantial, which can therefore only be something simple, since everything that is not simple is composite and hence accidental.

Whatever one makes of this argument, what is important for our purposes is to note how it goes beyond the argument introduced by Leibniz (and initially reaffirmed by Wolff in one of its versions). Leibniz's formulation of the argument in the 'New System' focused on how the (infinite) divisibility of a (continuous) spatial magnitude

---

[29] Ibid. 592–4.

is incompatible with the (discrete) unity required for being. Wolff's present argument, by contrast, embarks on a new line of reasoning by considering the accidental nature of composition and by assuming that accidents require substantiality.[30]

Despite the fact that Wolff's argument goes beyond what Leibniz explicitly asserts in print, it is noticeable that Wolff's 'new' argument is based not on principles completely foreign to Leibniz's system, but rather on resources already contained in Leibniz's position. For Leibniz does explicitly hold that composition is a contingent form of unity that can bestow only an accidental being on a plurality of entities. As a result, Wolff is not genuinely breaking with Leibniz, much less misreading Leibniz's position. Instead, he can be read as making more efficient use of the resources implicit in Leibniz's account, since his new argument broadens the scope of the views that are vulnerable to attack. For this argument applies not merely to those who accept a Cartesian account of body as consisting in extension alone, but also to anyone who accepts that bodies are composed of parts, since in the latter case features in addition to extension could be attributed to bodies, attributions that are ruled out by Cartesian conceptions. That is, this argument reveals more clearly what the fundamental issue is, namely not the narrowness of Descartes's conception of extension *per se*, but rather substantiality and its importance for the kind of composition that is proper to bodies.

Moreover, Wolff's understanding of the *nature* of the simples required by the arguments presented above is likewise different from Leibniz's in a subtle but important way. Whereas Leibniz, as we saw above, asserts that all unities or simples are like minds in so far as they have the power to represent the world (with varying degrees of

---

[30] Wolff's argument is different in so far as it turns on the distinction between accidents and substances and not simply on the relation between plurality and unity. In fact, though Wolff was presumably not aware of it, Leibniz suggests this argument briefly in a letter to Arnauld, 30 Apr. 1687: 'It also seems that what constitutes the essence of a being by aggregation is only a mode of the things of which it is composed. For example, what constitutes the essence of an army is only a mode of the men who compose it. This mode therefore presupposes a substance whose essence is not a mode of a substance' (Leibniz, *Essays*, 86). Perhaps surprisingly, Leibniz immediately continues on—without any break—with an argument based on the identity of being and unity.

clarity and distinctness), Wolff is agnostic about whether *all* simples must have such a power.

Now that I have distinctly established that the internal state of every simple thing refers to all the rest that exist in the world (§596) and Herr von Leibniz explains this in such a way that the whole world is represented in each simple thing according to the point where it is (§599), one can also understand further how everything in the world down to the smallest thing harmonizes with every other according to his opinion, and accordingly what he advances with his universal harmony of things, which, like all the rest that he has presented in this regard, appears to many as a puzzle that they believe to be unsolvable, since he has *neither explained nor proved it sufficiently*. However, because at the present time we *do not want to decide* what it really means for the inner state of simple things to refer to everything in the world, we shall let it *remain undecided* for the present in what the universal harmony of things consists, and it is enough for us that we have shown that it is present and that it can be explained in an intelligible manner according to the sense of Herr von Leibniz.[31]

Given the absence of any clear proof and the lack of an awareness of the internal state of other simples, Wolff is, at least 'for the present', agnostic about the nature of simples. In his so-called *Notations on Rational Thoughts* (*Der vernünfftigen Gedancken von Gott, der Welt und der Seele des Menschen, auch allen Dingen überhaupt, anderer Theil, bestehend in ausführlichen Anmerckungen*), which was published in 1724, only a few years after *Rational Thoughts*, and which contains comments on some of its most important and controversial paragraphs, Wolff explicitly notes that he had asked Leibniz for a proof of monads, but that Leibniz, who had claimed that he could provide a proper demonstration, never actually did so.[32] Wolff then comments that while he accepts that Leibniz has demonstratively proved the existence of simple things whose forces are responsible for their own changes, he still does 'not yet see the necessity of why all simple things must have one and the same kind of force and suspects rather that a force would have to be found in the elements of corporeal things from which the forces of

---

[31] Wolff, *Vernünfftige Gedancken*, §600, pp. 370–1; my emphasis.

[32] Leibniz has more to say about why true unities are minds than Wolff acknowledges, but this discrepancy may be due to the fact that Leibniz's most explicit views on the topic were not available to Wolff.

bodies ... can be derived in an intelligible manner'.[33] Wolff thus grants that at least some simples, namely souls, have the power to represent the world, but he notes that it has not yet been proved that all simples must have such a power, explicitly leaving open the possibility that some simples, e.g. those that underlie bodies, might have a different kind of intrinsic quality or primitive force. Moreover, Wolff explicitly recognizes—in a way reminiscent of the motivation underlying the second question raised in the previous section for Leibniz—that it would be advantageous if the simples of corporeal things were of such a nature that one could also derive the forces of bodies from them in an intelligible way.

If Wolff is agnostic about the nature of simples from 1719 to 1724, does he commit himself on the issue at a later time? In his *Philosophia prima; sive, Ontologia*, Wolff provides a lengthy list of characterizations of simples: as what have no parts, as indivisible, as not extended, as lacking size and shape, as not filling a space, as incapable of internal motion, as different from composites, and as being either necessary or, if contingent, then arising instantaneously owing to a necessary being *ex nihilo* and perishing instantaneously via annihilation.[34] In his Latin treatment of rational cosmology, *Cosmologia generalis*, first published in 1731, Wolff adds that 'Zenonical points are not the [simple] elements of material things' (§217), where Zenonical points are identified with mathematical points.[35]

What stands out about Wolff's later characterizations of simples is that they are almost exclusively negative and are generated by way of contrast with the properties of composite bodies. It is true that he provides more extensive analyses and arguments in his *Philosophia prima; sive, Ontologia*, but the characterizations of simples in these

---

[33] Christian Wolff, *Der vernünftigen Gedancken von Gott, der Welt und der Seele des Menschen, auch allen Dingen überhaupt, anderer Theil, bestehend in ausfürlichen Anmerckungen* ([Halle], 1724); repr. in Wolff, *Gesammelte Werke*, division 1, vol. iii (Hildesheim: Georg Olms 1983), §215, p. 369.

[34] These features of simples are defended and elaborated in *Ontologia*, §§673–702, pp. 511–29. Several of them are repeated in *Cosmologia generalis* ([Frankfurt and Leipzig], 1737); repr. in Wolff, *Gesammelte Werke*, division 2, vol. iv (Hildesheim: Georg Olms, 1964), §§182–5, esp. 184, pp. 146–8.

[35] Wolff's argument against simples being identified with mathematical points is different from Leibniz's (as presented above). For Wolff argues that mathematical points are not different from each other, whereas the simple elements of material bodies must be different (§216).

contexts are typically functional characterizations (such as that a simple must contain the sufficient reason for its next state), which do not give insight into the features simple substances have that would allow them to carry out their functions.[36] As a result, though Wolff accepts that simples must be endowed with a force, he is ultimately agnostic about the specific nature of the force and thus of the simple endowed with it.[37] As he remarks in the *Cosmologia generalis*: 'And from this it is clear why we do not inquire into the specific difference between the elements and other simple substances, and why we gladly relinquish the opinions of Leibniz regarding monads.'[38]

At this point, one could grant that Wolff's agnosticism about the nature of simples is different from Leibniz's position, but hold that this difference is ultimately insignificant. After all, in §600 of *Rational Thoughts* Wolff implicitly leaves open the possibility that Leibniz could be right about all substances having the power to represent the world. Further, the basic structure of his account of physics in the *Cosmologia generalis* is similar to Leibniz's. For he argues that the specific properties of bodies—e.g. size, shape, and motion—are to be accounted for in terms of motive force and the force of inertia, which he explicitly characterizes as derivative active and passive force, respectively, just as Leibniz does. Thus, it might appear as if the differences between Leibniz's and Wolff's positions on the nature of simples are unimportant to their broader accounts and can thus be disregarded.

However, such a view would mislead in unfortunate ways. For Wolff's agnosticism about the nature of simples does have important ramifications by placing significant limits on the kinds of explanation that involve these simples. Instead of being able to call on specific features of the representations that monads have (e.g. their degree of clarity and distinctness or the spatial features of the objects represented), Wolff is restricted to asserting merely that simples have some sort of intrinsic quality that distinguishes them. Specifically, this restriction makes an immediate difference to Wolff's explanation of space. Leibniz's explanation of space can be quite simple, at least

---

[36] See Wolff, *Cosmologia generalis*, esp. §§195–214 and §§703–95.
[37] See ibid., §196, for an explicit argument for the claim that simples are endowed with 'a certain force' (p. 152).
[38] Ibid., §243, p. 186.

in principle.[39] Space arises because monads' representations are, to a certain extent, confused. It is a limitation or imperfection of minds that they represent objects as spatially extended, when what is ultimately real is not. Moreover, because Leibniz explicitly adopts the 'world apart' doctrine, according to which I would have the very same representations I do even if only God and I existed, it follows that only the representations of a single finite monad are required to account for (my representation of) extension.

Wolff's explanation of extension, by contrast, requires a plurality of simples. In §602 of *Rational Thoughts*, he says of simples that,

> since each one of them refers to the rest in a special way according to its internal state (§595), it coexists with the rest in a special way such that none of them can exist with the rest in precisely this way. And thus not only is each one external to the others (§45), but many, taken together, also follow each other in an order (§132, 133), and thus many, taken together, fill a space (§46), although each one of them does not actually fill a space, but rather only has a certain point in it.

Wolff's argument here is that since the intrinsic qualities of simples, when taken together, stand in an ordering relationship and since space is nothing other than a certain ordering relationship, space is to be identified with the ordering relationship between the intrinsic qualities of simples.[40]

---

[39] In fact, Leibniz seems to have two separate lines of thought about space. On the one hand, in his correspondence with Clarke, Leibniz seems to hold that our representation of space is formed through abstraction, based on relations among bodies that we perceive existing in the world. On the other hand, in his correspondence with Des Bosses (5 Feb. 1712), for example, he clearly distinguishes between our subjective phenomena and the 'phenomena of God', *scientia visionis*, and holds (as he does in the *New Essays* as well) that both space—the order of coexisting things—and time—the order of successive things—are represented by God through innate ideas (in which we partake in so far as we have apodictically certain geometrical knowledge).

[40] Wolff provides essentially the same line of reasoning in his *Cosmologia generalis*, arguing that since the elements of material things are different (§219) and united to each other (§220), extension arises when they are aggregated (§221), given that extension is entailed by a plurality of distinct coexistent entities (*Ontologia*, §548). In neither treatise does Wolff's argument explain why spatiality rather than some other kind of relationship is required by the order that happens to exist between simples, but Leibniz's argument is not significantly different on this point, since the mere fact that monads must represent the world in ways that are not completely clear and distinct does not obviously entail spatiality rather than some other confused mode of representation. As a result, both Leibniz and Wolff can be understood as making the valid point that, given spatiality, one can provide at least a partial

Wolff's argument thus shows that his account of space, or extension, relies on the relation between simples rather than simply on the (representational) nature of the simples as Leibniz's might seem to. Moreover, this point is supported by Wolff's explicit account of the essence of composite entities in §789 of the *Prima philosophia; sive, Ontologia*, where, as we saw above, he asserts that the essence of a composite entity consists in mere accidents. But this same point applies not merely to extension (which obviously contains a plurality of distinct coexistent entities), but also to bodies and to their most basic properties as well, such as size (magnitude) and shape (figure). For bodies are not merely extended, but are themselves composite entities, whose essence and properties likewise depend on the accidental or contingent relations among the simple elements that constitute them, rather than only on the specific nature of such simple elements.[41] Also, since Leibniz denies that one should use the true unities 'to explain the particular problems of nature', it is open to Wolff as well to deny that the nature of the simples can be used to explain any features of the composites that they constitute.[42] As a result, Wolff's agnosticism about the nature of simples has important implications for several issues within his broader metaphysics and physics.

We have thus seen that Wolff's position differs from Leibniz's with respect to the nature of the simple elements that compose bodies and also with respect to the way in which simples figure into explanations of the nature and properties of bodies. And we have also seen that these differences are not based on a crude misunderstanding of Leibniz's position, but rather on Wolff quite reasonably not wanting to base his own philosophy on a claim about the nature of simples that lacks sufficient argumentative backing.[43] In light of these differences, one can

---

explanation of it in terms of non-extended simples, whether in terms of their intrinsic (representational) qualities or in terms of the order between their intrinsic qualities.

[41] See Wolff, *Cosmologia generalis*, §140, for his account of the essence of composite bodies.

[42] Leibniz, 'New System', in Leibniz, *Essays*, 139. In §243, Section II of the *Cosmologia generalis*, where Wolff is explaining the origin of bodies from the simple elements, he explicitly asserts that the qualities of the elements of material things should not be used in natural philosophy.

[43] Wolff may not have fully come to terms with the issues that Leibniz refers to as constituting the labyrinth of the continuum, and thus he may not be as clear as Leibniz was about the relations among unities and space, but Wolff's account of how unities and space

now consider whether Wolff might be able to offer different responses
to the three questions that were posed above for Leibniz's account.

First, because the simples (or true unities) that Leibniz posited to
explain bodies are minds, he is, as we saw above, paradoxically forced
to deny the reality of bodies in attempting to account for the reality
of bodies. Since Wolff, by contrast, does not assert that the simples
that constitute bodies must be minds, he is not immediately forced
into the same position. For if not all simples are endowed with the
force of representation, then the bodies that are constituted by such
non-mental simples (or the relations between them) need not for
that reason be ideal and the reality of bodies could be maintained.
Granted, Wolff's agnosticism about the nature of simples can entail
only agnosticism about the ontological status of bodies, but even such
a modest difference could be a welcome result.[44]

This alleged advantage notwithstanding, one might still object that,
compared to Leibniz's position, Wolff's agnosticism has a significant
cost for the following reason. As we saw above, Leibniz's explanation
of how one entity can bestow unity and thus reality on something
else depends on the specific nature of the entities that have unity
intrinsically and being *per se*. For it is because a mind perceives (or at
least represents) a certain relation among a number of entities that they
could be aggregated and thus viewed as a unified collection. The unity
(and hence being) of the collection was thus merely accidental rather
than intrinsic (and *per se*), but it is clearly significant that Leibniz can
give an intelligible explanation of how an entity that lacks being *per
se* could nonetheless have unity bestowed upon it and thus be given
being *per accidens*. But given that Wolff cannot rely on the mental
features of simples, he cannot simply repeat Leibniz's explanation of
how minds can bestow accidental unity and reality on bodies.

While it is true that Wolff cannot adopt every detail of Leibniz's
explanation of how simples can bestow unity on bodies, he can and,

---

are related may also lack detail sufficient to bring out significant differences between their
positions. For a helpful account of this issue in Leibniz, see the Introduction by Richard
Arthur to *The Labyrinth of the Continuum: Writings on the Continuum Problem, 1672–1686*, ed.
and tr. R. Arthur (New Haven: Yale University Press, 2001), pp. xxiii–lxxxviii.

[44] See Wolff, *Psychologia rationalis* ([Frankfurt and Leipzig], 1740); repr. in Wolff, *Gesammelte Werke*, division 2, vol. vi (Hildesheim: Georg Olms, 1972), §§36–7, pp. 550–1, and
614, for his discussion of materialism and idealism.

on some points, does tell a story that is similar to it in fundamental respects. Specifically, although Wolff does not explicitly draw Leibniz's distinction between being *per se* and being *per accidens*, he does assert that the essence of a composite consists in the contingent relations between its constituent parts, which is one of the main features of Leibniz's account.[45] What Wolff cannot endorse is Leibniz's claim that these contingent relations must be represented by a mind, but he could argue that this particular claim is not an *essential* part of an account of how simples (i.e. entities that have intrinsic unity) can bestow unity on entities that lack it as such (e.g. bodies). For he could hold that what explains the special status of something that has unity through something else and hence being *per accidens* is not the fact that it is represented by a mind, but rather the fact that its unity stems from its accidental, or contingent, relations. That is, from Wolff's perspective, Leibniz's claim that a mind represents entities as related in a certain way is an unnecessary element of an explanation of how composite bodies could have an accidental unity, an element that is also not required by Leibniz's idealist commitments, even though it fits in with them quite naturally. Accordingly, Wolff's agnostic stance on the nature of simples does not prevent him from adopting a broadly Leibnizian account of how they can bestow (an accidental) unity on composite entities, such as bodies, that lack intrinsic unity. In short, Wolff has no obvious disadvantage here, and, in fact, would even seem to have a modest advantage in so far as he is in a position to avoid the paradox that Leibniz faces.

Second, as we saw above, Leibniz's account encounters the following question: If true unities are perceptual or *mental*, how exactly are any of the *physical* states of bodies to be derived from them (given the heterogeneity of the mental and the physical)? Now Wolff might seem to have a quick and easy answer to this question, since simples, for him, are not necessarily mental, and he is not thereby committed to a heterogeneous derivation relationship between the mental and the physical. In fact, as we saw above, he explicitly acknowledges the desirability of being able to understand physical derivative forces on the basis of primitive forces. This advantage seems to disappear just as

---

[45] That Wolff does not explicitly draw the distinction between being *per se* and being *per accidens* may be due to the fact that the *New Essays* were not published until 1765.

quickly as it arose, however, when one recalls that Wolff denies that
simple elements have any of the same properties as material bodies—at
least in so far as 'the elements of material things are not extended, are
not endowed with shape and magnitude, fill no space, and are lacking
in internal motion'.[46] Even if Wolff's simples may not be mental,
they also cannot be physical *in the same sense* in which bodies are, and
therefore providing an intelligible explanation of how something that
is not physical is supposed to give rise to something else that is, would
seem to remain as serious a difficulty for him as for Leibniz.[47]

However, even if Wolff's agnosticism about the nature of simples as
such does not provide an answer to the second question raised for Leibniz's original position, a consequence that follows from it can. Recall
from above that one of the consequences of Wolff's agnosticism was
that both spatial extension and the physical properties of bodies were
to be explained not directly through the intrinsic features of simple
substances (since Wolff is agnostic about them), but rather in terms of
relations between these intrinsic features. But if the relations between
the intrinsic features of simple substances can plausibly be understood
as physical, then an explanation of the physical properties of bodies
in terms of the relations between the intrinsic features of simple substances can amount to a connection between homogeneous entities,
which can therefore be proportional and hence intelligible. In this
way, Wolff's agnosticism can also have a significant indirect pay-off.

Finally, there is also the difficulty of explaining how the *intrinsic*
features of simple substances are supposed to generate the *relational*
properties of bodies. Unfortunately, Wolff's agnosticism about the
nature of simples is of no significant help here, either directly or
indirectly. That is, even if one asserts merely that simples have some
unknown kind of intrinsic property, it remains unclear how relational
properties between simples are supposed to arise. To see how Wolff
skips over the difficulty, recall his account of the origin of space

[46] *Cosmologia generalis*, §184, p. 147.
[47] If one accepts this conclusion, one is essentially weakening the derivation and hence
intelligibility relationship between the primitive and derivative forces, a strategy Paul
Lodge pursues in 'Primitive and Derivative Forces in Leibnizian Bodies', in H. Poser and
E. Knobloch (eds.), *Nihil Sine Ratione. Mensch, Natur und Technik im Wirken von G. W.
Leibniz* (Hanover: Gottfried Wilhelm Leibniz Gesellschaft, 2001), 720–7, by claiming that
the derivation relation is not an inherence relation (despite the examples that Leibniz uses
to illustrate the distinction, such as point to line).

from the simple elements. On his account, since space is simply a unity of a plurality of coexistent things and since a plurality of simple elements stand in a certain ordering relationship in virtue of the intrinsic qualities of each, the ordering relationship is supposed to generate space. However, this begs the question in so far as it simply assumes that there must be an ordering relation between the intrinsic properties of the simple elements. For one, Wolff has not established that all simples have an intrinsic property of the same kind (as, for example, objects must all have some size in order for the 'taller than' relation to obtain). For another, even if every simple element did have an intrinsic property of the same kind (but with a different degree), it is still not clear that any order or relation between them is generated, given that Wolff has not established that and, more importantly, how these intrinsic properties must be 'taken together'. Why would they not be 'worlds apart'?

One might think that Leibniz has a slight advantage on this point in so far as the representational activities of his monads could, as we saw above, be construed as 'taking' several distinct entities 'together' and representing them as related in some respect. However, given the challenge Leibniz faces in providing a genuine sense in which distinct entities are actually related, and not merely represented as such, this advantage may well be merely apparent. For in the end, regardless of the specific nature of simple substances, it is difficult to see how the simples that are constituted by their intrinsic activities alone could ground relational properties of the kind that bodies have. Leibniz and Wolff face, it seems, similar difficulties on this point.

By investigating Wolff's arguments concerning the necessity and nature of simples, we have seen that his reaction to Leibniz's position is both sophisticated and insightful. He agrees with Leibniz that there must be simple substances and, early on, endorses one version of Leibniz's argument in support of that claim, but, upon further reflection and when faced with a significant objection to that argument, develops a second argument that is also broader in scope, while still being based on aspects of Leibniz's position. Further, since Wolff does not think that Leibniz has presented an argument establishing that the true unities or simple elements that are required for composite bodies *must* be minds, he is agnostic on the issue. But his agnosticism on the nature of simples is not simply a sign of a desire to avoid overstating conclusions, but also brings with it, as a consequence, several further differences between Leibniz's position and his own, especially regarding the way in which simples are invoked in explanations of the derivative phenomena of bodies. In particular, we saw that these differences helped to provide partial answers to several of the questions that naturally arise for Leibniz's position regarding simples and their place in his metaphysics. By illustrating in this way how one could reasonably be led to articulate a point of view that is slightly different from Leibniz's own while still remaining within a distinctively Leibnizian framework, Wolff's position represents an intelligible and, in fact, quite illuminating response to the situation that he encountered in his attempt to develop a comprehensive metaphysical system after Leibniz's death.

3. BAUMGARTEN

Alexander Baumgarten is relatively well known for his views on aesthetics, but his views on theoretical philosophy have fared much less well, typically receiving attention owing to the fact that Kant had used Baumgarten's *Metaphysica* (originally published in 1739) as a textbook for several decades, which gave rise to the hope that one could make sense of Kant's peculiar terminology by finding a clearer precursor. What is of interest in the present context, however, is Baumgarten's position on the necessity and nature of simples.

Baumgarten's argument for the necessity of simples represents an interesting twist on Leibniz's and Wolff's strategies. Whereas Leibniz and, at least initially, Wolff considered the implications of the spatial divisibility of bodies and the way in which unity is a requirement of reason for being, Baumgarten focuses exclusively on the nature of composition. After stating (in §224) that a composite thing is (by definition) a whole of parts outside of (*extra*) parts, he argues:

§231. Every part of a composite substance is either something substantial or something accidental. Accidents cannot exist outside of what is substantial (§196). Therefore, substantial parts of a composite substance are posited outside of each other.[48]

---

[48] Alexander Baumgarten, *Metaphysica*, 4th edn. (Frankfurt, 1757; first pub. 1739); repr. in Kant, *Gesammelte Schriften*, ed. Königlich Preussische Akademie der Wissenschaften (Berlin: de Gruyter, 1902–), xv. 5–54, xvii. 23–226, at 78; translations are my own.

Though Baumgarten's argument is extremely compressed, the basic idea is that a composite substance (such as a body) must be composed of at least some simple substances, since if it were not, then it would be composed exclusively of accidents, which is impossible, since accidents cannot exist independently of a substance.[49] It can be formalized as follows:

P1: A composite is a whole of parts outside of parts, i.e. parts that are distinct from each other.

P2: The (ultimate) parts of a composite that are distinct from each other are either accidents or simple substances.

C1: A composite is composed of parts that are either accidents or simple substances. (from P1 and P2)

P3: If a composite were composed solely of parts that are accidents, accidents would exist without a substance.

P4: An accident cannot exist without a substance.

C2: A composite is composed of parts at least one of which is a simple substance. (from C1, P3, and P4)

Baumgarten's argument for simples represents the endpoint of a shift in strategy that is quite striking, but at the same time fully intelligible if one keeps in mind the different audiences Leibniz, Wolff, and Baumgarten were addressing and the diverse aims they pursued as a result. Because Descartes's position was highly influential during most of Leibniz's career (or at least during his relatively early years in Paris in the 1670s), one of Leibniz's most pressing tasks was to show that matter cannot be understood as Descartes had proposed, namely as a substance whose principal attribute is extension (and extension alone). As a result, to establish his own position, it would make sense for Leibniz to begin with the nature of extension and then exploit the metaphysical implications of extension's infinite divisibility.

Since the most significant opposition Wolff faced in Germany in the 1720s and 1730s was not Cartesians, but rather Pietists whose position was primarily inspired by theological concerns, his main task

---

[49] Not only is the argument compressed, but the explicit conclusion that he draws seems to go well beyond the point that there must be simple substances, since it claims that the (presumably simple) substances that compose a composite substance must be posited 'outside of each other' (*extra se*), which raises a number of further issues (e.g. whether that is to be understood as spatial or not).

was to articulate and promulgate a systematic philosophy based on reason.[50] Thus, although the argument that he adopted early on in his *Rational Thoughts* was essentially the same as one strand of Leibniz's, he highlighted the importance of the principle of sufficient reason. Later, however, after the heat of direct battle with the Pietists was past and he was able to lay out the details of his systematic metaphysics in his *Prima philosophia; sive, Ontologia*, he was not under pressure to emphasize the role of reason and could explore in greater detail the rational basis for the necessity of simples. In doing so, he was clearly tempted to accept the quick inference that composites must ultimately be composed of non-composites, but he also articulated further reasons for accepting simples that were different from Leibniz's explicit argument, even if they could be seen as arising naturally from certain aspects of Leibniz's position.

Baumgarten, by contrast, was mainly interested in presenting a skeleton of metaphysics in a textbook for students, and he therefore focused exclusively on what is minimally necessary to understand fundamental metaphysical principles adequately.[51] Since simple substances belong to the first principles of ontology, he clearly had to develop an argument in support of them that does not draw on anything extraneous. He attempted to satisfy this demand by considering the ontological status of the distinct parts that are united in a composite, and the dependence of accidents on substances. Baumgarten's main focus thus departed from both Leibniz's and Wolff's. For an argument based on composition is more fundamental than what pertains to infinite divisibility, which is specific to spatiality (as Leibniz's argument was), and such an argument also did not need to rely

---

[50] For a more detailed account of the opposition Wolff faced from the Pietists and how he reacted, see Georg Volckmar Hartmann, *Anleitung zur Historie der Leibnitzisch–Wolffischen Philosophie* (1737); repr. in Christian Wolff, *Gesammelte Werke*, division 3, vol. iv (Hildesheim: Georg Olms, 1973); Max Wundt, *Die deutsche Schulphilosophie im Zeitalter der Aufklärung* (Tübingen: Mohr, 1945); Eduard Zeller, 'Wolff's Vertreibung aus Halle. Der Kampf des Pietismus mit der Philosophie', *Preussische Jahrbücher*, 10 (1862), 47–72; Konrad Cramer, 'Zur geistigen Situation der Zeit der Göttinger Universitätsgründung 1737', in *Göttinger Universitätsschriften*, xii (Göttingen: Vandenhoeck & Ruprecht, 1988), 101–43; as well as my 'From Pre-established Harmony to Physical Influx: Leibniz's Reception in Early Eighteenth Century Germany', *Perspectives on Science*, 6 (1998), 136–203.

[51] For a description of Baumgarten and the context in which he worked, see e.g. Bernhard Poppe, *Alexander Gottlieb Baumgarten. Seine Bedeutung und Stellung in der Leibniz–Wolffischen Philosophie und seine Beziehung zu Kant* (Leipzig: Buchdrückerei Robert Noske, 1907).

on considerations pertaining to what is contained in the essence of composition (as Wolff's later argument had).

What is even more interesting about Baumgarten's reflections on this particular issue, however, is his treatment of the nature of simples. Though Baumgarten agrees with Leibniz that all simple substances or monads have the power of representation, he also claims that monads are impenetrable:

§398. Each finite monad of this and any universe (§354), because it exists outside of all the rest that constitute the world with it (§192), cannot exist in the same total place along with any other (§282). *A substance whose place no other substance posited outside of it can occupy is impenetrable* (solid). Therefore, all substances, hence also all monads, of this and of every composite world are impenetrable (§230).[52]

On the one hand, ascribing impenetrability to monads might seem to be wholly inappropriate. After all, monads might seem to be impenetrable in precisely the same (vacuous) sense in which, say, numbers are. Since numbers do not occupy any extended region of space at all, it necessarily follows that nothing else could push them out of any given region of space, but to say that they are therefore impenetrable is vacuous in so far as one is not ascribing any causal power or real property to them. If monads are simply immaterial minds (as Leibniz held), then the same conclusion would follow for monads as well. Something, one suspects, is seriously amiss here.

On the other hand, there is a textual and philosophical basis for Baumgarten's ascription of impenetrability to monads. Near the beginning of the 'Specimen dynamicum', Leibniz says that primitive passive force is that force 'by virtue of which it happens that a body cannot be penetrated by another body, but presents an obstacle to it'.[53] That is, one could naturally (even if mistakenly) interpret Leibniz as claiming that impenetrability is a primitive rather than a derivative force, making it reasonable to assert that monads are impenetrable.[54] Further, both Leibniz and Wolff relate monads or simple elements to

---

[52] Baumgarten, *Metaphysica*, xvii. 110.   [53] Leibniz, *Essays*, 120.

[54] In retrospect, it is clear that such an interpretation does not reflect Leibniz's considered opinion. Impenetrability is a derivative force of bodies rather than a primitive force of monads—though impenetrability *depends* on the primitive forces of monads, which is all that this passage actually asserts.

points in space. In the 'New System', Leibniz remarks that the true
unities or metaphysical points for which he had argued are associated
both with particular organic bodies 'by an immediate presence' and
with 'points of view' from which they represent the world.[55] As we
saw above in the *Rational Thoughts*, Wolff similarly argues that each
simple element 'has a certain point in' space in virtue of the order that
exists between the intrinsic qualities of a plurality of simple elements.
If monads or simple elements are immediately present in, or have a
location at, particular points in space, then they are different from
numbers in an important way, since numbers are not associated with
particular locations in space. Moreover, this difference is crucial to
whether impenetrability can sensibly be said to be involved in each
case. For in the case of monads (or simple elements) that occupy points
in space, one would need a reason to exclude the possibility that two
of them could occupy the same point in space, and that reason would
be provided by the impenetrability (or primitive passive force) of the
relevant monads (or simple elements).

These reflections lead Baumgarten to an even bolder assertion in
the section that immediately follows his assertion that monads are
impenetrable:

§399. The monads of this and any composite, and hence extended, world
(§241, 393) are POINTS (§286), but not MATHEMATICAL points, in which
nothing other than the absence of extension is posited (§396–398). Nor, if
placed next to each other (*iuxta se positae*), are they congruent or do they
coincide (§70, 396). Rather, if a plurality of them have been posited as
coexisting, since any given one of them is impenetrable (§398), they are
placed simultaneously outside each other (*extra se*) in a certain order (§396,
78). Hence, in the aggregation of them is space. Therefore, every aggregate
of monads of this and every composite world is an extended thing (§241). If
a mathematical point, which is an abstract possibility, is imagined to exist, it
is a ZENONICAL POINT, which is a fiction. If by a PHYSICAL POINT you mean
an actual thing that is completely determined beyond its simplicity, then
certain monads of this universe, namely those the aggregation of which is an
extended thing, are physical points.[56]

---

[55] For difficulties in attributing a single coherent view to Leibniz, see Daniel Garber,
'What Leibniz Really Said?' (unpub.).

[56] Baumgarten, *Metaphysica*, xvii. 110.

In this passage Baumgarten is reacting to Leibniz and Wolff in a novel way. On the one hand, he follows Leibniz and Wolff in asserting that monads cannot be mathematical or Zenonical points. Mathematical points are, as Leibniz claims, merely abstract possibilities and hence fictions, not realities. Nor are they identical if they are posited simultaneously, since monads are distinguished by their intrinsic properties. On the other hand, Baumgarten departs from Leibniz and Wolff by explicitly describing monads as *physical points*. That is, Baumgarten *identifies* monads with (physical) points, whereas Leibniz and Wolff simply *associate* monads or simple elements with points in space—for Wolff, for example, each simple element *has* a certain point, as opposed to *being* a certain point. Moreover, although the precise details of Baumgarten's line of reasoning have been left implicit in the text, it is obviously supposed to be based directly on the impenetrability of monads.[57]

Baumgarten's position thus represents a significant departure from both Leibniz's and Wolff's. Leibniz's monads are metaphysical points, which he assimilates to minds, whereas Wolff is agnostic about the nature of his simple elements. Given Wolff's agnosticism, it is clear that he might not object to Baumgarten's position, even if he might not be persuaded by Baumgarten's argument for specifying the nature of simple substances as being physical. But what about Leibniz, who explicitly mentions physical points in the 'New System'? In the passage (quoted above) where Leibniz is discussing the nature of the true unities required by extended matter as consisting in metaphysical points, he remarks: 'But when corporeal substances are contracted, all their organs together constitute only a *physical point* relative to us. Thus physical points are indivisible only in appearance.' Unfortunately, Leibniz's remarks here are both brief and cryptic. He seems to be considering whether metaphysical points could be corporeal substances, and rejecting that possibility because corporeal substances can be represented as indivisible only if they are 'contracted'. That is, if one identified metaphysical points with corporeal substances, then it would appear that such substances would not be truly indivisible (given that organic corporeal substances would

---

[57] It is presumably because monads are impenetrable that they must be 'placed simultaneously outside each other in a certain order' and thus in different points in space.

be extended). In light of this difficulty, one might 'contract' or reduce corporeal substances down to physical points. This act of reduction would solve the problem of divisibility, but, Leibniz seems to be suggesting, it would do so at the cost of their reality, since such points would be indivisible 'only in appearance'. Leibniz's argument excludes in this way the possibility that metaphysical points could be corporeal substances.

However, if this passage from the 'New System' is to be read in this way, then it turns out that Leibniz does not even consider Baumgarten's suggestion that the true unities required for extended matter could be actual physical points. That is, since Leibniz discusses only the possibility that organic corporeal substances could be treated *as if* they were physical points, there is no evidence that he ever entertained the view that monads are simply real, indivisible physical points. And even if he had been aware of this view, it is not clear that he has sufficient argumentative resources to refute it. For if Leibniz were to present an argument establishing that true unities must be like minds (by having representations of the world), such an argument would still not immediately exclude the possibility that they were physical points as well. Further, his arguments in favour of monads necessarily being associated with points of view in space would presumably restrict what he could say against them being identical with such points. As a result, Baumgarten's position and argument are interestingly different from the positions that Leibniz and Wolff had explicitly taken into account.

Moreover, on the basis of these differences, Baumgarten's position can provide more satisfying answers to two of the three questions that were posed above regarding Leibniz's and Wolff's views on the nature of monads or simple elements. First, since Baumgarten identifies monads with physical points, he is free to claim that the bodies that are composed by physical points are just as real, actual, and physical as physical points are. Therefore, he need not deny the reality of bodies because they depend on minds, as Leibniz was forced to. Nor does he need to be agnostic on the issue, as Wolff was, which represented an advantage only in so far as it allowed one to set the issue to one side. While it is true that Baumgarten cannot appeal to all of the details of Leibniz's explanation of how the intrinsic unity of an entity having being *per se* could bestow accidental unity and hence being *per accidens* on an entity that lacked it as such, since his argument for the necessity of monads depended on the nature of composition, he can appeal to the same explanation that was available to Wolff.

Second, Baumgarten would appear to have an obvious and considerable advantage over Leibniz and Wolff concerning the relationship between monads and bodies. The issue for Leibniz was that this relationship is problematic if the primitive forces of monads are exclusively *mental* and hence heterogeneous with the derivative forces of *physical* bodies. Because Baumgarten's monads are *physical* points, however, they are homogeneous with *physical* bodies, and there is therefore no principled objection to providing intelligible explanations of the connections between them. Before granting Baumgarten too much, however, one might pause to consider what it is that makes monads physical (and thus homogeneous with bodies) on his account. For Baumgarten describes a physical point rather unusually as 'an actual thing that is completely determined beyond its simplicity'. He is surely contrasting physical with mathematical points by emphasizing that physical points are (i) actual and (ii) completely determined, because mathematical points are not actual (since mere abstractions or fictions) and are determined only by geometrical properties (which, if Wolff is right, do not suffice to distinguish one point from another, a problem that would not arise if points are completely determined). However, this description could still leave one curious as to what is physical about such points and, specifically, what would distinguish them from metaphysical points (or monads as Leibniz understands them). Physical points are, for Baumgarten, impenetrable, but without knowing what intrinsic feature of monads makes them impenetrable, it could still seem unclear what constitutes the specifically physical dimension of physical points. But even lacking such an account, Baumgarten's view still allows for some measure of homogeneity between monads and bodies, which could suffice to resolve the question about the mind—body relationship that seems to arise for Leibniz and, to a lesser degree, Wolff.

If Baumgarten's view of monads as physical points helps to address the first two questions that arose for Leibniz's and Wolff's positions, his innovations, unfortunately, do not seem to be of any help in answering the third. Whether points are physical or not, they are indivisible entities endowed with intrinsic properties of some sort, and as such, it is unclear how they can generate relational properties that would amount to more than purely logical relations. That is, without stating the nature of physical points in detail or how, specifically, they are completely determined, it seems difficult to say why they stand in any (non-logical or real) relations to each other.

While Baumgarten thus followed Leibniz and Wolff in accepting the necessity of simple substances, he developed an argument for this position that was original in so far as it focused exclusively on the ontological status of the parts of composite wholes. Moreover, he also proposed a novel understanding of the nature of simples by suggesting that they could be impenetrable physical points, an understanding that neither Leibniz nor Wolff explicitly considered and that helped to address two of the three questions that Leibniz and, to a lesser extent, Wolff had faced.

4. THE PRE-CRITICAL KANT

In 1756, some seventy years after Leibniz's first public criticism of Descartes's physics and just over sixty years after his sustained attack on Descartes's metaphysics, Immanuel Kant addressed several of these same issues in his *Metaphysicae cum geometria junctae usus in philosophia naturali, cuius specimen I. continet monadologiam physicam*, commonly referred to now simply as the *Physical Monadology*. Though Wolff and those sympathetic to his approach (such as Baumgarten) still dominated the philosophical landscape in Germany in the 1740s and early 1750s, his systematic position had come under serious and sustained attack in major publications by Christian August Crusius, a Pietist who advocated a strongly voluntaristic perspective, and in the writings and official activities of several highly influential members of the newly reformed Prussian Academy of Sciences in Berlin, such as Leonhard Euler and Pierre Maupertuis, who were both interested in the more scientific, and especially mathematical, dimension of natural philosophy. In light of these and other developments, it is not surprising that Kant did not simply accept Wolffian metaphysics without question during the first part of his career in the late 1740s and 1750s. Instead it makes sense in this context that he devoted his efforts to working out a position that would be able to reconcile a fully intelligible metaphysics with principles that seemed fundamental to the pre-eminent science of his day.

The *Physical Monadology* represents a prime instance of Kant's efforts to integrate metaphysics and science in a comprehensive natural philosophy. For he explicitly introduces his task as that of explaining how 'metaphysics can be married to geometry, when it seems easier to mate griffins with horses than to unite transcendental philosophy with geometry'.[58] Moreover, what stands in the way of such a marriage is that 'the former peremptorily denies that space is infinitely divisible, while the latter, with its usual certainty, asserts that it is infinitely divisible'.[59] Kant proposes to remove this obstacle by showing that 'the existence of physical monads is in agreement with geometry'.[60] He begins his task by arguing for the necessity of monads in the Theorem of Proposition II as follows:

Bodies consist of parts, each one of which has an enduring existence. Since, however, the composition of such parts is nothing but a relation, and hence a determination which is in itself contingent, and which can be denied without abrogating the existence of the things having this relation, it is plain that all composition of a body can be abolished, though all of the parts which were formerly combined together nonetheless continue to exist. After having abolished, however, all composition among the parts that still exist, they have no composition at all, and thus are completely free from [any] plurality of substances, [and are] hence simple. All bodies, whatever, therefore, consist of absolutely simple primitive parts, that is to say, monads.[61]

Kant's argument for the necessity of simples is similar to both Wolff's and Baumgarten's, without being entirely identical to either one. Like Wolff's argument, Kant's argument depends on the contingency of composition, though it does not rely on the essence of a composite consisting exclusively in accidents, as Wolff's does, and it also contains steps absent in Wolff's. It is similar to Baumgarten's argument in so far as it focuses on the ontological status of what remains after all composition has been removed, but it is different in so far as it stresses that composition must be contingent, given that it is simply a relation between various parts. At the same time, there is nothing fundamentally new in Kant's line of argument.

---

[58] Kant, *Gesammelte Schriften*, i. 475.
[59] Ibid.   [60] Ibid. i. 477.   [61] Ibid.

What is novel, however, is Kant's explanation of the relation
between monads and space, and the way in which it allows him
to reconcile the infinite divisibility of (bodies in) space with the
simplicity of monads. Whereas Wolff had asserted that the intrinsic
qualities of substances, when taken together, will give rise to a certain
order, which was then identified—without argument—with space,
Kant explicitly attributes this function to the activity of monads.
Specifically, he introduces the notion of a 'sphere of activity' by
means of which a monad can be present throughout an extended
region of space, despite the fact that it is itself an unextended point
in space.[62] What Kant clearly has in mind here is impenetrability,
since it is by means of a monad's sphere of activity that it 'hinders
the things external to it and present to it on both sides from moving
any closer to each other'.[63] Given that Baumgarten had already made
impenetrability available as a fundamental property of monads, Kant
is simply making explicit use of the metaphysical notion of activity
underlying it to account for the emergence of space.

However, because Kant, unlike Baumgarten, distinguishes between
the monad and the sphere of its activity, he can reconcile the infinite
divisibility of space with the simplicity of monads quite elegantly. The
basic move is as follows: Since a monad occupies space by means
of its sphere of activity on other monads, the divisibility of space
entails merely the divisibility of its relations to others, not that of
its own substance, and is thus no threat to its unity. Kant explains
how attributing a sphere of activity to monads can effect the desired
reconciliation of the infinite divisibility of space with the simplicity of
monads as follows:

But, you say, substance is to be found in this little space and is everywhere
present within it; so, if one divides space, does not one divide substance? I
answer: this space itself is the orbit of the external presence of its element.
Accordingly, if one divides space, one divides the extensive quantity of its
presence. But, in addition to external presence, that is to say, in addition to
the relational determinations of substance, there are other, internal determinations. If the latter did not exist, the former would have no subject in
which to inhere. But the internal determinations are not in space, precisely

---

because they are internal. Accordingly, they are not themselves divided by the division of the external determinations.[64]

Kant's reconciliation of the infinite divisibility of space with the simplicity of monads thus depends on monads having both relational and intrinsic properties and on the latter being in some measure independent of the former (even if the former, asymmetrically, depend on the latter). For (i) divisibility entails a change in the relational properties of space, (ii) simplicity (or unity) is an intrinsic property of monads, and (iii) what is required for the reconciliation of divisibility and simplicity is that a certain kind of change in the former kind of property not entail a change in the latter kind of property. Kant's reconciliation thus asserts that these conditions are satisfied, because dividing (bodies in) space simply entails a change in a monad's relational properties, which can leave its intrinsic properties, such as its simplicity, unaffected, since changes in the latter need not bring about any changes in the former.

What may not be immediately evident, however, is that Kant's reconciliation presupposes a view that Leibniz, Wolff, and Baumgarten explicitly reject. For whereas Leibniz, Wolff, and Baumgarten, as we saw above, explicitly assert that the intrinsic properties of monads, when taken together, give rise to a certain order, which (relational property) is then identified with space, Kant's reconciliation assumes that monads can generate space by means of their causal activities on each other. That is, Kant thinks that spatial relations depend on causal relations between monads, which Leibniz, Wolff, and Baumgarten all reject by accepting pre-established harmony.

The debate about whether finite substances can act on each other or only themselves was hotly contested at the time and involved a wide range of philosophical topics, from narrow metaphysical and logical concerns to issues at home in natural theology—topics that require extensive discussion in their own right.[65] What is important in the current context is to see how Kant adds descriptive content to the causal relations between monads and thereby characterizes the nature of monads in more detail. As we saw above, Kant's initial

---

[64] Ibid. i. 481.

[65] See my *Kant and the Metaphysics of Causality* (New York: Cambridge University Press, 2005), ch. 1, for discussion of this debate.

characterization of the sphere of activity that each monad has involved impenetrability. But in the course of the *Physical Monadology* it becomes clear that he understands impenetrability not in terms of solidity, but rather in terms of repulsive force, and he argues that monads must have an attractive force as well if they are to have a determinate volume.[66] Further, Kant ascribes to monads a force of inertia, which he identifies with mass and which he uses, along with attractive and repulsive forces, to account for both the nature and specific differences of bodies.[67] In short, Kant draws heavily on Newtonian forces to fill out the account of monads that he has taken over in certain central respects from Leibniz and Wolff, since attractive, repulsive, and inertial forces all form fundamental principles of Newtonian physics.

The way in which Kant incorporates Newtonian forces into his metaphysical account of monads is important, because it reveals several interesting points of contrast with the views of Leibniz, Wolff, and Baumgarten. The first point concerns their respective views on whether monads can be said to be physical and, if so, in what sense. In so far as Leibniz considered the possibility at all, he denied that monads could be physical, since they were perceptual or mental, while Wolff was agnostic about the nature of simple substances. Baumgarten advocated the possibility that monads might be physical, but was not in a position to say in what sense they were physical beyond the minimal sense that they were impenetrable and fully determinate (and thus different from mathematical points). Kant, by contrast, is able to provide a much richer description of why monads are physical, because on his view, they are the immediate seat of several basic physical forces, that is, of forces that are directly causally responsible for the physical properties of bodies. That is, given his interests in reconciling metaphysics and physics, Kant does not merely explore the possibility, apparently overlooked by others, that monads could be physical in some minimal sense; instead he wants to base his account of the most fundamental properties of bodies *directly* on physical monads and their basic forces. Physical monads thus play a fundamental role in his natural philosophy at the time. As Kant remarks at the end of the Introduction to the *Physical Monadology*: 'Anyone who is able to deduce these two principles [i.e. attractive and repulsive forces] from

---

[66] Kant, *Gesammelte Schriften*, i. 483.   [67] Ibid. i. 483–7.

the very nature and fundamental properties of the elements will have made a substantial contribution towards explaining the inner nature of bodies.'[68] His distinctive version of a physical monadology is of course supposed to do just that.

That Kant commits to physical monads in this way illustrates a second point of contrast, one that is perhaps even more fundamental than the first. By holding that what makes physical monads physical is their close relationship to physical forces, Kant applies in a very different way Leibniz's distinction between primitive and derivative forces (which Wolff had taken over, at least in certain respects, without any apparent hesitation).[69] Because attractive, repulsive, and inertial forces can both explain the fundamental properties of bodies (which is what was of primary interest to Kant at that time) and be immediately grounded in monads possessing unity, there is no need to invoke any other, more fundamental forces of monads. In short, Kant's proposal is to view physical forces, which Leibniz thinks of as instances of derivative forces, as fundamental and hence primitive.

Further, Kant is able to provide answers to the three questions raised above that differ significantly from those available to Leibniz, Wolff, and Baumgarten. First, because physical monads are not only physical, but physical in a robust sense—they are the seat of physical forces—the bodies that are generated through their activities (or forces) can be physical in a weighty sense as well. Accordingly, Kant can clearly avoid the paradoxical argument that Leibniz was saddled with, namely that the reality of bodies could be saved only by denying their reality in favour of their ideality. This result is especially important for Kant in so far as he explicitly rejects idealism at the time; in the *Nova dilucidatio*, the first consequence that he draws from the principle of succession is that a mind cannot cause a change in itself and thus must interact with external bodies if change is to be possible.[70]

Second, Kant also has a clear rebuttal to the charge that monads are heterogeneous with bodies such that no intelligible relation between

---

[68] Ibid. i. 476.

[69] Baumgarten does not discuss the distinction between primitive and derivative forces in detail, perhaps because he thought that the distinction is central not to the most fundamental principles of metaphysics, but rather to the details of general or rational cosmology.

[70] Kant, *Gesammelte Schriften*, i. 411.

the two is possible. Kant's monads may or may not have representations and thus be endowed with mental powers, but at least those monads that compose bodies must have physical forces and there can therefore be no lack of intelligibility between these forces and the physical properties of the bodies that they cause.[71] While Kant's response on this issue represents an obvious improvement over Leibniz and even Wolff, it is also stronger than Baumgarten's. For the only physical trait that Baumgarten could ascribe to monads was impenetrability. However, as we saw above, Baumgarten does not clarify what it is in a monad that makes it impenetrable to others. As a result, he may not have attributed enough physical content to his monads to avoid a charge of heterogeneity between them and the bodies to which they are supposed to give rise. Because Kant, by contrast, has provided a fuller account of the physical forces with which monads are endowed, he has no gap here at all, which allows him to answer this question quite straightforwardly.

Third, given the nature of his physical monadology, Kant can also address in a novel way the question of how the intrinsic features of monads can give rise to the relational properties of bodies. The basic idea behind Kant's response to this question is that the attractive and repulsive forces of physical monads are activities of the monads themselves, but monads can nonetheless have effects on other monads by means of these forces. In other words, physical monads have a nature (e.g. inertial mass) and causal powers (attractive and repulsive forces) that are intrinsic to them in the sense that physical monads have this nature and these causal powers regardless of what else exists in the world. At the same time, when these monads are placed in a

---

[71] Instead, one might be concerned about vacuity. For it could appear to be meaningless to be told that a monad has an attractive force after seeing that it attracts other monads. It may well be true that it has an attractive force, but one knows nothing about the monad itself that one did not already know after seeing its effect. While Kant's response to this charge is more complex than can be treated adequately here, it is important to note two basic points. First, Kant's position is not simply that a physical monad has a force to bring about x (where x is some particular state), but rather that a physical monad has a force to bring about X (where X is a general kind of state, such as attraction). In other words, forces have generality built into them in such a way that inferring the existence of a force from a given effect is not completely vacuous. Second, it is an important part of scientific practice, according to Kant, that one attempt to reduce the forces that must be posited to account for all of the different effects that occur to as small a number as possible, a task that likewise shows that the inference from effect to force is not vacuous or trivial.

certain relation to other substances, they can, through the exercise of their causal powers in accordance with their nature and circumstances, have a certain 'sphere of activity' and thereby bring about changes in each other. By distinguishing in this way between the intrinsic activity of the cause and the relational character of the effect it brings about, one can understand how it is that activities intrinsic to monads can give rise to causal relations between substances.

One should not forget, however, what it is that allows Kant to provide such answers to questions that one might naturally raise for Leibnizian positions, namely a constellation of factors that were established in different ways by Leibniz, Wolff, and Baumgarten. Leibniz's philosophy provided many of the main elements of Kant's basic metaphysical framework (e.g. the concept of substance, the intuition that there must be simples, the idea that physics requires metaphysics, etc.). Wolff creates space for further Leibnizian possibilities by noting that not all simple substances have to be minds and drawing certain consequences from this point. Baumgarten makes use of this space by suggesting (but not developing in detail) the idea that simple substances might be impenetrable physical points, since neither Leibniz nor Wolff raises any explicit criticisms of such a point of view and it would have considerable advantages for explaining the properties of bodies. Kant seizes on this possibility and develops it in detail by combining it with Newtonian forces and his own distinctive views on causality so as to articulate an extensive and original natural philosophy. In this way, one can understand how a series of small changes in the thinking of post-Leibnizian thinkers made possible a shift of considerable magnitude from Leibniz's idealistic to the pre-Critical Kant's physical monadology.

5. CONCLUDING REFLECTIONS

If we are thus now in possession of a historically accurate and philosophically well motivated explanation of the transition from Leibniz's idealistic to the pre-Critical Kant's physical monadology, what fresh insights can be gained? Three points can, I think, be seen more clearly from this perspective. The first point, which is especially relevant to distinctively Leibnizian positions, focuses on the systematic importance of activity, the second point is particularly revealing in regard to Leibniz's position, illustrating the centrality to his philosophy of the distinction between primitive and derivative forces, while the third point represents a very different view of the nature of Kant's Critical turn.

First, one can see quite clearly how fundamental the notion of activity is to any account that can be viewed as distinctively Leibnizian. For it is now clear that what is required as a link between the unity of simple substances and the plurality of (parts of) extended bodies is not necessarily a *mind* and its *representations*, but rather an *activity* that in some way *unifies* a multitude. As we saw above, Leibniz argued against Descartes that the infinite divisibility of space, and thus the plurality of the parts of matter that occupies any space, requires that true unities, or simples, exist. What was not immediately clear, however, was how a plurality of beings that, as such, lacked unity could be given reality by simples. How could a true unity bestow unity and hence being on another? Leibniz's ultimate answer was to note that *minds* are able to bestow unity and thus being on a multitude by *representing* them as related in a particular way (e.g. in virtue of similarities in their properties). Leibniz may have assumed that first-person introspection into one's own mind could reveal the structure of substances in general, and then inferred as a result that all simple substances are minds (or at least mindlike) and that in principle all substances could bestow unity on multitudes in the way that minds do.[72]

What we have seen, however, by investigating the positions developed by Wolff, Baumgarten, and the pre-Critical Kant is that the crucial intermediary between unity and plurality need not be specifically mental, but can rather be the activity of a simple entity. For what is required is that something *act* so as to *take* a plurality of beings *together* such that relational properties emerge that can unify the various relata. The necessity of activity is implicit in Wolff, who repeatedly remarked that a plurality of simple beings must be 'taken together' for spatial extension to result, though his agnosticism about the nature of simples kept him from providing a detailed account of how exactly this is to occur. The point is illustrated more explicitly, however, by the position developed by the pre-Critical

---

[72] See Donald Rutherford, 'Idealism Declined: Leibniz and Christian Wolff', in Lodge (ed.), *Leibniz and his Correspondents*, 214–37, esp. 230.

Kant, since his physical monads establish relations between each other by means of the exercise of their attractive and repulsive forces (i.e. their sphere of activity), which are clearly physical, not mental, activities.

Now one might counter that Leibniz had already publicly emphasized the importance of activity in 'On Nature Itself'. As he stressed there, it is the activity of finite substances that allows him to distinguish his position from that of the occasionalists and to articulate at least one fundamental criticism of their position. For according to Leibniz, finite substances must be the active cause of their own states at each and every moment such that activity serves as a criterion for identifying which states belong to a given substance. As a result, if finite substances were not active (as occasionalists maintain), then there would be, Leibniz thinks, no reason to prevent one from ascribing all states to God. Thus, Leibniz not only has a concept of activity available to him, but even gives it pride of place in his systematic metaphysics on grounds that are independent of the issues discussed above.[73]

However, this rejoinder fails to acknowledge that activity plays an additional role that is fundamental to Leibnizian metaphysics. For the notion of activity is crucial for explaining not only how a plurality of *states* can be ascribed to a single substance (instead of to God), but also what binds a plurality of *substances* together into a larger unity.[74] Leibniz does make clear that (mental) activity is important for understanding how aggregates (e.g. organisms) are to be understood, but he does not seem to emphasize the systematic importance of such activities for comprehending the unity of the world as a whole. Leibniz suggests that monads must represent all other monads in the world, but he does not present a detailed argument for this point and does not suggest that one needs a principle to unify a plurality of independently existing entities such that they can belong

[73] Leibniz also conceives of activity as what is distinctive of substantiality, in contrast to the Cartesian conception of substance in terms of (relative) ontological independence.

[74] This line of thought naturally leads to a further question: How is it that activity is able to bestow unity on a plurality of beings? How is activity to be understood such that it can accomplish this task? By means of what features? My own hypothesis is that what distinguishes an activity from any more generic state of affairs is that activities are governed by rules, and it is the rules that are the source of the unity, though the causal component of activity is also required to bring the unity about.

to one and the same world.[75] Though Kant similarly recognizes the importance of activity early in his career, he does not explicitly recognize the *systematic* importance of this kind of larger unity until his Inaugural Dissertation, when he makes causal activity (in the form of mutual interaction) into the principle of the form of the world.[76]

A second point that is revealed by reflecting on how Leibniz's position on the necessity and nature of simples was received and modified by Wolff, Baumgarten, and the pre-Critical Kant concerns the distinction between primitive and derivative forces. Leibniz's reasoning on this issue started out with a comparatively modest point. To account for the reality of matter one cannot take matter to be extension alone, as Descartes had; rather, one must also accept the existence of something else that has the unity that extension lacks. This argument thus establishes a distinction between primitive and derivative entities in a very minimal sense, namely extension is derivative in the sense that it cannot exist on its own, but rather requires something else that is therefore prior to it. As Leibniz articulated further the nature of simples and the way in which they relate to extended bodies, he committed himself to a somewhat fuller account of the distinction. Thus, in the 'Specimen dynamicum' Leibniz characterizes the distinction in terms of forces, asserting that the simples have primitive forces, that derivative forces are limitations of primitive forces, and that derivative forces are directly responsible for the physical properties of bodies. In other contexts, Leibniz maintains further that derivative entities are nothing more than well-founded phenomena.[77] At the same time, Leibniz does not provide an especially detailed public description of the exact nature of the dependence of derivative on primitive forces. In particular, he seems not to address clearly enough two central questions: (1) Can primitive forces be described as the cause of derivative forces (and if so, in

---

[75] One might also think that Leibniz's 'world apart' doctrine stands in tension with the idea that representations as such unite monads into a single world.

[76] See §2 of *De mundi sensibilis atque intelligibilis forma et principiis*, repr. in Kant, *Gesammelte Schriften*, ii. 390–1.

[77] See Leibniz's reply to Foucher's objection published in the *Journal des Savants* (Apr. 1696), where he explicitly uses the term 'well-founded phenomena' in this sense (Leibniz, *Essays*, 147).

what sense)?[78] (2) Can the latter be understood on the basis of the former? Leibniz's main line of response for these questions is, it seems, that there is a pre-established harmony between these primitive and derivative forces that defies detailed explanation.

One can then view Wolff, Baumgarten, and the pre-Critical Kant as exploring more specific conceptions of the relationship between primitive and derivative forces and as developing their overall positions in accordance with the particular conceptions they have adopted. Thus Wolff accepted the idea that derivative forces are caused by, and should also be intelligible on the basis of, primitive forces; his doubts about whether Leibniz had proved the necessity of understanding simple substances as being mental were expressed in the context of his expectation that the forces of bodies *ought* to be derivable in an intelligible manner from the elements of corporeal things. However, Wolff also denied that we have an adequate grasp of the specific nature of primitive forces, which forced him to admit that we cannot understand in any specific way how derivative forces derive from primitive forces and, in fact, cannot even positively claim that the relationship between primitive and derivative forces is intelligible. At the same time, he could still reasonably hold that being ignorant of these matters is better than having to acknowledge that this relation is, in principle, heterogeneous, unintelligible, and therefore as standing in need of the special kind of connection that only pre-established harmony can provide.

Baumgarten, by contrast, saw a way in which to understand the nature of primitive forces such that one *can* positively establish the possibility of an intelligible explanation of derivative forces on the basis of primitive forces. By understanding points as physical rather than metaphysical and by characterizing physical points as fully determined entities (which suffices to distinguish them from mathematical points), he could accept a limited, but still genuine, sense in which the derivative forces of physical bodies can seem to be homogeneous with physical points, which establishes the possibility of an intelligible explanation of the one on the basis of the other. However, because of

---

[78] In the 'Specimen dynamicum', Leibniz does clearly state that the primitive forces are the grounds of the derivative forces, which are modes of the primitive forces, but the use of the terms 'grounds' and 'modes' does not, by itself, clarify the relevant issues sufficiently.

the purely formal way in which points are characterized, he cannot in fact provide any specific explanation.

The pre-Critical Kant then completed the trend that Wolff and Baumgarten had begun, by actually attempting to deliver a detailed explanation of the relation between physical monads and bodies that would allow it be fully intelligible. The main move here is to view attractive and repulsive forces as primitive rather than derivative, and the motivation for this step is as follows. Because the nature of attractive and repulsive forces is characterized in terms of their effects on bodies at a derivative level, one can give an intelligible explanation of how they cause particular physical states. Yet because the (intrinsic activities of the) forces themselves (as opposed to their effects) are viewed as primitive, the demands (for intrinsic unity and being *per se*) characteristic of Leibnizian metaphysics can still be satisfied. In this way, the pre-Critical Kant worked out a detailed understanding of the relation between primitive and derivative forces that has a greater degree of intelligibility than do those described by Leibniz, Wolff, and Baumgarten.

This description thus illustrates in a very concrete way not only how the distinction between primitive and derivative forces is central to Leibnizian philosophy, but also how different conceptions of it can give rise to a range of positions that differ from Leibniz's position, while still being recognizably Leibnizian (in a sufficiently broad sense). At the same time, it allows us to observe, from a somewhat more systematic point of view, the basic structure of these different positions and what motivations lead to them. What Leibniz, Wolff, Baumgarten, and the pre-Critical Kant agree on is that the primitive forces of monads are in some sense the causes of the derivative forces (and states) of bodies. The main disagreement concerns whether, and to what extent, this causal relation can be made intelligible. Since Leibniz holds that what happens at the level of the primitive forces of monads (according to teleological principles) and what happens at the level of derivative forces of bodies (according to mechanical, efficient principles) are related by pre-established harmony, and that neither level can be reduced to the other, he is committed to the claim that we can have no specific insights into any intelligible relation between the two. The pre-Critical Kant, by contrast, maintains that he can specify in detail an intelligible relation between the primitive forces of (physical) monads and the derivative states of bodies and without losing anything essential to his metaphysics.

Had Leibniz lived to encounter such a position, he might have responded that the pre-Critical Kant overestimated what can be accomplished by failing to draw a crucial distinction between different kinds of causality. For Leibniz thought that primitive forces are merely *formal* causes of the derivative states of bodies and thus are able to explain only very general features of bodies, while derivative forces alone can serve as *efficient* causes of the particular states of bodies. On this view, Kant's account confuses different kinds of causation by having primitive forces function as (partial) efficient causes. However, from a pre-Critical Kantian perspective, Leibniz's response could seem merely to push the query back one step. For Leibniz has not argued against the possibility of what Kant is in effect suggesting, namely that one ought to be able to, and in fact can, understand how formal and efficient causality cooperate to bring about the specific states of bodies. Whether or not the details of Kant's particular way of developing this suggestion are ultimately feasible, it does raise an interesting issue for the fundamental possibilities inherent in Leibniz's (and Leibnizian) metaphysics.

These reflections on the transition from Leibniz's idealistic monadology to the pre-Critical Kant's physical monadology also shed light on a third point of interest by providing a new context for understanding Kant's position in the Critical period. For instead of being forced to accept at face value the Critical Kant's claim to have initiated a completely novel and allegedly revolutionary way of thinking, and to view his meta-philosophical arguments concerning the possibility of synthetic a priori knowledge as evidence counting in its favour, we can take into account the changes from the pre-Critical to the Critical period, and pose more specific questions about the exact nature and motivation for his Critical position.

Prior to considering Wolff's, Baumgarten's, and the pre-Critical Kant's positions, one might have thought that, on the issue of idealism, the Critical Kant was following Leibniz's lead and simply adding some twists and turns of his own (by, for example, developing innovative considerations concerning space and time and perhaps inflating his differences with Leibniz to mask their fundamental similarities). For Leibniz and Kant are both deeply committed to a number of controversial metaphysical claims: spatio-temporal bodies are phenomenal or ideal, and not noumenal or real, a status that is reserved for radically different kinds of beings, namely agents that operate not in accordance with mechanical laws, but rather in accordance with their conception of the good. And, viewed from this particular perspective, Kant and Leibniz also seem to be motivated on this issue by the same philosophical considerations in so far as Kant's Thesis and Antithesis arguments in the Second Antinomy cover ground that we are already familiar with from Leibniz. The Thesis argument claims that there must be simples, a view that Leibniz argues for in the 'New System' and then gives pride of place to in *The Monadology*, while the Antithesis argument asserts that bodies must be infinitely divisible on the grounds that anything spatial must be divisible into further parts that are themselves spatial and thus divisible, a line of thought that Leibniz explicitly endorses in 'A New System of Nature'. Finally, since Transcendental Idealism's distinction between things in themselves and appearances allows one to relegate infinitely divisible bodies to the realm of mere appearances, while still holding out hope that noumenal substances are simple, the reasoning behind Kant's resolution to this antinomy can sound very similar to Leibniz's as well (even if it requires setting aside some differences merely terminological in nature). In short, if one considers the views of only Leibniz and the Critical Kant, the question one immediately faces is simply whether Kant's meta-philosophical reflections concerning the possibility of synthetic a priori cognition and his arguments (e.g. from geometry) for viewing space and time as merely subjective forms of intuition suffice to make the Critical philosophy as revolutionary as he claims.

After having investigated the views of Wolff, Baumgarten, and the pre-Critical Kant, however, we can see that a different question is actually more pressing. The question can be posed in one form as follows: Why did Kant ultimately turn to idealism when he had been familiar with such a position for several decades and had consistently rejected it (on grounds that had seemed adequate to him)? What this question reveals is that Kant's acceptance of idealism is to be viewed not as something that he inherited as an unquestioned (though not therefore unmodified) element of Leibniz's legacy, but rather as a fundamental reversal of position that requires positive explanation against a particular historical background, and it is quite noticeable that such an explanation does not currently exist in so far as interpretations of Kant's familiar arguments for the ideality of space and time in the Transcendental Aesthetic do not immediately address more encompassing questions that would have arisen immediately and quite naturally in such a context, such as whether all of the properties of objects that appear in space and time must be ideal, just as space and time are.[79]

The same question can be raised from another perspective as follows: What reason did Kant have for becoming dissatisfied with his pre-Critical physical monadology? It may be that the kind of argument typically advanced on Kant's behalf for Transcendental Idealism (e.g. his meta-philosophical reflections on geometry and the possibility of synthetic a priori knowledge) is relevant to understanding what he found objectionable about his early view, but it is striking, from our current vantage point, that standard discussions of Kant's 'Critical turn' have not explicitly addressed this particular issue at all. Further, it is worth noting that answering this question on the basis of the general arguments in favour of Transcendental Idealism that are most often discussed does not promise to be an especially easy or trivial task, given that the Critical Kant retains a number of the central claims of his earlier physical monadology. For example, Kant argues at length (in the *Metaphysical Foundations of Natural Science*) that attractive and repulsive forces are causes of the properties of bodies; he also holds that noumena, the ultimate level of reality, must be intelligible (since they are, by definition, beings of thought that we represent by means of reason), and also the cause of what appears to us at the level of bodies (even if we cannot cognize the specific ways in which such causation occurs); and Kant even repeatedly asserts that we must think (though we cannot know) that reality is ultimately composed of simple substances. At this level of detail, what changes in Kant's view is instead that attractive and repulsive forces are, to speak with Leibniz, no longer primitive, but rather derivative; to put the point in Kant's own terminology, the substances that are endowed with attractive and repulsive forces are not noumenal, but rather phenomenal and thus not

---

[79] For a preliminary discussion of this issue, see my 'Transcendental Idealism and the Categories', *History of Philosophy Quarterly*, 19 (2002), 191–215.

simple. Since perhaps the central difference between the pre-Critical and the Critical Kant that is relevant to this issue—whether particular forces should be ascribed to phenomenal or noumenal substances—is not a topic that is the immediate focus of more standard discussions of Transcendental Idealism, considerable conceptual manoeuvring will be required to forge the requisite link, if such a link is even possible at this level of generality.

These remarks about Transcendental Idealism, as well as the other two points just mentioned, are, of course, extremely sketchy and preliminary in nature, and would need to be treated in much greater detail for us to be able to draw definitive conclusions from them. Still, they do reveal how focusing on the specific arguments and positions of Wolff, Baumgarten, and the pre-Critical Kant concerning the necessity and nature of simples can not only render intelligible how the transition from an idealistic to a physical monadology could have occurred quite naturally in certain historical circumstances, but also provide us with a novel perspective from which we can discern important aspects of Leibniz's and Kant's own philosophies with greater clarity.[80]

University of California, San Diego

[80] I thank Karl Ameriks, Daniel Garber, Rick Grush, Michael Hardimon, Matt Kisner, Sukjae Lee, James Messina, Sam Rickless, Donald Rutherford, Tad Schmaltz, and an anonymous referee for helpful comments on earlier versions of this chapter.

10

Review Essay
Descartes's Theory of Mind
Desmond M. Clarke
(Oxford: Clarendon Press, 2003)

DENNIS DES CHENE

The physicist and physiologist have no reason to read Descartes. Descartes said that the solar system is filled with subtle matter moving in circular vortices. It isn't. He said that the nexus of sensation and action in animals is the pineal gland. It isn't. He said that matter is extension. It isn't. His errors are not worth repeating; the truths of which he had some grasp are more accessibly and usably expressed elsewhere. Philosophers, of course, still read Descartes. But why?

You might, of course, read the *Meditations* just for inspiration. A temple inscription, the plays of Nestroy, or the Upanishads would do as well. The use of a text for inspiration requires no exegesis, no reconstruction, no setting in context. And yet with Descartes we explicate, reconstruct, supply context, at length. What for? The *Meditations* is a curious artefact; but so too are the works of Kircher and Wolff. Curiosity is, perhaps, a sufficient motive in history. Paul Veyne thought so. But philosophers typically have, or would like to have, a more serious motive. Some think that Descartes, even if mistaken in details, got hold of something basic: in the *cogito*, for example, the centrality of self-awareness to thought; or, in the stages of doubt of the First Meditation, the disturbing possibility that my experience could be just as it is even if its causes were quite other than what I believe them to be. Others think that Descartes, though fundamentally wrong, was not only influentially but instructively wrong, and thus still worth studying.

Desmond Clarke is of both opinions in his book *Descartes's Theory of Mind*. His Descartes is correspondingly bifurcated. Descartes the working scientist was right, not only about how inquiry into nature should be conducted, but in supposing that the functions of the soul could be 'naturalized'. That Descartes is worth recovering. The other Descartes, the metaphysician, issued dubious and dispensable judgements about substances, God, freedom, and so forth. What is worth retaining from Descartes the metaphysician is only the *ne plus ultra* presented by certain properties of the mind to his, and our, naturalistic psychology.

To approach a text with the aim of recuperation, of extracting what you consider to be a kernel of truth from the shroud of obscurities and falsehoods that surround it, is evidently to read *from* the present, or a near future, of which you and your author are the prophets. The recuperator will often argue that what has been recovered is the essential, even the real, thought of the author; that disparities are mere contingencies, forced upon the author by his situation; that where the author seems at odds with what is taken to be the kernel of truth in his work he is unserious, or confused, or dissembling.

Reading Descartes as Clarke would have us read him requires a shift in perspective (*Descartes's Theory*, 9), a change of emphasis that in itself I regard as salutary, though at this point not especially innovative. Clarke reminds us that Descartes's œuvre up to the time of the *Meditations* consisted almost entirely in works in mathematics and natural philosophy. We are to suppose that Descartes found himself, sometime in the 1630s, in the position of having to reconcile his properly scientific work with the terms and doctrines of a Christian philosophy from which he did not wish to diverge. He had, moreover, come to realize that the physiology of the *Treatise on Man* was not up to the task of explaining all the operations of the human mind. On both accounts it was necessary to retain the soul, or rather (as Clarke believes) mental properties. Descartes thereby remained in nominal agreement with the teachings of the Catholic Church and at the same time acknowledged the limits of his natural philosophy.

I. DOING HISTORIES

I'll skip to Clarke's conclusion: the recuperated Descartes is a failed substance dualist but a successful property dualist. His dualism is not a metaphysical thesis. It is a recognition of the limits of mechanical explanation. This same Descartes has an entirely materialist theory of sensation. He regards the will as free only in so far as reflection enables us to order and modify our passions. The use of language alone distinguishes us from the beasts, providing the basis upon which to credit us with mental properties while denying them to the rest of creation.

Historically considered, the object of Clarke's work is ambiguous. The texts are Descartes's. The doctrines just mentioned are ascribed to the actual Descartes. But the working assumption of Clarke's interpretation is inspired by Sellars's distinction between the manifest and the scientific image of the world. Clarke, following Sellars, holds that 'the scientific image provides our most reliable access to reality and the best reasons for adopting one ontology rather than another' (*Descartes's Theory*, 10). If Descartes's ontology was not 'inherited uncritically from his predecessors', then our only route to his new ontology is to infer from his natural philosophy 'the theoretical entities that are required for an adequate explanation of all the realities' in a Cartesian universe (*Descartes's Theory*, 11).

The question by which the reading of Descartes's whole philosophy is to be guided thus becomes: to which entities has the working scientist Descartes committed himself in his natural philosophy by way of the particular explanations he gives? His explicit claims about what there is will be interpreted in light of the answer to that question. If, for example, his psychology turns out not to be committed to mental substance, but only to mental properties, then Descartes the working scientist is effectively a property dualist, whatever he may have said by way of making his ontology explicit.

Many historians agree that the vocabulary of late scholasticism was ill-suited to express conceptions of body emerging in the new natural philosophies of the seventeenth century. The alternatives were to avoid as much as possible the more heavily marked terms of the Schools, like "substance" and "form"; to replace the scholastic vocabulary with another, as Gassendi did in adapting Epicurean logic and physics; or to endeavour to cancel the unwanted implications of scholastic terms so as to avoid inconsistency and misunderstanding. In the *Regulae* and the *Meditations*, for example, Descartes uses the term *res*, rather than *substantia*, in referring to bodies and minds. Substances are *res*; but in scholastic usage qualities and modes are *res* too. When, in the *Principles of Philosophy*, he adopts the term "substance", he defines it, taking as primary from among the features attributed to substances by late scholastics the feature of independent existence. *Res* was an ontologically less specific, less loaded term than *substantia*, and thus preferable in a context where the connotations of that term were unwanted; and when *substantia* was used, it had to be explicitly defined so as to filter out those unwanted connotations.

In considering Clarke's project, it is worth reflecting for a moment on the methods and aims of the history of philosophy. Descartes writes in the *Discourse on Method* that the acts recorded in works of histories, if read with discretion, help to form the judgement, and that reading good books generally is 'like a conversation with the finest people of past centuries' (AT vi. 5; cf. vi. 6; all translations are mine). The aim of consulting the works of the past is to find worthy interlocutors—to generate matter for discussion in the present. As Clarke notes, many philosophers have found suitable matter only in the *Meditations* and in corresponding passages elsewhere in the Cartesian corpus. They have dismissed the natural philosophy on the grounds that it is obsolete. The result, however, is unsatisfactory: it is that familiar bogeyman, the arch-dualist Descartes, who is mentioned only to be dismissed as 'an obvious dead end' (*Descartes's Theory*, 2).

Clarke, in the interest of finding a more worthy interlocutor, gives the natural philosophy pride of place in his interpretation. The metaphysics becomes a kind of afterthought—a diversion at best, a distraction at worst. Language that would apparently entail that the mind is a substance distinct from the body is to be interpreted in the light of the project initiated in the *Treatise on Man*. There Descartes promises to explain the functions of living things mechanistically, that is, by reference only to a limited collection of properties held to exist in bodies, and by invoking only the arrangements or 'dispositions' of parts of the body and the efficient-causal production of effects from those arrangements. We are to read the Cartesian corpus in the light of that starting point. In particular, Descartes's apparent dualism is to be treated as a 'solution' to the problem presented by the failure of the methods of the *Treatise* to explain mental phenomena: it is here, if anywhere, that we would find genuine *reasons* for holding that the mind is a substance really distinct from the body—a posteriori grounds, that is, to postulate such a substance (*Descartes's Theory*, 18).

So far we have a historical thought experiment. Suppose that Descartes had been only a natural philosopher: what sort of ontology would he have been committed to? Clarke, however, holds that the views we attribute to Descartes on the basis of that thought experiment are those of the *historical* Descartes, the author of the *Meditations*. That is a more contentious claim. Descartes had arrived, according to Clarke, at the view that scholastic appeals to forms and qualities are never 'genuinely explanatory'—and are thus to be avoided everywhere, not only in physics and physiology. The objections raised against forms and qualities remain valid 'even when explaining mental phenomena' (*Descartes's Theory*, 20). 'We should therefore expect that, in constructing a theory of mind, Descartes would not revert spontaneously to the failed concept of explanation against which he had argued so successfully'; instead, substance dualism, if indeed that was Descartes's considered view, would be a consequence of the failure of the new philosophy and its new methods successfully to treat mental phenomena (ibid. 17).[1]

---

[1] Clarke may well believe that on the basis of the arguments for it the proscription of forms ought to apply everywhere, and that Descartes should have believed that too, because excluding the mind is arbitrary; but to show that the historical Descartes denied the utility of appeals to forms in explaining human action requires argument. One might well suppose that disparate domains call for disparate methods, and that Descartes regarded the phenomena of the mind and those of nature as disparate. Here are a few brief points in support of that claim: (i) Descartes recognizes what we would call the intentionality of thoughts. Thoughts have *objects*, bodies don't. (ii) The attribution of ends is not permitted in reasoning about the phenomena of nature; but Descartes does attribute ends to the powers of the mind, and to the 'instituted' relations between motions in the brain and certain kinds of thought (Meditation 6, AT vii. 87). The five primitive passions other than wonder have the natural use (*usage naturel*) of 'inciting the soul to consent and contribute to actions that may serve to conserve the body and render it in some way more perfect' (*Passions of the soul*, pt. 2, art. 137, AT xi. 430). (iii) Descartes indicates here and there that the laws of nature apply only to *res extensae* (e.g. at *Principles of Philosophy*, II. 40, AT viiia. 65). His version of mechanism is accompanied, from the time of his collaboration with Beeckman onward, by the conception of law. Mechanistic explanations rest ultimately on the derivation of the motions of bodies from assumptions about their size and shape and the laws of nature. It would not be surprising, then, if (supposing minds are not subject to those laws) Descartes excluded the explanation of mental phenomena from his strictures against form. On the scope of the laws of nature, see Daniel Garber, 'Mind, Body, and the Laws of Nature in Descartes and Leibniz', in Garber, *Descartes Embodied* (Cambridge: Cambridge University Press, 2001), 133–67, esp. 150–2.

Clarke is correct in holding that we should not treat the historical Descartes a priori as a substance dualist. Preconceived opinions are out of place in history as in science. It is a mistake, for example, to argue that because Descartes was a dualist, he excluded the mind from his strictures on forms and qualities—a mistake, that is, if there are not independent grounds for asserting that Descartes was a dualist. The standard account, as Clarke calls it, bases itself on certain of Descartes's texts, notably the *Meditations* and the first book of the *Principles*. It also appeals to the context in which Descartes constructed his metaphysics, and to features of Descartes's response to that context: his scholastic education, for example, or his evident intention to avoid overt conflict with the pronouncements of the Church.

The hope is to discover the causes or, more modestly, the causal conditions under which an agent like Descartes would have produced the texts that the actual Descartes produced. In the case of conclusions arrived at by argument, we look first of all at the reasons explicitly offered (following a general principle to the effect that if a rational agent holds that p, and p is known by that agent to have the consequence q, then holding p suffices to explain why that agent holds that q). In other cases, when the arguments would be unsound even by the agent's own lights, or when we suspect that the agent is not sincere, we look rather for *motives* than *reasons*. Motives determine in part not only the conclusions that an agent wants to reach, but the weight assigned to various reasons for and against that conclusion. Descartes's treatment of the motion of the earth in the *Principles* is a case in point (*Principles of Philosophy*, III. 28; AT viiia. 90). We suspect that the conclusion (which is that properly speaking the earth does not move) is motivated by the intention to remain in agreement with the judgement issued against Galileo, and that Descartes found what he may or may not have regarded as adequate reasons for a conclusion held independently of them.

Clarke gives us not only motives but a reason for Descartes's apparent dualism. The motives are the ones usually attributed to Descartes. He wished, for example, to 'render intelligible the Christian doctrine of the immortality of human souls' (Clarke, *Descartes's Theory*, 208; cf. 5), and to preserve some notion of moral responsibility in voluntary action (ibid. 154). The reason is that 'Cartesian matter in motion could not deliver the kind of explanation' that Descartes thought of as genuine. Descartes's mind, on this account, is a 'mind of the gaps': a signpost at the limits of science.

2. FORMS, QUALITIES, EXPLANATIONS

Clarke's basic argument against the standard account of Descartes's theory of mind is this. Descartes rules out appeals to forms everywhere (or at least his arguments against appealing to forms can be seen to hold regardless of subject matter). Forms explain nothing. The mind or soul, considered as a substance, would be a form. Therefore if we are not to find that Descartes's theory of mind is violently at odds with his model of explanation, we should try to find a reading of that theory in which it is not a form. For Clarke, the result is that there is no such thing as mental substance, but only mental properties, which themselves are, if not identical to physical properties, at least supervenient upon the body. That is the view he would like to attribute, as much as possible, to Descartes himself.

In what follows I will first discuss the Cartesian brief against forms and qualities. Then I will take up particular issues concerning the mind. After a quick look at Clarke's treatment of intellectual memory, I examine Descartes's treatment of sensation, his doctrine of substance, and finally the question of dualism. Brevity requires that I omit what Clarke has to say about the passions, the will, and language; there is much of interest in those chapters, but I think that the main line of argument will be clear from the parts I discuss.

It is apparent to anyone who has studied Aristotelian natural philosophy that Descartes has altered not only the content but the aims of natural philosophy. Though in both the overall aim is knowledge of the natural world, what is to count as knowing differs. The Aristotelian considers a thing, or rather a kind of thing, known if its nature is specified; its nature is specified by first classifying its powers, especially its active powers, and then showing, to whatever extent possible, that those powers are realized in the matter of things of that kind. The human species, for example, is distinguished first of all as a living thing, and then placed in a class by itself in virtue of the powers commonly attributed to the 'rational' part of the soul: abstract reasoning and free will. Powers that the human soul shares with animals, sensation for example, require a material substrate, a suitably disposed matter; a structural description of the organ of hearing, for example, according to which it is a chamber filled with fluid, shows how it is possible for sounds to affect the body, and thus how the soul can receive the 'species' of sound. Needless to say, the anatomy and physiology is by our lights primitive—though not so primitive that Descartes does not avail himself of it. But if one is looking for what Descartes (and Clarke) would regard as a genuine explanation of hearing, that is what approaches it most closely. The classification and analysis of powers and the discovery of the manners in which they are realized are in Aristotelian natural philosophy complementary, not competing, pursuits.[2]

Descartes, in the *Treatise on Man* and subsequent works in physiology, does not so much reject the Aristotelian account of the powers of the human soul as take it for granted. Animals breathe, digest, move themselves, sense, imagine, remember, and undergo the bodily correspondents of human passion, just as the commentaries on Aristotle say they do. But Descartes does not believe that there is anything more to an animal's having the power of vision than that its organ of sight has a certain 'disposition' or arrangement of parts, themselves described in accordance with a limited list of qualities attributable to matter, and that an organ so disposed will yield certain specified effects when acted upon by light.

The Jesuit Aristotelians with whom Descartes was familiar would have distinguished between the power and its realization. Descartes does not. The ascription of a power is only a prelude to a mechanistic, efficient-causal explanation of the *effects* of the thing to which that power is ascribed. Boyle writes, in his *Free Enquiry into the Vulgarly Received Notion of Nature* (published in 1686 but begun some twenty years before), that 'to explicate a phenomenon, it is not enough to ascribe it to one general efficient, but we must intelligibly show the particular manner how that general cause produces the proposed effect' (*Free Enquiry*, 150; quoted in Clarke, *Descartes's Theory*, 24).[3]

---

[2] For a modern version of this distinction, see Robert Cummins, *The Nature of Psychological Explanation* (Cambridge, Mass.: MIT Press, 1982), and for a defence of capacities in natural science, see Nancy Cartwright, *Nature's Capacities and their Measurement* (Oxford: Clarendon Press, 1989).

[3] Robert Boyle, *A Free Enquiry into the Vulgarly Received Notion of Nature* [*Free Enquiry*], ed. Edward B. Davis and Michael Hunter (Cambridge: Cambridge University Press, 1996; first pub. 1686).

Boyle applies the principle to souls: knowing in detail what the parts of a watch are, and how they act so as to move the hour hand, we no longer need to suppose 'that it has a soul or life to be the internal principle of its motions or operations'. The supposed soul of the watch, if you want to retain that term, consists in nothing other than the arrangement of its parts.

On this view, adducing a power, or a form considered as the ground of the characteristic powers of a kind, is a stopgap, an indication of what needs explaining. Animals move themselves: you may, if you like, attribute to them a 'locomotive power', but only by way of indicating (i) a characteristic *action* and (ii) that the action is to be explained by reference to properties of the animal itself (and not, for example, to external forces, as would be the case with a marionette).

Boyle, I should note, understands that substantial forms *were* held to explain certain features of natural things. In 'The Origin of Forms and Qualities', Boyle takes on some of the standard physical arguments on behalf of substantial form.[4] The postulation of forms was thought, for example, to be required in order to explain the difference between generation (change of substance) and alteration (change of quality). One argument is that if in bodies there were only collocations of qualities, then we would not observe, say, in the transformation of water into air that the qualities characteristic of water are *simultaneously* replaced by those characteristic of air. Boyle has a response to this (in addition to his constant refrain that forms are not explanatory): he introduces, on the one hand, the notion of *texture*, which is an arrangement of the basic corpuscles of matter, and on the other, the notion of a *denominating state*, *essential modification*, or *stamp*, which is a recurrent (and stable) texture on the basis of whose effects we distinguish one kind of natural body from another (Boyle, 'Origin', 30, 40). Postulated textures do for Boyle what postulated forms did for the Aristotelians.[5]

---

[4] Robert Boyle, 'The Origin of Forms and Qualities' ['Origin'], in Boyle, *Selected Philosophical Papers*, ed. M. A. Stewart (Indianapolis: Hackett, 1991), 1–96.

[5] One might well ask, as Alan Gabbey does, why question-begging hypotheses about dispositions or textures are preferable to question-begging hypotheses about forms and qualities. See Gabbey, 'Explanatory Structures and Models in Descartes' Physics', in G. Belgioioso, G. Cimino, P. Costabel, and G. Papuli (eds.), *Descartes: Il metodo e i saggi* (Rome: Istituto della Enciclopedia Italiana), i. 273–86, esp. 279, 282. Clarke cites Gabbey but

Clarke ascribes to Descartes the project of 'testing the applicability' of his new methods of explanation to the human mind (*Descartes's Theory*, 17). Only, it would seem, *after* discovering the limits of those methods did Descartes take up the option of relying on the otherwise *verboten* powers and forms. 'One would expect those limits to emerge rather quickly given the minimal knowledge of the human brain with which Descartes was working' (ibid.). Perhaps so, but when?

Descartes's earliest extant systematic work in physiology is the *Treatise on Man*, begun after 1630. That work specifically exempts those operations of the human mind that involve thought from its purview. It begins by dividing the human being into a soul and a body. There is no record in the correspondence from that period that Descartes ever entertained the notion of explaining human reason or the will by the same means he uses in the *Treatise* to explain those powers we share with animals. What we have instead from that period is some letters to Mersenne that, in addition to answering questions in natural philosophy, expound Descartes's doctrine on the creation of the eternal truths. A 'little treatise' on metaphysics is mentioned in 1629; its contents are unknown to us, although in the *Discourse* Descartes dates the reflections recorded in Part IV to that period. Descartes extravagantly describes, in the letters to Mersenne as in the sixth part of the *Discourse*, the tasks he thinks he can accomplish with his new philosophy: none of them can be construed as rendering the mind superfluous.

It is possible that Descartes did include all the phenomena of the mind in his project. It is possible he recognized that his project if successful would imply the redundancy of the soul (as later philosophers came to believe), or realized that it was not going to succeed entirely, and then devised the arguments we find in the *Meditations* as a precaution or a *pis aller*. But this is conjecture. The documents do not permit us to say more than that Descartes did not consider the question of the immateriality of the soul in any depth until 1629 or after.

---

misunderstands, I think, his point: it is not only that Cartesian explanations are deficient, but that some of the very same criticisms made of scholastic explanations by the mechanists could be urged against theirs. 'Dormitive disposition' (i.e. being of such a *texture* as to produce sleep) is not much better than 'dormitive virtue' (which, in the scholastics, would be cashed out in terms of a temperament or mixture of elementary qualities).

He seems to have regarded many of the Aristotelian arguments on that question to be either irrelevant or insufficient. Aside from the indivisibility of the mind and certain suggestive claims on the limitations of corporeal substances, Descartes retains almost nothing from the usual array. The arguments of the Schools were inadequate; materialism, never entirely vanquished, was again a live possibility thanks to the revival of Epicureanism; Descartes's own physiology had done away with the vegetative and sensitive parts of the Aristotelian soul: it is not surprising that Descartes, not only to forestall objections to his philosophy but perhaps also to aid the Church in its defence of the immortality of the soul, should have endeavoured to find new arguments to show that the rational part of the soul does not depend on the body for its existence.

So far there don't seem to be compelling reasons to deny that Descartes was a substance dualist. Much of Clarke's interpretation devotes itself to showing that Descartes's theories of the powers of the mind—sensation, imagination, memory, and the will—do not commit him to dualism. Much of what he says about the mind could, *mutatis mutandis*, be taken over by a materialist or a property dualist. Clarke's argument is not that the *content* of his psychology is inconsistent with an immaterial soul, but that Descartes's *method* ought to have led him to reject dualism.

3. MEMORY AND SENSATION

By way of illustrating Clarke's manner in dealing with texts that seem to imply a dualist view, I will look briefly at intellectual memory before turning to his treatment of sensation.

Intellectual memory, as its name implies, is a kind of memory associated not with the sensitive soul but with the rational. The Aristotelian holds that the rational soul is the immortal part of the soul; a soul without a body, if we had only corporeal memory, would remember nothing; but since it was thought that we do remember things in the afterlife, there must be some sort of memory that, like the intellect, has no organ. The phenomenon is, of course, not of this world; Clarke dismisses it. Descartes's supposition of an intellectual memory is, in his letter to Huygens and in similar contexts, 'a tentative conclusion from a theological doctrine about the afterlife', and not a conclusion derived from his theory of mind (Clarke, *Descartes's Theory*, 101, on Descartes to Huygens, 10 October 1642, AT iii. 798). It is rather a 'concession' to the theologians. The working scientist Descartes is not in the business of accounting for phenomena vouched for only by faith or revelation.

Among the phenomena of experience for which Descartes adduces intellectual memory as a cause is the recognition of novelty which is part of his account of memory (of the sort we would call 'episodic'). It is not enough that the mind should now be affected by a trace persisting from some earlier sensation; the mind must also recognize that the trace 'has not always been in us, but rather arrived sometime for the first time'. Only an intellectual memory would be capable of noticing that the thing we are observing has not been observed before, because 'there can be no corporeal vestige of that novelty' (Descartes to Arnauld, 29 July 1648, AT v. 220).

Clarke sees no good reason to insist that only intellectual memory could perform the feat of recognizing the novelty of an experience. In the *Passions of the Soul*, Descartes puts as the cause of wonder first of all 'the impression one has in the brain, which represents the object as rare and consequently as worthy of great consideration'. This in turn causes the animal spirits to rush towards the part of the brain where the impression is located (AT xi. 380–1). The force of wonder arises from the sudden and unexpected arrival of the impression that changes the course of the spirits, and depends in part on novelty (AT xi. 382). In principle, then, the recognition of novelty could be based somehow on impressions and changes in the flow of the animal spirits.

References to intellectual memory, then, are otiose for the theory of mind required in natural philosophy, and are otherwise motivated by theological doctrines. Those doctrines, says Clarke, cannot decide the fate of theories in natural philosophy because doing so 'would reverse the order in which we acquire and use concepts': we are most confident in applying them to ordinary experience, we extend them to supposed spiritual beings 'only by analogy and with due caution'.[6] The most Clarke is willing to grant is that some acts of memory

---

[6] If this is supposed to be Descartes's view, I think Clarke is mistaken. The *order of acquisition* and the *order of certainty* are quite distinct in Descartes. The idea of God, for example, is the clearest and most distinct of all (Meditation 3, AT vii. 46); the ideas of geometry, whether (as Clarke seems to think) they arise by abstraction from the perceptions

depend less on brain traces than others; but all acts of memory depend on them somehow (*Descartes's Theory*, 105).

I won't defend intellectual memory here. Instead I use this discussion to illustrate a systematic puzzle presented by Clarke's interpretation. Suppose we grant that Descartes, had he been on the ball, would have come to see that intellectual memory has no role in explaining human actions and thoughts. This Descartes, however, is not only a working scientist Descartes but an *ideal* working scientist Descartes. The historical Descartes thought he had good reasons for postulating an intellectual memory. It is, no doubt, peripheral to his natural philosophy: most of Descartes's efforts at explanation were directed to faculties that depend on the body for their operation. But if it is not part of his theory of mind I don't know where else to put it.

Sensation is, for Descartes as for most philosophers in the period, an operation that cannot occur, save by miracle, except through the mediation of corporeal organs. Clarke's question is whether for Descartes the explanation of sensing in humans requires us to suppose that humans have not only physical but mental properties; and then, if the answer to that question is yes, whether the mental properties can be attributed to a subject that also has the physical properties we attribute to humans.

In the Second Meditation and again in the *Sixth Replies*, Descartes holds that sensation loosely speaking includes operations of the intellect. In the *Sixth Replies* Descartes distinguishes three grades of sensation: (i) certain bodily changes of which some external object is normally the proximate cause; (ii) changes in the mind, the causal

---

or not, and the truths we formulate using them, are more certain than any truth of experience.

Descartes does regularly use comparisons to things of ordinary experience in his accounts of phenomena in natural philosophy. But those comparisons are of something *unfamiliar* (a hypothetical, often microscopic, mechanism) with something *familiar*. It is not clear that the more familiar thing is in fact *better understood*. Descartes doesn't know how fermentation works, for example; he has no hydrodynamics worth the name, no theory of materials by which to explain the rigidity of some objects and the malleability of others even though he appeals to such properties in his comparisons. Rather than being a strength of Descartes's theory, his expectation that the most fundamental things in the world would be the simplest and easiest to understand (as the *Regulae* would have it) is a weakness. Quarks are only 'easy' if you have studied a great deal of mathematical physics; the comparisons that physicists or popularizers sometimes use to give the lay reader some sort of impression of what they are have no role in physical reasoning.

condition for which is the union of the mind with the body, and whose
proximate particular cause is those bodily changes; (iii) judgements we
make concerning the size, shape, and distance of that which we take
to be the cause of those changes in the mind. The first is evidently
corporeal; the third Descartes attributes 'to the intellect alone' (AT
vii. 438). I will call the first 'bodily sensings'; the second 'sensations
proper', and the third 'perceptions'.

Only those changes in the mind which are *immediately* caused by
bodily changes by virtue of the union belong properly to sense. Clarke
finds that claim strange (*Descartes's Theory*, 66, quoting AT vii. 437).
But Descartes probably has in mind the Aristotelian *sensus communis*,
to which sensations of figure, size, and distance are referred. The
sensus communis is assigned to the sensitive part of the soul (its bodily
organ is one of the ventricles of the brain), and is therefore corporeal.
Descartes denies that the thoughts we have concerning the figure and
so forth of the things we take to be the causes of sensations proper are
really *sensations* at all: they are *judgements*, and they are effected not by
a 'common sense' but by the intellect. Even the *incorrect* judgements
we are accustomed to make since childhood are to be attributed to
the intellect: not only the educated judgement according to which a
baton half-submerged in water is affirmed to be in fact straight, but
also the naive judgement that it is bent. We, like the philosophers
of the Schools, tend to attribute the naive judgements to sense, and
to attribute only those judgements that involve a noticeable effort of
thought to the intellect. But that is a mistake.

Descartes refers here to the account of distance perception he
devised in the *Dioptrics*. What that account shows is that (i) the
distance of an object can be calculated, using the angle–side–angle
theorem, from the angles of the axes of the eyeballs relative to the plane
perpendicular to the line between them; (ii) those angles, together
perhaps with the distance between the eyes (which is the side of the
triangle whose altitude is being calculated), could be represented in
the brain by mechanisms similar to the mechanisms by which the
figures of objects, projected onto the retina, are sensed. In the *Sixth
Replies* Descartes says that the perception of size, distance, and shape
'by reasoning alone (*per solam ratiocinationem*)' was demonstrated in the
earlier work (AT vii. 438); reasoning he here attributes to the intellect,
not to the senses themselves.

It is a consequence of the account of perception in the *Sixth Replies* that, if animals lack an intellect, they cannot properly be said to have perceptions of distance. To understand what goes on in their case, it will be helpful to consider what Descartes says generally about certain kinds of bodily sensing. Consider colours. The datum Descartes has in mind in the *Dioptrics* and the *Treatise on Man* is that animals (and humans in what we do without thinking) *discriminate* among those objects we perceive as having distinct colours. The squirrel devours a red tomato while ignoring the green. Bodies, however, have no colours: in bodies there are only certain configurations that, under normal circumstances, produce in the mind ideas of colours. In a perfected psychology of squirrels, colours would never appear: only those configurations and their effects on the brain would be mentioned.

Several times over in the *Treatise* Descartes attempts to show that differences in bodies affecting this or that sense will bring about different physical states in the brain and the pineal gland. As we learn both in the *Treatise* and in the fourth part of the *Dioptrics*, the 'encoding' (I take this term from Jean-Luc Marion's analyses[7]) of physical states of things affecting the senses into physical states of the brain is not based on resemblance: it is an arbitrary system of physical symbols corresponding one-to-one with different physical states in their external causes. Those symbols, as we would say, carry information about their causes without resembling them. That suffices (so Descartes argues) to account for discrimination in animals. We may suppose that in the squirrel's brain the projected figure of the tomato is encoded together with a code for green or red; the difference between the two colour codes will result in different actions. The same goes for differences in distance: it suffices, in understanding how an action of reaching, say, is caused, to know that the angles of the eyes are encoded together with the projected figure; that, together with suitable hard-wired connections between impressions on the pineal gland and flows of spirits into the motor nerves, *suffices* to explain the action. There is in all this no judging but only sensing; indeed there is in the animal-machine no explicit representation of distance at all, no calculating except in so far as a balance, for example, might be said to 'calculate' the relative weights of items.

[7] Jean-Luc Marion, *La Théologie blanche de Descartes* (Paris: PUF, 1981), 231–63.

What I've said so far is consistent with a materialist theory of
perceiving and acting. It had better be: it is, after all, a theory of
vision in *animals*. What then would lead Descartes to postulate in the
human case an additional act of judging, attributed to a faculty lacking
in animals? Consider the wax example in the Second Meditation.
Descartes argues that only by the intellect do we come to know that
the hard white thing we start with is identical to the soft clear thing
we end with. The key point is that the *kind* of thing we conceive to
endure through the changes is an *extended* thing. Only by representing
the wax to ourselves as extended could we conclude that it remains
the same thing. That representation 'is not by seeing, by touching, or
by imagining ... but through inspection by the mind alone' (AT vii.
31). The human mind represents to itself the visible thing as extended;
and that, according to Descartes, is an act of intellect alone.

There is as yet nothing in this argument to show that the intellect
is not corporeal; Descartes does not offer it as an argument on behalf
of the real distinction. By way of arguing that Descartes's treatment of
sensation is materialist, Clarke adduces two passages from the letters.
In a response to Henry More, after arguing that animals do not,
properly speaking, have language, Descartes adds:

I would like to note that I am speaking of thought, not life or sense (*de
cogitatione, non de vitâ, vel sensu*): I deny no animal life, which I hold to consist
only in the heat of the heart; nor do I deny sense, insofar as it depends on a
corporeal organ. (Descartes to More, 5 February 1649, AT v. 278)

It seems to me clear that Descartes's intention here is not to deny that
sensation proper is a mode of thought. Descartes says that *if* by "life"
you mean "the heat of the heart", then animals have life. Likewise
if by "sense" you mean "the capacity of receiving impressions in the
sense organs", then animals have sense. But if you mean sensation
proper, animals don't have sense.

The human body is an automaton, not needing even the soul to
operate in the manner of animals. In a letter to the Marquess of
Newcastle, Descartes notes that we do many things without thinking;
in that case, our acts are to be explained solely by reference to the
body-machine, just as similar acts in animals are to be explained
(Descartes to Newcastle, 23 November 1646, AT iv. 573–4). Those
acts can be complex: 'when swallows return in the spring, in doing so

they act like clocks'. All the instances traditionally adduced in favour of attributing reason to animals are instances of 'instinct' (which in this context denotes a disposition of the machine), not of thought (AT iv. 576).[8] It is often argued, Descartes notes, that because the organs of animals are like ours, there must be some thought 'joined to those organs', less perfect perhaps than ours, but thought nevertheless. Descartes's reply is entirely unoriginal: if animals have thought, they have an immortal soul; there is no reason to attribute thought to some without attributing it to all, even though oysters and the like are very imperfect. As Pierre Bayle would argue later, the upshot of this exchange is not that humans alone have souls, but that either animals do or we don't.[9]

Clarke takes Descartes's insistence that animals have no souls to be an instance of his general proscription against appealing to forms or powers in natural philosophy. The 'logic' of Descartes's physiology was to push mechanistic explanation 'to its limits', even to the elimination of the human soul (Clarke, *Descartes's Theory,* 77). That is an apt description of what was to come; and there is no doubt that Descartes meant to explain mechanistically everything that in natural philosophy the Schools had explained by other means—including all the phenomena we observe in living things other than ourselves. But it is not evident that Descartes ever wished to extend mechanistic explanation to those phenomena that had always been attributed to the rational soul—that is, to discursive reason and the exercise of the will.

4. EXCURSUS ON SUBSTANCE

The argument of the later part of Clarke's book is that although, in a Cartesian framework, certain phenomena require us to postulate mental properties by way of acknowledging their inexplicability within

---

[8] The term "instinct" is just the sort of promissory note that Clarke takes Cartesian mind to be. It denotes the mechanism or mechanisms, whatever they may be, by which the behaviour in question is to be explained.

[9] Pierre Bayle, 'Rorarius', in Bayle, *Dictionnaire historique et critique* (Amsterdam, 1740), *Œuvres diverses,* ed. E. Labrousse (Hildesheim: Georg Olms, 1982), suppl. 1, pt. 2, pp. 970–81. See Dennis Des Chene, ' "Animal" as Category: Bayle's "Rorarius" ', in Justin Smith (ed.), *The Problem of Animal Generation in Modern Philosophy* (Cambridge: Cambridge University Press, 2006).

that framework, there are no grounds for postulating any *substance* distinct from matter, in part because there is no coherent conception of substance in Descartes's philosophy. It's an odd sort of argument if you think it is intended to yield conclusions about the historical Descartes—rather like saying that because there is no alkahest, the chemists who are said to have searched for it must really have been doing something else. As a matter of fact, those who said they had made it *did* make something else; but they remain alkahest-searchers and not something-else-makers. So too Descartes may have failed to be a dualist by virtue of having no coherent conception of substance; but he remains a would-be *substance* dualist, not an actual *property* dualist. Only the ideal working scientist Descartes, a figure of fiction, could be said to be a property dualist.

The aim of this excursus is to remove from Descartes's conception the stigma of incoherence. Whether his conception does any explanatory work in his natural philosophy is a separate issue. Even if it doesn't, the conclusion to be drawn is at most that Descartes the natural philosopher has no need of substance. The historical Descartes, however, was not only a natural philosopher. He did say that we shouldn't make a habit of metaphysics. Just once does anyone need to go through the arguments for the existence of God and the immortality of the soul. Afterward, having impressed not only those truths on our memory but also the fact that we have removed them from all doubt, we can recall and retain certain of them. But just as baptism, which we undergo just once, is nonetheless necessary to salvation, so too for intellectual salvation—for releasing ourselves from the *praejudicia* we acquire in childhood—we must demonstrate to ourselves the truths of metaphysics.

Clarke notes that substance has many uses in the seventeenth century (*Descartes's Theory*, 209). For our purposes, only two matter, and of those two primarily the notion defined in the *Principles*. The first part of that work is Descartes's most systematic treatment, and whatever variation may be found elsewhere, it is to that treatment we should turn in deciding whether he had a coherent notion.

Aristotelian philosophers notice two notions of substance. The first, or logical, notion is that of an ultimate subject of predication. "Bald" is said of Socrates, but "Socrates" is not said of anything.[10] The second, metaphysical, notion is that of a thing whose existence is independent of the existence of any other thing. Descartes notes that strictly speaking only God is substance according to the second notion. The existence of all created things is dependent on that of God, the only *necessarily* existing thing. A created thing is a substance just in case its existence is independent of the existence of any other thing save God. (Any thing which is not a substance is a mode.) Descartes acknowledges that the term cannot be unequivocally applied both to creatures and to God; we may—and Spinoza did—insist that it be used unequivocally, but there is nothing *incoherent* in saying of a thing that its existence is independent of the existence of all other things save God. Independence here, as Descartes's subsequent discussion of the real distinction makes clear, is (by way of reference to God's absolute power) *logical* independence. If it is logically possible that *x* should exist even on the supposition that nothing else but God exists, then *x* is a substance.[11]

The real distinction which is said to hold between thinking substance and extended substance is also defined in terms of independence. A thing is really distinct from another just in case it is possible for it to exist without that other (Descartes adds 'by the power of God', but in this context that is a way of distinguishing logical from *natural*, or as we would say, *physical* possibility). Using this definition of the real distinction we can restate the definition of substance as follows: a thing is a substance just in case it is really distinct from everything else; to which, in the case of created substances, we add 'except God'. (An obvious question arises here: is it true no created substance is, on this account, really distinct from God? Again we seem to be moving towards Spinoza. For present purposes, however, it won't matter much how that question is resolved.)

To show, then, that the mind is a substance requires *inter alia* showing that it is really distinct from the body, and indeed from every

---

[10] The logical definition of substance is used in the 'geometric' version of the argument of the *Meditations* in the *Second Replies* (AT vii. 161).

[11] Clarke says of substance so construed that it has 'the unwelcome implication that, if any second substance exists, then God exists' (*Descartes's Theory*, 216). Unwelcome to whom? Descartes, after all, argues from the *duration* of created things to the existence of God; and duration is nothing other than the thing itself considered as existing over several instants of time (*Principles of Philosophy*, I. 21, 45, AT viiia. 13, 26).

body. Descartes's basic argument (I do not claim it is sound) can be summarized as follows:[12]

(1) In order to determine whether the existence of a thinking sub-
    stance is independent of the existence of extended substances,
    we consider whether any of the *modes* we ascribe to thinking
    substance is such that only if an extended substance existed
    could that mode exist.

(2) There is, for each substance, a mode of that substance upon
    which all its other modes depend: this mode Descartes calls the
    attribute of that substance. All the created substances we know of
    have one or the other of two attributes, thought and extension.

(3) The question in (1) thus becomes: is it the case that a thing can
    have the attribute of extension alone, or the attribute of thought
    alone, without having the other attribute? Our assurance that it
    is possible is based on the *completeness* of our ideas of extension
    and thought: we can see (Descartes says) that a thing which has
    the attribute of extension has 'all it needs to exist', and similarly
    for a thing which has the attribute of thought. The idea of a
    triangle, on the other hand, is not complete: in order to exist,
    a triangular thing must be extended.

(4) The argument of (3) yields not only the conclusion that an
    extended or thinking thing is a substance merely by virtue of
    being extended or thinking, but also that by virtue of being
    extended a thing is really distinct from every thinking thing,
    and that by virtue of being thought a thing is really distinct
    from every extended thing.

To say of a thing that it is a substance cannot explain why it has
any of the modes it has. The causal interactions of a thing with other
things are determined by its modes, not the fact of its existence, and
still less by the possibility of its existing even if no other created thing
exists. In particular the effect of a thing on the mind is determined by
its modes, not by its substancehood; and even the mind's awareness
of itself is always the awareness of a mode of thought. We would
not expect, therefore, that the concept of substance should enter

---

[12] See the very complete analysis of Descartes on the real distinction in Marleen
Rozemond, *Descartes's Dualism* (Cambridge, Mass.: Harvard University Press, 1998).

directly into causal explanations. Even in proving, say, the *existence* of the 'channelled particles' responsible for magnetism, what is proved is that certain modes of other bodies follow from the assumption that particles of a certain *shape* move through their pores. We infer that such particles exist by way of an argument that only they could produce the observed phenomena.

My being angry is a mode of me, considered as a thinking substance. That is to say: were I to cease to exist, my anger would likewise cease to exist. But I may well not be angry—not have *that* individual mode—one day. We could cast this into the form of an explanation: the datum is that today I am angry and tomorrow I, the very same person, am not angry; and the explanation of how that is possible is that the anger is a mode of me rather than the other way around. Note the 'possible': Descartes's metaphysics is intended to help us think clearly about certain *modal* claims, chiefly the claim that possibly my mind exists but my body does not. Unless all this is somehow not seriously meant, it is, I think, quite difficult to take the historical Descartes to be other than a substance dualist.

It does happen on occasion even in natural philosophy that the substancehood of a thing becomes a genuine question. Some people used to think that heat was a distinct stuff, a fluid, and that bodies could contain more or less of this fluid. The 'specific heat' of a body was a measure of the amount of fluid a particular kind of body could hold per unit volume. It turns out, of course, that heat is not a fluid but a statistical measure of the motion of molecules; in Descartes's scheme, heat would not be a substance, nor even a mode, exactly, but rather a quantity derived from the modes of molecules taken in large ensembles. That, I take it, was a genuine discovery: the claim "heat is a substance" was decisively refuted.

Clarke proposes that "substance" in Descartes's natural philosophy be taken to mean no more than "thing", and that what counts as a thing depends on which properties we have in mind: 'the predication of thinghood would follow the properties that are the focus of attention' (*Descartes's Theory*, 233). A clock is a thing with respect to telling time; its parts are things with respect to being made of metal or wood.

I'm not sure whether this is meant to be a description of Descartes's own notion of thinghood or an original contribution of Clarke's.

The word "thing" here is clearly not Descartes's *res*. Properties (that is, modes) are *res*; but Clarke's *things* depend on properties. *Res*, moreover, in Descartes's usage as in that of the Schools, denotes only those entities whose nature does not depend on the manner of our conceiving them, but Clarke's *things* (and their natures, if they have natures) do depend on our manner of conceiving them.[13]

Consider, moreover, the exemplary things of Cartesian physics: bodies. That a certain portion of *res extensa* is not an individual body but only part of one is not a matter of which properties we have in mind. That portion is united with the rest of the individual body it belongs to by virtue of being at rest with respect to them, and in particular with respect to those with which it shares a boundary (*Principles of Philosophy*, II. 25; AT viiia. 53–4). Descartes is not so conventionalist as to make the distinction between one individual body and another depend on our conception.[14]

Having said that, I would agree with Clarke that the distinction between 'things' (i.e. bearers of properties) and substances (i.e. things

---

[13] In the paragraph leading into this proposal, Clarke notes a passage in which Descartes takes up the phrase *substantia incompleta* (*Fourth Replies*, AT vii. 222). If by "incomplete" is meant 'that which cannot exist by itself alone', then "incomplete substance" is contradictory. But if by "incomplete substance" is meant a substance—i.e. a thing that can exist by itself alone—which, 'insofar as it is referred to another substance, with which it composes [a thing which is] *unum per se*', then the hand, for example, can be called an incomplete substance with respect to the body of which it is part. Clarke calls this a 'verbal manœuvre' (Clarke, *Descartes's Theory*, 232). It is to the extent that Descartes is showing Arnauld how he would understand the phrase *substantia incompleta* when in the Schools it is applied to mind and body. But what is arbitrary in the examples is not the *substantiality* of the hand or the mind; it is whether they are to be called *complete*. Descartes doesn't care much whether you call the hand complete or not; what matters is that, considered in itself, it can exist by itself. The truth or falsity of that proposition is not a matter of convention or of which properties of the hand we attend to. There is indeed 'no philosophical problem' when Descartes describes both material objects and their parts as substances (Clarke, *Descartes's Theory*, 233): considered in themselves, a sphere and each of its hemispheres can exist even if nothing else does (provided that we understand, for the sphere, that its parts are *not* something else), and are therefore substances. Substance and individual are different notions: the hemispheres are distinct substances but (supposing them to be mutually at rest) they are *not* distinct individuals.

[14] It is true that in the paragraph to which I have just referred, Descartes says that we understand by 'one part of matter' even a collection of parts, provided that they move together. But in any particular physical situation there are what might be called primordial parts, whose own parts are mutually at rest, and derivative parts, so called because their primordial parts are moving together. Even if derivative parts are arbitrary, primordial parts are not: that this portion of matter is moving, i.e. separating from those which are contiguous to it, is not a matter of our conception.

that exist independently of other things) is of secondary importance in Descartes's natural philosophy. Natural philosophy—Descartes's and that of the Schools alike—concerns itself with properties, not with substances *per se.* As Descartes says, the existence of a thing—and so too its being substance or mode—does not of itself determine its effects on other things; it is a necessary condition for having any effect at all, but once we are given *that,* natural philosophical explanation concerns itself with properties (or modes).

5. DUALISMS

Having established that Descartes the working scientist has no use for substances but only for a rough-and-ready distinction between properties and things, Clarke concludes that Descartes the working scientist was not a *substance* dualist. He was, as it turns out, a *property* dualist, but even that is camouflage behind which we find only the inability to 'provide the kind of structural explanation of thinking that his philosophy required' (*Descartes's Theory,* 234).

What would that explanation have looked like? Consider first of all the explananda. They include the motions of certain bodies—our own and other people's—and those things of which we are aware by virtue of thinking them (under this heading I include pains and sensations, which we 'think' simply by having them occur in our thoughts). The motions of people's bodies, if they are not to be explained as we explain those of animals' bodies, will be explained by reference—the *Discourse* tells us—to the intellect, and perhaps also the will; that is, they are explained by reference to certain phenomena of thought. As for the phenomena of thought, these would in principle be explained (if I understand Clarke correctly) by first telling the usual causal story about the course of events that leads from the sense organ to the pineal gland, and then completing the story by showing that the state of the pineal gland is identical to our sensation of, say, colour (Clarke, *Descartes's Theory,* 255). (I note in passing that if the phenomena of thought just are physical states, then in the explanation of behaviour mental descriptions simply drop out.)

Clarke gives short shrift to the argument for the real distinction outlined above. He notes that Descartes acknowledges that in many cases I have distinct ideas of what is in fact just one thing. I can, for example, think of a thing merely as existing or as existing through some time: the latter I call its 'duration', but the duration of a thing, its existence, and the thing itself are all one. The inference from a distinction of ideas to a distinction of the things they are ideas of requires something more. In the case of the ideas of thought and extension, the additional feature is that those ideas are *complete*, which means that in thinking of a thing as extended, for example, I understand of my conception that nothing more need be added to it for me to have the idea of an *existing* thing. Each extended thing has a certain size, shape, and motion; but once I have considered it to have some determinate of each of those modes, I can (so Descartes thinks) conceive of God creating a thing with just those modes such that that thing exists independently of all other things.

The evident difficulty with the argument is that even if a thing having only modes of thought can exist independently of any thing having only modes of body, still one thing—perhaps me—could have both. Spinoza, like some of the objectors to the *Meditations*, noted that according to Descartes's own conception no mode of thought is *contrary* to any mode of body. We cannot show, it would seem, that I am not *also* a body, but only that possibly a thing like me in certain respects is not a body.

Something stronger must be shown than what is shown by the complete ideas argument: namely, that there are some modes for which we have good reason to believe that they exist independently of any bodily mode, *and* that a mind that had only those modes would still be a substance. Clarke considers the likely candidates: the operations of the intellect and those of the will. He finds no good grounds for denying that those powers could be found in a body.

Aristotelian authors did assert that some properties of the soul could not exist in any body: the spontaneity of the will, for example, or the power of reflection. Descartes avails himself of only two such arguments. In the *Discourse* he holds that reason, being a 'universal instrument', cannot be realized in any machine: it is 'morally impossible that there should be sufficiently many different [dispositions] in one machine to make it act on all occasions in life in the same way our reason makes us act' (Discourse 5, AT vi. 57). Clarke, I think, would point to the primitive condition of Descartes's science; we now have ample reason to think that one machine can be endowed with all the 'dispositions' required to emulate a reasoning creature like us. We have some reason to think that Descartes was wrong. But Descartes put the argument forward to show that the intellect is not reducible to the dispositions of a machine, and that in turn implies (given that machines are the sole means by which the operations of human beings can be simulated even to the extent that they can be) that the human mind is not realizable by bodies. He was convinced of its soundness, even if we aren't. (Clarke agrees that Descartes did not think he could give a mechanistic explanation of the intellect; but he denies that an *ideal* Descartes would have inferred from this that the mind, rather than consisting in certain irreducible properties possessed by human bodies, is a separate substance.)

The other is that the soul is indivisible but every body is divisible (Meditation 6, AT vii. 86)—an old argument. I won't evaluate it; I note only that Descartes, in offering it, clearly *intends* it to be yet another proof of *substance* dualism.

6. CONCLUSION

Clarke's book shows that a number of passages in Descartes's writings that might be thought to entail substance dualism needn't be read that way. A Descartes who asserted, moreover, only what (by our lights) he was *entitled* to assert would have given us a less ambitious version of the *Treatise on Man*; about the mind he would have said only that much remains to be explained. I'm not sure that this Descartes is of much interest. The science is obsolete; the philosophical arguments long since digested and superseded.

I am not persuaded that Descartes, after having tried and failed to explain all the operations of the mind by the methods of the *Treatise*, reverted to dualism (of whatever sort) by way of acknowledging (or camouflaging) the limits of his natural philosophy. I'm not persuaded even that he tried. Descartes did see, I think, that others might, upon seeing what he had accomplished, come to believe that the human soul would suffer the fate of occult powers, final causes, and hylomorphism. He saw too that speculations of that sort might jeopardize the new philosophy, and to forestall that possibility began to construct arguments for what had been (I think) a rather conventional dualist opinion.

The dualism Descartes defends is—and here I think Clarke's work is instructive—more conservative, more like that of his teachers, than some interpreters have made it out to be. Like theirs, his is based primarily on the powers of what had been the rational part of the soul, and especially upon the operations of the understanding, which takes over those aspects of perception that cannot be explained mechanistically. From the standpoint of natural philosophy, the *only* argument for dualism is the argument of the *Discourse*, which invokes the understanding to explain how some animal-machines manage to behave appropriately in 'all the occurrences of life' (AT vi. 57). But that argument yields only property dualism, not substance dualism. The co-presence in the same individual of physical and mental properties cannot be ruled out by its means.

Nevertheless, I cannot agree with Clarke that Descartes—the historical Descartes not the ideal working scientist—'was a property dualist' (*Descartes's Theory*, 258). Clarke is not convinced by the arguments of the *Meditations* and the *Principles*. But there is no reason to suppose that Descartes wasn't, or that he was other than sincere in offering them. He may not have been justified in judging mind and body to be really distinct substances. But he did.

Washington University, St Louis

Index of Names

Notes to Contributors

1. Articles may be submitted at any time of year. It is strongly preferred that they be submitted by email attachment to one of the editors. Normally, articles should be submitted in MS Word (either Macintosh or PC version) or in RTF format. Diagrams and illustrations can be submitted either as computer files or in hard copy. The editors should be alerted if there are any special requirements with respect to characters or fonts. If it is not possible to submit an article by email attachment, please send two copies to one of the editors, double-spaced, clearly printed on one side of the page with reasonable margins. Notes should be given at the end, though in the published version they will be printed at the bottom of the page. The notes should also be double-spaced with reasonable margins. Wherever possible, references should be built into the text.

2. The first time a book is referred to in the notes, give at least the first name or initial of the author, the place and date of publication, and for books published after 1900, the publisher; where you are abbreviating the title in subsequent citations, give the abbreviation in square brackets. Thus for an initial citation:

Robert M. Adams, *Leibniz: Determinist, Theist, Idealist* [*Leibniz*] (Oxford: Oxford University Press, 1994), 138.

For a later citation:

Adams, *Leibniz*, 28–9.

Do *not* use the author-and-date style of reference:

Adams 1994: 28–9.

3. For articles in journals, give the full citation in the first occurrence. The full extents of articles should be given, and where the reference is to a specific page or pages, that should be indicated. In subsequent citations, use only author and brief title as indicated in square brackets in the original citation. Thus for an initial citation:

Michael R. Ayers, 'Mechanism, Superaddition, and the Proofs of God's Existence in Locke's *Essay*' ['Mechanism'], *Philosophical Review*, 90 (1981), 210–51, at 221–2.

For a later citation:

Ayers, 'Mechanism', 225.

4. For chapters in collected volumes, follow a similar format. Thus for an initial citation:

Christia Mercer, 'The Vitality and Importance of Early Modern Aristotelianism' ['Vitality and Importance'], in Tom Sorell (ed.), *The Rise of Modern Philosophy* (Oxford: Oxford University Press, 1997), 33–67, at 52.

For a later citation:

Mercer, 'Vitality and Importance', 38.

5. Volumes of *Oxford Studies in Early Modern Philosophy* contain lists of conventional abbreviations for standard works and editions, as well as citation conventions for each work. Please consult these when preparing your text.

EDITORS

Daniel Garber
Department of Philosophy
1879 Hall
Princeton University
Princeton, New Jersey 08544-1006
dgarber@princeton.edu

Steven Nadler
Department of Philosophy
5185 Helen C. White Hall
600 North Park Street
University of Wisconsin-Madison
Madison, Wisconsin 53706
smnadler@wisc.edu